CCST®

Cisco Certified
Support Technician
Study Guide

CCST®
Cisco Certified Support Technician
Study Guide
Networking Exam

Todd Lammle

Donald Robb

A Wiley Brand

Acknowledgments

Many people helped me build the new Cisco certification books in 2023 and 2024. Kenyon Brown helped me put together the book direction. He managed the internal editing at Wiley, so thank you, Ken, for working diligently for many months to keep these books moving.

Kim Wimpsett is always such a pleasure to work with that I get excited when she is assigned to work with me on a new project because I know the project will be okay. As a developmental editor, Kim is top-notch, low-key, and she helps keep everyone calm and on track. Not an easy thing in this field!

Thanks to Donald Robb, who is helping me assemble the CCST series! He was instrumental in helping me build the table of contents of both books and helped with some chapters in this book. He is writing most of the Cyber CCST book as well.

This is the first time I have worked with John Sleeva as CE, and he has done an excellent job, keeping edits to the minimum so as not to lose the voicing created for this book series. Thank you, John! Looking forward to working with you on the rest of the series.

The technical editor I used for the first book in the CCST series was Jon Buhagiar, who read each chapter in the entire series multiple times, making extraordinary discoveries both technically and editorially. Thank you, Jon!

About the Authors

Todd Lammle is the authority on Cisco certification and internetworking and is certified in most Cisco certification categories. He is a world-renowned author, speaker, trainer, and consultant. Todd has three decades of experience working with LANs, WANs, and large enterprise licensed and unlicensed wireless networks, and lately he's been implementing large Cisco Security networks using Firepower/FTD and ISE.

His years of real-world experience are evident in his writing; he is not just an author but an experienced networking engineer with very practical experience from working on the largest networks in the world, at such companies as Xerox, Hughes Aircraft, Texaco, AAA, Cisco, and Toshiba, among many others.

Todd has published over 130 books, including the very popular *CCNA: Cisco Certified Network Associate Study Guide, CCNA Wireless Study Guide, CCNA Data Center Study Guide, and CCNP Security*—among over a hundred more—all from Sybex. He runs an international consulting and training company based in northern Idaho, where he spends his free time in the mountains playing with his golden retrievers.

You can reach Todd through his website at www.lammle.com.

Donald Robb, also known as the-packet-thrower, has become very well known in the networking and security field for his ability to thrive in complex environments during his 15+ years in the industry. He has worked with practically every major vendor in the industry and has earned more than 100 certifications, including a Juniper JNCIE and many Cisco certifications.

Donald is an author, a trainer who frequently works with Todd Lammle, and a consultant. He currently works as a principal network architect for a world-wide company. In his free time, he enjoys playing with his kitties and explaining to his wife that she needs to read this book to know why Netflix isn't working.

About the Technical Editor

Jon Buhagiar (Network+, A+, CCNA, MCSA, MCSE, BS/ITM) is an information technology professional with two decades of experience in higher education. During the past 23 years, he has been responsible for Network Operations at Pittsburgh Technical College and has lead several projects, such as virtualization (server and desktop), VoIP, Microsoft 365, and many other projects supporting the quality of education at the college. He has achieved several certifications from Cisco, CompTIA, and Microsoft, and has taught many of the certification paths. He is the author of several books, including Sybex's *CompTIA A+ Complete Study Guide: Core 1 Exam 220-1101 and Core 2 Exam 220-1102* (2022), *CompTIA Network+ Review Guide: Exam N10-008* (2021) and *CCNA Certification Practice Tests: Exam 200-301* (2020).

Contents at a Glance

Contents

Introduction

Welcome to the exciting world of internetworking and your path towards Cisco certification. If you've picked up this book because you want to improve yourself and your life with a better, more satisfying, and secure job, you've chosen well!

Whether you're striving to enter the thriving, dynamic IT sector or seeking to enhance your skill set and advance your position within it, being Cisco certified can seriously stack the odds in your favor to help you attain your goals. This book is a great start.

Cisco certifications are powerful instruments of success that also markedly improve your grasp of all things internetworking. As you progress through this book, you'll gain a strong, foundational understanding of networking that reaches far beyond Cisco devices. And when you finish this book, you'll be ready to tackle the next step toward Cisco certification.

Essentially, by beginning your journey towards becoming Cisco certified, you're proudly announcing that you want to become an unrivaled networking expert, a goal that this book will help get you underway to achieving.

Congratulations in advance for taking the first step towards your brilliant future!

 To find bonus material, including Todd Lammle videos and extra practice questions, please see www.lammle.com/ccst.

Cisco's CCST Certifications

It used to be that to secure the holy grail of Cisco certifications—the CCIE—you passed only one written test before being faced with a grueling, formidable hands-on lab. This intensely daunting, all-or-nothing approach made it nearly impossible to succeed and predictably didn't work out too well for most people.

Cisco responded to this issue by creating a series of new certifications, which not only created a sensible, stepping-stone-path to the highly coveted CCIE prize but also gave employers a way to accurately rate and measure the skill levels of prospective and current employees.

The CCNA and CCNP exams were born and are still the most popular certifications in the world. This exciting paradigm shift in Cisco's certification path truly opened doors that few were allowed through before!

Now Cisco has reached down and created a new introductory-level certification program, below the CCNA, called the Cisco Certified Support Technician (CCST). There are two exams/certifications: Networking and Cybersecurity.

The Cisco Certified Support Technician (CCST) Networking certification validates an individual's skills and knowledge of entry-level networking concepts and topics. The certification demonstrates foundational knowledge and skills needed to show how networks operate, including the devices, media, and protocols that enable network communications.

The Networking certification is also a first step toward working on achieving your CCNA Certification.

The Cisco Certified Support Technician (CCST) Cybersecurity certification validates a candidate's skills and knowledge of entry-level cybersecurity concepts and topics, including security principles, network security and endpoint security concepts, vulnerability assessment and risk management, and incident handling. The Cybersecurity certification is also a first step toward CyberOps Associate certification.

This book is a powerful tool to get you started in your Cisco certification studies, and it's vital to understand the material in it before you go on to conquer any other certifications!

 Exam policies can change from time to time. We highly recommend that you check both Cisco and Certiport (www.certiport.com) sites for the most up-to-date information when you begin your preparing when you register, and then again a few days before your scheduled exam date.

Tips for Taking the CCST Network Exam

Here are some general tips for taking your exam successfully (assuming you are going in person, as online testing is available as well):

- This is not like the CCNA or other Cisco certification tests that are available on www .vue.com. You need to instead go to www.certiport.com/locator to both register and pay for your exam. You can take the exams in person at a center or in your home or office, under direct video and audio supervision. For exams at home information and to sign up, call (800) 589-6871.

- Bring two forms of ID with you. One must be a photo ID, such as a driver's license. The other can be a major credit card or a passport. Both forms must include a signature.

- Arrive early at the exam center so that you can relax and review your study materials, particularly tables and lists of exam-related information. After you are ready to enter the testing room, you will need to leave everything outside; you won't be able to bring any materials into the testing area.

- Read the questions carefully. Don't be tempted to jump to an early conclusion. Make sure you know exactly what each question is asking.

- Don't leave any questions unanswered. Unanswered questions are scored against you. There will be questions with multiple correct responses. When there is more than one correct answer, a message at the bottom of the screen will prompt you to either "choose two" or "choose all that apply." Be sure to read the messages displayed to know how many correct answers you must choose.

- When answering multiple-choice questions you're not sure about, use a process of elimination to get rid of the obviously incorrect answers first. Doing so will improve your odds if you need to make an educated guess.

Who Should Read This Book?

You—if want to pass the CCST Networking exam confidently! This book is chock-full of the exact information you need and directly maps to CCST Networking exam objectives, so if you use it to study for the exam, your odds of passing shoot way up.

In addition to including every bit of knowledge you need to learn to pass the exam, I've included some really great tips and solid wisdom to equip you even further to successfully work in the real IT world.

What's Included in the Book

I've included several study tools throughout the book:

Assessment Test   At the end of this Introduction is an assessment test that you can use to check your readiness for the exam. Take this test before you start reading the book; it will help you determine the areas you might need to brush up on. The answers to the assessment test questions appear on a separate page after the last question of the test. Each answer includes an explanation and a note telling you the chapter in which the material appears.

Objective Map and Opening List of Objectives   This Introduction includes a detailed exam objective map showing you where each of the exam objectives is covered in the book. In addition, each chapter opens with a list of the exam objectives it covers. Use these to see exactly where each exam topic is covered.

Exam Essentials   Each chapter, just after the summary, includes a number of exam essentials. These are the key topics you should take from the chapter in terms of areas to focus on when preparing for the exam.

Chapter Review Questions   To test your knowledge as you progress through the book, there are review questions at the end of each chapter. As you finish each chapter, answer the review questions and check your answers; the correct answers and explanations are in Appendix. You can go back to reread the section that deals with each question you got wrong to ensure that you correctly answer the next time you're tested on the material.

Interactive Online Learning Environment and Test Bank

The interactive online learning environment that accompanies this book provides a test bank with study tools to help you prepare for the certification exam and increase your chances of passing it the first time! The test bank includes the following tools:

Sample Tests   All of the questions in this book are provided, including the assessment test, which you'll find at the end of this Introduction, and the chapter tests that include the review questions at the end of each chapter. In addition, there is an online practice exam.

Use these questions to test your knowledge of the study guide material. The online test bank runs on multiple devices.

Flashcards   Approximately 100 questions are provided in digital flashcard format (a question followed by a single correct answer). You can use the flashcards to reinforce your learning and provide last-minute test prep before the exam.

Other Study Tools   A glossary of key terms from this book is available as a fully searchable PDF.

Go to www.wiley.com/go/sybextestprep to register and gain access to this interactive online learning environment and test bank.

How to Use This Book

If you want a solid foundation for the serious effort of preparing for the Cisco CCST Networking exam, then look no further, because I've spent countless hours putting together this book with the sole intention of helping you pass it!

This book is loaded with valuable information, and you will get the most out of your study time if you understand how I put the book together. Here's a list that describes how to approach studying:

1. Take the assessment test immediately following this Introduction. (The answers are at the end of the test, but no peeking!) It's okay if you don't know any of the answers—that's what this book is for. Carefully read over the explanations for any question you get wrong and make note of the chapters where that material is covered.

2. Study each chapter carefully, making sure you fully understand the information and the exam objectives listed at the beginning of each one. Again, pay extra-close attention to any chapter that includes material covered in questions you missed on the assessment test.

3. Answer all the review questions related to each chapter. Specifically note any questions that confuse you and study the corresponding sections of the book again. And don't just skim these questions—make sure you understand each answer completely.

4. Before you take your test, be sure to visit my website www.lammle.com for questions, videos, audios, and other useful information.

5. Test yourself using all the electronic flashcards. This is a brand-new and updated flashcard program to help you prepare for the latest Cisco CCST Network exam, and it is a great study tool.

I tell you no lies—learning every bit of the material in this book is going to require applying yourself with a good measure of discipline. So, try to set aside the same time period every day to study, and select a comfortable and quiet place to do so. If you work hard, you will be surprised at how quickly you learn this material.

The figures in this book are in black and white in the print edition; however, in the e-book, they are all in color.

What Does This Book Cover?

This book covers everything you need to know to solidly prepare you for getting into your CCST studies. Be advised that just because much of the material in this book won't be official Cisco CCST objectives in the future, that doesn't mean you won't be tested on it. Understanding the foundational, real-world networking information and skills offered in this book is critical to your certifications and your career!

Here's a snapshot of what you'll learn as you move through the book:

Chapter 1: Internetworking   In Chapter 1, you'll learn the basics of the Open Systems Interconnection (OSI) model the way Cisco wants you to learn it.

Chapter 2: Introduction to TCP/IP   Chapter 2 provides you with the background necessary for success on the CCST/CCNA/NP exams, as well as in the real world, with a thorough presentation of TCP/IP. It's an in-depth chapter that covers the very beginnings of the Internet Protocol stack and moves all the way to IP addressing. You'll gain an understanding of the difference between a network address and a broadcast address before finally ending with valuable network troubleshooting tips.

Chapter 3: Easy Subnetting   Believe it or not, you'll actually be able to subnet a network in your head after reading this chapter! Success will take a little determination, but you can do it.

Chapter 4: Network Address Translation (NAT) and IPv6   Network Address Translation (NAT) is very useful in today's world. Maybe people believed that IPv6 would take over the world, but because of NAT, it's still not as prevalent as IPv4. After learning about NAT, you'll find a small but powerful section on IPv6. You'll love it!

Chapter 5: IP Routing   This is a super fun chapter because you will learn about static, default, and dynamic routing. The fundamentals covered in this chapter are probably the most important in the book because understanding the IP routing process is what Cisco is all about! It's actually assumed that you solidly possess this knowledge when you get into the CCNA and CCNP studies, but rest assured, I wrote this as an introduction chapter.

Chapter 6: Switching   In Chapter 6, you'll learn how switches break up large collision domains into smaller ones and that a collision domain is a network segment with two or more devices sharing the same bandwidth. You will learn how switch ports create one collision domain per host. The chapter also surveys and compares how networks were designed before and after switching technologies were introduced.

Chapter 7: Cables and Connectors   Chapter 7 discusses the various types of devices and technologies that are used to create networks, as well as the basic network topologies and how they work together. Ethernet cabling is important, and this chapter covers that fully.

Chapter 8: Wireless Technologies   Chapter 8 begins by defining a basic wireless network as well as basic wireless principles. I'll also talk about different types of wireless networks, the minimum devices required to create a simple wireless network, and some basic wireless topologies. Finally, I'll get into basic security by covering WPA, WPA2, and WPA3.

Chapter 9: Cisco Devices   This chapter covers both network infrastructure and diagnosing problems. You need to be able to look at a basic Cisco device and understand some simple lights and their meaning, as well as be able to understand various type of cables and how they will be used for connecting to devices using different types of ports. I'll also cover how to connect and access local and remote network devices, as well as some basic Cisco IOS commands to help you find and diagnose problems.

Chapter 10: Security   This chapter covers authentication, authorization, and accounting, or AAA. AAA is a technology that gives us substantial control over users and what they're permitted to do inside our networks. That's just the beginning—there are more tools in the box! RADIUS and TACACS+ and security servers, like Identity Services Engine (ISE), help us implement a centralized security plan by recording network events to the security server, or to a Syslog server via logging.

Chapter 11: Cloud & IoT   Basically, cloud computing can provide virtualized processing, storage, and computing resources to users remotely, making the resources transparently available regardless of the user connection. Chapter 11 starts by discussing cloud computing and then moves on to cloud concepts and IoT endpoints.

Chapter 12: Troubleshooting   Chapter 12 discusses the help desk, including its purpose, policies and procedures, ticking, documentation, and information gathering. From there, you need to understand documentation and that maintaining updated documents is a large part of working a help desk. You also need to know Cisco's seven steps for helping help-desk personnel find and solve problems. In addition, Wireshark is an important objective, so I'll introduce that product to you. Lastly, you'll learn some important Cisco IP and network troubleshooting techniques to ensure that you're well equipped with these key skills.

Exam Objectives

You're probably pretty curious about the CCST Networking exam's objectives, right? Cisco asked groups of IT professionals to fill out a survey rating the skills they felt were important in their jobs, and the results were grouped into objectives for the exam.

The following table lists the objectives and which chapter discusses them. Note that a single objective can be covered in multiple chapters.

Objective	Chapter
1. Standards and Concepts	**1, 2, 7, 11, 12**
1.1. Identify the fundamental conceptual building blocks of networks.	**1, 2**
▪ TCP/IP model, OSI model, frames and packets, addressing	1, 2
1.2. Differentiate between bandwidth and throughput.	**12**
▪ Latency, delay, speed test vs. Iperf	12
1.3. Differentiate between LAN, WAN, MAN, CAN, PAN, and WLAN.	**7**
▪ Identify and illustrate common physical and logical network topologies	7
1.4. Compare and contrast cloud and on-premises applications and services.	**11**
▪ Public, private, hybrid, SaaS, PaaS, IaaS, remote work/hybrid work	11
1.5. Describe common network applications and protocols.	**2**
▪ TCP vs. UDP (connection-oriented vs. connectionless), FTP, SFTP, TFTP, HTTP, HTTPS, DHCP, DNS, ICMP, NTP	2
2. Addressing and Subnet Formats	**3, 4**
2.1. Compare and contrast private addresses and public addresses.	**3, 4**
▪ Address classes, NAT concepts	3, 4
2.2. Identify IPv4 addresses and subnet formats.	**3**
▪ Subnet concepts, Subnet Calculator, slash notation, and subnet mask; broadcast domain	3
2.3. Identify IPv6 addresses and prefix formats.	**3, 4**
▪ Types of addresses, prefix concepts	3, 4
3. Endpoints and Media Types	**7, 8, 11**
3.1. Identify cables and connectors commonly used in local area networks.	**7**
▪ Cable types: fiber, copper, twisted pair; Connector types: coax, RJ-45, RJ-11, fiber connector types	7
3.2. Differentiate between Wi-Fi, cellular, and wired network technologies.	**8**
▪ Copper, including sources of interference; fiber; wireless, including 802.11 (unlicensed, 2.4GHz, 5GHz, 6GHz), cellular (licensed), sources of interference	8

How to Contact the Publisher

If you believe you have found a mistake in this book, please bring it to our attention. At John Wiley & Sons, we understand how important it is to provide our customers with accurate content, but even with our best efforts an error may occur.

In order to submit your possible errata, please email it to our Customer Service Team at wileysupport@wiley.com with the subject line "Possible Book Errata Submission."

Assessment Test

1. In which of the following layers of the OSI model are MAC addresses defined?

   A. Data Link

   B. Presentation

   C. Transport

   D. Physical

2. Which of the following is a function of an access point (AP)?

   A. To automatically handle the configuration of wireless access points

   B. To monitor and control the incoming and outgoing network traffic

   C. To allow wireless devices to connect to a wireless network and connect to wired resources

   D. To connect networks and intelligently choose the best paths between networks

3. Which of the following statements regarding ICMP packets are true? (Choose two.)

   A. ICMP guarantees datagram delivery.

   B. ICMP can provide hosts with information about network problems.

   C. ICMP is encapsulated within layer 3 packets.

   D. ICMP is encapsulated within UDP datagrams.

4. What is the address range of a Class A network address in binary?

   A. 01*xxxxxx*

   B. 0*xxxxxxx*

   C. 10*xxxxxx*

   D. 110*xxxxx*

5. You have an interface on a router with the IP address of 192.168.192.20/29. What is the broadcast address on this LAN?

   A. 192.168.192.23

   B. 192.168.192.31

   C. 192.168.192.63

   D. 192.168.192.127

   E. 192.168.192.255

6. You need to subnet a network that has 10 subnets, each with at least 10 hosts. Which classful subnet mask would you use?

   A. 255.255.255.192

   B. 255.255.255.224

   C. 255.255.255.240

   D. 255.255.255.248

7. Which of the following descriptions about IPv6 is correct?

    A. Addresses are not hierarchical and are assigned at random.

    B. Broadcasts have been eliminated and replaced with multicasts.

    C. There are 2.7 billion addresses.

    D. An interface can be configured with only one IPv6 address.

8. In NAT, an inside global address is which of the following?

    A. The inside host's address before translation

    B. The inside host's address after translation

    C. The address that inside hosts use to get to the Internet

    D. The outside address used by the external router port

9. What does the 99 at the end of the following command mean?

    `Router(config)#ip route 192.168.13.0 255.255.255.0 10.31.2.4 99`

    A. Metric

    B. Administrative distance

    C. Hop count

    D. Cost

10. A network administrator views the output from the `show ip route` command. A network that is advertised by both RIP and OSPF appears in the routing table flagged as an OSPF route. Why is the RIP route to this network not used in the routing table?

    A. OSPF has a faster update timer.

    B. OSPF has a lower administrative distance.

    C. RIP has a higher metric value for that route.

    D. The OSPF route has fewer hops.

    E. The RIP path has a routing loop.

11. You log into a switch CLI and type a command. What command generated the following output?

    ```
    Vlan Mac Address Type Ports]]>
    ---- ----------- -------- -----
    All 0100.0ccc.cccc STATIC CPU
    [output cut]
    1 000e.83b2.e34b DYNAMIC Fa0/1
    1 0011.1191.556f DYNAMIC Fa0/1
    1 0011.3206.25cb DYNAMIC Fa0/1
    1 001a.2f55.c9e8 DYNAMIC Fa0/1
    1 001a.4d55.2f7e DYNAMIC Fa0/1
    1 001c.575e.c891 DYNAMIC Fa0/1
    1 b414.89d9.1886 DYNAMIC Fa0/5
    1 b414.89d9.1887 DYNAMIC Fa0/6
    ```

12. Spanning Tree Protocol (STP) is used on layer 2 switches to solve problems. Which of the following problems are addressed by STP? (Choose three.)

   A. Broadcast storms

   B. Layer 2 loops

   C. A device receiving multiple copies of the same frame

   D. Gateway redundancy

13. Your boss asks you if you need to put single-mode fiber (SMF) or multimode fiber (MMF) between buildings. What is the difference between the two?

   A. Electrical signals

   B. Number of light rays

   C. Number of digital signals

   D. That signal-mode can be run a shorter distance

14. You have a group of accountants who have their computers and printers all connected into a single switch. What is this logical grouping of network users and resources called?

   A. WAN

   B. LAN

   C. MPLS

   D. Host

15. Two workers have established wireless communication directly between their wireless laptops. You need to create a wireless topology so that two finance employees can connect their laptops directly only to each other. What type of network is this?

   A. IBSS

   B. SSID

   C. BSS

   D. ESS

16. You start a new job and find that the company is running the older wireless security standard WPA instead of WPA2 or 3. What defines this WPA standard? (Choose two.)

   A. It requires that all devices must use the same encryption key.

   B. It specifies the use of dynamic encryption keys that change throughout the users connection time.

   C. Static keys must be used.

   D. It can use PSK authentication.

17. Which of the following is a network protocol that is designed as a secure alternative to command-based utilities such as Telnet?

   A. SSL

   B. SSH

   C. STP

   D. STFP

18. Which of the following commands provides a quick overview of all a device's interfaces, including the logical address and interface status at layers 1 and 2?

   A. `show running-config`

   B. `show processes`

   C. `show ip interface brief`

   D. `show mac address-table`

   E. `show interfaces`

19. You need to secure your Cisco routers and switches with security protocols. Which of the following security server protocols are supported by Cisco routers and switches? (Choose three.)

   A. AAA

   B. RADIUS

   C. Kerberos

   D. DIA

   E. TACACS+

20. Your boss asks you in a meeting of executives to define an exploit. What do you tell them?

   A. This is when antivirus software uses definition files that identify known malware.

   B. This is a system of ranking vulnerabilities that are discovered based on predefined metrics.

   C. This is when a threat agent takes advantage of a vulnerability and uses it to advance an attack.

   D. This is when a hacker confuses an internal user and gets them to turn over their credentials.

21. You want to move part of your data center to another location that is managed by someone else. You only want to move the server VMs. What is this called?

   A. SaaS

   B. PaaS

   C. IaaS

   D. DaaS

22. You want to move your data center and have the data center run the operating systems and the network infrastructure, and you can then load and run your own applications. What is this called?

   A. SaaS

   B. DaaS

   C. IaaS

   D. PaaS

23. Which of the following would you do after analyzing the problem described in the trouble ticket you are working on?

   A. Gather information.

   B. Eliminate possible causes.

   C. Solve the problem.

   D. Define the problem.

24. You just loaded the Wireshark program on your computer. What is the first thing you need to do before starting to capture packets?

   A. Read the first frame you receive for license info.

   B. Save the file.

   C. Open all TCP packets, which always show the problem.

   D. Choose the interface on which you want to receive the packets.

Answers to Assessment Test

1. A. The IEEE Ethernet Data Link layer has two sublayers: the Media Access Control (MAC) layer and the Logical Link Control (LLC) layer. MAC addresses are defined in the MAC sublayer. See Chapter 1 for more information.

2. C. Wireless APs are very popular today. The idea behind these devices (which are layer 2 bridge devices) is to connect wireless products to a wired Ethernet network. See Chapter 1 for more information.

3. B, C. ICMP is used for diagnostics and destination unreachable messages. ICMP is encapsulated within IP datagrams, and, because it is used for diagnostics, it will provide hosts with information about network problems. See Chapter 2 for more information.

4. B. The range of a Class A network address is 0–127. This makes our binary range 00000000 – 01111111. See Chapter 2 for more information.

5. A. A /29 (255.255.255.248) has a block size of 8 in the fourth octet. This means the subnets are 0, 8, 16, 24, etc. 20 is in the 16 subnet. The next subnet is 24, so 23 is the broadcast address. See Chapter 3 for more information.

6. C. You need 10 subnets, each with at least 10 hosts. The mask 255.255.255.224 provides 8 subnets, each with 30 hosts—this will not work. The mask 255.255.255.240 provides 16 subnets with 14 hosts. This is the best answer. See Chapter 3 for more information.

7. B. There are no broadcasts with IPv6. Unicast, multicast, anycast, global, and link-local unicast addresses are used. See Chapter 4 for more information.

8. C. An inside local address is an inside host address before translation. An inside global address is the address an inside host will use to get to the Internet or out of the local network. See Chapter 4 for more information.

9. B. The 99 at the end changes the default administrative distance (AD) of 1 to 99. See Chapter 5 for more information.

10. B. RIP has an administrative distance (AD) of 120, whereas OSPF has an administrative distance of 110, so the router will choose the route with a lower AD to the same network. See Chapter 5 for more information.

11. `show mac address-table`

    This command displays the forward filter table, also called a content-addressable memory (CAM) table. See Chapter 6 for more information.

12. A, B, C. STP provides loop protection in layer 2 switched networks, which also stops multiple frame copies and broadcast storms. Gateway redundancy issues can be solved with Hot Standby Router Protocol (HSRP), which provides dynamic default gateways. See Chapter 6 for more information.

13. B. The difference between single-mode fibers and multimode fibers is in the number of light rays (and thus the number of signals) they can carry. Generally speaking, multimode fiber is used for shorter-distance applications, and single-mode fiber for longer distances. See Chapter 7 for more information.

14. B. A logical grouping of hosts is called a LAN, and you typically group them by connecting them to a hub or switch. See Chapter 7 for more information.

15. A. Two wireless hosts directly connected wirelessly is no different from two hosts connecting with a crossover cable. They are both ad hoc networks, but in wireless, we call this an independent basic service set (IBSS). See Chapter 8 for more information.

16. B, D. WPA, although using the same RC4 encryption that WEP uses, provides enhancements to the WEP protocol by using dynamic keys that change constantly. It also provides a pre-shared key (PSK) method of authentication. See Chapter 8 for more information.

17. B. Secure Shell (SSH) creates a secure channel between devices and provides confidentiality and integrity of the data transmission. It uses public-key cryptography to authenticate the remote computer and allows the remote computer to authenticate the user, if necessary. See Chapter 9 for more information.

18. C. The output of the Cisco IOS command show ip interface brief is very useful, providing all the device's interfaces, including the logical address and interface status at layers 1 and 2. See Chapter 9 for more information.

19. B, C, E. RADIUS, TACACS+, and Kerberos are the three types of security server protocols supported by Cisco routers. See Chapter 10 for more information.

20. C. An exploit occurs when a threat agent takes advantage of a vulnerability and uses it to advance an attack. Snort rules are created to stop hackers from attacking a known vulnerability. See Chapter 10 for more information.

21. C. IaaS delivers computer infrastructure—a platform virtualization environment where you can load your own server VMs. This is where the customer has the most control and management capability. See Chapter 11 for more information.

22. D. The vendor provides the hardware platform or data center and the software running on the platform, allowing customers to develop, run, and manage applications without the complexity of building and maintaining the infrastructure typically associated with developing and launching an application. An example is Windows Azure. See Chapter 11 for more information.

23. B. Cisco has created a seven-step troubleshooting process for help desk technicians to have a step-by-step approach to help find and fix issues. See Chapter 12 for more information.

24. D. Once the Wireshark program loads, you need to select which interface you want to do a packet capture on. If you have multiple interfaces in your computer, then you'll need to select the one that would have the traffic you are interested in seeing. See Chapter 12 for more information.

Chapter

1

Internetworking

THE CCST EXAM TOPICS COVERED IN THIS CHAPTER INCLUDE THE FOLLOWING:

✓ **1.0 Standards and Concepts**

- 1.1. Identify the fundamental conceptual building blocks of networks.

  - TCP/IP model, OSI model, frames and packets, addressing

Welcome to the exciting world of internetworking. This first chapter will serve as an internetworking review by focusing on how to connect networks together using Cisco routers and switches, and I've written it with the assumption that you have some simple basic networking knowledge.

Let's start by defining exactly what an internetwork is: You create an internetwork when you connect two or more networks via a router and configure a logical network addressing scheme with a protocol such as IP or IPv6.

This chapter will also describe in detail each part of the Open Systems Interconnection (OSI) model. Understanding the OSI model is key for the solid foundation you'll need to build upon with the more advanced Cisco networking knowledge gained as you become increasingly more skilled.

The OSI model has seven hierarchical layers, which were developed to enable different networks to communicate reliably between disparate systems.

To find up-to-the-minute updates for this chapter, please see www.lammle.com/ccst.

Internetworking Basics

Before exploring internetworking models and the OSI model's specifications, you need to grasp the big picture and the answer to this burning question: Why is it so important to learn Cisco internetworking anyway?

Networks and networking have grown exponentially over the past 20 years, and understandably so. They've had to evolve at light speed just to keep up with huge increases in basic, mission-critical user needs (e.g., the simple sharing of data and printers) as well as greater burdens like multimedia remote presentations and conferencing. Unless everyone who needs to share network resources is located in the same office space—an increasingly uncommon situation—the challenge is to connect relevant networks so that all users can share the wealth of whatever services and resources are required.

Figure 1.1 shows a basic *local area network (LAN)* that's connected using a *hub*, which is basically just an antiquated device that connects wires together. Keep in mind that a simple network like this would be considered one collision domain and one broadcast domain. No worries if you have no idea what I mean by that, because coming up soon I'm going to talk about collision and broadcast domains enough to make you dream about them!

FIGURE 1.1   A very basic network

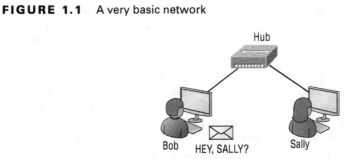

Things really can't get much simpler than this. And, yes, though you can still find this configuration in some home networks, even many of those as well as the smallest business networks are more complicated today. As we move through this book, I'll just keep building upon this tiny network a bit at a time until we arrive at some really nice, robust, and current network designs—the types that will help you get your certification and a job!

But as I said, we'll get there one step at a time, so let's get back to the network shown in Figure 1.1 with this scenario: Bob wants to send Sally a file, and to complete that goal in this kind of network, he'll simply broadcast that he's looking for her, which is basically just shouting out over the network. Think of it like this: Bob walks out of his house and yells down a street called Chaos Court in order to contact Sally. This might work if Bob and Sally were the only ones living there, but not so much if it's crammed with homes and all the others living there are always hollering up and down the street to their neighbors, just like Bob. Nope, Chaos Court would absolutely live up to its name, with all those residents going off whenever they felt like it—and believe it or not, our networks actually still work this way to a degree! So, given a choice, would you stay in Chaos Court, or would you pull up stakes and move on over to a nice new modern community called Broadway Lanes, which offers plenty of amenities and room for your home plus future additions, all on nice, wide streets that can easily handle all present and future traffic? If you chose the latter, good choice—so did Sally, and she now lives a much quieter life, getting letters (packets) from Bob instead of a headache!

The scenario I just described brings me to the basic point of what this book and the Cisco certification objectives are really all about. My goal of showing you how to create efficient networks and segment them correctly in order to minimize all the chaotic yelling and screaming going on in them is a universal theme throughout my CCST and CCNA series books.

At some point you will inevitably have to break up a large network into a bunch of smaller ones to match a network's equally inevitable growth. As that expansion occurs, user response time will simultaneously dwindle to a frustrating crawl. If you master the vital technology and skills I have in store for you in this series, however, you'll be well equipped to rescue your network and its users by creating an efficient new network neighborhood to give them key amenities like the bandwidth they need to meet their evolving demands.

And this is no joke; most of us think of growth as good—and it can be—but as many of us experience daily when commuting to work, school, etc., it can also mean your LAN's traffic congestion can reach critical mass and grind to a complete halt! Again, the solution to this problem begins with breaking up a massive network into a number of smaller ones—something called *network segmentation*. This concept is a lot like planning a new community or modernizing an existing one. More streets are added, complete with new intersections and traffic signals, plus post offices are built, with official maps documenting all those street names and directions on how to get to each. You'll need to effect new laws to keep order to it all, and provide a police station to protect this nice new neighborhood. In a networking neighborhood environment, all of this is carried out using devices like *routers, switches,* and *bridges.*

So let's take a look at our new neighborhood now, because the word has gotten out; many more hosts have moved into it, so it's time to upgrade that new high-capacity infrastructure that we promised to handle the increase in population. Figure 1.2 shows a network that's been segmented with a switch, making each network segment that connects to the switch its own separate collision domain. Doing this results in a lot less yelling!

FIGURE 1.2 A switch can break up collision domains

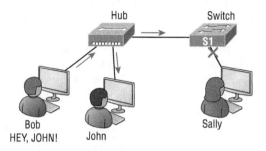

This is a great start, but I really want you to make note of the fact that this network is still one, single broadcast domain, meaning that we've really only decreased our screaming and yelling, not eliminated it. For example, if there's some sort of vital announcement that everyone in our neighborhood needs to hear about, it will definitely still get loud! You can see that the hub used in Figure 1.2 just extended the one collision domain from the switch port. The result is that John received the data from Bob, but, happily, Sally did not. This is good because Bob intended to talk with John directly, and if he had needed to send a broadcast instead, everyone, including Sally, would have received it, possibly causing unnecessary congestion.

Here's a list of some of the things that commonly cause LAN traffic congestion:

- Too many hosts in a collision or broadcast domain
- Broadcast storms
- Too much multicast traffic
- Low bandwidth
- Adding hubs for connectivity to the network
- A bunch of ARP broadcasts

Take another look at Figure 1.2 and make sure you see that I extended the main hub from Figure 1.1 to a switch in Figure 1.2. I did that because hubs don't segment a network; they just connect network segments. Basically, it's an inexpensive way to connect a couple of PCs, and again, that's great for home use and troubleshooting, but that's about it!

As our planned community starts to grow, we'll need to add more streets with traffic control, and even some basic security. We'll achieve this by adding routers, because these convenient devices are used to connect networks and route packets of data from one network to another. Cisco became the de facto standard for routers because of its unparalleled selection of high-quality router products and fantastic service. So never forget that, by default, routers are basically employed to efficiently break up a *broadcast domain*—the set of all devices on a network segment that are allowed to "hear" all broadcasts sent out on that specific segment.

Figure 1.3 depicts a router in our growing network, creating an internetwork and breaking up broadcast domains.

FIGURE 1.3   Routers create an internetwork

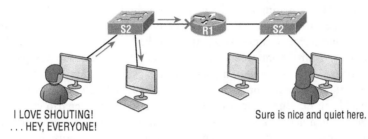

I LOVE SHOUTING!
. . . HEY, EVERYONE!

Sure is nice and quiet here.

The network in Figure 1.3 is actually a pretty cool little network. Each host is connected to its own collision domain because of the switch, and the router has created two broadcast domains. So now our Sally is happily living in peace in a completely different neighborhood, no longer subjected to Bob's incessant shouting. If Bob wants to talk with Sally, he has to send a packet with a destination address using her IP address—he cannot broadcast for her!

But there's more. Routers provide connections to *wide area network (WAN)* services as well via a serial interface for WAN connections—specifically, a V.35 physical interface on a Cisco router. (Note that a serial V.35 is an older interface, but you still may find some in use.)

Let me make sure you understand why breaking up a broadcast domain is so important. When a host or server sends a network broadcast, every device on the network must read and process that broadcast—unless you have a router. When the router's interface receives this broadcast, it can respond by basically saying, "Thanks, but no thanks," and discard the broadcast without forwarding it on to other networks. Even though routers are known for breaking up broadcast domains by default, it's important to remember that they break up collision domains as well.

There are two advantages to using routers in your network:

- They don't forward broadcasts by default.
- They can filter the network based on layer 3 (Network layer) information such as an IP address.

Here are four ways a router functions in your network:

- Packet switching
- Packet filtering
- Internetwork communication
- Path selection

I'll tell you all about the various layers later in this chapter, but for now it's helpful to think of routers as layer 3 switches. Unlike plain-vanilla layer 2 switches, which forward or filter frames, routers (layer 3 switches) use logical addressing and provide an important capacity called *packet switching*. Routers can also provide packet filtering via access lists, and when routers connect two or more networks together and use logical addressing (IP or IPv6), you then have an *internetwork*. Finally, routers use a routing table, which is essentially a map of the internetwork, to make the best path selections for getting data to its proper destination and properly forwarding packets to remote networks.

Conversely, we don't use layer 2 switches to create internetworks, because they don't break up broadcast domains by default. Instead, they're employed to add functionality to a network LAN. The main purpose of these switches is to make a LAN work better—to optimize its performance—providing more bandwidth for the LAN's users. Also, these switches don't forward packets to other networks like routers do. Instead, they only "switch" frames from one port to another within the switched network. And, don't worry, even though you're probably thinking, "Wait—what are frames and packets?" I promise to completely fill you in later in this chapter. For now, think of a packet as a package containing data.

Okay, so by default, switches break up collision domains, but what are these things? A *collision domain* is an Ethernet term used to describe a network scenario in which one device sends a packet out on a network segment and every other device on that same segment is forced to pay attention, no matter what. This isn't very efficient, because if a different device tries to transmit at the same time, a collision will occur, requiring both devices to retransmit, one at a time—not good! This happens a lot in a hub environment, where each host segment connects to a hub that represents only one collision domain and a single broadcast domain. By contrast, each and every port on a switch represents its own collision domain, allowing network traffic to flow much more smoothly.

> **NOTE** Switches create separate collision domains within a single broadcast domain. Routers provide a separate broadcast domain for each interface. Don't let this ever confuse you!

The term *bridging* was introduced before routers and switches were implemented, so it's pretty common to hear people referring to switches as bridges. That's because bridges and switches basically do the same thing—break up collision domains on a LAN. Note to self that you cannot buy physical bridges these days, only LAN switches, which use bridging technologies. This does not mean that you won't still hear Cisco and others refer to LAN switches as multiport bridges now and then.

But does it mean that a switch is just a multiple-port bridge with more brainpower? Well, pretty much, only there are still some key differences. Switches do provide a bridging function, but they do that with greatly enhanced management ability and features. Plus, most bridges had only two or four ports, which is severely limiting. Of course, it was possible to get your hands on a bridge with up to 16 ports, but that's nothing compared to the hundreds of ports available on some switches!

Figure 1.4 shows how a network would look with all these internetwork devices in place. Remember, a router doesn't just break up broadcast domains for every LAN interface, it breaks up collision domains too.

FIGURE 1.4   Internetworking devices

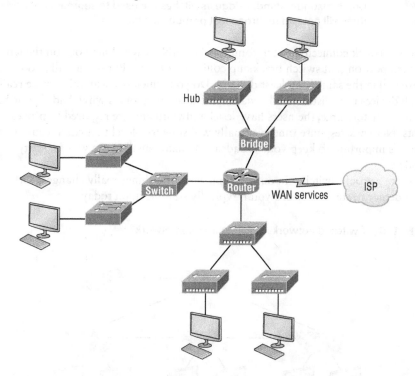

Looking at Figure 1.4, did you notice that the router has the center stage position and connects each physical network together? I'm stuck with using this layout because of the ancient bridges and hubs involved. I really hope you don't run across a network like this, but it's still really important to understand the strategic ideas that this figure represents!

See that bridge up at the top of our internetwork shown in Figure 1.4? It's there to connect the hubs to a router. The bridge breaks up collision domains, but all the hosts connected to both hubs are still crammed into the same broadcast domain. That bridge also created only three collision domains, one for each port, which means that each device connected to a hub is in the same collision domain as every other device connected to that same hub. This is really lame and to be avoided if possible, but it's still better than having one collision domain for all hosts! So don't do this at home; it's a great museum piece and a wonderful example of what not to do, but this inefficient design would be terrible for use in today's networks! However, it does show us how far we've come, and, again, the foundational concepts it illustrates are really important for you to get.

And I want you to notice something else: The three interconnected hubs at the bottom of the figure also connect to the router. This setup creates one collision domain and one broadcast domain and makes that bridged network, with its two collision domains, look majorly better by contrast!

Don't misunderstand: Bridges/switches are used to segment networks, but they will not isolate broadcast or multicast packets.

The best network connected to the router is the LAN switched network on the left. Why? Because each port on that switch breaks up collision domains. But it's not all good—all devices are still in the same broadcast domain. Do you remember why this can be really bad? Because all devices must listen to all broadcasts transmitted, that's why! And if your broadcast domains are too large, the users have less bandwidth and are required to process more broadcasts. Network response time eventually will slow to a level that could cause riots and strikes, so it's important to keep your broadcast domains small in the vast majority of networks today.

Once there are only switches in our example network, things really change a lot! Figure 1.5 demonstrates a network you'll typically stumble upon today.

FIGURE 1.5   Switched networks creating an internetwork

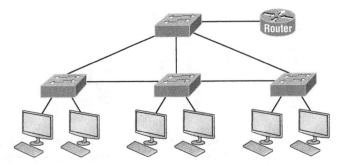

Here, I've placed the LAN switches at the center of this network world, with the router connecting the logical networks. If I went ahead and implemented this design, I'll have created something called virtual LANs, or VLANs, which are used when you logically break up broadcast domains in a layer 2, switched network. It's really important to understand that even in a switched network environment, you still need a router to provide communication between VLANs. Don't forget that!

Still, clearly the best network design is the one that's perfectly configured to meet the business requirements of the specific company or client it serves, and it's usually one in which LAN switches exist in harmony with routers strategically placed in the network. It's my hope that this book will help you understand the basics of routers and switches so you can make solid, informed decisions on a case-by-case basis and be able to achieve that goal! But I digress.

So let's go back to Figure 1.4 now for a minute and really scrutinize it, because I want to ask you this question: How many collision domains and broadcast domains are really there in this internetwork? I hope you answered nine collision domains and three broadcast domains! The broadcast domains are definitely the easiest to spot, because only routers break up broadcast domains by default, and since there are three interface connections, that gives you three broadcast domains. But do you see the nine collision domains? Just in case that's a no, I'll explain. The all-hub network at the bottom is one collision domain; the bridge network on top equals three collision domains. Add in the switch network of five collision domains—one for each switch port—and you get a total of nine!

While we're at this, back in Figure 1.5, each port on the switch is a separate collision domain, and each VLAN would be a separate broadcast domain. So how many collision domains do you see here? I'm counting 12—remember that connections between the switches are considered a collision domain! Since the figure doesn't show any VLAN information, we can assume the default of one broadcast domain is in place.

Before we move on to internetworking models, let's take a look at a few more network devices that we'll find in pretty much every network today (see Figure 1.6).

FIGURE 1.6   Other devices typically found in our internetworks today

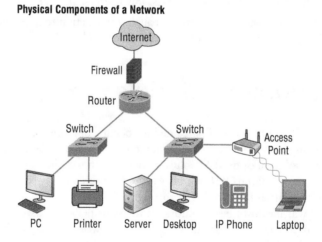

Taking off from the switched network in Figure 1.5, you'll find wireless LAN (WLAN) devices, including access points (APs) and wireless controllers, and firewalls. You'd be hardpressed not to find these devices in your networks today. Let's look closer at these devices:

- **WLAN devices:** These devices connect wireless devices such as computers, printers, and tablets to the network. Since pretty much every device manufactured today has a wireless network interface card (NIC), you just need to configure a basic access point (AP) to connect to a traditional wired network.

- **Access points (APs):** These devices allow wireless devices to connect to a wired network and extend a collision domain from a switch, and are typically in their own broadcast domain, or what we'll refer to as a virtual LAN (VLAN). An AP can be a simple standalone device, but today they are usually managed by wireless controllers either in house or through the Internet.

- **WLAN controllers:** These are the devices that network administrators or network operations centers use to manage access points in medium to large to extremely large quantities.

  The WLAN controller automatically handles the configuration of wireless access points and was typically used only in larger enterprise systems. However, with Cisco's acquisition of Meraki systems, you can easily manage a small- to medium-sized wireless network via the cloud using their simple-to-configure web controller system.

- **Firewalls:** These devices are network security systems that monitor and control the incoming and outgoing network traffic based on predetermined security rules and are usually part of an intrusion protection system (IPS). Cisco Adaptive Security Appliance (ASA) firewall typically establishes a barrier between a trusted, secure internal network and the Internet, which is neither secure nor trusted. Cisco's new acquisition of Sourcefire put them in the top of the market with next-generation firewalls (NGFWs) and next-generation IPS (NGIPS), which Cisco now just calls Secure Firewall for what was once known as Firepower. Cisco's Secure Firewall (also called Firepower) runs on dedicated management appliances, Cisco's ASAs, ISR routers, and even on Meraki products.

Okay, so now that you've gotten a pretty thorough introduction to internetworking and the various devices that populate an internetwork, it's time to explore the internetworking models.

Internetworking Models

First a little history: When networks first came into being, computers could typically communicate only with computers from the same manufacturer. For example, companies ran either a complete DECnet solution or an IBM solution, never both together. In the late 1970s, the *Open Systems Interconnection (OSI) reference model* was created by the International Organization for Standardization (ISO) to break through this barrier.

The OSI model was meant to help vendors create interoperable network devices and software in the form of protocols so that different vendor networks could work in peaceable accord with each other. Like world peace, it'll probably never happen completely, but it's still a great goal!

Anyway, the OSI model is the primary architectural model for networks. It describes how data and network information are communicated from an application on one computer through the network media to an application on another computer. The OSI reference model breaks this approach into layers.

Coming up next, I'll explain the layered approach plus how we can use it to help us troubleshoot our internetworks.

The Layered Approach

Understand that a *reference model* is a conceptual blueprint of how communications should take place. It addresses all the processes required for effective communication and divides them into logical groupings called *layers*. When a communication system is designed in this manner, it's known as a hierarchical or *layered architecture*.

Think of it like this: You and some friends want to start a company. One of the first things you'll do is sort out every task that must be done and decide who will do what. You would move on to determine the order in which you would like everything to be done, with careful consideration of how all your specific operations relate to each other. You would then organize everything into departments (e.g., sales, inventory, and shipping), with each department dealing with its specific responsibilities and keeping its own staff busy enough to focus on their own particular area of the enterprise.

In this scenario, the departments are a metaphor for the layers in a communication system. For things to run smoothly, the staff of each department has to trust in and rely heavily upon those in the other departments to do their jobs well. During planning sessions, you would take notes, recording the entire process to guide later discussions and clarify standards of operation, thereby creating your business blueprint—your own reference model.

And once your business is launched, your department heads, each armed with the part of the blueprint relevant to their own department, will develop practical ways to implement their distinct tasks. These practical methods, or protocols, will then be compiled into a standard operating procedures manual and followed closely, because each procedure will have been included for different reasons, delimiting their various degrees of importance and implementation. All of this will become vital if you form a partnership or acquire another company, because then it will be really important that the new company's business model is compatible with yours!

Models happen to be really important to software developers too. They often use a reference model to understand computer communication processes so they can determine which functions should be accomplished on a given layer. This means that if someone is creating a protocol for a certain layer, they only need to be concerned with their target layer's function. Software that maps to another layer's protocols and is specifically designed to be deployed there will handle additional functions. The technical term for this idea is *binding*. The communication processes that are related to each other are bound, or grouped together, at a particular layer.

Advantages of Reference Models

The OSI model is hierarchical, and there are many advantages that can be applied to any layered model, but as I said, the OSI model's primary purpose is to allow different vendors' networks to interoperate.

Here's a list of some of the more important benefits of using the OSI layered model:

- It divides the network communication process into smaller and simpler components, facilitating component development, design, and troubleshooting.
- It allows multiple-vendor development through the standardization of network components.
- It encourages industry standardization by clearly defining which functions occur at each layer of the model.
- It allows various types of network hardware and software to communicate.
- It prevents changes in one layer from affecting other layers to expedite development.

The OSI Reference Model

One of the best gifts the OSI specifications give us is paving the way for the data transfer between disparate hosts running different operating systems, like Unix hosts, Windows machines, Macs, smartphones, and so on.

And remember, the OSI is a logical model, not a physical one. It's essentially a set of guidelines that developers can use to create and implement applications to run on a network. It also provides a framework for creating and implementing networking standards, devices, and internetworking schemes.

The OSI has seven different layers, divided into two groups. The top three layers define how the applications within the end stations will communicate with each other as well as with users. The bottom four layers define how data is transmitted end to end.

Figure 1.7 shows the three upper layers and their functions.

FIGURE 1.7   The upper layers

Application	• Provides a user interface
Presentation	• Presents data • Handles processing such as encryption
Session	• Keeps different applications' data separate

When looking at Figure 1.7, understand that users interact with the computer at the Application layer and that the upper layers are responsible for applications communicating between hosts. None of the upper layers knows anything about networking or network addresses, because that's the responsibility of the four bottom layers.

In Figure 1.8, which shows the four lower layers and their functions, you can see that it's these four bottom layers that define how data is transferred through physical media like wire, cable, fiber optics, switches, and routers. These bottom layers also determine how to rebuild a data stream from a transmitting host to a destination host's application.

FIGURE 1.8   The lower layers

Transport	• Provides reliable or unreliable delivery • Performs error correction before retransmit
Network	• Provides logical addressing, which routers use for path determination
Data Link	• Combines packets into bytes and bytes into frames • Provides access to media using MAC address • Performs error detection, not correction
Physical	• Moves bits between devices • Specifies voltage, wire speed, and pinout of cables

The following network devices operate at all seven layers of the OSI model:

- Network management stations (NMSs)
- Web and application servers
- Gateways (not default gateways)
- Servers
- Network hosts

Basically, the ISO is pretty much the Emily Post of the network protocol world. Just as Ms. Post wrote the book setting the standards—or protocols—for human social interaction, the ISO developed the OSI reference model as the precedent and guide for an open network protocol set. Defining the etiquette of communication models, it remains the most popular means of comparison for protocol suites today.

The OSI reference model has the following seven layers:

- Application layer (layer 7)
- Presentation layer (layer 6)
- Session layer (layer 5)
- Transport layer (layer 4)
- Network layer (layer 3)
- Data Link layer (layer 2)
- Physical layer (layer 1)

Some people like to use a mnemonic to remember the seven layers, such as **All People Seem To Need Data Processing**. Figure 1.9 shows a summary of the functions defined at each layer of the OSI model.

FIGURE 1.9   OSI layer functions

Application	• File, print, message, database, and application services
Presentation	• Data encryption, compression, and translation services
Session	• Dialog control

Transport	• End-to-end connection
Network	• Routing

Data Link	• Framing
Physical	• Physical topology

I've separated the seven-layer model into three different functions: the upper layers, the middle layers, and the bottom layers. The upper layers communicate with the user interface and application, the middle layers do reliable communication and routing to a remote network, and the bottom layers communicate to the local network.

With this in hand, you're now ready to explore each layer's function in detail.

The Application Layer

The *Application layer* of the OSI model marks the spot where users actually communicate to the computer and comes into play only when it's clear that access to the network will be needed soon. Take the case of Internet Explorer (IE). You could actually uninstall every trace of networking components like TCP/IP, the network interface card (NIC) card, and so on and still use IE to view a local HTML document. But things would get ugly if you tried to do things like view a remote HTML document that must be retrieved, because IE and other browsers act on these types of requests by attempting to access the Application layer. So basically, the Application layer is working as the interface between the actual application program and the next layer down by providing ways for the application to send information down through the protocol stack. This isn't actually part of the layered structure, because browsers don't live in the Application layer, but they interface with it as well as the relevant protocols when asked to access remote resources.

Identifying and confirming the communication partner's availability and verifying the required resources to permit the specified type of communication to take place also occurs at the Application layer. This is important because, like the lion's share of browser functions, computer applications sometimes need more than desktop resources. It's more typical than you would think for the communicating components of several network applications to come together to carry out a requested function. Here are a few good examples of these kinds of events:

- File transfers
- Email
- Enabling remote access
- Network management activities
- Client/server processes
- Information location

Many network applications provide services for communication over enterprise networks, but for present and future internetworking, the need is fast developing to reach beyond the limits of current physical networking.

NOTE The Application layer works as the interface between actual application programs. This means end-user programs like Microsoft Word don't reside at the Application layer; they interface with the Application layer protocols. In Chapter 2, "Introduction to TCP/IP," I'll talk in detail about a few important programs that actually reside at the Application layer, like Telnet, FTP, and TFTP.

The Presentation Layer

The *Presentation layer* gets its name from its purpose: It presents data to the Application layer and is responsible for data translation and code formatting. Think of it as the OSI model's translator, providing coding and conversion services. One very effective way of ensuring a successful data transfer is to convert the data into a standard format before transmission. Computers are configured to receive this generically formatted data and then reformat it back into its native state to read it. An example of this type of translation service occurs when translating old Extended Binary Coded Decimal Interchange Code (EBCDIC) data to ASCII, the American Standard Code for Information Interchange (often pronounced "askee"). So just remember that by providing translation services, the Presentation layer ensures that data transferred from the Application layer of one system can be read by the Application layer of another one.

With this in mind, it follows that the OSI would include protocols that define how standard data should be formatted, so key functions like data compression, decompression, encryption, and decryption are also associated with this layer. Some Presentation layer standards are involved in multimedia operations as well.

The Session Layer

The *Session layer* is responsible for setting up, managing, and dismantling sessions between Presentation layer entities and keeping user data separate. Dialog control between devices also occurs at this layer.

Communication between hosts' various applications at the Session layer, as from a client to a server, is coordinated and organized via three different modes: *simplex*, *half-duplex*, and *full-duplex*. Simplex is simple one-way communication, kind of like saying something and not getting a reply. Half-duplex is actual two-way communication, but it can take place in only one direction at a time, preventing the interruption of the transmitting device. It's like when pilots and ship captains communicate over their radios, or even a walkie-talkie. But full-duplex is exactly like a real conversation where devices can transmit and receive at the same time, much like two people arguing or interrupting each other during a telephone conversation.

The Transport Layer

The *Transport layer* segments and reassembles data into a single data stream. Services located at this layer take all the various data received from upper-layer applications, then combine it into the same, concise data stream. These protocols provide end-to-end data transport services and can establish a logical connection between the sending host and destination host on an internetwork.

A pair of well-known protocols called TCP and UDP are integral to this layer, but no worries if you're not already familiar with them, because I'll bring you up to speed later, in Chapter 2. For now, understand that although both work at the Transport layer, TCP is known as a reliable service, but UDP is not. This distinction gives application developers more options because they have a choice between the two protocols when they are designing products for this layer.

The Transport layer is responsible for providing mechanisms for multiplexing upper-layer applications, establishing sessions, and tearing down virtual circuits. It can also hide the details of network-dependent information from the higher layers as well as provide transparent data transfer.

 The term *reliable networking* can be used at the Transport layer. Reliable networking requires that acknowledgments, sequencing, and flow control will all be used.

The Transport layer can be either connectionless or connection-oriented, but because Cisco really wants you to understand the connection-oriented function of the Transport layer, I'm going to go into that in more detail here.

Connection-Oriented Communication

For reliable transport to occur, a device that wants to transmit must first establish a connection-oriented communication session with a remote device—its peer system—known as a *call setup* or the *three-way handshake*. Once this process is complete, the data transfer occurs, and when it's finished, a call termination takes place to tear down the virtual circuit.

Figure 1.10 depicts a typical reliable session taking place between sending and receiving systems. You can see that both hosts' application programs begin by notifying their individual operating systems that a connection is about to be initiated. The two operating systems communicate by sending messages over the network confirming that the transfer is approved and that both sides are ready for it to take place. After all of this required synchronization takes place, a connection is fully established, and the data transfer begins. And by the way, it's really helpful to understand that this virtual circuit setup is often referred to as *overhead*.

FIGURE 1.10   Establishing a connection-oriented session

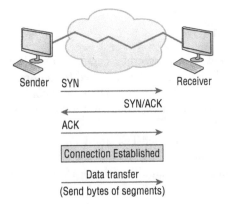

Okay, now while the information is being transferred between hosts, the two machines periodically check in with each other, communicating through their protocol software to ensure that all is going well and that the data is being received properly.

Here's a summary of the steps in the connection-oriented session—that three-way handshake—pictured in Figure 1.10:

- The first "connection agreement" segment is a request for *synchronization (SYN)*.

- The next segments *acknowledge (ACK)* the request and establish connection parameters—the rules—between hosts. These segments request that the receiver's sequencing is synchronized here as well so that a bidirectional connection can be formed.

- The final segment is also an acknowledgment, which notifies the destination host that the connection agreement has been accepted and that the actual connection has been established. Data transfer can now begin.

Sounds pretty simple, but things don't always flow so smoothly. Sometimes during a transfer, congestion can occur because a high-speed computer is generating data traffic a lot faster than the network itself can process it! And a whole bunch of computers simultaneously sending datagrams through a single gateway or destination can also jam things up pretty badly. In the latter case, a gateway or destination can become congested even though no single source caused the problem. Either way, the problem is basically akin to a freeway bottleneck—too much traffic for too small a capacity. It's not usually one car that's the problem; it's just that there are way too many cars on that freeway at once!

But what actually happens when a machine receives a flood of datagrams too quickly for it to process? It stores them in a memory section called a *buffer*. Sounds great; it's just that this buffering action can solve the problem only if the datagrams are part of a small burst. If the datagram deluge continues, eventually exhausting the device's memory, its flood capacity will be exceeded, and it will dump any and all additional datagrams it receives just like an inundated overflowing bucket!

Flow Control

Since floods and losing data can both be tragic, we have a fail-safe solution in place known as *flow control*. Its job is to ensure data integrity at the Transport layer by allowing applications to request reliable data transport between systems. Flow control prevents a sending host on one side of the connection from overflowing the buffers in the receiving host. Reliable data transport employs a connection-oriented communications session between systems, and the protocols involved ensure that the following will be achieved:

- The segments delivered are acknowledged back to the sender upon their reception.

- Any segments not acknowledged are retransmitted.

- Segments are sequenced back into their proper order upon arrival at their destination.

- A manageable data flow is maintained in order to avoid congestion, overloading, or, worse, data loss.

The purpose of flow control is to provide a way for the receiving device to control the amount of data sent by the sender.

Because of the transport function, network flood control systems really work well. Instead of dumping and losing data, the Transport layer can issue a "not ready" indicator to the sender, or potential source of the flood. This mechanism works kind of like a stoplight, signaling the sending device to stop transmitting segment traffic to its overwhelmed peer. After the peer receiver processes the segments already in its memory reservoir (its buffer), it sends out a "ready" transport indicator. When the machine waiting to transmit the rest of its datagrams receives this "go" indicator, it resumes its transmission. Figure 1.11 illustrates the process.

FIGURE 1.11   Transmitting segments with flow control

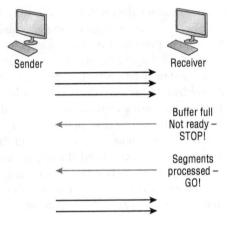

In a reliable, connection-oriented data transfer, datagrams are delivered to the receiving host hopefully in the same sequence they're transmitted. A failure will occur if any data segments are lost, duplicated, or damaged along the way—a problem solved by having the receiving host acknowledge that it has received each and every data segment.

A service is considered connection-oriented if it has the following characteristics:

- A virtual circuit, or "three-way handshake," is set up.
- It uses sequencing.
- It uses acknowledgments.
- It uses flow control.

The types of flow control are buffering, windowing, and congestion avoidance.

Windowing

Ideally, data throughput happens quickly and efficiently. And as you can imagine, it would be painfully slow if the transmitting machine had to actually wait for an acknowledgment after sending each and every segment! The quantity of data segments, measured in bytes, that the transmitting machine is allowed to send without receiving an acknowledgment is called a *window*.

> Windows are used to control the amount of outstanding, unacknowledged data segments.

The size of the window controls how much information is transferred from one end to the other before an acknowledgement is required. While some protocols quantify information depending on the number of packets, TCP/IP measures it by counting the number of bytes.

As you can see in Figure 1.12, there are two window sizes—one set to 1 and one set to 3.

FIGURE 1.12   Windowing

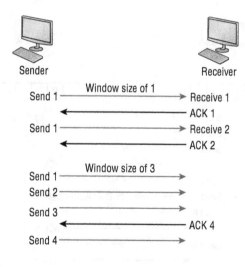

If you've configured a window size of 1, the sending machine will wait for an acknowledgment for each data segment it transmits before transmitting another one but will allow three to be transmitted before receiving an acknowledgement if the window size is set to 3.

In this simplified example, both the sending and receiving machines are workstations. Remember that in reality, the transmission isn't based on simple numbers but on the amount of bytes that can be sent!

If a receiving host fails to receive all the bytes that it should acknowledge, the host can improve the communication session by decreasing the window size.

Acknowledgments

Reliable data delivery ensures the integrity of a stream of data sent from one machine to the other through a fully functional data link. It guarantees that the data won't be duplicated or lost. This is achieved through something called *positive acknowledgment with retransmission*—a technique that requires a receiving machine to communicate with the transmitting source by sending an acknowledgment message back to the sender when it receives data. The sender documents each segment measured in bytes, then sends and waits for this acknowledgment before sending the next segment. Also important is that when it sends a segment, the transmitting machine starts a timer and will retransmit if it expires before it gets an acknowledgment back from the receiving end. Figure 1.13 shows this process.

FIGURE 1.13   Transport layer reliable delivery

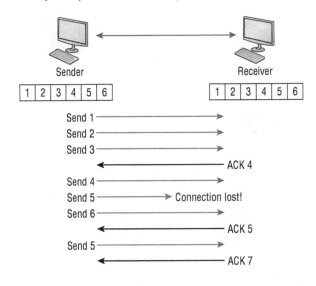

In the figure, the sending machine transmits segments 1, 2, and 3. The receiving node acknowledges that it has received them by requesting segment 4 (what it is expecting next). When it receives the acknowledgment, the sender then transmits segments 4, 5, and 6.

If segment 5 doesn't make it to the destination, the receiving node acknowledges that event with a request for the segment to be resent. The sending machine will then resend the lost segment and wait for an acknowledgment, which it must receive in order to move on to the transmission of segment 7.

The Transport layer, working in tandem with the Session layer, also separates the data from different applications, an activity known as *session multiplexing*, and it happens when a client connects to a server with multiple browser sessions open. This is exactly what's taking place when you go someplace online like Amazon and click multiple links, opening them simultaneously to get information when comparison shopping. The client data from each browser session must be separate when the server application receives it, which is pretty slick technologically speaking, and it's the Transport layer to the rescue for that juggling act!

The Network Layer

The *Network layer*, or layer 3, manages device addressing, tracks the location of devices on the network, and determines the best way to move data. This means that it's up to the Network layer to transport traffic between devices that aren't locally attached. Routers, which are layer 3 devices, are specified at this layer and provide the routing services within an internetwork.

Here's how that works: First, when a packet is received on a router interface, the destination IP address is checked. If the packet isn't destined for that particular router, it will look up the destination network address in the routing table. Once the router chooses an exit interface, the packet will be sent to that interface to be framed and sent out on the local network. If the router can't find an entry for the packet's destination network in the routing table, the router drops the packet.

Data and route update packets are the two types of packets used at the Network layer:

Data Packets   These are used to transport user data through the internetwork. Protocols used to support data traffic are called routed protocols, and IP and IPv6 are key examples. I'll cover IP addressing in Chapter 2 and Chapter 3, "Easy Subnetting."

Route Update Packets   These packets are used to update neighboring routers about the networks connected to all routers within the internetwork. Protocols that send route update packets are called routing protocols; the most common ones for CCST and the CCNA are RIPv2, EIGRP, and OSPF. Route update packets are used to help build and maintain routing tables.

Figure 1.14 shows an example of a routing table. The routing table each router keeps and refers to includes the following information:

FIGURE 1.14 A routing table used in a router

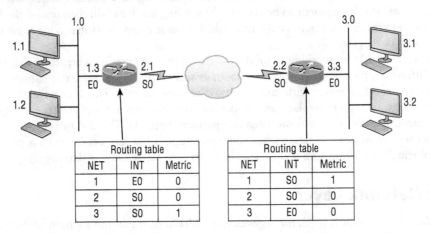

Routing table		
NET	INT	Metric
1	E0	0
2	S0	0
3	S0	1

Routing table		
NET	INT	Metric
1	S0	1
2	S0	0
3	E0	0

Network Addresses The network address would be either an IPv4 or IPv6 network address. A router must maintain a routing table for individual routing protocols because each routed protocol keeps track of a network with a different addressing scheme. For example, the routing tables for IP and IPv6 are completely different, so the router keeps a table for each one. Think of it as a street sign in each of the different languages spoken by the American, Spanish, and French people living on a street; the street sign would read Cat/Gato/Chat.

Interface The interface variable is the exit interface a packet will take when destined for a specific network.

Metric A metric is the distance to the remote network. Different routing protocols use different ways of computing this distance. I'm going to cover routing protocols thoroughly in Chapter 5, "IP Routing." For now, know that some routing protocols like the Routing Information Protocol, or RIP, use hop count, which refers to the number of routers a packet passes through en route to a remote network. Others use bandwidth, delay of the line, or even tick count (1/18 of a second) to determine the best path for data to get to a given destination.

And as I mentioned earlier, routers break up broadcast domains, which means that by default, broadcasts aren't forwarded through a router. Do you remember why this is a good thing? Routers also break up collision domains, but you can also do that using layer 2 (Data Link layer) switches. Because each interface in a router represents a separate network, it must be assigned unique network identification numbers, and each host on the network connected to that router must use the same network number. Figure 1.15 shows how a router works in an internetwork.

FIGURE 1.15   A router in an internetwork. Each router LAN interface is a broadcast domain. Routers break up broadcast domains by default and provide WAN services.

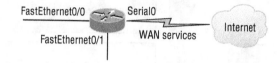

Here are some router characteristics that you should never forget:

- Routers, by default, will not forward any broadcast or multicast packets.

- Routers use the logical address in a Network layer header to determine the next-hop router to forward the packet to.

- Routers can use access lists, created by an administrator, to control security based on the types of packets allowed to enter or exit an interface.

- Routers can provide layer 2 bridging functions if needed and can simultaneously route through the same interface.

- Layer 3 devices—in this case, routers—provide connections between *virtual LANs (VLANs)*.

- Routers can provide *quality of service (QoS)* for specific types of network traffic.

The Data Link Layer

The *Data Link layer* provides for the physical transmission of data and handles error notification, network topology, and flow control. This means that the Data Link layer will ensure that messages are delivered to the proper device on a LAN using hardware addresses and will translate messages from the Network layer into bits for the Physical layer to transmit.

The Data Link layer formats the messages, each called a *data frame*, and adds a customized header containing the hardware destination and source address. This added information forms a sort of capsule that surrounds the original message in much the same way that engines, navigational devices, and other tools were attached to the lunar modules of the Apollo project. These various pieces of equipment were useful only during certain stages of space flight and were stripped off the module and discarded when their designated stage was completed. The process of data traveling through networks is similar.

Figure 1.16 shows the Data Link layer with the Ethernet and IEEE specifications. When you check it out, notice that the IEEE 802.2 standard is used in conjunction with and adds functionality to the other IEEE standards.

FIGURE 1.16   The Data Link layer

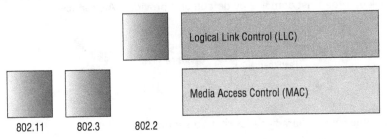

It's important for you to understand that routers, which work at the Network layer, don't care at all about where a particular host is located. They're only concerned about where networks are located and the best way to reach them—including remote ones. Routers are totally obsessive when it comes to networks, which in this case is a good thing! It's the Data Link layer that's responsible for the actual unique identification of each device that resides on a local network.

For a host to send packets to individual hosts on a local network as well as transmit packets between routers, the Data Link layer uses hardware addressing. Each time a packet is sent between routers, it's framed with control information at the Data Link layer, but that information is stripped off at the receiving router, and only the original packet is left completely intact. This framing of the packet continues for each hop until the packet is finally delivered to the correct receiving host. It's really important to understand that the packet itself is never altered along the route; it's only encapsulated with the type of control information required for it to be properly passed on to the different media types.

The IEEE Ethernet Data Link layer has two sublayers:

Media Access Control (MAC)   The MAC sublayer defines how packets are placed on the media. Contention for media access is "first come/first served" access where everyone shares the same bandwidth—hence the name. Physical addressing is defined here as well as logical topologies. What's a logical topology? It's the signal path through a physical topology. Line discipline, error notification (but not correction), the ordered delivery of frames, and optional flow control can also be used at this sublayer.

Logical Link Control (LLC)   The LLC sublayer is responsible for identifying Network layer protocols and then encapsulating them. An LLC header tells the Data Link layer what to do with a packet once a frame is received. It works like this: A host receives a frame and looks in the LLC header to find out where the packet is destined—for instance, the IP protocol at the Network layer. The LLC can also provide flow control and sequencing of control bits.

The switches and bridges I talked about near the beginning of the chapter both work at the Data Link layer and filter the network using hardware (MAC) addresses. I'll talk about these next.

As data is encoded with control information at each layer of the OSI model, the data is named with something called a protocol data unit (PDU). At the Transport layer, the PDU is called a segment; at the Network layer, a packet; at the Data Link, a frame; and at the Physical layer, it's called bits.

Switches and Bridges at the Data Link Layer

Layer 2 switching is considered hardware-based bridging because it uses specialized hardware called an *application-specific integrated circuit (ASIC)*. ASICs can run up to high gigabit speeds with very low latency rates.

Latency is the time measured from when a frame enters a port to when it exits a port.

Bridges and switches read each frame as it passes through the network. The layer 2 device then puts the source hardware address in a filter table and keeps track of which port the frame was received on. This information (logged in the bridge's or switch's filter table) is what helps the machine determine the location of the specific sending device.

Figure 1.17 shows a switch in an internetwork and how John is sending packets to the Internet and Sally doesn't hear his frames because she is in a different collision domain. The destination frame goes directly to the default gateway router, and Sally doesn't see John's traffic, much to her relief.

FIGURE 1.17   A switch in an internetwork

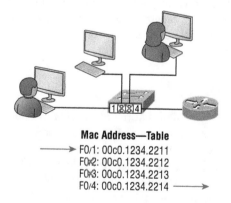

Mac Address—Table
F0/1: 00c0.1234.2211
F0/2: 00c0.1234.2212
F0/3: 00c0.1234.2213
F0/4: 00c0.1234.2214

The real estate business is all about location, location, location, and it's the same way for both layer 2 and layer 3 devices. Though both need to be able to negotiate the network, it's crucial to remember that they're concerned with very different parts of it. Primarily, layer 3 machines (such as routers) need to locate specific networks, whereas layer 2 machines (switches and bridges) need to eventually locate specific devices. So, networks are to routers as individual devices are to switches and bridges. And routing tables that "map" the internetwork are for routers as filter tables that "map" individual devices are for switches and bridges.

After a filter table is built on the layer 2 device, it will forward frames only to the segment where the destination hardware address is located. If the destination device is on the same segment as the frame, the layer 2 device will block the frame from going to any other segments. If the destination is on a different segment, the frame can be transmitted only to that segment. This is called *transparent bridging*.

When a switch interface receives a frame with a destination hardware address that isn't found in the device's filter table, it will forward the frame to all connected segments. If the unknown device that was sent the "mystery frame" replies to this forwarding action, the switch updates its filter table regarding that device's location. But in the event the destination address of the transmitting frame is a broadcast address, the switch will forward all broadcasts to every connected segment by default.

All devices that the broadcast is forwarded to are considered to be in the same broadcast domain. This can be a problem because layer 2 devices propagate layer 2 broadcast storms that can seriously choke performance, and the only way to stop a broadcast storm from propagating through an internetwork is with a layer 3 device—a router!

The biggest benefit of using switches instead of hubs in your internetwork is that each switch port is actually its own collision domain. Remember that a hub creates one large collision domain, which is not a good thing! But even armed with a switch, you still don't get to just break up broadcast domains by default, because neither switches nor bridges will do that. They'll simply forward all broadcasts instead.

Another benefit of LAN switching over hub-centered implementations is that each device on every segment plugged into a switch can transmit simultaneously. Well, at least they can as long as there's only one host on each port, and there isn't a hub plugged into a switch port! As you might have guessed, this is because hubs allow only one device per network segment to communicate at a time.

The Physical Layer

Finally arriving at the bottom, we find that the *Physical layer* does two things: It sends bits and receives bits. Bits come only in values of 1 or 0—a Morse code with numerical values. The Physical layer communicates directly with the various types of actual communication media. Different kinds of media represent these bit values in different ways. Some use audio tones, while others employ *state transitions*—changes in voltage from high to low and low to high. Specific protocols are needed for each type of media to describe the proper bit patterns to be used, how data is encoded into media signals, and the various qualities of the physical media's attachment interface.

The Physical layer specifies the electrical, mechanical, procedural, and functional requirements for activating, maintaining, and deactivating a physical link between end systems.

This layer is also where you identify the interface between the *data terminal equipment (DTE)* and the *data communication equipment (DCE)*. (Some old phone-company employees still call DCE "data circuit-terminating equipment.") The DCE is usually located at the service provider, while the DTE is the attached device. The services available to the DTE are most often accessed via a modem or *channel service unit/data service unit (CSU/DSU)*.

The Physical layer's connectors and different physical topologies are defined by the OSI as standards, allowing disparate systems to communicate. The Cisco exam objectives are interested only in the IEEE Ethernet standards.

Hubs at the Physical Layer

A hub is really a multiple-port repeater. A repeater receives a digital signal, reamplifies or regenerates that signal, and then forwards the signal out the other port without looking at any data. A hub does the same thing across all active ports: Any digital signal received from a segment on a hub port is regenerated or reamplified and transmitted out all other ports on the hub. This means all devices plugged into a hub are in the same collision domain as well as in the same broadcast domain. Figure 1.18 shows a hub in a network and how when one host transmits, all other hosts must stop and listen.

FIGURE 1.18   A hub in a network

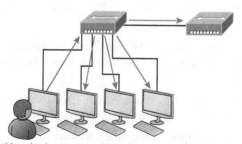

I love it when everyone has to listen to everything I say!

Hubs, like repeaters, don't examine any of the traffic as it enters or before it's transmitted out to the other parts of the physical media. And every device connected to the hub, or hubs, must listen if a device transmits. A physical star network, where the hub is a central device and cables extend in all directions out from it, is the type of topology a hub creates. Visually, the design really does resemble a star, whereas Ethernet networks run a logical bus topology, meaning that the signal has to run through the network from end to end.

Hubs and repeaters can be used to enlarge the area covered by a single LAN segment, but I really do not recommend going with this configuration! LAN switches are affordable for almost every situation and will make you much happier.

Topologies at the Physical layer

One last thing I want to discuss at the Physical layer is topologies, both physical and logical. Understand that every type of network has both a physical and a logical topology.

- The physical topology of a network refers to the physical layout of the devices, but mostly the cabling and cabling layout.

- The logical topology defines the logical path on which the signal will travel on the physical topology.

  Figure 1.19 shows the four types of topologies.

FIGURE 1.19   Physical vs. logical topologies

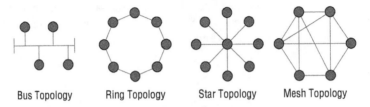

- Physical topology is the physical layout of the devices and cabling.
- The primary physical topology categories are bus, ring, star, and mesh.

Bus Topology   Ring Topology   Star Topology   Mesh Topology

Here are the topology types, although the most common and pretty much the only network we use today is a physical star, logical bus technology, which is considered a hybrid topology (think Ethernet):

- **Bus:** In a bus topology, every workstation is connected to a single cable, meaning every host is directly connected to every other workstation in the network.

- **Ring:** In a ring topology, computers and other network devices are cabled together in a way that the last device is connected to the first to form a circle or ring.

- **Star:** The most common physical topology is a star topology, which is your Ethernet switching physical layout. A central cabling device (switch) connects the computers and other network devices together. This category includes star and extended star topologies. Physical connection is commonly made using twisted-pair wiring.

- **Mesh:** In a mesh topology, every network device is cabled together with a connection to each other. Redundant links increase reliability and self-healing. The physical connection is commonly made using fiber or twisted-pair wiring.

- **Hybrid:** Ethernet uses a physical star layout (cables come from all directions), and the signal travels end to end, like a bus route.

Summary

Whew! I know this seemed like the chapter that wouldn't end, but it did—and you made it through! You're now armed with a ton of fundamental information; you're ready to build upon it and are well on your way to certification.

I started by discussing simple, basic networking and the differences between collision and broadcast domains.

I then discussed the OSI model—the seven-layer model used to help application developers design applications that can run on any type of system or network. Each layer has its special jobs and select responsibilities within the model to ensure that solid, effective communications do, in fact, occur. I provided you with complete details of each layer and discussed how Cisco views the specifications of the OSI model.

In addition, each layer in the OSI model specifies different types of devices, and I described the different devices used at each layer.

Remember that hubs are Physical layer devices and repeat the digital signal to all segments except the one from which it was received. Switches segment the network using hardware addresses and break up collision domains. Routers break up broadcast domains as well as collision domains and use logical addressing to send packets through an internetwork.

Exam Essentials

Identify the possible causes of LAN traffic congestion.   Too many hosts in a broadcast domain, broadcast storms, multicasting, and low bandwidth are all possible causes of LAN traffic congestion.

Describe the difference between a collision domain and a broadcast domain.   *Collision domain* is an Ethernet term used to describe a network collection of devices in which one particular device sends a packet on a network segment, forcing every other device on that same segment to pay attention to it. With a *broadcast domain*, a set of all devices on a network hears all broadcasts sent on all segments.

Differentiate a MAC address and an IP address and describe how and when each address type is used in a network.   A MAC address is a hexadecimal number identifying the physical connection of a host. MAC addresses are said to operate on layer 2 of the OSI model. IP addresses, which can be expressed in binary or decimal format, are logical identifiers that are said to be on layer 3 of the OSI model. Hosts on the same physical segment locate one another with MAC addresses, while IP addresses are used when they reside on different LAN segments or subnets.

Understand the difference between a hub, a bridge, a switch, and a router.   A hub creates one collision domain and one broadcast domain. A bridge breaks up collision domains but creates one large broadcast domain. They use hardware addresses to filter the network. Switches are really just multiple-port bridges with more intelligence; they break up collision domains but create one large broadcast domain by default. Bridges and switches use hardware addresses to filter the network. Routers break up broadcast domains (and collision domains) and use logical addressing to filter the network.

Identify the functions and advantages of routers.   Routers perform packet switching, filtering, and path selection, and they facilitate internetwork communication. One advantage of routers is that they reduce broadcast traffic.

Differentiate connection-oriented and connectionless network services and describe how each is handled during network communications.   Connection-oriented services use acknowledgments and flow control to create a reliable session. More overhead is used than in a connectionless network service. Connectionless services are used to send data with no acknowledgments or flow control. This is considered unreliable.

Define the OSI layers, understand the function of each, and describe how devices and networking protocols can be mapped to each layer.   You must remember the seven layers of the OSI model and what function each layer provides. The Application, Presentation, and Session layers are upper layers and are responsible for communicating from a user interface to an application. The Transport layer provides segmentation, sequencing, and virtual circuits. The Network layer provides logical network addressing and routing through an internetwork. The Data Link layer provides framing and placing of data on the network medium. The Physical layer is responsible for taking 1s and 0s and encoding them into a digital signal for transmission on the network segment.

Review Questions

The following questions are designed to test your understanding of this chapter's material. For more information on how to get additional questions, please see www.lammle.com/ccst.

You can find the answers to these questions in Appendix, "Answers to Review Questions."

1. With respect to the OSI model, which one of the following is the correct statement about PDUs?

   A. A segment contains IP addresses.

   B. A packet contains IP addresses.

   C. A segment contains MAC addresses.

   D. A packet contains MAC addresses.

2. You are the Cisco administrator for your company. A new branch office is opening and you are selecting the necessary hardware to support the network. There will be two groups of computers, each organized by department. The Sales group computers will be assigned IP addresses ranging from 192.168.1.2 to 192.168.1.50. The Accounting group will be assigned IP addresses ranging from 10.0.0.2 to 10.0.0.50. What type of device should you select to connect the two groups of computers so that data communication can occur?

   A. Hub

   B. Switch

   C. Router

   D. Bridge

3. The most effective way to mitigate congestion on a LAN would be to _____.

   A. Upgrade the network cards

   B. Change the cabling to CAT 6

   C. Replace the hubs with switches

   D. Upgrade the CPUs in the routers

4. What is the function of the WLAN controller?

   A. To monitor and control the incoming and outgoing network traffic

   B. To automatically handle the configuration of wireless access points

   C. To allow wireless devices to connect to a wired network

   D. To connect networks and intelligently choose the best paths between networks

5. What is the function of a firewall?

   A. To automatically handle the configuration of wireless access points

   B. To allow wireless devices to connect to a wired network

C. To monitor and control the incoming and outgoing network traffic

D. To connect networks and intelligently choose the best paths between networks

6. Which layer in the OSI reference model is responsible for determining the availability of the receiving program and checking to see whether enough resources exist for that communication?

A. Transport

B. Network

C. Presentation

D. Application

7. Which of the following correctly describes steps in the OSI data encapsulation process? (Choose two.)

A. The Transport layer divides a data stream into segments and may add reliability and flow control information.

B. The Data Link layer adds physical source and destination addresses and a Frame Check Sequence (FCS) field to the segment.

C. Packets are created when the Network layer encapsulates a frame with source and destination host addresses and protocol-related control information.

D. Packets are created when the Network layer adds layer 3 addresses and control information to a segment.

E. The Presentation layer translates bits into voltages for transmission across the physical link.

8. Which of the following layers of the OSI model was later subdivided into two layers?

A. Presentation

B. Transport

C. Data Link

D. Physical

9. What is a function of an access point (AP)?

A. To monitor and control the incoming and outgoing network traffic

B. To automatically handle the configuration of wireless access point

C. To allow wireless devices to connect to a wired network

D. To connect networks and intelligently choose the best paths between networks

10. A _____ is an example of a device that operates only at the physical layer.

A. Hub

B. Switch

C. Router

D. Bridge

Chapter 2

Introduction to TCP/IP

THE CCST EXAM TOPICS COVERED IN THIS CHAPTER INCLUDE THE FOLLOWING:

✓ **1.0 Standards and Concepts**

- 1.1. Identify the fundamental conceptual building blocks of networks.

    - TCP/IP model, OSI model, frames and packets, addressing

- 1.5. Describe common network applications and protocols.

    - TCP vs. UDP (connection-oriented vs. connectionless), FTP, SFTP, TFTP, HTTP, HTTPS, DHCP, DNS, ICMP, NTP

The *Transmission Control Protocol/Internet Protocol (TCP/IP)* suite was designed and implemented by the Department of Defense (DoD) to ensure and preserve data integrity as well as maintain communications in the event of catastrophic war. So it follows that if designed and implemented correctly, a TCP/IP network can be a secure, dependable, and resilient one. In this chapter, I'll cover the protocols of TCP/IP, and throughout this book, you'll learn how to create a solid TCP/IP network with Cisco routers and switches.

We'll begin by exploring the DoD's version of TCP/IP, then compare that version and its protocols with the OSI reference model that we discussed earlier.

Once you understand the protocols and processes used at the various levels of the DoD model, we'll take the next logical step by delving into the world of IP addressing and the different classes of IP addresses used in networks today.

To find up-to-the-minute updates for this chapter, please see www.lammle.com/ccst.

Introducing TCP/IP

TCP/IP is at the very core of all things networking, so I really want to ensure that you have a comprehensive and functional command of it. I'll start by giving you the whole TCP/IP backstory, including its inception, and then move on to describe the important technical goals as defined by its original architects. And, of course, I'll include how TCP/IP compares to the theoretical OSI model.

A Brief History of TCP/IP

TCP first came on the scene way back in 1973. In 1978, it was divided into two distinct protocols: TCP and IP. Later, in 1983, TCP/IP replaced the Network Control Protocol (NCP) and was authorized as the official means of data transport for anything connecting to ARPAnet, the Internet's ancestor. The DoD's Advanced Research Projects Agency (ARPA) created this ancient network way back in 1957, in a cold war reaction to the Soviet's launching of *Sputnik*. Also in 1983, ARPA was redubbed DARPA and divided into ARPAnet and MIL-NET, until both were finally dissolved in 1990.

It may be counterintuitive, but most of the development work on TCP/IP happened at UC Berkeley in Northern California, where a group of scientists were simultaneously working on the Berkeley version of UNIX, which soon became known as the Berkeley Software Distribution (BSD) series of UNIX versions. Of course, because TCP/IP worked so well, it was packaged into subsequent releases of BSD Unix and offered to other universities and institutions if they bought the distribution tape. So basically, BSD Unix bundled with TCP/IP began as shareware in the world of academia. As a result, it became the foundation for the tremendous success and unprecedented growth of today's Internet as well as smaller, private and corporate intranets.

As usual, what started as a small group of TCP/IP aficionados evolved, and as it did, the US government created a program to test any new published standards and make sure they passed certain criteria. This was to protect TCP/IP's integrity and to ensure that no developer changed anything too dramatically or added any proprietary features. It's this very quality— this open-systems approach to the TCP/IP family of protocols—that sealed its popularity, because this quality guarantees a solid connection between myriad hardware and software platforms with no strings attached.

TCP/IP and the DoD Model

The DoD model is basically a condensed version of the OSI model that comprises four instead of seven layers:

- Process/Application layer
- Host-to-Host layer or Transport layer
- Internet layer
- Network Access layer or Link layer

Figure 2.1 offers a comparison of the DoD model and the OSI reference model. As you can see, the two models are similar in concept, but each has a different number of layers with different names. Cisco may at times use different names for the same layer, such as both "Host-to-Host" and "Transport" to describe the layer above the Internet layer, as well as "Network Access" and "Link" to describe the bottom layer.

FIGURE 2.1   The DoD and OSI models

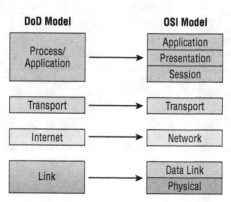

When the different protocols in the IP stack are discussed, the layers of the OSI and DoD models are interchangeable. In other words, be prepared for the exam objectives to call the Host-to-Host layer the Transport layer!

A vast array of protocols join forces at the DoD model's *Process/Application layer*. These processes integrate the various activities and duties spanning the focus of the OSI's corresponding top three layers (Application, Presentation, and Session). We'll focus on a few of the most important applications found in the CCST objectives. In short, the Process/Application layer defines protocols for node-to-node application communication and controls user-interface specifications.

The *Host-to-Host layer or Transport layer* parallels the functions of the OSI's Transport layer, defining protocols for setting up the level of transmission service for applications. It tackles issues like creating reliable end-to-end communication and ensuring the error-free delivery of data. It handles packet sequencing and maintains data integrity.

The *Internet layer* corresponds to the OSI's Network layer, designating the protocols relating to the logical transmission of packets over the entire network. It takes care of the addressing of hosts by giving them an IP (Internet Protocol) address and handles the routing of packets among multiple networks.

At the bottom of the DoD model, the *Network Access layer or Link layer* implements the data exchange between the host and the network. The equivalent of the Data Link and Physical layers of the OSI model, the Network Access layer oversees hardware addressing and defines protocols for the physical transmission of data. The reason TCP/IP became so popular is because there were no set physical layer specifications, so it could run on any existing or future physical network!

The DoD and OSI models are alike in design and concept and have similar functions in similar layers. Figure 2.2 shows the TCP/IP protocol suite and how its protocols relate to the DoD model layers.

FIGURE 2.2   The TCP/IP protocol suite

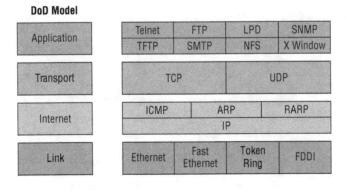

The following sections discuss the different protocols in more detail, beginning with those found at the Process/Application layer.

The Process/Application Layer Protocols

Coming up, I'll describe the different applications and services typically used in IP networks, and although there are many more protocols defined here, I'll focus on the protocols most relevant to the CCST objectives. Here's a list of the protocols and applications I'll cover in this section:

- Telnet
- SSH
- FTP
- SFTP
- TFTP
- SNMP
- HTTP
- HTTPS
- NTP
- DNS
- DHCP/BootP
- APIPA

Telnet

Telnet was one of the first Internet standards, developed in 1969, and is the chameleon of protocols—its specialty is terminal emulation. It allows a user on a remote client machine, called the Telnet client, to access the resources of another machine, the Telnet server, in order to access a command-line interface. Telnet achieves this by pulling a fast one on the Telnet server and making the client machine appear as though it were a terminal directly attached to the local network. This projection is actually a software image—a virtual terminal that can interact with the chosen remote host. A drawback is that no encryption techniques are available within the Telnet protocol, so everything must be sent in clear text, including passwords! Figure 2.3 shows an example of a Telnet client trying to connect to a Telnet server.

FIGURE 2.3   Telnet

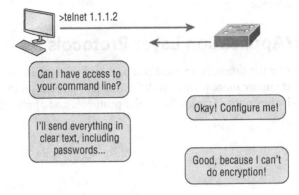

These emulated terminals are of the text-mode type and can execute defined procedures such as displaying menus that give users the opportunity to choose options and access the applications on the duped server. Users begin a Telnet session by running the Telnet client software and then logging into the Telnet server. Telnet uses an 8-bit, byte-oriented data connection over TCP, which makes it very thorough. It's still in use today because it is so simple and easy to use, with very low overhead—but again, with everything sent in clear text, it's not recommended in production.

Secure Shell

Secure Shell (SSH) protocol sets up a secure session that's similar to Telnet over a standard TCP/IP connection and is employed for doing things like logging into systems, running programs on remote systems, and moving files from one system to another. And it does all of this while maintaining an encrypted connection. Figure 2.4 shows an SSH client trying to connect to an SSH server. The client must send the data encrypted!

FIGURE 2.4   Secure Shell

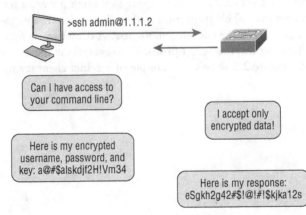

You can think of SSH as the new-generation protocol that's now used in place of the antiquated and very unused commands of remote shell (`rsh`) and remote login (`rlogin`)—even Telnet.

File Transfer Protocol

File Transfer Protocol (FTP) actually lets us transfer files, and it can accomplish this between any two machines using it. But FTP isn't just a protocol; it's also a program. Operating as a protocol, FTP is used by applications. As a program, it's employed by users to perform file tasks by hand. FTP also allows for access to both directories and files and can accomplish certain types of directory operations, such as relocating into different ones (Figure 2.5).

FIGURE 2.5   FTP

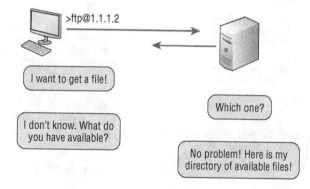

But accessing a host through FTP is only the first step. Users must then be subjected to an authentication login that's usually secured with passwords and usernames implemented by system administrators to restrict access. You can get around this somewhat by adopting the username *anonymous*, but you'll be limited in what you'll be able to access.

Even when employed by users manually as a program, FTP's functions are limited to listing and manipulating directories, typing file contents, and copying files between hosts. It can't execute remote files as programs.

Secure File Transfer Protocol

Secure File Transfer Protocol (SFTP) is used when you need to transfer files over an encrypted connection. It uses an SSH session (more on this later), which encrypts the connection, and SSH uses port 22, hence the port 22 for SFTP.

Apart from the secure part, it's used just as FTP is—for transferring files between computers on an IP network, such as the Internet.

Trivial File Transfer Protocol

Trivial File Transfer Protocol (TFTP) is the stripped-down, stock version of FTP, but it's the protocol of choice if you know exactly what you want and where to find it because it's fast and so easy to use!

But TFTP doesn't offer the abundance of functions that FTP does because it has no directory-browsing abilities, meaning that it can only send and receive files (Figure 2.6). Still, it's heavily used for managing file systems on Cisco devices.

FIGURE 2.6   TFTP

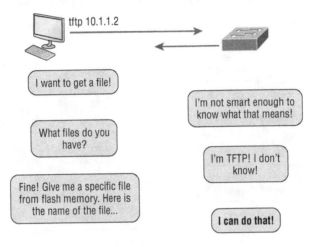

This compact little protocol also skimps in the data department, sending much smaller blocks of data than FTP. Also, there's no authentication, as with FTP, so it's even more insecure, and few sites support it because of the inherent security risks.

Simple Network Management Protocol

Simple Network Management Protocol (SNMP) collects and manipulates valuable network information, as shown in Figure 2.7. It gathers data by polling the devices on the network from a network management station (NMS) at fixed or random intervals, requiring them to disclose certain information, or even asking for certain information from the device. In addition, network devices can inform the NMS station about problems as they occur so the network administrator is alerted.

FIGURE 2.7   SNMP

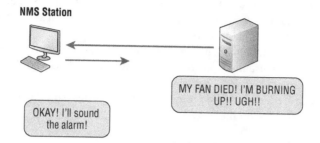

When all is well, SNMP receives something called a *baseline*—a report delimiting the operational traits of a healthy network. This protocol can also stand as a watchdog over the network, quickly notifying managers of any sudden turn of events. These network watchdogs are called *agents*, and when aberrations occur, agents send an alert called a *trap* to the management station.

SNMP Versions 1, 2, and 3

SNMP versions 1 and 2 are pretty much obsolete. This doesn't mean you won't see them in a network now and then, but you'll only come across v1 rarely, if ever. SNMPv2 provided improvements, especially in performance, but one of the best additions was called GETBULK, which allowed a host to retrieve a large amount of data at once. Even so, v2 never really caught on in the networking world, and SNMPv3 is now the standard. Unlike v1, which used only UDP, v3 uses both TCP and UDP and added even more security, message integrity, authentication, and encryption.

Hypertext Transfer Protocol

All those snappy websites comprising a mélange of graphics, text, links, ads, and so on rely on the *Hypertext Transfer Protocol (HTTP)* to make it all possible (Figure 2.8). It's used to manage communications between web browsers and web servers and opens the right resource when you click a link, wherever that resource may actually reside.

FIGURE 2.8   HTTP

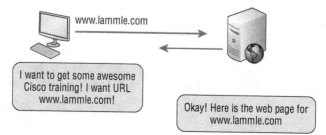

In order for a browser to display a web page, it must find the exact server that has the right web page, plus the exact details that identify the information requested. This information must be then be sent back to the browser. Nowadays, it's highly doubtful that a web server would have only one page to display!

Your browser can understand what you need when you enter a Uniform Resource Locator (URL), which we usually refer to as a web address, such as www.lammle.com/order-our-books and www.lammle.com/blog.

So, basically, each URL defines the protocol used to transfer data, the name of the server, and the particular web page on that server.

Hypertext Transfer Protocol Secure

Hypertext Transfer Protocol Secure (HTTPS) is also known as Secure Hypertext Transfer Protocol. It uses Secure Sockets Layer (SSL). Sometimes you'll see it referred to as SHTTP or S-HTTP, which were slightly different protocols, but since Microsoft supported HTTPS, it became the de facto standard for securing web communication. But no matter—as indicated, it's a secure version of HTTP that arms you with a whole bunch of security tools for keeping transactions between a web browser and a server secure.

It's what your browser needs to fill out forms, sign in, authenticate, and encrypt an HTTP message when you do things online like make a reservation, access your bank, or buy something.

Network Time Protocol

Kudos to Professor David Mills of the University of Delaware for coming up with this handy protocol that's used to synchronize the clocks on our computers to one standard time source (typically, an atomic clock). *Network Time Protocol (NTP)* works by synchronizing devices to ensure that all computers on a given network agree on the time (Figure 2.9).

FIGURE 2.9   NTP

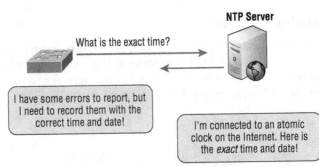

This may sound pretty simple, but it's very important because so many of the transactions done today are time and date stamped. Think about databases—a server can get messed up pretty badly and even crash if it's out of sync with the machines connected to it by even mere seconds! You can't have a transaction entered by a machine at, say, 1:50 a.m. when the server records that transaction as having occurred at 1:45 a.m. So, basically, NTP works to prevent a "back to the future *sans* DeLorean" scenario from bringing down the network—very important indeed!

Domain Name Service

Domain Name Service (DNS) resolves hostnames—specifically, Internet names, such as www .lammle.com to an IP address. But you don't have to actually use DNS. You just type in the IP address of any device you want to communicate with and find the IP address of a URL by using the Ping program. For example, >ping www.cisco.com will return the IP address resolved by DNS.

An IP address identifies hosts on a network and the Internet as well, but DNS was designed to make our lives easier. Think about this: What would happen if you wanted to move your web page to a different service provider? The IP address would change and no one would know what the new one is. DNS allows you to use a domain name to specify an IP address. You can change the IP address as often as you want, and no one will know the difference.

To resolve a DNS address from a host, you'd typically type in the URL from your favorite browser, which would hand the data to the Application layer interface to be transmitted on the network. The application would look up the DNS address and send a UDP request to your DNS server to resolve the name (Figure 2.10).

FIGURE 2.10 DNS

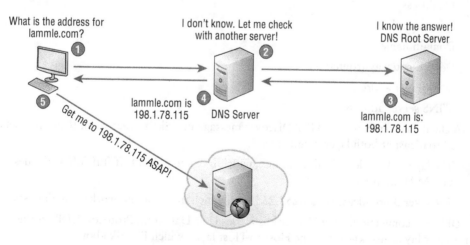

If your first DNS server doesn't know the answer to the query, then the DNS server forwards a TCP request to its root DNS server. Once the query is resolved, the answer is transmitted back to the originating host, which means the host can now request the information from the correct web server.

If you want to resolve the name *todd*, you either must type in the fully qualified domain name (FQDN) of todd .lammle.com or have a device such as a PC or router add the suffix for you. For example, on a Cisco router, you can use the command ip domain-name lammle.com to append each request with the lammle.com domain. If you don't do that, you'll have to type in the FQDN to get DNS to resolve the name.

> An important thing to remember about DNS is that if you can ping a device with an IP address but cannot use its FQDN, then you might have some type of DNS configuration failure.

Dynamic Host Configuration Protocol/Bootstrap Protocol

Dynamic Host Configuration Protocol (DHCP) assigns IP addresses to hosts. It allows for easier administration and works well in small to very large network environments. Many types of hardware can be used as a DHCP server, including a Cisco router.

DHCP differs from BootP in that BootP assigns an IP address to a host but the host's hardware address must be entered manually in a BootP table. You can think of DHCP as a dynamic BootP. But remember that BootP is also used to send an operating system that a host can boot from. DHCP can't do that.

But there's still a lot of information a DHCP server can provide to a host when the host is requesting an IP address from the DHCP server. Here's a list of the most common types of information a DHCP server can provide:

- IP address
- Subnet mask
- Domain name
- Default gateway (routers)
- DNS server address
- WINS server address

A client that sends out a DHCP Discover message in order to receive an IP address sends out a broadcast at both layer 2 and layer 3.

- The layer 2 broadcast is all *F*s in hex, which looks like this: ff:ff:ff:ff:ff:ff as the destination MAC address.
- The layer 3 broadcast is 255.255.255.255, which means all networks and all hosts.

DHCP is connectionless, which means it uses User Datagram Protocol (UDP) at the Transport layer, also known as the Host-to-Host layer, which I'll talk about later.

Seeing is believing, so here's an example of output from my analyzer showing the layer 2 and layer 3 broadcasts:

```
Ethernet II, Src: 0.0.0.0 (00:0b:db:99:d3:5e),Dst: Broadcast(ff:ff:ff:ff:ff:ff)
Internet Protocol, Src: 0.0.0.0 (0.0.0.0),Dst: 255.255.255.255(255.255.255.255)
```

The Data Link and Network layers are both sending out "all hands" broadcasts saying, "Help—I don't know my IP address!"

Figure 2.11 shows the process of a client/server relationship using a DHCP connection.

FIGURE 2.11 DHCP client four-step process

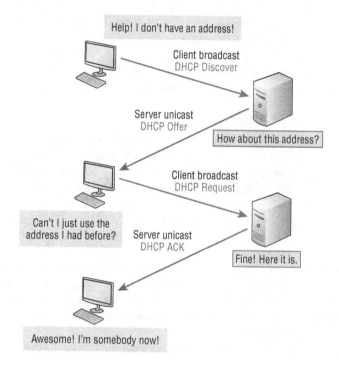

This is the four-step process a client takes to receive an IP address from a DHCP server:

1. The DHCP client broadcasts a DHCP Discover message looking for a DHCP server (port 67).

2. The DHCP server that received the DHCP Discover message sends a layer 2 unicast DHCP Offer message back to the host.

3. The client then broadcasts to the server a DHCP Request message asking for the offered IP address and possibly other information.

4. The server finalizes the exchange with a unicast DHCP Acknowledgment message.

DHCP Conflicts

A DHCP address conflict occurs when two hosts use the same IP address. This sounds bad, and it is! We'll never even have to discuss this problem once we get to the Chapter 3, "Easy Subnetting," on IPv6.

During IP address assignment, a DHCP server checks for conflicts using the Ping program to test the availability of the address before it's assigned from the pool. If no host replies, then the DHCP server assumes that the IP address is not already allocated. This helps the server know that it's providing a good address, but what about the host? To provide extra protection against that terrible IP conflict issue, the host can broadcast for its own address!

A host uses something called a gratuitous ARP to help avoid a possible duplicate address. The DHCP client sends an ARP broadcast out on the local LAN or VLAN using its newly assigned address to solve conflicts before they occur.

So, if an IP address conflict is detected, the address is removed from the DHCP pool (scope), and it's really important to remember that the address will not be assigned to a host until the administrator resolves the conflict by hand!

Automatic Private IP Addressing

Okay, so what happens if you have a few hosts connected together with a switch or hub and you don't have a DHCP server? You can add IP information by hand, known as *static IP addressing*, but later Windows operating systems provide a feature called Automatic Private IP Addressing (APIPA). With APIPA, clients can automatically self-configure an IP address and subnet mask—basic IP information that hosts use to communicate—when a DHCP server isn't available. The IP address range for APIPA is 169.254.0.1 through 169.254.255.254. The client also configures itself with a default Class B subnet mask of 255.255.0.0.

But when you're in your corporate network working and you have a DHCP server running, and your host shows that it's using this IP address range, it means that either your DHCP client on the host is not working or the server is down or can't be reached due to some network issue. Believe me—I don't know anyone who's seen a host in this address range and has been happy about it!

Now, let's take a look at the Transport layer, or what the DoD calls the Host-to-Host layer.

 If you see an IP address starting with the first two octets of 169.254.x.x, then you either don't have a working DHCP server on the subnet or you have a network connectivity issue.

The Host-to-Host or Transport Layer Protocols

The main purpose of the Host-to-Host layer is to shield the upper-layer applications from the complexities of the network. This layer says to the upper layer, "Just give me your data stream, with any instructions, and I'll begin the process of getting your information ready to send."

Coming up, I'll introduce you to the two protocols at this layer:

- Transmission Control Protocol (TCP)
- User Datagram Protocol (UDP)

In addition, I'll discuss some of the key host-to-host protocol concepts as well as the port numbers.

 Remember, this is still considered layer 4, and layer 4 can use acknowledgments, sequencing, and flow control.

Transmission Control Protocol

Transmission Control Protocol (TCP) takes large blocks of information from an application and breaks them into segments. It numbers and sequences each segment so that the destination's TCP stack can put the segments back into the order the application intended. After these segments are sent on the transmitting host, TCP waits for an acknowledgment of the receiving end's TCP virtual circuit session, retransmitting any segments that aren't acknowledged.

Before a transmitting host starts to send segments down the model, the sender's TCP stack contacts the destination's TCP stack to establish a connection. This creates a *virtual circuit*, and this type of communication is known as *connection-oriented*. During this initial handshake, the two TCP layers also agree on the amount of information that's going to be sent before the recipient's TCP sends back an acknowledgment. With everything agreed upon in advance, the path is paved for reliable communication to take place.

TCP is a full-duplex, connection-oriented, reliable, and accurate protocol, but establishing all these terms and conditions, in addition to error checking, is no small task. TCP is very complicated, and so not surprisingly, it's costly in terms of network overhead. And since today's networks are much more reliable than those of yore, this added reliability is often unnecessary. Most programmers use TCP because it removes a lot of programming work, but for real-time video and VoIP, *User Datagram Protocol (UDP)* is often better because using it results in less overhead.

TCP Segment Format

Since the upper layers just send a data stream to the protocols in the Transport layers, I'll use Figure 2.12 to demonstrate how TCP segments a data stream and prepares it for the Internet layer. When the Internet layer receives the data stream, it routes the segments as packets through an internetwork. The segments are handed to the receiving host's Host-to-Host layer protocol, which rebuilds the data stream for the upper-layer applications or protocols.

FIGURE 2.12   TCP segment format

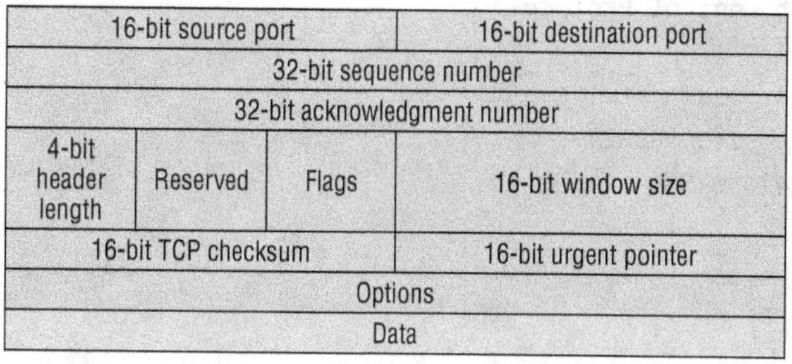

16-bit source port			16-bit destination port	
32-bit sequence number				
32-bit acknowledgment number				
4-bit header length	Reserved	Flags	16-bit window size	
16-bit TCP checksum			16-bit urgent pointer	
Options				
Data				

Figure 2.12 shows the TCP segment format and shows the different fields within the TCP header. This isn't important to memorize for the Cisco exam objectives, but you need to understand it well because it's really good foundational information.

The TCP header is 20 bytes long, or up to 24 bytes with options. You need to understand what each field in the TCP segment is in order to build a strong educational foundation:

Source Port   The port number of the application on the host sending the data, which I'll talk about more thoroughly a little later in this chapter.

Destination Port   The port number of the application requested on the destination host.

Sequence Number   A number used by TCP that puts the data back in the correct order or retransmits missing or damaged data during a process called sequencing.

Acknowledgment Number   The TCP octet that is expected next.

Header Length   The number of 32-bit words in the TCP header, which indicates where the data begins. The TCP header (even one including options) is an integral number of 32 bits in length.

Reserved   Always set to zero.

Code Bits/Flags   Controls functions used to set up and terminate a session.

Window   The window size the sender is willing to accept, in octets.

Checksum   The cyclic redundancy check (CRC), used because TCP doesn't trust the lower layers and checks everything. The CRC checks the header and data fields.

Urgent   A valid field only if the Urgent pointer in the code bits is set. If so, this value indicates the offset from the current sequence number, in octets, where the segment of nonurgent data begins.

Options   May be 0, meaning that no options have to be present, or a multiple of 32 bits. However, if any options are used that do not cause the option field to total a multiple of 32 bits, padding of 0s must be used to make sure the data begins on a 32-bit boundary. These boundaries are known as words.

Data   Handed down to the TCP protocol at the Transport layer, which includes the upper-layer headers.

Let's take a look at a TCP segment copied from a network analyzer:

```
TCP - Transport Control Protocol
Source Port: 5973
Destination Port: 23
Sequence Number: 1456389907
Ack Number: 1242056456
Offset: 5
Reserved: %000000
Code: %011000
```

```
Ack is valid
Push Request
Window: 61320
Checksum: 0x61a6
Urgent Pointer: 0
No TCP Options
TCP Data Area:
vL.5.+.5.+.5.+.5 76 4c 19 35 11 2b 19 35 11 2b 19 35 11
2b 19 35 +. 11 2b 19
Frame Check Sequence: 0x0d00000f
```

Did you notice that everything I talked about earlier is in the segment? As you can see from the number of fields in the header, TCP creates a lot of overhead. Again, this is why application developers may opt for efficiency over reliability to save overhead and go with UDP instead. It's also defined at the Transport layer as an alternative to TCP.

User Datagram Protocol

User Datagram Protocol (UDP) is basically the scaled-down economy model of TCP, which is why UDP is sometimes referred to as a thin protocol. Like a thin person on a park bench, a thin protocol doesn't take up a lot of room—or in this case, require much bandwidth on a network.

UDP doesn't offer all the bells and whistles of TCP either, but it does do a fabulous job of transporting information that doesn't require reliable delivery, using far less network resources. (UDP is covered thoroughly in request for comments [RFC] 768.)

So, clearly there are times when it's wise for developers to opt for UDP rather than TCP, one of them being when reliability is already taken care of at the Process/Application layer. Network File System (NFS) handles its own reliability issues, making the use of TCP both impractical and redundant. Ultimately, however, it's up to the application developer to opt for using UDP or TCP, not the user who wants to transfer data faster!

UDP does *not* sequence the segments and does not care about the order in which the segments arrive at the destination. UDP just sends the segments off and forgets about them. It doesn't follow through, check up on them, or even allow for an acknowledgment of safe arrival—complete abandonment. Because of this, it's referred to as an unreliable protocol. This does not mean that UDP is ineffective, only that it doesn't deal with reliability issues at all.

Furthermore, UDP doesn't create a virtual circuit, nor does it contact the destination before delivering information to it. Because of this, it's also considered a *connectionless* protocol. Since UDP assumes that the application will use its own reliability method, it doesn't use any itself. This presents an application developer with a choice when running the Internet Protocol stack: TCP for reliability or UDP for faster transfers.

It's important to know how this process works because if the segments arrive out of order, which is commonplace in IP networks, they'll simply be passed up to the next layer in whatever order they were received. This can result in some seriously garbled data! On the other hand, TCP sequences the segments so they get put back together in exactly the right order, which is something UDP just can't do.

UDP Segment Format

Figure 2.13 clearly illustrates UDP's markedly lean overhead as compared to TCP's hungry requirements. Look at the figure carefully—can you see that UDP doesn't use windowing or provide acknowledgments in the UDP header?

FIGURE 2.13   UDP segment

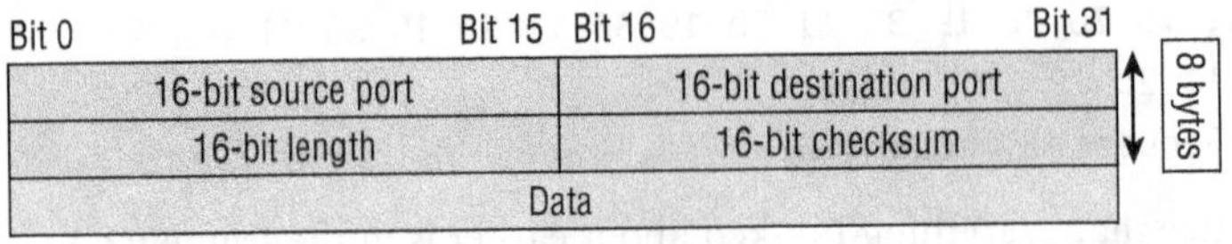

It's important to understand what each field in the UDP segment is.

Source Port   The port number of the application on the host sending the data.

Destination Port   The port number of the application requested on the destination host.

Length   This is the length of the UDP header and UDP data.

Checksum   The checksum of both the UDP header and UDP data fields.

Data   The upper-layer data.

UDP, like TCP, doesn't trust the lower layers and runs its own CRC. Remember that the checksum is the field that houses the CRC, which is why you can see the checksum information.

The following shows a UDP segment caught on a network analyzer:

```
UDP - User Datagram Protocol
Source Port: 1085
Destination Port: 5136
Length: 41
Checksum: 0x7a3c
UDP Data Area:
..Z......00 01 5a 96 00 01 00 00 00 00 00 11 0000 00
...C..2._C._C 2e 03 00 43 02 1e 32 0a 00 0a 00 80 43 00 80
Frame Check Sequence: 0x00000000
```

Notice that low overhead! Try to find the sequence number, ack number, and window size in the UDP segment. You can't, because they just aren't there!

Key Concepts of Host-to-Host Protocols

Since you've now seen both a connection-oriented (TCP) and connectionless (UDP) protocol in action, it's a good time to summarize the two here. Table 2.1 highlights some of the key concepts about these two protocols for you to memorize.

TABLE 2.1　Key features of TCP and UDP

TCP	UDP
Sequenced	Unsequenced
Reliable	Unreliable
Connection-oriented	Connectionless
Virtual circuit	Low overhead
Acknowledgments	No acknowledgment
Windowing flow control	No windowing or flow control of any type

And if all this isn't quite clear yet, a telephone analogy will really help you understand how TCP works. Most of us know that before you speak to someone on a phone, you must first establish a connection with that other person, no matter where they are. This is akin to establishing a virtual circuit with the TCP protocol. If you were giving someone important information during your conversation, you might say things like, "You know?" or "Did you get that?" Saying things like this is a lot like a TCP acknowledgment—it's designed to get you verification. From time to time, especially on mobile phones, people ask, "Are you still there?" People end their conversations with a "Goodbye" of some kind, putting closure on the phone call, which you can think of as tearing down the virtual circuit that was created for your communication session. TCP performs these types of functions.

Conversely, using UDP is more like sending a postcard. To do that, you don't need to contact the other party first, you simply write your message, address the postcard, and send it off. This is analogous to UDP's connectionless orientation. Since the message on the postcard is probably not a matter of life or death, you don't need an acknowledgment of its receipt. Similarly, UDP does not involve acknowledgments.

Let's take a look at another figure, one that includes TCP, UDP, and the applications associated to each protocol: Figure 2.14 (discussed in the next section).

FIGURE 2.14　Port numbers for TCP and UDP

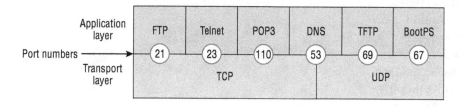

Port Numbers

TCP and UDP must use *port numbers* to communicate with the upper layers because these are what keep track of different conversations crossing the network simultaneously. Originating-source port numbers are dynamically assigned by the source host and will equal some number starting at 1024. Port number 1023 and below are defined in RFC 3232 (or just see www.iana.org), which discusses what we call well-known port numbers.

Virtual circuits that don't use an application with a well-known port number are assigned port numbers randomly from a specific range instead. These port numbers identify the source and destination application or process in the TCP segment.

 The requests for comments (RFCs) form a series of notes about the Internet (originally, the ARPAnet) started in 1969. These notes discuss many aspects of computer communication, focusing on networking protocols, procedures, programs, and concepts, but they also include meeting notes, opinions, and sometimes even humor. You can find the RFCs by visiting www.iana.org.

Figure 2.14 illustrates how both TCP and UDP use port numbers. I'll cover the different port numbers that can be used next:

- Numbers below 1024 are considered well-known port numbers and are defined in RFC 3232.

- Numbers 1024 and above are used by the upper layers to set up sessions with other hosts and by TCP and UDP to use as source and destination addresses in the segment.

TCP Session: Source Port

Let's take a minute to check out analyzer output showing a TCP session I captured with my analyzer software session:

```
TCP - Transport Control Protocol
Source Port: 5973
Destination Port: 23
Sequence Number: 1456389907
Ack Number: 1242056456
Offset: 5
Reserved: %000000
Code: %011000
Ack is valid
Push Request
Window: 61320
Checksum: 0x61a6
Urgent Pointer: 0
No TCP Options
```

```
TCP Data Area:
vL.5.+.5.+.5.+.5 76 4c 19 35 11 2b 19 35 11 2b 19 35 11
2b 19 35 +. 11 2b 19
Frame Check Sequence: 0x0d00000f
```

Notice that the source host makes up the source port, which in this case is 5973. The destination port is 23, which is used to tell the receiving host the purpose of the intended connection (Telnet).

By looking at this session, you can see that the source host makes up the source port by using numbers from 1024 to 65535. But why does the source make up a port number? It does so in order to differentiate between sessions with different hosts, because how would a server know where information is coming from if it didn't have a different number from a sending host? TCP and the upper layers don't use hardware and logical addresses to understand the sending host's address, as the Data Link and Network layer protocols do; instead, they use port numbers.

TCP Session: Destination Port

You'll sometimes look at an analyzer and see that only the source port is above 1024 and the destination port is a well-known port, as shown in the following trace:

```
TCP - Transport Control Protocol
Source Port: 1144
Destination Port: 80 World Wide Web HTTP
Sequence Number: 9356570
Ack Number: 0
Offset: 7
Reserved: %000000
Code: %000010
Synch Sequence
Window: 8192
Checksum: 0x57E7
Urgent Pointer: 0
TCP Options:
Option Type: 2 Maximum Segment Size
Length: 4
MSS: 536
Option Type: 1 No Operation
Option Type: 1 No Operation
Option Type: 4
Length: 2
Opt Value:
No More HTTP Data
Frame Check Sequence: 0x43697363
```

And, sure enough, the source port is over 1024, but the destination port is 80, indicating an HTTP service. The server, or receiving host, will change the destination port if it needs to.

In the preceding trace, a "SYN" packet is sent to the destination device. This Synch (as shown in the output) sequence is what's used to inform the remote destination device that it wants to create a session.

TCP Session: Syn Packet Acknowledgment

The next trace shows an acknowledgment to the SYN packet:

```
TCP - Transport Control Protocol
Source Port: 80 World Wide Web HTTP
Destination Port: 1144
Sequence Number: 2873580788
Ack Number: 9356571
Offset: 6
Reserved: %000000
Code: %010010
  Ack is valid
  Synch Sequence
Window: 8576
Checksum: 0x5F85
Urgent Pointer: 0
TCP Options:
  Option Type: 2 Maximum Segment Size
  Length: 4
  MSS: 1460
No More HTTP Data
Frame Check Sequence: 0x6E203132
```

Notice the Ack is valid, which means that the source port was accepted and the device agreed to create a virtual circuit with the originating host.

Here again, you can see that the response from the server shows that the source is 80 and the destination is the 1144 sent from the originating host—all's well!

Table 2.2 provides a list of the typical applications used in the TCP/IP suite by showing their well-known port numbers and the Transport layer protocols used by each application or process. It's really key to memorize this table.

TABLE 2.2   Key protocols that use TCP and UDP

TCP	UDP
Telnet 23	SNMP 161
SMTP 25	TFTP 69
HTTP 80	DNS 53
FTP 20, 21	BooTP/DHCP 67
DNS 53	
HTTPS 443	NTP 123
SSH 22	
POP3 110	
IMAP4 143	

Notice that DNS uses both TCP and UDP. Whether it opts for one or the other depends on what it's trying to do. Even though it's not the only application that can use both protocols, it's certainly one that you should make sure to remember.

NOTE   What makes TCP reliable is sequencing, acknowledgments, and flow control (windowing). UDP does not have reliability.

Okay, I want to discuss one more item before we move down to the Internet layer—session multiplexing. Session multiplexing is used by both TCP and UDP and basically allows a single computer, with a single IP address, to have multiple sessions occurring simultaneously. Say you go to www.lammle.com and are browsing and then click a link to another page. Doing this opens another session to your host. Now you go to www.lammle.com/self-paced-online from another window, and that site opens a window as well. Now you have three sessions open using one IP address because the Session layer is sorting the separate requests based on the Transport layer port number. This is the job of the Session layer: to keep application layer data separate!

The Internet Layer Protocols

In the DoD model, there are two main reasons for the Internet layer's existence: routing and providing a single network interface to the upper layers.

None of the other upper- or lower-layer protocols have any functions relating to routing—that complex and important task belongs entirely to the Internet layer. The Internet layer's second duty is to provide a single network interface to the upper-layer protocols. Without this layer, application programmers would need to write "hooks" into every one of their applications for each different Network Access protocol. This would not only be a pain in the neck, but it would lead to different versions of each application—one for Ethernet, another one for wireless, and so on. To prevent this, IP provides one single network interface for the upper-layer protocols. With that mission accomplished, it's then the job of IP and the various Network Access protocols to get along and work together.

All network roads don't lead to Rome—they lead to IP. And all the other protocols at this layer, as well as all those at the upper layers, use it. Never forget that. All paths through the DoD model go through IP. Here's a list of the important protocols at the Internet layer that I'll cover individually in detail coming up:

- Internet Protocol (IP)

- Internet Control Message Protocol (ICMP)

- Address Resolution Protocol (ARP)

Internet Protocol

Internet Protocol (IP) essentially is the Internet layer. The other protocols found here merely exist to support it. IP holds the big picture and could be said to "see all," because it's aware of all the interconnected networks. It can do this because all the machines on the network have a software, or logical, address called an IP address, which I'll discuss more thoroughly later in this chapter.

For now, understand that IP looks at each packet's address. Then, using a routing table, it decides where a packet is to be sent next, choosing the best path to send it upon. The protocols of the Network Access layer at the bottom of the DoD model don't possess IP's enlightened scope of the entire network; they deal only with physical links (local networks).

Identifying devices on networks requires answering these two questions: Which network is it on? And what is its ID on that network? The first answer is the *software address*, or *logical address*. You can think of this as the part of the address that specifies the correct street. The second answer is the hardware address, which goes a step further to specify the correct mailbox. All hosts on a network have a logical ID called an IP address. This is the software, or logical, address and contains valuable encoded information, greatly simplifying the complex task of routing. (IP is discussed in RFC 791.)

IP receives segments from the Host-to-Host layer and fragments them into datagrams (packets) if necessary. IP then reassembles datagrams back into segments on the receiving side. Each datagram is assigned the IP address of the sender and that of the recipient. Each router or switch (layer 3 device) that receives a datagram makes routing decisions based on the packet's destination IP address.

Figure 2.15 shows an IP header. This will give you a picture of what the IP protocol has to go through every time user data that is destined for a remote network is sent from the upper layers.

FIGURE 2.15   An IP header

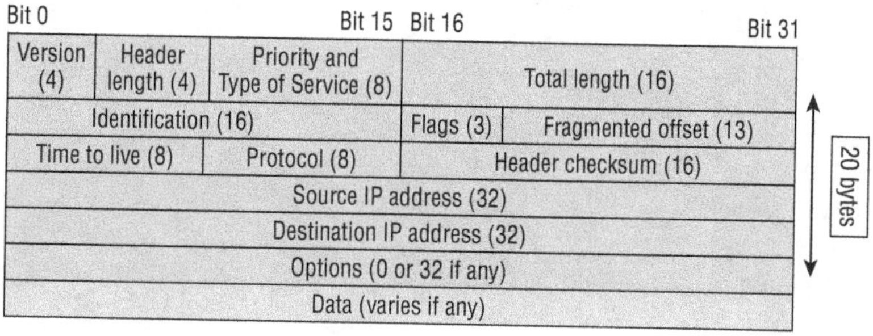

| Bit 0 | | Bit 15 | Bit 16 | | Bit 31 |

Version (4)	Header length (4)	Priority and Type of Service (8)	Total length (16)		
Identification (16)			Flags (3)	Fragmented offset (13)	
Time to live (8)		Protocol (8)	Header checksum (16)		
Source IP address (32)					
Destination IP address (32)					
Options (0 or 32 if any)					
Data (varies if any)					

20 bytes

The following fields make up the IP header:

Version   The IP version number.

Header Length   The header length (HLEN), in 32-bit words.

Priority and Type of Service   Type of Service tells how the datagram should be handled. The first 3 bits are the priority bits, now called the differentiated services bits.

Total Length   The length of the packet, including header and data.

Identification   A unique IP-packet value used to differentiate fragmented packets from different datagrams.

Flags   Specifies whether fragmentation should occur.

Fragment Offset   Provides fragmentation and reassembly if the packet is too large to put in a frame. It also allows different maximum transmission units (MTUs) on the Internet.

Time To Live   The time to live (TTL) is set into a packet when it is originally generated. If it doesn't get to where it's supposed to go before the TTL expires, boom—it's gone. This stops IP packets from continuously circling the network looking for a home.

Protocol   The port of the upper-layer protocol; for example, TCP is port 6 or UDP is port 17. Also supports Network layer protocols, like ARP and ICMP, and can be referred to as the Type field in some analyzers. I'll talk about this field more in a minute.

Header Checksum   The cyclic redundancy check (CRC) on the header only.

Source IP Address   The 32-bit IP address of the sending station.

Destination IP Address   The 32-bit IP address of the station this packet is destined for.

Options   Used for network testing, debugging, security, and more.

Data   After the IP option field, will be the upper-layer data.

Here's a snapshot of an IP packet caught on a network analyzer. Notice that all the header information discussed previously appears here:

```
IP Header - Internet Protocol Datagram
Version: 4
Header Length: 5
Precedence: 0
Type of Service: %000
Unused: %00
Total Length: 187
Identifier: 22486
Fragmentation Flags: %010 Do Not Fragment
Fragment Offset: 0
Time To Live: 60
IP Type: 0x06 TCP
Header Checksum: 0xd031
Source IP Address: 10.7.1.30
Dest. IP Address: 10.7.1.10
No Internet Datagram Options
```

The Type field is typically a Protocol field, but this analyzer sees it as an IP Type field. This is important. If the header didn't carry the protocol information for the next layer, IP wouldn't know what to do with the data carried in the packet. The preceding example clearly tells IP to hand the segment to TCP.

Figure 2.16 demonstrates how the Network layer sees the protocols at the Transport layer when it needs to hand a packet up to the upper-layer protocols.

FIGURE 2.16   The Protocol field in an IP header

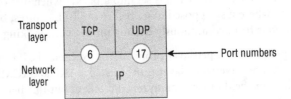

In this example, the Protocol field tells IP to send the data to either TCP port 6 or UDP port 17. But it will be UDP or TCP only if the data is part of a data stream headed for an upper-layer service or application. It could just as easily be destined for Internet Control Message Protocol (ICMP), Address Resolution Protocol (ARP), or some other type of Network layer protocol.

Table 2.3 lists some other popular protocols that can be specified in the Protocol field.

TABLE 2.3 Possible protocols found in the Protocol field of an IP header

Protocol	Protocol Number
ICMP	1
IP in IP (tunneling)	4
TCP	6
UDP	17
EIGRP	88
OSPF	89
IPv6	41
GRE	47
Layer 2 tunnel (L2TP)	115

You can find a complete list of Protocol field numbers at www.iana.org/assignments/protocol-numbers.

Internet Control Message Protocol

Internet Control Message Protocol (ICMP) works at the Network layer and is used by IP for many different services. ICMP is basically a management protocol and messaging service provider for IP. Its messages are carried as IP datagrams. RFC 1256 is an annex to ICMP, which gives hosts extended capability in discovering routes to gateways.

ICMP packets have the following characteristics:

- They can provide hosts with information about network problems.
- They are encapsulated within IP datagrams.

The following are some common events and messages that ICMP relates to:

Destination Unreachable If a router can't send an IP datagram any further, it uses ICMP to send a message back to the sender, advising it of the situation. For example, take a look at Figure 2.17, which shows that interface e0 of the Lab_B router is down.

FIGURE 2.17   An ICMP error message sent to the sending host from the remote router

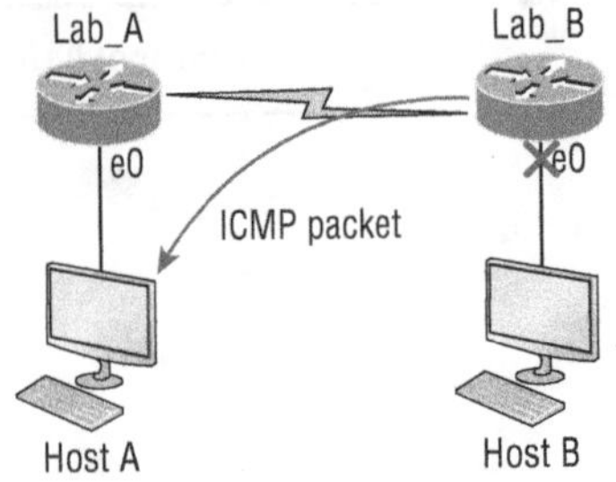

When Host A sends a packet destined for Host B, the Lab_B router will send an "ICMP destination unreachable" message back to the sending device, which is Host A in this example.

Buffer Full/Source Quench   If a router's memory buffer for receiving incoming datagrams is full, it will use ICMP to send out this message alert until the congestion abates.

Hops/Time Exceeded   Each IP datagram is allotted a certain number of routers, called hops, to pass through. If it reaches its limit of hops before arriving at its destination, the last router to receive that datagram deletes it. The executioner router then uses ICMP to send an obituary message, informing the sending machine of the demise of its datagram.

Ping   Packet Internet Groper (Ping) uses ICMP echo request and reply messages to check the physical and logical connectivity of machines on an internetwork.

Traceroute   Using ICMP time-outs, Traceroute is used to discover the path a packet takes as it traverses an internetwork.

> Traceroute is usually just called trace. Microsoft Windows uses tracert to
> allow you to verify address configurations in your internetwork.

The following data is from a network analyzer catching an ICMP echo request:

```
Flags: 0x00
Status: 0x00
Packet Length: 78
Timestamp: 14:04:25.967000 12/20/03
Ethernet Header
Destination: 00:a0:24:6e:0f:a8
Source: 00:80:c7:a8:f0:3d
Ether-Type: 08-00 IP
```

```
IP Header - Internet Protocol Datagram
Version: 4
Header Length: 5
Precedence: 0
Type of Service: %000
Unused: %00
Total Length: 60
Identifier: 56325
Fragmentation Flags: %000
Fragment Offset: 0
Time To Live: 32
IP Type: 0x01 ICMP
Header Checksum: 0x2df0
Source IP Address: 100.100.100.2
Dest. IP Address: 100.100.100.1
No Internet Datagram Options
ICMP - Internet Control Messages Protocol
ICMP Type: 8 Echo Request
Code: 0
Checksum: 0x395c
Identifier: 0x0300
Sequence Number: 4352
ICMP Data Area:
abcdefghijklmnop 61 62 63 64 65 66 67 68 69 6a 6b 6c 6d 6e 6f 70
qrstuvwabcdefghi 71 72 73 74 75 76 77 61 62 63 64 65 66 67 68 69
Frame Check Sequence: 0x00000000
```

Notice anything unusual? Did you catch the fact that even though ICMP works at the Internet (Network) layer, it still uses IP to do the Ping request? The IP Type field in the IP header is 0x01, which specifies that the data we're carrying is owned by the ICMP protocol. Remember, just as all roads lead to Rome, all segments or data *must* go through IP!

The Ping program uses the alphabet in the data portion of the packet as a payload, typically around 100 bytes by default, unless, of course, you are pinging from a Windows device, which thinks the alphabet stops at the letter *W* (and doesn't include *X*, *Y*, or *Z*) and then starts at *A* again. Go figure!

We'll move on soon, but before we get into the ARP protocol, let's take another look at ICMP in action. Figure 2.18 shows an internetwork—it has a router, so it's an internetwork, right?

FIGURE 2.18 ICMP in action

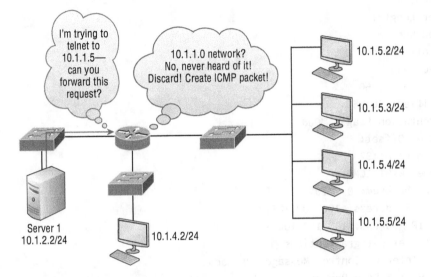

Server 1 (10.1.2.2) telnets to 10.1.1.5 from a DOS prompt. What do you think Server 1 will receive as a response? Server 1 will send the Telnet data to the default gateway, which is the router, and the router will drop the packet because there isn't a network 10.1.1.0 in the routing table. Because of this, Server 1 will receive an ICMP destination unreachable back from the router.

Address Resolution Protocol

Address Resolution Protocol (ARP) finds the hardware address of a host from a known IP address. Here's how it works: When IP has a datagram to send, it must inform a Network Access protocol, such as Ethernet or wireless, of the destination's hardware address on the local network. Remember that it has already been informed by upper-layer protocols of the destination's IP address. If IP doesn't find the destination host's hardware address in the ARP cache, it uses ARP to find this information.

As IP's detective, ARP interrogates the local network by sending out a broadcast asking the machine with the specified IP address to reply with its hardware address. So basically, ARP translates the software (IP) address into a hardware address—for example, the destination machine's Ethernet adapter address—and from it, deduces its whereabouts on the LAN by broadcasting for this address. Figure 2.19 shows how an ARP broadcast looks to a local network.

FIGURE 2.19   A local ARP broadcast

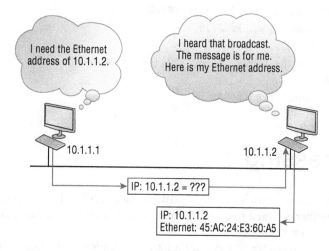

 ARP resolves IP addresses to Ethernet (MAC) addresses.

The following trace shows an ARP broadcast—notice that the destination hardware address is unknown and is all *F*s in hex (all 1s in binary)—and is a hardware address broadcast:

Flags: 0x00
Status: 0x00
Packet Length: 64
Timestamp: 09:17:29.574000 12/06/03
Ethernet Header
Destination: FF:FF:FF:FF:FF:FF Ethernet Broadcast
Source: 00:A0:24:48:60:A5
Protocol Type: 0x0806 IP ARP
ARP - Address Resolution Protocol
Hardware: 1 Ethernet (10Mb)
Protocol: 0x0800 IP
Hardware Address Length: 6
Protocol Address Length: 4
Operation: 1 ARP Request
Sender Hardware Address: 00:A0:24:48:60:A5

```
Sender Internet Address: 172.16.10.3
Target Hardware Address: 00:00:00:00:00:00 (ignored)
Target Internet Address: 172.16.10.10
Extra bytes (Padding):
............... 0A 0A 0A 0A 0A 0A 0A 0A 0A 0A 0A 0A 0A
0A 0A 0A 0A 0A
Frame Check Sequence: 0x00000000
```

IP Addressing

One of the most important topics in any discussion of TCP/IP is IP addressing. An *IP address* is a numeric identifier assigned to each machine on an IP network. It designates the specific location of a device on the network.

An IP address is a software address, not a hardware address—the latter is hard-coded on a network interface card (NIC) and used for finding hosts on a local network. IP addressing was designed to allow hosts on one network to communicate with a host on a different network regardless of the type of LANs the hosts are participating in.

Before we get into the more complicated aspects of IP addressing, you need to understand some of the basics. First, I'm going to explain some of the fundamentals of IP addressing and its terminology. Then, you'll learn about the hierarchical IP addressing scheme and private IP addresses.

IP Terminology

Throughout this chapter you're being introduced to several important terms that are vital to understanding the Internet Protocol. Here are a few to get you started:

Bit   A bit is one digit, either a 1 or a 0.

Byte   A byte is 7 or 8 bits, depending on whether parity is used. For the rest of this chapter, always assume a byte is 8 bits.

Octet   An octet, made up of 8 bits, is just an ordinary 8-bit binary number. In this chapter, the terms *byte* and *octet* are completely interchangeable.

Network Address   This is the designation used in routing to send packets to a remote network—for example, 10.0.0.0, 172.16.0.0, and 192.168.10.0.

Broadcast Address   The address used by applications and hosts to send information to all nodes on a network is called the broadcast address. Examples of layer 3 broadcasts include 255.255.255.255, which is any network, all nodes; 172.16.255.255, which is all subnets and hosts on network 172.16.0.0; and 10.255.255.255, which broadcasts to all subnets and hosts on network 10.0.0.0.

The Hierarchical IP Addressing Scheme

An IP address consists of 32 bits of information. These bits are divided into four sections, referred to as octets or bytes, with each containing 1 byte (8 bits). You can depict an IP address using one of three methods:

- Dotted-decimal, as in 172.16.30.56
- Binary, as in 10101100.00010000.00011110.00111000
- Hexadecimal, as in AC.10.1E.38

All these examples represent the same IP address. Pertaining to IP addressing, hexadecimal isn't used as often as dotted-decimal or binary, but you still might find an IP address stored in hexadecimal in some programs.

The 32-bit IP address is a structured or hierarchical address, as opposed to a flat or non-hierarchical address. Although either type of addressing scheme could have been used, *hierarchical addressing* was chosen for a good reason. The advantage of this scheme is that it can handle a large number of addresses, namely 4.3 billion. (A 32-bit address space with two possible values for each position—either 0 or 1—gives you 2^{32}, or 4,294,967,296.) The disadvantage of the flat addressing scheme—and the reason it's not used for IP addressing— relates to routing. If every address were unique, all routers on the Internet would need to store the address of each and every machine on the Internet! This would make efficient routing impossible, even if only a fraction of the possible addresses were used.

The solution to this problem is to use a two- or three-level hierarchical addressing scheme that is structured by network and host or by network, subnet, and host.

This two- or three-level scheme can also be compared to a telephone number. The first section, the area code, designates a very large area. The second section, the prefix, narrows the scope to a local calling area. The final segment, the customer number, zooms in on the specific connection. IP addresses use the same type of layered structure. Rather than all 32 bits being treated as a unique identifier, as in flat addressing, a part of the address is designated as the network address and the other part is designated as either the subnet and host or just the node address.

Next, I'll cover IP network addressing and the different classes of address we can use to address our networks.

Network Addressing

The *network address* (which can also be called the network number) uniquely identifies each network. Every machine on the same network shares that network address as part of its IP address. For example, in the IP address 172.16.30.56, the 172.16 is the network address.

The *node address* is assigned to, and uniquely identifies, each machine on a network. This part of the address must be unique because it identifies a particular machine—an individual—as opposed to a network, which is a group. This number can also be referred to as a *host address*. In the sample IP address 172.16.30.56, the 30.56 specifies the node address.

The designers of the Internet decided to create classes of networks based on network size. For the small number of networks possessing a very large number of nodes, they created the rank *Class A network*. At the other extreme is the *Class C network*, which is reserved for the numerous networks with a small number of nodes. The class distinction for networks between very large and very small is predictably called the *Class B network*.

Subdividing an IP address into a network and node address is determined by the class designation of one's network. Figure 2.20 summarizes the three classes of networks used to address hosts—a subject I'll explain in much greater detail throughout this chapter.

FIGURE 2.20   A summary of the three classes of networks

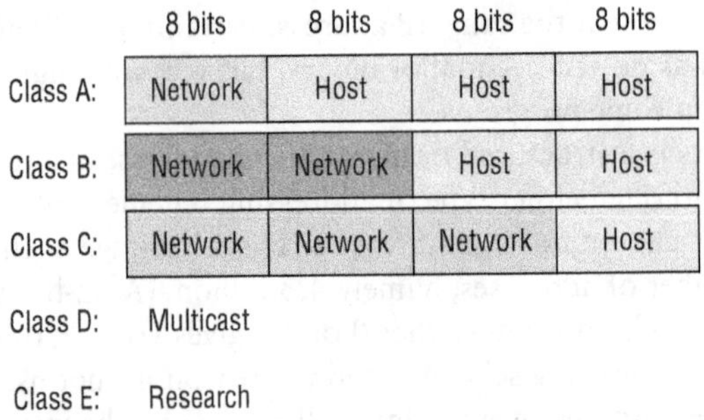

To ensure efficient routing, Internet designers defined a mandate for the leading-bits section of the address for each different network class. For example, since a router knows that a Class A network address always starts with a 0, the router might be able to speed a packet on its way after reading only the first bit of its address. This is where the address schemes define the difference between a Class A, a Class B, and a Class C address. Coming up, I'll discuss the differences between these three classes, followed by a discussion of the Class D and Class E addresses. Classes A, B, and C are the only ranges that are used to address hosts in our networks.

Network Address Range: Class A

The designers of the IP address scheme decided that the first bit of the first byte in a Class A network address must always be off, or 0. This means a Class A address must be between 0 and 127 in the first byte, inclusive.

Consider the following network address:

0xxxxxxx

If we turn the other 7 bits all off and then turn them all on, we'll find the Class A range of network addresses:

```
00000000 = 0
01111111 = 127
```

So, a Class A network is defined in the first octet between 0 and 127, and it can't be less or more. Understand that 0 and 127 are not valid in a Class A network, because they're reserved addresses, which I'll explain soon.

Network Address Range: Class B

In a Class B network, the RFCs state that the first bit of the first byte must always be turned on but the second bit must always be turned off. If you turn the other 6 bits all off and then all on, you will find the range for a Class B network:

```
10000000 = 128
10111111 = 191
```

As you can see, a Class B network is defined when the first byte is configured from 128 to 191.

Network Address Range: Class C

For Class C networks, the RFCs define the first 2 bits of the first octet as always turned on, but the third bit can never be on. Following the same process as the previous classes, convert from binary to decimal to find the range. Here's the range for a Class C network:

```
11000000 = 192
11011111 = 223
```

So, if you see an IP address that starts at 192 and goes to 223, you'll know it is a Class C IP address.

Network Address Ranges: Classes D and E

The addresses between 224 and 255 are reserved for Class D and E networks. Class D (224–239) is used for multicast addresses and Class E (240–255) for scientific purposes, but I'm not going into these types of addresses, because they are beyond the scope of knowledge you need to gain from this book.

Network Addresses: Special Purpose

Some IP addresses are reserved for special purposes, so network administrators can't ever assign these addresses to nodes. Table 3.4 lists the members of this exclusive little club and the reasons why they're included in it.

TABLE 2.4   Reserved IP addresses

Address	Function
Network address of all 0s	Interpreted to mean "this network or segment."
Network address of all 1s	Interpreted to mean "all networks."
Network 127.0.0.1	Reserved for loopback tests. Designates the local node and allows that node to send a test packet to itself without generating network traffic.
Node address of all 0s	Interpreted to mean "network address" or any host on a specified network.

TABLE 2.4 Reserved IP addresses *(continued)*

Address	Function
Node address of all 1s	Interpreted to mean "all nodes" on the specified network; for example, 128.2.255.255 means "all nodes" on network 128.2 (Class B address).
Entire IP address set to all 0s	Used by Cisco routers to designate the default route. Could also mean "any network."
Entire IP address set to all 1s (same as 255.255.255.255)	Broadcast to all nodes on the current network; sometimes called an "all 1s broadcast" or local broadcast.

Class A Addresses

In a Class A network address, the first byte is assigned to the network address, and the three remaining bytes are used for the node addresses. The Class A format is as follows:

`network.node.node.node`

For example, in the IP address 49.22.102.70, the 49 is the network address, and the 22.102.70 is the node address. Every machine on this particular network would have the distinctive network address of 49.

Class A network addresses are 1 byte long, with the first bit of that byte reserved and the 7 remaining bits available for manipulation (addressing). As a result, the maximum number of Class A networks that can be created is 128. Why? Because each of the 7 bit positions can be either a 0 or a 1—thus 2^7, or 128.

To complicate matters further, the network address of all 0s (0000 0000) is reserved to designate the default route (refer to Table 2.4 in the previous section). Additionally, the address 127, which is reserved for diagnostics, can't be used either, which means that you can really only use the numbers 1 to 126 to designate Class A network addresses. This means the actual number of usable Class A network addresses is 128 minus 2, or 126.

> The IP address 127.0.0.1 is used to test the IP stack on an individual node and cannot be used as a valid host address. However, the loopback address creates a shortcut method for TCP/IP applications and services that run on the same device to communicate with each other.

Each Class A address has 3 bytes (24-bit positions) for the node address of a machine. This means there are 2^{24}—or 16,777,216—unique combinations and, therefore, precisely that many possible unique node addresses for each Class A network. Because node addresses with the two patterns of all 0s and all 1s are reserved, the actual maximum usable number of nodes for a Class A network is 2^{24} minus 2, which equals 16,777,214. Either way, that's a huge number of hosts on a single network segment!

Class A Valid Host IDs

Here's an example of how to figure out the valid host IDs in a Class A network address:

- All host bits off is the network address: 10.0.0.0.
- All host bits on is the broadcast address: 10.255.255.255.

The valid hosts are the numbers in between the network address and the broadcast address: 10.0.0.1 through 10.255.255.254. Notice that 0s and 255s can be valid host IDs. All you need to remember when trying to find valid host addresses is that the host bits can't all be turned off or on at the same time.

Class B Addresses

In a Class B network address, the first 2 bytes are assigned to the network address and the remaining 2 bytes are used for node addresses. The format is as follows:

network.network.node.node

For example, in the IP address 172.16.30.56, the network address is 172.16, and the node address is 30.56.

With a network address being 2 bytes (8 bits each), you get 2^{16} unique combinations. But the Internet designers decided that all Class B network addresses should start with the binary digit 1, then 0. This leaves 14 bit positions to manipulate, therefore 16,384, or 2^{14} unique Class B network addresses.

A Class B address uses 2 bytes for node addresses. This is 2^{16}, minus the two reserved patterns of all 0s and all 1s, for a total of 65,534 possible node addresses for each Class B network.

Class B Valid Host IDs

Here's an example of how to find the valid hosts in a Class B network:

- All host bits turned off is the network address: 172.16.0.0.
- All host bits turned on is the broadcast address: 172.16.255.255.

The valid hosts would be the numbers in between the network address and the broadcast address: 172.16.0.1 through 172.16.255.254.

Class C Addresses

The first 3 bytes of a Class C network address are dedicated to the network portion of the address, with only 1 measly byte remaining for the node address. Here's the format:

network.network.network.node

Using the example IP address 192.168.100.102, the network address is 192.168.100, and the node address is 102.

In a Class C network address, the first three bit positions are always the binary 110. The calculation is as follows: 3 bytes, or 24 bits, minus 3 reserved positions leaves 21 positions. Hence, there are 2^{21}, or 2,097,152, possible Class C networks.

Each unique Class C network has 1 byte to use for node addresses. This leads to 2^8, or 256, minus the two reserved patterns of all 0s and all 1s, for a total of 254 node addresses for each Class C network.

Class C Valid Host IDs

Here's an example of how to find a valid host ID in a Class C network:

- All host bits turned off is the network ID: 192.168.100.0.

- All host bits turned on is the broadcast address: 192.168.100.255.

The valid hosts would be the numbers in between the network address and the broadcast address: 192.168.100.1 through 192.168.100.254.

Private IP Addresses (RFC 1918)

The people who created the IP addressing scheme also created private IP addresses. These addresses can be used on a private network, but they're not routable through the Internet. This is designed for the purpose of creating a measure of well-needed security, but it also conveniently saves valuable IP address space.

If every host on every network was required to have real routable IP addresses, we would have run out of IP addresses to hand out years ago. But by using private IP addresses, ISPs, corporations, and home users only need a relatively tiny group of bona fide IP addresses to connect their networks to the Internet. This is economical because they can use private IP addresses on their inside networks and get along just fine.

To accomplish this task, the ISP and the corporation—the end user, no matter who they are—need to use something called *Network Address Translation (NAT)*, which basically takes a private IP address and converts it for use on the Internet. Many people can use the same real IP address to transmit out onto the Internet. Doing things this way saves megatons of address space—good for us all!

The reserved private addresses are listed in Table 2.5.

TABLE 2.5   Reserved IP address space

Address Class	Reserved Address Space
Class A	10.0.0.0 through 10.255.255.255
Class B	172.16.0.0 through 172.31.255.255
Class C	192.168.0.0 through 192.168.255.255

IPv4 Address Types

Most people use the term *broadcast* as a generic term, and most of the time, we understand what they mean—but not always! For example, you might say, "The host broadcasted through a router to a DHCP server," but, well, it's pretty unlikely that this would ever really happen. What you probably mean—using the correct technical jargon—is, "The DHCP client broadcasted for an IP address, and a router then forwarded this as a unicast packet to the DHCP server." Oh, and remember that with IPv4, broadcasts are pretty important, but with IPv6, there aren't any broadcasts sent at all.

Okay, I've referred to IP addresses numerous times, and I even showed you some examples, but I really haven't gone into the different terms and uses associated with them yet, and it's about time I did. So here are the address types that I'd like to define for you:

Loopback (Localhost)   This address is used to test the IP stack on the local computer. It can be any address from 127.0.0.1 through 127.255.255.254.

Layer 2 Broadcasts   These are sent to all nodes on a LAN.

Layer 3 Broadcasts   These are sent to all nodes on the network.

Unicast   This is an address for a single interface and is used to send packets to a single destination host.

Multicast   These are packets sent from a single source and transmitted to many devices on different networks. Referred to as "one-to-many."

Layer 2 Broadcasts

Layer 2 broadcasts are also known as hardware broadcasts—they only go out on a LAN, but they don't go past the LAN boundary (router).

The typical hardware address is 6 bytes (48 bits) and looks something like 45:AC:24:E3:60:A5. The broadcast would be all 1s in binary, which would be all *F*s in hexadecimal, as in ff:ff:ff:ff:ff:ff and shown in Figure 2.21.

FIGURE 2.21   Local layer 2 broadcasts

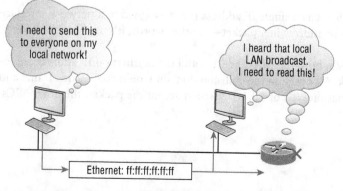

I need to send this to everyone on my local network!

I heard that local LAN broadcast. I need to read this!

Ethernet: ff:ff:ff:ff:ff:ff

Every network interface card (NIC) will receive and read the frame, including the router, since this was a layer 2 broadcast, but the router would never, ever forward this!

Layer 3 Broadcasts

Then there are the plain old broadcast addresses at layer 3. Broadcast messages are meant to reach all hosts on a broadcast domain. These are the network broadcasts that have all host bits on.

Here's an example that you're already familiar with: The network address of 172.16.0.0 255.255.0.0 would have a broadcast address of 172.16.255.255—all host bits on. Broadcasts can also be "any network and all hosts," as indicated by 255.255.255.255 and shown in Figure 2.22.

FIGURE 2.22 Layer 3 broadcasts

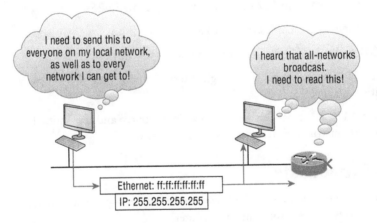

In Figure 2.22, all hosts on the LAN will get this broadcast on their NIC, including the router, but by default the router would never forward this packet.

Unicast Address

A unicast is defined as a single IP address that's assigned to a network interface card and is the destination IP address in a packet—in other words, it's used for directing packets to a specific host.

In Figure 2.23, both the MAC address and the destination IP address are for a single NIC on the network. All hosts on the collision domain would receive this frame and accept it. Only the destination NIC of 10.1.1.2 would accept the packet; the other NICs would discard the packet.

FIGURE 2.23   Unicast address

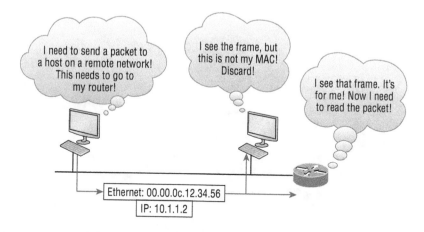

Multicast Address

Multicast is a different beast entirely. At first glance, it appears to be a hybrid of unicast and broadcast communication, but that isn't quite the case. Multicast does allow point-to-multipoint communication, which is similar to broadcasts, but it happens in a different manner. The crux of *multicast* is that it enables multiple recipients to receive messages without flooding the messages to all hosts on a broadcast domain. However, this is not the default behavior—it's what we *can* do with multicasting if it's configured correctly!

Multicast works by sending messages or data to IP *multicast group* addresses. Unlike with broadcasts, which aren't forwarded, routers then forward copies of the packet out to every interface that has hosts *subscribed* to that group address. This is where multicast differs from broadcast messages—with multicast communication, copies of packets, in theory, are sent only to subscribed hosts. For example, when I say "in theory," I mean that the hosts will receive a multicast packet destined for 224.0.0.10. This is an EIGRP packet, and only a router running the EIGRP protocol will read these. All hosts on the broadcast LAN—and Ethernet is a broadcast multi-access LAN technology—will pick up the frame, read the destination address, and then immediately discard the frame, unless they're in the multicast group.

This saves PC processing, not LAN bandwidth. Be warned, though—multicasting can cause some serious LAN congestion if it's not implemented carefully! Figure 2.24 shows a Cisco router sending an EIGRP multicast packet on the local LAN, and only the other Cisco router will accept and read this packet.

FIGURE 2.24 An EIGRP multicast example

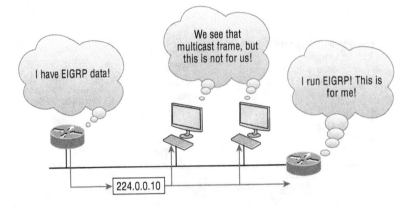

There are several different groups that users or applications can subscribe to. The range of multicast addresses starts with 224.0.0.0 and goes through 239.255.255.255. As you can see, this range of addresses falls within IP Class D address space based on classful IP assignment.

Summary

If you made it this far and understood everything the first time through, you should be extremely proud of yourself! This chapter covered a lot of ground, but understand that the information in it is critical to being able to navigate well through the rest of this book.

If you didn't get a complete understanding the first time around, don't stress. It really wouldn't hurt you to read this chapter more than once. There is still a lot of ground to cover, so make sure you've got this material all nailed down. That way, you'll be ready for more—and just so you know, there's a lot more! What we're doing up to this point is building a solid foundation to build upon as you advance.

With that in mind, after you learned about the DoD model, the layers, and associated protocols, you learned about the oh-so-important topic of IP addressing. I discussed in detail the difference between each address class, how to find a network address and broadcast address, and what denotes a valid host address range. I can't stress enough how important it is for you to have this critical information unshakably understood before moving on to Chapter 3!

Since you've already come this far, there's no reason to stop now and waste all those brainwaves and new neural connections. So don't stop—go through the written labs and review questions at the end of this chapter and make sure you understand each answer's explanation. The best is yet to come!

Exam Essentials

Differentiate between the DoD and the OSI network models.   The DoD model is a condensed version of the OSI model, composed of four layers instead of seven, but is nonetheless like the OSI model in that it can be used to describe packet creation and devices and protocols can be mapped to its layers.

Identify Process/Application layer protocols.   Telnet is a terminal emulation program that allows you to log into a remote host and run programs. File Transfer Protocol (FTP) is a connection-oriented service that allows you to transfer files. Trivial FTP (TFTP) is a connectionless file transfer program. Simple Mail Transfer Protocol (SMTP) is a sendmail program.

Identify Host-to-Host layer protocols.   Transmission Control Protocol (TCP) is a connection-oriented protocol that provides reliable network service by using acknowledgments and flow control. User Datagram Protocol (UDP) is a connectionless protocol that provides low overhead and is considered unreliable.

Identify Internet layer protocols.   Internet Protocol (IP) is a connectionless protocol that provides network addressing and routing through an internetwork. Address Resolution Protocol (ARP) finds a hardware address from a known IP address.

Describe the functions of DNS and DHCP in the network.   Dynamic Host Configuration Protocol (DHCP) provides network configuration information (including IP addresses) to hosts, eliminating the need to perform the configurations manually. Domain Name Service (DNS) resolves hostnames—both Internet names such as www.lammle.com and device names such as Workstation 2—to IP addresses, eliminating the need to know the IP address of a device for connection purposes.

Identify what is contained in the TCP header of a connection-oriented transmission.   The fields in the TCP header include the source port, destination port, sequence number, acknowledgment number, header length, a field reserved for future use, code bits, window size, checksum, urgent pointer, options field, and finally, the data field.

Identify what is contained in the UDP header of a connectionless transmission.   The fields in the UDP header include only the source port, destination port, length, checksum, and data. The smaller number of fields as compared to the TCP header comes at the expense of providing none of the more advanced functions of the TCP frame.

Identify what is contained in the IP header.   The fields of an IP header include version, header length, priority or type of service, total length, identification, flags, fragment offset, time to live, protocol, header checksum, source IP address, destination IP address, options, and finally, data.

Compare and contrast UDP and TCP characteristics and features.   TCP is connection-oriented, acknowledged, and sequenced and has flow and error control, while UDP is connectionless, unacknowledged, and not sequenced and provides no error or flow control.

Understand the role of port numbers.   Port numbers are used to identify the protocol or service that is to be used in the transmission.

Identify the role of ICMP. Internet Control Message Protocol (ICMP) works at the Network layer and is used by IP for many different services. ICMP is a management protocol and messaging service provider for IP.

Define the Class A IP address range. The IP range for a Class A network is 1 through 126. This provides 8 bits of network addressing and 24 bits of host addressing by default.

Define the Class B IP address range. The IP range for a Class B network is 128 through 191. Class B addressing provides 16 bits of network addressing and 16 bits of host addressing by default.

Define the Class C IP address range. The IP range for a Class C network is 192 through 223. Class C addressing provides 24 bits of network addressing and 8 bits of host addressing by default.

Identify the private IP ranges. The Class A private address range is 10.0.0.0 through 10.255.255.255. The Class B private address range is 172.16.0.0 through 172.31.255.255. The Class C private address range is 192.168.0.0 through 192.168.255.255.

Understand the difference between a broadcast, unicast, and multicast address. A broadcast is to all devices in a subnet; a unicast is to one device; and a multicast is to some but not all devices.

Review Questions

NOTE The following questions are designed to test your understanding of this chapter's material. For more information on how to get additional questions, please see www.lammle.com/ccst.

You can find the answers to these questions in Appendix, "Answers to Review Questions."

1. Which of the following Application layer protocols sets up a secure session that's similar to Telnet?
   - **A.** FTP
   - **B.** SSH
   - **C.** DNS
   - **D.** DHCP

2. Which protocol is used to find the hardware address of a local device?
   - **A.** RARP
   - **B.** ARP
   - **C.** IP
   - **D.** ICMP
   - **E.** BootP

3. Which of the following are layers in the TCP/IP model? (Choose three.)
   - **A.** Application
   - **B.** Session
   - **C.** Transport
   - **D.** Internet
   - **E.** Data Link
   - **F.** Physical

4. Which class of IP address provides a maximum of only 254 host addresses per network ID?
   - **A.** Class A
   - **B.** Class B
   - **C.** Class C
   - **D.** Class D
   - **E.** Class E

5. Which of the following describe the DHCP Discover message? (Choose two.)

    A. It uses ff:ff:ff:ff:ff:ff as a layer 2 broadcast.

    B. It uses UDP as the Transport layer protocol.

    C. It uses TCP as the Transport layer protocol.

    D. It does not use a layer 2 destination address.

6. Which layer 4 protocol is used for a Telnet connection?

    A. IP

    B. TCP

    C. TCP/IP

    D. UDP

    E. ICMP

7. Private IP addressing was specified in RFC _____.

8. Which of the following services use TCP? (Choose three.)

    A. DHCP

    B. SMTP

    C. SNMP

    D. FTP

    E. HTTP

    F. TFTP

9. Which of the following is an example of a multicast address?

    A. 10.6.9.1

    B. 192.168.10.6

    C. 224.0.0.10

    D. 172.16.9.5

10. If you use either Telnet or FTP, which layer are you using to generate the data?

    A. Application

    B. Presentation

    C. Session

    D. Transport

11. The DoD model (also called the TCP/IP stack) has four layers. Which layer of the DoD model is equivalent to the Network layer of the OSI model?

    A. Application

    B. Host-to-Host

    C. Internet

    D. Network Access

12. Which of the following are private IP addresses? (Choose two.)

    A. 12.0.0.1

    B. 168.172.19.39

    C. 172.20.14.36

    D. 172.33.194.30

    E. 192.168.24.43

13. What layer in the TCP/IP stack is equivalent to the Transport layer of the OSI model?

    A. Application

    B. Host-to-Host

    C. Internet

    D. Network Access

14. Which statements are true regarding ICMP packets? (Choose two.)

    A. ICMP guarantees datagram delivery.

    B. ICMP can provide hosts with information about network problems.

    C. ICMP is encapsulated within IP datagrams.

    D. ICMP is encapsulated within UDP datagrams

15. What is the address range of a Class B network address in binary?

    A. 01*xxxxxx*

    B. 0*xxxxxxx*

    C. 10*xxxxxx*

    D. 110*xxxxx*

Chapter

3

Easy Subnetting

THE CCST EXAM TOPICS COVERED IN THIS CHAPTER INCLUDE THE FOLLOWING:

✓ **2.0 Addressing and Subnet Formats**

- 2.1. Compare and contrast private addresses and public addresses.
  - Address classes, NAT concepts
- 2.2. Identify IPv4 addresses and subnet formats.
  - Subnet concepts, Subnet Calculator, slash notation, and subnet mask; broadcast domain
- 2.3. Identify IPv6 addresses and prefix formats.
  - Types of addresses, prefix concepts

We'll pick up right where we left off in the previous chapter and continue to explore the world of IP addressing. I'll open this chapter by telling you how to subnet an IP network—an indispensable crucial skill that's central to mastering networking in general! Forewarned is forearmed, so prepare yourself, because being able to subnet quickly and accurately is pretty challenging and you'll need time to practice what you've learned to really nail it. So be patient and don't give up on this key aspect of networking until your skills are seriously sharp. I'm not kidding—this chapter is so important you should really just graft it into your brain!

So be ready because we're going to hit the ground running and thoroughly cover IP subnetting from the very start. And though I know this will sound weird to you, you'll be much better off if you just try to forget everything you've learned about subnetting before reading this chapter—especially if you've been to an official Cisco or Microsoft class! I think these forms of special torture often do more harm than good and sometimes even scare people away from networking completely. Those who survive and persevere usually at least question the sanity of continuing to study in this field. If this is you, relax, breathe, and know that you'll find that the way I tackle the issue of subnetting is relatively painless, because I'm going to show you a whole new, much easier method to conquer this monster!

After working through this chapter, you'll be able to tame the IP addressing/subnetting beast—just don't give up! I promise that you'll be really glad you didn't. It's one of those things that once you get it down, you'll wonder why you used to think it was so hard!

To find up-to-the-minute updates for this chapter, please see www.lammle.com/ccst.

Subnetting Basics

In Chapter 2, "Introduction to TCP/IP," you learned how to define and find the valid host ranges used in a Class A, Class B, and Class C network address by turning the host bits all off and then all on. This is very good, but here's the catch: You were defining only one network, as shown in Figure 3.1.

By now you know that having one large network is not a good thing, because the first two chapters you just read were veritably peppered with me incessantly telling you that! But how would you fix the out-of-control problem that Figure 3.1 illustrates? Wouldn't it be nice to be able to break up that one, huge network address and create four manageable networks from it? You betcha it would, but to make that happen, you would need to apply the infamous trick of *subnetting*, because it's the best way to break up a giant network into a bunch of smaller ones. Take a look at Figure 3.2 and see how this might look.

FIGURE 3.1   One network

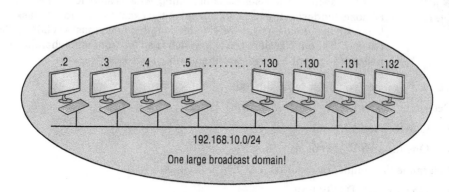

192.168.10.0/24

One large broadcast domain!

FIGURE 3.2   Multiple networks connected together

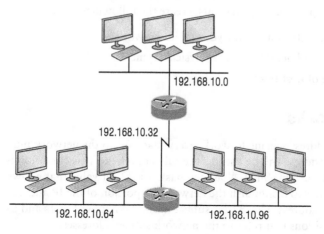

What are those 192.168.10.*x* addresses shown in the figure? Well, that is what this chapter will explain—how to make one network into many networks!

Let's take off from where we left in Chapter 2 and start working in the host section (host bits) of a network address, where we can borrow bits to create subnets.

How to Create Subnets

Creating subnetworks is essentially the act of taking bits from the host portion of the address and reserving them to define the subnet address instead. Clearly, this will result in fewer bits being available for defining your hosts, which is something you'll always want to keep in mind.

Later in this chapter, I'll guide you through the entire process of creating subnets, starting with Class C addresses. As always in networking, before you actually implement anything, including subnetting, you must first determine your current requirements and make sure to plan for future conditions as well.

> This first section discusses classful routing, which refers to the fact that all hosts (nodes) in the network are using the exact same subnet mask. Later, when I move on to cover variable-length subnet masks (VLSMs), I'll tell you all about classless routing, which is an environment wherein each network segment *can* use a different subnet mask.

To create a subnet, you must fulfill the following three steps:

1. Determine the number of required network IDs:
   - One for each LAN subnet
   - One for each WAN connection
2. Determine the number of required host IDs per subnet:
   - One for each TCP/IP host
   - One for each router interface
3. Based on the previous requirements, create the following:
   - A unique subnet mask for your entire network
   - A unique subnet ID for each physical segment
   - A range of host IDs for each subnet

Subnet Masks

For the subnet address scheme to work, every machine on the network must know which part of the host address will be used as the subnet address. This condition is met by assigning a *subnet mask* to each machine. A subnet mask is a 32-bit value that allows the device that's receiving IP packets to distinguish the network ID portion of the IP address from the host ID portion of the IP address. This 32-bit subnet mask is composed of 1s and 0s, where the 1s represent the positions that refer to the network subnet addresses.

Not all networks need subnets, and if not, it really means that they're using the default subnet mask, which is basically the same as saying that a network doesn't have a subnet address. Table 3.1 shows the default subnet masks for Classes A, B, and C.

TABLE 3.1   Default subnet mask

Class	Format	Default Subnet Mask
A	*network.node.node.node*	255.0.0.0
B	*network.network.node.node*	255.255.0.0
C	*network.network.network.node*	255.255.255.0

Although you can use any mask in any way on an interface, typically it's not usually good to mess with the default masks. In other words, you don't want to make a Class B subnet mask read 255.0.0.0, and some hosts won't even let you type it in. But these days, most devices will. For a Class A network, you wouldn't change the first byte in a subnet mask, because it should read 255.0.0.0 at a minimum. Similarly, you wouldn't assign 255.255.255.255, because this is all 1s, which is a broadcast address. A Class B address starts with 255.255.0.0, and a Class C starts with 255.255.255.0. For the CCST especially, there is no reason to change the defaults!

Understanding the Powers of 2

Powers of 2 are important to understand and memorize for use with IP subnetting. Remember that when you see a number noted with an exponent, it means you should multiply the number by itself as many times as the upper number specifies. For example, 2^3 is $2 \times 2 \times 2$, which equals 8. Here's a list of powers of 2 to commit to memory:

$2^1 = 2$

$2^2 = 4$

$2^3 = 8$

$2^4 = 16$

$2^5 = 32$

$2^6 = 64$

$2^7 = 128$

$2^8 = 256$

$2^9 = 512$

$2^{10} = 1,024$

$2^{11} = 2,048$

$2^{12} = 4,096$

$2^{13} = 8,192$

$2^{14} = 16,384$

Memorizing these powers of 2 is a good idea, but it's not absolutely necessary. Just remember that since you're working with powers of 2, each successive power of 2 is double the previous one.

It works like this—all you have to do to remember the value of 2^9 is to first know that $2^8 = 256$. Why? Because when you double 2 to the eighth power (256), you get 2^9 (or 512). To determine the value of 2^{10}, simply start at $2^8 = 256$, and then double it twice.

You can go the other way as well. If you needed to know what 2^6 is, for example, you just cut 256 in half two times: once to reach 2^7 and then one more time to reach 2^6.

Classless Inter-Domain Routing (CIDR)

Another term you need to familiarize yourself with is *Classless Inter-Domain Routing (CIDR)*. It's basically the method that Internet service providers (ISPs) use to allocate a number of addresses to a company, a home—their customers. They provide addresses in a certain block size, something I'll talk about in greater detail soon.

When you receive a block of addresses from an ISP, what you get will look something like this: 192.168.10.32/28. This is telling you what your subnet mask is. The slash notation (/) means how many bits are turned on (1s). Obviously, the maximum could only be /32, because a byte is 8 bits and there are 4 bytes in an IP address: (4 × 8 = 32). But keep in mind that regardless of the class of address, the largest subnet mask available relevant to the Cisco exam objectives can only be a /30, because you've got to keep at least 2 bits for host bits.

Take, for example, a Class A default subnet mask, which is 255.0.0.0. This tells us that the first byte of the subnet mask is all ones (1s), or 11111111. When referring to a slash notation, you need to count all the 1 bits to figure out your mask. The 255.0.0.0 is considered a /8 because it has 8 bits that are 1s—that is, 8 bits that are turned on.

A Class B default mask would be 255.255.0.0, which is a /16 because 16 bits are ones (1s): 11111111.11111111.00000000.00000000.

Table 3.2 lists every available subnet mask and its equivalent CIDR slash notation.

TABLE 3.2   CIDR values

Subnet Mask	CIDR Value
255.0.0.0	/8
255.128.0.0	/9
255.192.0.0	/10
255.224.0.0	/11
255.240.0.0	/12
255.248.0.0	/13
255.252.0.0	/14
255.254.0.0	/15
255.255.0.0	/16
255.255.128.0	/17
255.255.192.0	/18
255.255.224.0	/19

Subnet Mask	CIDR Value
255.255.240.0	/20
255.255.248.0	/21
255.255.252.0	/22
255.255.254.0	/23
255.255.255.0	/24
255.255.255.128	/25
255.255.255.192	/26
255.255.255.224	/27
255.255.255.240	/28
255.255.255.248	/29
255.255.255.252	/30

The /8 through /15 can be used only with Class A network addresses. /16 through /23 can be used by Class A and B network addresses. /24 through /30 can be used by Class A, B, and C network addresses. This is a big reason why most companies use Class A network addresses. Since they can use all subnet masks, they get the maximum flexibility in network design.

 NOTE   No, you cannot configure a Cisco router using this slash format. But wouldn't that be nice? Nevertheless, it's *really* important for you to know subnet masks in the slash notation (CIDR).

IP Subnet-Zero

Even though `ip subnet-zero` is not a new command, Cisco courseware and Cisco exam objectives didn't used to cover it. Know that Cisco certainly covers it now! This command allows you to use the first and last subnet in your network design. For instance, the Class C mask of 255.255.255.192 provides subnets 64 and 128, another facet of subnetting that I'll discuss more thoroughly later in this chapter. But with the `ip subnet-zero` command, you now get to use subnets 0, 64, 128, and 192. It may not seem like a lot, but this provides two more subnets for every subnet mask you use.

By using the command show running-config from a Cisco router prompt, you can see the active configuration on a router. Let's take a look at the top of a Cisco router configuration:

```
Router#sh running-config
Building configuration...
Current configuration : 827 bytes
!
hostname Pod1R1
!
ip subnet-zero
!
```

This router output shows that the command ip subnet-zero is enabled on the router. Cisco has turned on this command by default starting with Cisco IOS version 12.*x*, and now we're running 15.*x* code.

When taking your Cisco exams, make sure you read very carefully to see if Cisco is asking you *not* to use ip subnet-zero. There are actually instances where this may happen.

Subnetting Class C Addresses

There are many different ways to subnet a network. The right way is the way that works best for you. In a Class C address, only 8 bits are available for defining the hosts. Remember that subnet bits start at the left and move to the right, without skipping bits. This means that the only Class C subnet masks can be the following:

```
Binary Decimal CIDR
---------------------------------------------------------
00000000 = 255.255.255.0 /24
10000000 = 255.255.255.128 /25
11000000 = 255.255.255.192 /26
11100000 = 255.255.255.224 /27
11110000 = 255.255.255.240 /28
11111000 = 255.255.255.248 /29
11111100 = 255.255.255.252 /30
```

You can't use a /31 or /32 because, as I've said, you must have at least 2 host bits for assigning IP addresses to hosts. But this is only mostly true. Certainly you can never use a /32, because that would mean zero host bits available, yet Cisco has various forms of the IOS, as well as the new Cisco Nexus switches operating system, that support the /31 mask.

Coming up, I'm going to teach you that significantly less painful method of subnetting I promised at the beginning of this chapter, which makes it ever so much easier to subnet larger numbers in a flash. Excited? Good! Because I'm not kidding when I tell you that you absolutely need to be able to subnet quickly and accurately in order to succeed in the networking real world—and on the exam!

Subnetting a Class C Address—The Fast Way!

When you've chosen a possible subnet mask for your network and need to determine the number of subnets, valid hosts, and the broadcast addresses of a subnet that mask will provide, all you need to do is answer five simple questions:

- How many subnets does the chosen subnet mask produce?
- How many valid hosts per subnet are available?
- What are the valid subnets?
- What's the broadcast address of each subnet?
- What are the valid hosts in each subnet?

This is where you'll be really glad you followed my advice and took the time to memorize your powers of 2. If you didn't, now would be a good time. Just refer back to the sidebar "Understanding the Powers of 2" earlier if you need to brush up. Here's how you arrive at the answers to those five big questions:

- *How many subnets?* 2^x = number of subnets. x is the number of masked bits, or the 1s. For example, in 11000000, the number of 1s gives us 2^2 subnets. So, in this example, there are 4 subnets.

- *How many hosts per subnet?* $2^y - 2$ = number of hosts per subnet. y is the number of unmasked bits, or the 0s. For example, in 11000000, the number of 0s gives us $2^6 - 2$ hosts, or 62 hosts per subnet. You need to subtract 2 for the subnet address and the broadcast address, which are not valid hosts.

- *What are the valid subnets?* 256 – subnet mask = block size, or increment number. An example would be the 255.255.255.192 mask, where the interesting octet is the fourth octet (interesting because that is where our subnet numbers are). Just use this math: 256 – 192 = 64. The block size of a 192 mask is always 64. Start counting at zero in blocks of 64 until you reach the subnet mask value, and these are your subnets in the fourth octet: 0, 64, 128, 192. Easy, huh?

- *What's the broadcast address for each subnet?* Now here's the really easy part. Since we counted our subnets in the last section as 0, 64, 128, and 192, the broadcast address is always the number right before the next subnet. For example, the 0 subnet has a broadcast address of 63 because the next subnet is 64. The 64 subnet has a broadcast address of 127 because the next subnet is 128, and so on. Remember, the broadcast address of the last subnet is always 255.

- *What are the valid hosts?* Valid hosts are the numbers between the subnets, omitting the all-0s and all-1s. For example, if 64 is the subnet number and 127 is the broadcast address, then 65–126 is the valid host range. Your valid range is *always* the group of numbers between the subnet address and the broadcast address.

If you're still confused, don't worry, because it really isn't as hard as it seems to be at first—just hang in there! To help lift any mental fog, try a few of the practice examples next.

Subnetting Practice Examples: Class C Addresses

Here's your opportunity to practice subnetting Class C addresses using the method I just described. This is so cool. We're going to start with the first Class C subnet mask and work through every subnet that we can, using a Class C address. When we're done, I'll show you how easy this is with Class A and B networks too!

Practice Example #1C: 255.255.255.128 (/25)

Since 128 is 10000000 in binary, there is only 1 bit for subnetting and 7 bits for hosts. We're going to subnet the Class C network address 192.168.10.0.

192.168.10.0 = Network address

255.255.255.128 = Subnet mask

Now, let's answer the big five:

- *How many subnets?* Since 128 is 1 bit on (10000000), the answer would be $2^1 = 2$.

- *How many hosts per subnet?* We have 7 host bits off (10000000), so the equation would be $2^7 - 2 = 126$ hosts. Once you figure out the block size of a mask, the amount of hosts is always the block size minus 2. No need to do extra math if you don't need to!

- *What are the valid subnets?* $256 - 128 = 128$. Remember, we'll start at zero and count in our block size, so our subnets are 0, 128. By just counting your subnets when counting in your block size, you really don't need to do steps 1 and 2. We can see we have two subnets, and in the step before this one, just remember that the amount of hosts is always the block size minus 2, and in this example, that gives us 2 subnets, each with 126 hosts.

- *What's the broadcast address for each subnet?* The number right before the value of the next subnet is all host bits turned on and equals the broadcast address. For the zero subnet, the next subnet is 128, so the broadcast address of the 0 subnet is 127.

- *What are the valid hosts?* These are the numbers between the subnet and broadcast address. The easiest way to find the hosts is to write out the subnet address and the broadcast address, which makes valid hosts completely obvious. The following table shows the 0 and 128 subnets, the valid host ranges of each, and the broadcast address of both subnets:

Subnet	0	128
First host	1	129
Last host	126	254
Broadcast	127	255

Looking at a Class C /25, it's pretty clear that there are two subnets. But so what—why is this significant? Actually, it's not, because that's not the right question. What you really want to know is what you would do with this information!

I know this isn't exactly everyone's favorite pastime, but what we're about to do is really important, so bear with me; we're going to talk about subnetting—period. The key to understanding subnetting is to understand the very reason you need to do it, and I'm going to demonstrate this by going through the process of building a physical network.

Okay, because we added that router shown in Figure 3.3, in order for the hosts on our internetwork to communicate, they must now have a logical network addressing scheme. We could use IPv6, but IPv4 is still the most popular for now. It's also what we're studying at the moment, so that's what we're going with.

FIGURE 3.3 Implementing a Class C /25 logical network

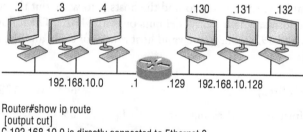

```
Router#show ip route
[output cut]
C 192.168.10.0 is directly connected to Ethernet 0
C 192.168.10.128 is directly connected to Ethernet 1
```

Looking at Figure 3.3, you can see that there are two physical networks, so we're going to implement a logical addressing scheme that allows for two logical networks. As always, it's a really good idea to look ahead and consider likely short- and long-term growth scenarios, but for this example in this book, a /25 gets it done.

Figure 3.3 shows that both subnets have been assigned to a router interface, which creates our broadcast domains and assigns our subnets. Use the command show ip route to see the routing table on a router. Notice that instead of one large broadcast domain, there are now two smaller broadcast domains, providing for up to 126 hosts in each. The C in the router output translates to "directly connected network," and we can see we have two of those with two broadcast domains and that we created and implemented them. So congratulations—you did it! You have successfully subnetted a network and applied it to a network design. Nice! Let's do it again.

Practice Example #2C: 255.255.255.192 (/26)

This time, we're going to subnet the network address 192.168.10.0 using the subnet mask 255.255.255.192.

192.168.10.0 = Network address

255.255.255.192 = Subnet mask

Now, let's answer the big five:

- *How many subnets?* Since 192 is 2 bits on (**11000000**), the answer would be $2^2 = 4$ subnets.
- *How many hosts per subnet?* We have 6 host bits off (**11000000**), giving us $2^6 - 2 = 62$ hosts. The amount of hosts is always the block size minus 2.
- *What are the valid subnets?* 256 – 192 = 64. Remember to start at zero and count in our block size. This means our subnets are 0, 64, 128, and 192. We can see we have a block size of 64, so we have 4 subnets, each with 62 hosts.
- *What's the broadcast address for each subnet?* The number right before the value of the next subnet is all host bits turned on and equals the broadcast address. For the zero subnet, the next subnet is 64, so the broadcast address for the zero subnet is 63.
- What are the valid hosts? These are the numbers between the subnet and broadcast address. As I said, the easiest way to find the hosts is to write out the subnet address and the broadcast address, which clearly delimits our valid hosts. The following table shows the 0, 64, 128, and 192 subnets, the valid host ranges of each, and the broadcast address of each subnet:

	0	64	128	192
The subnets (Do this first.)	0	64	128	192
Our first host (Perform host addressing last.)	1	65	129	193
Our last host	62	126	190	254
The broadcast address (Do this second.)	63	127	191	255

Again, before getting into the next example, you can see that we can now subnet a /26 as long as we can count in increments of 64. And what are you going to do with this fascinating information? Implement it! We'll use Figure 3.4 to practice a /26 network implementation.

The /26 mask provides four subnetworks, and we need a subnet for each router interface. With this mask, in this example, we actually have room with a spare subnet to add to another router interface in the future. Always plan for growth if possible!

Practice Example #3C: 255.255.255.224 (/27)

This time, we'll subnet the network address 192.168.10.0 and subnet mask 255.255.255.224.

192.168.10.0 = Network address

255.255.255.224 = Subnet mask

- *How many subnets?* 224 is 11100000, so our equation would be $2^3 = 8$.
- *How many hosts?* $2^5 - 2 = 30$.
- *What are the valid subnets?* 256 – 224 = 32. We just start at zero and count to the subnet mask value in blocks (increments) of 32: 0, 32, 64, 96, 128, 160, 192, and 224.

FIGURE 3.4   Implementing a class C /26 (with three networks)

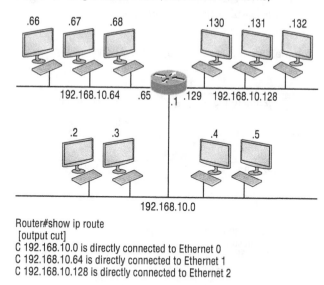

Router#show ip route
[output cut]
C 192.168.10.0 is directly connected to Ethernet 0
C 192.168.10.64 is directly connected to Ethernet 1
C 192.168.10.128 is directly connected to Ethernet 2

- *What's the broadcast address for each subnet (always the number right before the next subnet)?*

- *What are the valid hosts (the numbers between the subnet number and the broadcast address)?*

To answer the last two questions, first just write out the subnets, then write out the broadcast addresses—the number right before the next subnet. Last, fill in the host addresses. The following table gives you all the subnets for the 255.255.255.224 Class C subnet mask:

The subnet address	0	32	64	96	128	160	192	224
The first valid host	1	33	65	97	129	161	193	225
The last valid host	30	62	94	126	158	190	222	254
The broadcast address	31	63	95	127	159	191	223	255

In practice example #3C, we're using a 255.255.255.224 (/27) network, which provides eight subnets, as shown previously. We can take these subnets and implement them as shown in Figure 3.5 using any of the subnets available.

Notice that I used six of the eight subnets available for my network design. The lightning bolt symbol in the figure represents a wide area network (WAN) such as a T1 or other serial connection through an ISP or telco. In other words, something you don't own but is still a subnet, just like any LAN connection on a router. As usual, I used the first valid host in each subnet as the router's interface address. This is just a rule of thumb; you can use any address in the valid host range as long as you remember what address you configured so you can set the default gateways on your hosts to the router address.

FIGURE 3.5   Implementing a Class C /27 logical network

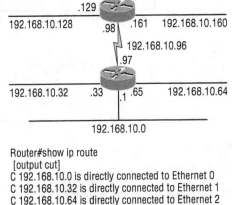

```
Router#show ip route
[output cut]
C 192.168.10.0 is directly connected to Ethernet 0
C 192.168.10.32 is directly connected to Ethernet 1
C 192.168.10.64 is directly connected to Ethernet 2
C 192.168.10.96 is directly connected to Serial 0
```

Practice Example #4C: 255.255.255.240 (/28)

Let's practice another one:

> 192.168.10.0 = Network address
>
> 255.255.255.240 = Subnet mask

- *Subnets?* 240 is 11110000 in binary. $2^4 = 16$.
- *Hosts?* 4 host bits, or $2^4 - 2 = 14$.
- *Valid subnets?* 256 – 240 = 16. Start at 0: 0 + 16 = 16. 16 + 16 = 32. 32 + 16 = 48. 48 + 16 = 64. 64 + 16 = 80. 80 + 16 = 96. 96 + 16 = 112. 112 + 16 = 128. 128 + 16 = 144. 144 + 16 = 160. 160 + 16 = 176. 176 + 16 = 192. 192 + 16 = 208. 208 + 16 = 224. 224 + 16 = 240.
- *Broadcast address for each subnet?*
- *Valid hosts?*

To answer the last two questions, check out the following table. It gives you the subnets, valid hosts, and broadcast addresses for each subnet. First, find the address of each subnet using the block size (increment). Second, find the broadcast address of each subnet increment, which is always the number right before the next valid subnet, and then just fill in the host addresses. The following table shows the available subnets, hosts, and broadcast addresses provided from a Class C 255.255.255.240 mask.

Subnet	0	16	32	48	64	80	96	112	128	144	160	176	192	208	224	240
First host	1	17	33	49	65	81	97	113	129	145	161	177	193	209	225	241
Last host	14	30	46	62	78	94	110	126	142	158	174	190	206	222	238	254
Broadcast	15	31	47	63	79	95	111	127	143	159	175	191	207	223	239	255

Practice Example #5C: 255.255.255.248 (/29)

Let's keep practicing:

192.168.10.0 = Network address

255.255.255.248 = Subnet mask

- *Subnets?* 248 in binary = 11111000. 2^5 = 32.
- *Hosts?* $2^3 - 2 = 6$.
- *Valid subnets?* 256 − 248 = 0, 8, 16, 24, 32, 40, 48, 56, 64, 72, 80, 88, 96, 104, 112, 120, 128, 136, 144, 152, 160, 168, 176, 184, 192, 200, 208, 216, 224, 232, 240, and 248.
- *Broadcast address for each subnet?*
- *Valid hosts?*

Take a look at the following table. It shows some of the subnets (first four and last four only), valid hosts, and broadcast addresses for the Class C 255.255.255.248 mask.

Subnet	0	8	16	24	...	224	232	240	248
First host	1	9	17	25	...	225	233	241	249
Last host	6	14	22	30	...	230	238	246	254
Broadcast	7	15	23	31	...	231	239	247	255

If you try to configure a router interface with the address 192.168.10.6 255.255.255.248 and receive the following error, it means that ip subnet-zero is not enabled:

```
Bad mask /29 for address 192.168.10.6
```

You must be able to subnet in order to see that the address used in this example is in the zero subnet!

Practice Example #6C: 255.255.255.252 (/30)

Okay—just one more:

192.168.10.0 = Network address

255.255.255.252 = Subnet mask

- *Subnets? 64.*
- *Hosts? 2.*
- *Valid subnets?* 0, 4, 8, 12, etc., all the way to 252.
- *Broadcast address for each subnet?* (Always the number right before the next subnet.)
- *Valid hosts?* (The numbers between the subnet number and the broadcast address.)

The following table shows you the subnet, valid host, and broadcast address of the first four and last four subnets in the 255.255.255.252 Class C subnet:

Subnet	0	4	8	12	. . .	240	244	248	252
First host	1	5	9	13	. . .	241	245	249	253
Last host	2	6	10	14	. . .	242	246	250	254
Broadcast	3	7	11	15	. . .	243	247	251	255

Subnetting in Your Head: Class C Addresses

It really is possible to subnet in your head? Yes, and it's not all that hard either. Consider the following example:

192.168.10.50 = Node address

255.255.255.224 = Subnet mask

First, determine the subnet and broadcast address of the network in which the previous IP address resides. You can do this by answering question 3 of the big 5 questions: 256 – 224 = 32. 0, 32, 64, and so on. The address of 50 falls between the two subnets of 32 and 64 and must be part of the 192.168.10.32 subnet. The next subnet is 64, so the broadcast address of the 32 subnet is 63. Don't forget that the broadcast address of a subnet is always the number right before the next subnet. The valid host range equals the numbers between the subnet and broadcast address, or 33–62. This is too easy!

Let's try another one. We'll subnet another Class C address:

192.168.10.50 = Node address

255.255.255.240 = Subnet mask

What is the subnet and broadcast address of the network of which the previous IP address is a member? 256 – 240 = 16. Now just count by our increments of 16 until we pass the host address: 0, 16, 32, 48, 64. Bingo—the host address is between the 48 and 64 subnets. The subnet is 192.168.10.48, and the broadcast address is 63 because the next subnet is 64. The valid host range equals the numbers between the subnet number and the broadcast address, or 49–62.

Let's do a couple more to make sure you have this down.

You have a node address of 192.168.10.174 with a mask of 255.255.255.240. What is the valid host range?

The mask is 240, so we'd do a 256 – 240 = 16. This is our block size. Just keep adding 16 until we pass the host address of 174, starting at zero, of course: 0, 16, 32, 48, 64, 80, 96, 112, 128, 144, 160, 176. The host address of 174 is between 160 and 176, so the subnet is 160. The broadcast address is 175; the valid host range is 161–174. That was a tough one!

One more, just for fun. This one is the easiest of all Class C subnetting:

192.168.10.17 = Node address

255.255.255.252 = Subnet mask

What is the subnet and broadcast address of the subnet in which the previous IP address resides? 256 – 252 = 4 (always start at zero unless told otherwise). 0, 4, 8, 12, 16, 20, etc. You've got it! The host address is between the 16 and 20 subnets. The subnet is 192.168.10.16, and the broadcast address is 19. The valid host range is 17–18.

Now that you're all over Class C subnetting, let's move on to Class B subnetting. But before we do, let's go through a quick review.

What Do We Know?

Okay, here's where you can really apply what you've learned so far and begin committing it all to memory. This is a very cool section that I've been using in my classes for years. It will really help you nail down subnetting for good!

When you see a subnet mask or slash notation (CIDR), you should know the following:

/25   What do we know about a /25?

- 128 mask
- 1 bit on and 7 bits off (10000000)
- Block size of 128
- Subnets 0 and 128
- 2 subnets, each with 126 hosts

/26   What do we know about a /26?

- 192 mask
- 2 bits on and 6 bits off (11000000)
- Block size of 64
- Subnets 0, 64, 128, 192
- 4 subnets, each with 62 hosts

/27   What do we know about a /27?

- 224 mask

- 3 bits on and 5 bits off (11100000)
- Block size of 32
- Subnets 0, 32, 64, 96, 128, 160, 192, 224
- 8 subnets, each with 30 hosts

/28 What do we know about a /28?

- 240 mask
- 4 bits on and 4 bits off
- Block size of 16
- Subnets 0, 16, 32, 48, 64, 80, 96, 112, 128, 144, 160, 176, 192, 208, 224, 240
- 16 subnets, each with 14 hosts

/29 What do we know about a /29?

- 248 mask
- 5 bits on and 3 bits off
- Block size of 8
- Subnets 0, 8, 16, 24, 32, 40, 48, etc.
- 32 subnets, each with 6 hosts

/30 What do we know about a /30?

- 252 mask
- 6 bits on and 2 bits off
- Block size of 4
- Subnets 0, 4, 8, 12, 16, 20, 24, etc.
- 64 subnets, each with 2 hosts

Table 3.3 puts all of the previous information into one compact little table. You should practice writing this table out on scratch paper, and if you can do it, write it down before you start your exam!

TABLE 3.3 What do you know?

CIDR Notation	Mask	Bits	Block Size	Subnets	Hosts
/25	128	1 bit on and 7 bits off	128	0 and 128	2 subnets, each with 126 hosts
/26	192	2 bits on and 6 bits off	64	0, 64, 128, 192	4 subnets, each with 62 hosts

CIDR Notation	Mask	Bits	Block Size	Subnets	Hosts
/27	224	3 bits on and 5 bits off	32	0, 32, 64, 96, 128, 160, 192, 224	8 subnets, each with 30 hosts
/28	240	4 bits on and 4 bits off	16	0, 16, 32, 48, 64, 80, 96, 112, 128, 144, 160, 176, 192, 208, 224, 240	16 subnets, each with 14 hosts
/29	248	5 bits on and 3 bits off	8	0, 8, 16, 24, 32, 40, 48, etc.	32 subnets, each with 6 hosts
/30	252	6 bits on and 2 bits off	4	0, 4, 8, 12, 16, 20, 24, etc.	64 subnets, each with 2 hosts

Regardless of whether you have a Class A, Class B, or Class C address, the /30 mask will provide you with only two hosts, ever. As suggested by Cisco, this mask is suited almost exclusively for use on point-to-point links.

If you can memorize this "What Do We Know?" section, you'll be much better off in your day-to-day job and in your studies. Try saying it out loud, which helps you memorize things—yes, your significant other and/or coworkers will think you've lost it, but they probably already do if you're in the networking field anyway. And if you're not yet in the networking field but are studying all this to break into it, get used to it!

It's also helpful to write these on some type of flashcards and have people test your skill. You'd be amazed at how fast you can get subnetting down if you memorize block sizes as well as this "What Do We Know?" section.

Using a Subnet Calculator

Before we move on to class B and then A subnetting, most people use a subnet calculator to help them achieve the valid hosts and don't bother doing any math at all. This doesn't work for most or all Cisco certification exams, so it's best to know how to do the math.

My website offers a free subnet calculator. Simply visit `http://bit.ly/subnetpractice`.

Of course, a simple Google search of "ip subnet calculator" yields more than 1.6 million results, so take your pick.

Subnetting Class B Addresses

Before we dive into this, let's look at all the possible Class B subnet masks. Notice that we have a lot more possible subnet masks than we do with a Class C network address:

```
255.255.0.0   (/16)
255.255.128.0 (/17) 255.255.255.0   (/24)
255.255.192.0 (/18) 255.255.255.128 (/25)
255.255.224.0 (/19) 255.255.255.192 (/26)
255.255.240.0 (/20) 255.255.255.224 (/27)
255.255.248.0 (/21) 255.255.255.240 (/28)
255.255.252.0 (/22) 255.255.255.248 (/29)
255.255.254.0 (/23) 255.255.255.252 (/30)
```

We know the Class B network address has 16 bits available for host addressing. This means we can use up to 14 bits for subnetting, because we need to leave at least 2 bits for host addressing. Using a /16 means you are not subnetting with Class B, but it *is* a mask you can use!

The process of subnetting a Class B network is pretty much the same as it is for a Class C, except that you have more host bits and you start in the third octet.

Use the same subnet numbers for the third octet with Class B that you used for the fourth octet with Class C, but add a zero to the network portion and a 255 to the broadcast section in the fourth octet. The following table shows an example host range of two subnets used in a Class B 240 (/20) subnet mask:

Subnet address	16.0	32.0
Broadcast address	31.255	47.255

Just add the valid hosts between the numbers, and you're set!

NOTE   The preceding example is true only until you get up to /24. After that, it's numerically exactly like Class C.

Subnetting Practice Examples: Class B Addresses

The following sections will give you an opportunity to practice subnetting Class B addresses. Again, I have to mention that this is the same as subnetting with Class C, except that we start in the third octet—with the exact same numbers!

Practice Example #1B: 255.255.128.0 (/17)

172.16.0.0 = Network address

255.255.128.0 = Subnet mask

- *Subnets?* $2^1 = 2$ (same amount as Class C).
- *Hosts?* $2^{15} - 2 = 32,766$ (7 bits in the third octet, and 8 in the fourth).
- *Valid subnets?* 256 – 128 = 128. 0, 128. Remember that subnetting is performed in the third octet, so the subnet numbers are really 0.0 and 128.0, as shown in the next table. These are the exact numbers we used with Class C; we use them in the third octet and add a 0 in the fourth octet for the network address.

- *Broadcast address for each subnet?*
- *Valid hosts?*

The following table shows the two subnets available, the valid host range, and the broadcast address of each:

Subnet	0.0	128.0
First host	0.1	128.1
Last host	127.254	255.254
Broadcast	127.255	255.255

Notice that we just added the fourth octet's lowest and highest values and came up with the answers. Again, it's done exactly the same way as for a Class C subnet. We just used the same numbers in the third octet and added 0 and 255 in the fourth octet. Pretty simple, huh? I really can't say this enough: It's just not that hard. The numbers never change; we just use them in different octets!

Question: Using the previous subnet mask, do you think 172.16.10.0 is a valid host address? What about 172.16.10.255? Can 0 and 255 in the fourth octet ever be a valid host address? The answer is absolutely, yes, those are valid hosts! Any number between the subnet number and the broadcast address is always a valid host.

Practice Example #2B: 255.255.192.0 (/18)

172.16.0.0 = Network address

255.255.192.0 = Subnet mask

- *Subnets?* $2^2 = 4$.
- *Hosts?* $2^{14} - 2 = 16,382$ (6 bits in the third octet, and 8 in the fourth).
- *Valid subnets?* 256 – 192 = 64. 0, 64, 128, 192. Remember that the subnetting is performed in the third octet, so the subnet numbers are really 0.0, 64.0, 128.0, and 192.0, as shown in the next table.
- *Broadcast address for each subnet?*
- *Valid hosts?*

The following table shows the four subnets available, the valid host range, and the broadcast address of each:

Subnet	0.0	64.0	128.0	192.0
First host	0.1	64.1	128.1	192.1
Last host	63.254	127.254	191.254	255.254
Broadcast	63.255	127.255	191.255	255.255

Again, it's pretty much the same as it is for a Class C subnet—we just added 0 and 255 in the fourth octet for each subnet in the third octet.

Practice Example #3B: 255.255.240.0 (/20)

172.16.0.0 = Network address

255.255.240.0 = Subnet mask

- *Subnets?* $2^4 = 16$.
- *Hosts?* $2^{12} - 2 = 4094$.
- *Valid subnets?* 256 – 240 = 0, 16, 32, 48, etc., up to 240. Notice that these are the same numbers as a Class C 240 mask—we just put them in the third octet and add a 0 and 255 in the fourth octet.
- *Broadcast address for each subnet?*
- *Valid hosts?*

The following table shows the first four subnets, valid hosts, and broadcast addresses in a Class B 255.255.240.0 mask:

Subnet	0.0	16.0	32.0	48.0
First host	0.1	16.1	32.1	48.1
Last host	15.254	31.254	47.254	63.254
Broadcast	15.255	31.255	47.255	63.255

Practice Example #4B: 255.255.248.0 (/21)

172.16.0.0 = Network address

255.255.248.0 = Subnet mask

- *Subnets?* $2^5 = 32$.
- *Hosts?* $2^{11} - 2 = 2046$.
- *Valid subnets?* 256 – 248 = 0, 8, 16, 24, 32, etc., up to 248.
- *Broadcast address for each subnet?*
- *Valid hosts?*

The following table shows the first five subnets, valid hosts, and broadcast addresses in a Class B 255.255.248.0 mask:

Subnet	0.0	8.0	16.0	24.0	32.0
First host	0.1	8.1	16.1	24.1	32.1
Last host	7.254	15.254	23.254	31.254	39.254
Broadcast	7.255	15.255	23.255	31.255	39.255

Practice Example #5B: 255.255.252.0 (/22)

  172.16.0.0 = Network address

  255.255.252.0 = Subnet mask

- *Subnets? 2^6 = 64.*
- *Hosts? $2^{10} - 2$ = 1022.*
- *Valid subnets? 256 – 252 = 0, 4, 8, 12, 16, etc., up to 252.*
- *Broadcast address for each subnet?*
- *Valid hosts?*

The following table shows the first five subnets, valid hosts, and broadcast addresses in a Class B 255.255.252.0 mask:

Subnet	0.0	4.0	8.0	12.0	16.0
First host	0.1	4.1	8.1	12.1	16.1
Last host	3.254	7.254	11.254	15.254	19.254
Broadcast	3.255	7.255	11.255	15.255	19.255

Practice Example #6B: 255.255.254.0 (/23)

  172.16.0.0 = Network address

  255.255.254.0 = Subnet mask

- *Subnets? 2^7 = 128.*
- *Hosts? $2^9 - 2$ = 510.*
- *Valid subnets? 256 – 254 = 0, 2, 4, 6, 8, etc., up to 254.*
- *Broadcast address for each subnet?*
- *Valid hosts?*

The following table shows the first five subnets, valid hosts, and broadcast addresses in a Class B 255.255.254.0 mask:

Subnet	0.0	2.0	4.0	6.0	8.0
First host	0.1	2.1	4.1	6.1	8.1
Last host	1.254	3.254	5.254	7.254	9.254
Broadcast	1.255	3.255	5.255	7.255	9.255

Practice Example #7B: 255.255.255.0 (/24)

Contrary to popular belief, 255.255.255.0 used with a Class B network address is not called a Class B network with a Class C subnet mask. It's amazing how many people see this mask used in a Class B network and think it's a Class C subnet mask. This is a Class B subnet mask with 8 bits of subnetting—it's logically different from a Class C mask. Subnetting this address is fairly simple:

> 172.16.0.0 = Network address

> 255.255.255.0 = Subnet mask

- *Subnets?* $2^8 = 256$.
- *Hosts?* $2^8 - 2 = 254$.
- *Valid subnets?* $256 - 255 = 1$. 0, 1, 2, 3, etc., all the way to 255.
- *Broadcast address for each subnet?*
- *Valid hosts?*

The following table shows the first four and last two subnets, the valid hosts, and the broadcast addresses in a Class B 255.255.255.0 mask:

Subnet	0.0	1.0	2.0	3.0	. . .	254.0	255.0
First host	0.1	1.1	2.1	3.1	. . .	254.1	255.1
Last host	0.254	1.254	2.254	3.254	. . .	254.254	255.254
Broadcast	0.255	1.255	2.255	3.255	. . .	254.255	255.255

Practice Example #8B: 255.255.255.128 (/25)

This is actually one of the hardest subnet masks you can play with. And worse, it actually is a really good subnet to use in production because it creates over 500 subnets with 126 hosts for each subnet—a nice mixture. So, don't skip over it!

> 172.16.0.0 = Network address

> 255.255.255.128 = Subnet mask

- *Subnets?* $2^9 = 512$.
- *Hosts?* $2^7 - 2 = 126$.
- *Valid subnets?* Now for the tricky part. $256 - 255 = 1$. 0, 1, 2, 3, etc., for the third octet. But you can't forget the one subnet bit used in the fourth octet. Remember when I showed you how to figure one subnet bit with a Class C mask? You figure this the same way. You actually get two subnets for each third octet value, hence the 512 subnets. For example, if the third octet is showing subnet 3, the two subnets would actually be 3.0 and 3.128.
- *Broadcast address for each subnet?* The numbers right before the next subnet.
- *Valid hosts?* The numbers between the subnet numbers and the broadcast address.

The following graphic shows how you can create subnets, valid hosts, and broadcast addresses using the Class B 255.255.255.128 subnet mask. The first eight subnets are shown, followed by the last two subnets:

Subnet	0.0	0.128	1.0	1.128	2.0	2.128	3.0	3.128	...	255.0	255.128
First host	0.1	0.129	1.1	1.129	2.1	2.129	3.1	3.129	...	255.1	255.129
Last host	0.126	0.254	1.126	1.254	2.126	2.254	3.126	3.254	...	255.126	255.254
Broadcast	0.127	0.255	1.127	1.255	2.127	2.255	3.127	3.255	...	255.127	255.255

Practice Example #9B: 255.255.255.192 (/26)

Now, this is where Class B subnetting gets easy. Since the third octet has a 255 in the mask section, whatever number is listed in the third octet is a subnet number. And now that we have a subnet number in the fourth octet, we can subnet this octet just as we did with Class C subnetting. Let's try it out:

172.16.0.0 = Network address

255.255.255.192 = Subnet mask

- *Subnets?* 2^{10} = 1024.
- *Hosts?* $2^6 - 2$ = 62.
- *Valid subnets?* 256 − 192 = 64. The subnets are shown in the following table. Do these numbers look familiar?
- *Broadcast address for each subnet?*
- *Valid hosts?*

The following table shows the first eight subnet ranges, valid hosts, and broadcast addresses:

Subnet	0.0	0.64	0.128	0.192	1.0	1.64	1.128	1.192
First host	0.1	0.65	0.129	0.193	1.1	1.65	1.129	1.193
Last host	0.62	0.126	0.190	0.254	1.62	1.126	1.190	1.254
Broadcast	0.63	0.127	0.191	0.255	1.63	1.127	1.191	1.255

Notice that for each subnet value in the third octet, you get subnets 0, 64, 128, and 192 in the fourth octet.

Practice Example #10B: 255.255.255.224 (/27)

This one is done the same way as the preceding subnet mask, except that we just have more subnets and fewer hosts per subnet available.

172.16.0.0 = Network address

255.255.255.224 = Subnet mask

- *Subnets?* $2^{11} = 2048$.
- *Hosts?* $2^5 - 2 = 30$.
- *Valid subnets?* $256 - 224 = 32$. 0, 32, 64, 96, 128, 160, 192, 224.
- *Broadcast address for each subnet?*
- *Valid hosts?*

The following table shows the first eight subnets:

Subnet	0.0	0.32	0.64	0.96	0.128	0.160	0.192	0.224
First host	0.1	0.33	0.65	0.97	0.129	0.161	0.193	0.225
Last host	0.30	0.62	0.94	0.126	0.158	0.190	0.222	0.254
Broadcast	0.31	0.63	0.95	0.127	0.159	0.191	0.223	0.255

This next table shows the last eight subnets:

Subnet	255.0	255.32	255.64	255.96	255.128	255.160	255.192	255.224
First host	255.1	255.33	255.65	255.97	255.129	255.161	255.193	255.225
Last host	255.30	255.62	255.94	255.126	255.158	255.190	255.222	255.254
Broadcast	255.31	255.63	255.95	255.127	255.159	255.191	255.223	255.255

Subnetting in Your Head: Class B Addresses

Are you nuts? Subnet Class B addresses in our heads? It's actually easier than writing it out—I'm not kidding! Let me show you how:

Question: What is the subnet and broadcast address of the subnet in which 172.16.10.33 /27 resides?

Answer: The interesting octet is the fourth one. $256 - 224 = 32$. $32 + 32 = 64$. You've got it: 33 is between 32 and 64. But remember that the third octet is considered part of the subnet, so the answer would be the 10.32 subnet. The broadcast is 10.63, since 10.64 is the next subnet. That was a pretty easy one.

Question: What subnet and broadcast address is the IP address 172.16.66.10 255.255.192.0 (/18) a member of?

Answer: The interesting octet here is the third octet instead of the fourth one. $256 - 192 = 64$. 0, 64, 128. The subnet is 172.16.64.0. The broadcast must be 172.16.127.25, because 128.0 is the next subnet.

Question: What subnet and broadcast address is the IP address 172.16.50.10 255.255.224.0 (/19) a member of?

Answer: 256 – 224 = 0, 32, 64 (remember, we always start counting at 0). The subnet is 172.16.32.0, and the broadcast must be 172.16.63.255, because 64.0 is the next subnet.

Question: What subnet and broadcast address is the IP address 172.16.46.255 255.255.240.0 (/20) a member of?

Answer: 256 – 240 = 16. The third octet is important here: 0, 16, 32, 48. This subnet address must be in the 172.16.32.0 subnet, and the broadcast must be 172.16.47.255, because 48.0 is the next subnet. So, yes, 172.16.46.255 is a valid host.

Question: What subnet and broadcast address is the IP address 172.16.45.14 255.255.255.252 (/30) a member of?

Answer: Where is our interesting octet? 256 – 252 = 0, 4, 8, 12, 16—the fourth. The subnet is 172.16.45.12, with a broadcast of 172.16.45.15, because the next subnet is 172.16.45.16.

Question: What is the subnet and broadcast address of the host 172.16.88.255/20?

Answer: What is a /20 written out in dotted decimal? If you can't answer this, you can't answer this question, can you? A /20 is 255.255.240.0, gives us a block size of 16 in the third octet, and since no subnet bits are on in the fourth octet, the answer is always 0 and 255 in the fourth octet: 0, 16, 32, 48, 64, 80, 96. Because 88 is between 80 and 96, the subnet is 80.0 and the broadcast address is 95.255.

Question: A router receives a packet on an interface with a destination address of 172.16.46.191/26. What will the router do with this packet?

Answer: Discard it. Do you know why? 172.16.46.191/26 is a 255.255.255.192 mask, which gives us a block size of 64. Our subnets are then 0, 64, 128 and 192. 191 is the broadcast address of the 128 subnet, and a router will discard any broadcast packets by default.

Subnetting Class A Addresses

You don't go about Class A subnetting any differently than Classes B and C, but there are 24 bits to play with instead of the 16 in a Class B address and the 8 in a Class C address.

Let's start by listing all the Class A masks:

```
255.0.0.0 (/8)
255.128.0.0 (/9)   255.255.240.0 (/20)
255.192.0.0 (/10)  255.255.248.0 (/21)
255.224.0.0 (/11)  255.255.252.0 (/22)
255.240.0.0 (/12)  255.255.254.0 (/23)
```

```
255.248.0.0 (/13) 255.255.255.0 (/24)
255.252.0.0 (/14) 255.255.255.128 (/25)
255.254.0.0 (/15) 255.255.255.192 (/26)
255.255.0.0 (/16) 255.255.255.224 (/27)
255.255.128.0 (/17) 255.255.255.240 (/28)
255.255.192.0 (/18) 255.255.255.248 (/29)
255.255.224.0 (/19) 255.255.255.252 (/30)
```

That's it. You must leave at least 2 bits for defining hosts. I hope you can see the pattern by now. Remember, we're going to do this the same way as a Class B or C subnet. It's just that, again, we simply have more host bits and we just use the same subnet numbers we used with Class B and C, but we start using these numbers in the second octet. However, the reason Class A addresses are so popular to implement is because they give the most flexibility. You can subnet in the second, third, or fourth octet. I'll show you this in the next examples.

Subnetting Practice Examples: Class A Addresses

When you look at an IP address and a subnet mask, you must be able to distinguish the bits used for subnets from the bits used for determining hosts. This is imperative. If you're still struggling with this concept, please reread the section "IP Addressing" in Chapter 2. It shows you how to determine the difference between the subnet and host bits and should help clear things up.

Practice Example #1A: 255.255.0.0 (/16)

Class A addresses use a default mask of 255.0.0.0, which leaves 22 bits for subnetting, because you must leave 2 bits for host addressing. The 255.255.0.0 mask with a Class A address is using 8 subnet bits:

- *Subnets?* $2^8 = 256$.
- *Hosts?* $2^{16} - 2 = 65,534$.
- *Valid subnets?* What is the interesting octet? $256 - 255 = 1$. 0, 1, 2, 3, etc. (all in the second octet). The subnets would be 10.0.0.0, 10.1.0.0, 10.2.0.0, 10.3.0.0, etc., up to 10.255.0.0.
- *Broadcast address for each subnet?*
- *Valid hosts?*

The following table shows the first two and the last two subnets, the valid host range and the broadcast addresses for the private Class A 10.0.0.0 network:

Subnet	10.0.0.0	10.1.0.0	. . .	10.254.0.0	10.255.0.0
First host	10.0.0.1	10.1.0.1	. . .	10.254.0.1	10.255.0.1
Last host	10.0.255.254	10.1.255.254	. . .	10.254.255.254	10.255.255.254
Broadcast	10.0.255.255	10.1.255.255	. . .	10.254.255.255	10.255.255.255

Practice Example #2A: 255.255.240.0 (/20)

255.255.240.0 gives us 12 bits of subnetting and leaves us 12 bits for host addressing.

- *Subnets?* 2^{12} = 4096.
- *Hosts?* 2^{12} − 2 = 4094.
- *Valid subnets?* What is the interesting octet? 256 − 240 = 16. The subnets in the second octet are a block size of 1, and the subnets in the third octet are 0, 16, 32, etc.
- *Broadcast address for each subnet?*
- *Valid hosts?*

The following table shows some examples of the host ranges—the first three subnets and the last subnet:

Subnet	10.0.0.0	10.0.16.0	10.0.32.0	. . .	10.255.240.0
First host	10.0.0.1	10.0.16.1	10.0.32.1	. . .	10.255.240.1
Last host	10.0.15.254	10.0.31.254	10.0.47.254	. . .	10.255.255.254
Broadcast	10.0.15.255	10.0.31.255	10.0.47.255	. . .	10.255.255.255

Practice Example #3A: 255.255.255.192 (/26)

Let's do one more example using the second, third, and fourth octets for subnetting:

- *Subnets?* 2^{18} = 262,144.
- *Hosts?* 2^6 − 2 = 62.
- *Valid subnets?* In the second and third octet, the block size is 1, and in the fourth octet, the block size is 64.
- *Broadcast address for each subnet?*
- *Valid hosts?*

The following table shows the first four subnets and their valid hosts and broadcast addresses in the Class A 255.255.255.192 mask:

Subnet	10.0.0.0	10.0.0.64	10.0.0.128	10.0.0.192
First host	10.0.0.1	10.0.0.65	10.0.0.129	10.0.0.193
Last host	10.0.0.62	10.0.0.126	10.0.0.190	10.0.0.254
Broadcast	10.0.0.63	10.0.0.127	10.0.0.191	10.0.0.255

This table shows the last four subnets and their valid hosts and broadcast addresses:

Subnet	10.255.255.0	10.255.255.64	10.255.255.128	10.255.255.192
First host	10.255.255.1	10.255.255.65	10.255.255.129	10.255.255.193
Last host	10.255.255.62	10.255.255.126	10.255.255.190	10.255.255.254
Broadcast	10.255.255.63	10.255.255.127	10.255.255.191	10.255.255.255

Subnetting in Your Head: Class A Addresses

Again, I know this sounds hard, but as with Class C and Class B, the numbers are the same; we just start in the second octet. What makes this easy? You only need to worry about the octet that has the largest block size, which is typically called the interesting octet, and one that is something other than 0 or 255, such as 255.255.240.0 (/20) with a Class A network. The second octet has a block size of 1, so any number listed in that octet is a subnet. The third octet is a 240 mask, which means we have a block size of 16 in the third octet. If your host ID is 10.20.80.30, what is your subnet, broadcast address, and valid host range?

The subnet in the second octet is 20 with a block size of 1, but the third octet is in block sizes of 16, so we'll just count them out: 0, 16, 32, 48, 64, 80, 96. . .voilà! By the way, you can count by 16s by now, right? Good! This makes our subnet 10.20.80.0, with a broadcast address of 10.20.95.255, because the next subnet is 10.20.96.0. The valid host range is 10.20.80.1 through 10.20.95.254. And, yes, no lie! You really can do this in your head if you just get your block sizes nailed!

Let's practice on one more, just for fun!

Host IP: 10.1.3.65/23

First, you can't answer this question if you don't know what a /23 is. It's 255.255.254.0. The interesting octet here is the third one: 256 − 254 = 2. Our subnets in the third octet are 0, 2, 4, 6, etc. The host in this question is in subnet 2.0, and the next subnet is 4.0, so that makes the broadcast address 3.255. And any address between 10.1.2.1 and 10.1.3.254 is considered a valid host.

Summary

Did you read Chapters 2 and 3 and understand everything on the first pass? If so, that is fantastic. Congratulations! However, you probably really did get lost a couple of times. No worries, because as I told you, that's what usually happens. Don't waste time feeling bad if you must read each chapter more than once, or even 10 times, before you're truly good to go. If you do have to read the chapters more than once, you'll be seriously better off in the long run, even if you were comfortable the first time through!

This chapter provided you with an important understanding of IP subnetting—the painless way! And when you've got the key material presented in this chapter really nailed down, you should be able to subnet IP addresses in your head.

This chapter is extremely essential to your Cisco certification process, so if you just skimmed it, please go back, read it thoroughly, and don't forget to do all the written labs too!

Exam Essentials

Identify the advantages of subnetting. Benefits of subnetting a physical network include reduced network traffic, optimized network performance, simplified management, and facilitated spanning of large geographical distances.

Describe the effect of the *ip subnet-zero* command. This command allows you to use the first and last subnet in your network design.

Identify the steps to subnet a classful network. Understand how IP addressing and subnetting work. First, determine your block size by using the 256-subnet mask math. Then count your subnets and determine the broadcast address of each subnet—it is always the number right before the next subnet. Your valid hosts are the numbers between the subnet address and the broadcast address.

Determine possible block sizes. This is an important part of understanding IP addressing and subnetting. The valid block sizes are always 2, 4, 8, 16, 32, 64, 128, etc. You can determine your block size by using the 256-subnet mask math.

Describe the role of a subnet mask in IP addressing. A subnet mask is a 32-bit value that allows the recipient of IP packets to distinguish the network ID portion of the IP address from the host ID portion of the IP address.

Understand and apply the $2^x - 2$ formula. Use this formula to determine the proper subnet mask for a particular size network given the application of that subnet mask to a particular classful network.

Review Questions

The following questions are designed to test your understanding of this chapter's material. For more information on how to get additional questions, please see www.lammle.com/ccst.

You can find the answers to these questions in Appendix, "Answers to Review Questions."

1. What is the maximum number of IP addresses that can be assigned to hosts on a local subnet that uses the 255.255.255.224 subnet mask?

    A. 14

    B. 15

    C. 16

    D. 30

    E. 31

    F. 62

2. You have a network that needs 29 subnets while maximizing the number of host addresses available on each subnet. How many bits must you borrow from the host field to provide the correct subnet mask?

    A. 2

    B. 3

    C. 4

    D. 5

    E. 6

    F. 7

3. What is the subnetwork address for a host with the IP address 200.10.5.68/28?

    A. 200.10.5.56

    B. 200.10.5.32

    C. 200.10.5.64

    D. 200.10.5.0

4. The network address of 172.16.0.0/19 provides how many subnets and hosts?

    A. 7 subnets, 30 hosts each

    B. 7 subnets, 2,046 hosts each

    C. 7 subnets, 8,190 hosts each

    D. 8 subnets, 8,190 hosts each

    E. 8 subnets, 2,046 hosts each

    F. 8 subnets, 8,190 hosts each

5. Which two statements describe the IP address 10.16.3.65/23? (Choose two.)

    A. The subnet address is 10.16.3.0 255.255.254.0.

    B. The lowest host address in the subnet is 10.16.2.1 255.255.254.0.

    C. The last valid host address in the subnet is 10.16.2.254 255.255.254.0.

    D. The broadcast address of the subnet is 10.16.3.255 255.255.254.0.

    E. The network is not subnetted.

6. If a host on a network has the address 172.16.45.14/30, what is the subnetwork this host belongs to?

    A. 172.16.45.0

    B. 172.16.45.4

    C. 172.16.45.8

    D. 172.16.45.12

    E. 172.16.45.16

7. Which mask should you use on point-to-point links in order to reduce the waste of IP addresses?

    A. /27

    B. /28

    C. /29

    D. /30

    E. /31

8. What is the subnetwork number of a host with an IP address of 172.16.66.0/21?

    A. 172.16.36.0

    B. 172.16.48.0

    C. 172.16.64.0

    D. 172.16.0.0

9. You have an interface on a router with the IP address of 192.168.192.10/29. Including the router interface, how many hosts can have IP addresses on the LAN attached to the router interface?

    A. 6

    B. 8

    C. 30

    D. 62

    E. 126

10. You need to configure a server that is on the subnet 192.168.19.24/29. The router has the first available host address. Which of the following should you assign to the server?

    A. 192.168.19.0 255.255.255.0

    B. 192.168.19.33 255.255.255.240

    C. 192.168.19.26 255.255.255.248

    D. 192.168.19.31 255.255.255.248

    E. 192.168.19.34 255.255.255.240

11. You have an interface on a router with the IP address of 192.168.192.10/29. What is the broadcast address the hosts will use on this LAN?

    A. 192.168.192.15

    B. 192.168.192.31

    C. 192.168.192.63

    D. 192.168.192.127

    E. 192.168.192.255

12. You need to subnet a network that has 5 subnets, each with at least 16 hosts. Which classful subnet mask would you use?

    A. 255.255.255.192

    B. 255.255.255.224

    C. 255.255.255.240

    D. 255.255.255.248

13. You configure a router interface with the IP address 192.168.10.62 255.255.255.192 and receive the following error:

```
Bad mask /26 for address 192.168.10.62
```

Why did you receive this error?

    A. You typed this mask on a WAN link, and that is not allowed.

    B. This is not a valid host and subnet mask combination.

    C. `ip subnet-zero` is not enabled on the router.

    D. The router does not support IP.

14. If an Ethernet port on a router were assigned an IP address of 172.16.112.1/25, what would be the valid subnet address of this interface?

    A. 172.16.112.0

    B. 172.16.0.0

    C. 172.16.96.0

    D. 172.16.255.0

    E. 172.16.128.0

15. The network ID is 192.168.10.0/28, and you need to use the last available IP address in the range. What would be a valid host IP address if you were using the first subnet? Again, the zero subnet should not be considered valid for this question.

    A. 192.168.10.16

    B. 192.168.10.62

    C. 192.168.10.30

    D. 192.168.10.127

Chapter

4

Network Address Translation (NAT) & IPv6

THE CCST EXAM TOPICS COVERED IN THIS CHAPTER INCLUDE THE FOLLOWING:

✓ **2.0 Addressing and Subnet Formats**

- 2.1. Compare and contrast private addresses and public addresses.

    - Address classes, NAT concepts

- 2.3. Identify IPv6 addresses and prefix formats.

    - Types of addresses, prefix concepts

In this short and concise chapter, we're going to dig into Network Address Translation (NAT), Dynamic NAT, and Port Address Translation (PAT), also known as NAT Overload. Of course, it's important to understand the Cisco objectives for this chapter. They are very straightforward: You have hosts on your inside corporate network using RFC 1918 addresses, and you need to allow those hosts access to the Internet by configuring NAT translations. With that objective in mind, that will be my direction with this chapter.

However, what if Network Address Translation isn't good enough to use in your cloud-based applications or your network is just too big, like enterprise worldwide big? This is where IPv6 sings and can be used to solve these types of business case issues. So I'll end the chapter by discussing IPv6, formats, and concepts.

To find up-to-the-minute updates for this chapter, please see www.lammle.com/ccst.

When Do We Use NAT?

Network Address Translation (NAT) is similar to Classless Inter-Domain Routing (CIDR) in that the original intention for NAT was to slow the depletion of available IP address space by allowing multiple private IP addresses to be represented by a much smaller number of public IP addresses.

Since then, it's been discovered that NAT is also a useful tool for network migrations and mergers, server load sharing, and creating "virtual servers." This chapter describes the basics of NAT functionality and the terminology common to NAT.

Because NAT really decreases the overwhelming amount of public IP addresses required in a networking environment, it comes in handy when two companies that have duplicate internal addressing schemes merge. NAT is also a great tool to use when an organization changes its Internet service provider (ISP), but the networking manager needs to avoid the hassle of changing the internal address scheme.

Here's a list of situations when NAT can be especially helpful:

- When you need to connect to the Internet and your hosts don't have globally unique IP addresses
- When you've changed to a new ISP that requires you to renumber your network
- When you need to merge two intranets with duplicate addresses

You typically use NAT on a border router. For example, in Figure 4.1, NAT is used on the corporate router connected to the Internet.

FIGURE 4.1   Where to configure NAT

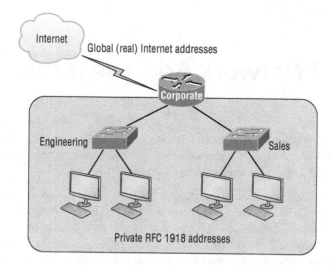

You may be thinking, "NAT's totally cool and I just gotta have it!" But don't get too excited yet because there are some serious snags related to using NAT that you need to understand first. Don't get me wrong—it can truly be a lifesaver sometimes, but NAT has a bit of a dark side you need to know about too. For the pros and cons linked to using NAT, check out Table 4.1.

TABLE 4.1   Advantages and disadvantages of implementing NAT

Advantages	Disadvantages
Conserves legally registered addresses	Results in switching path delays.
Remedies address overlap events	Causes loss of end-to-end IP traceability.
Increases flexibility when connecting to the Internet	Certain applications will not function with NAT enabled.
Eliminates address renumbering as a network evolves	Complicates tunneling protocols such as IPsec because NAT modifies the values in the header.

The most obvious advantage associated with NAT is that it allows you to conserve your legally registered address scheme. But a version of it known as Port Address Translation (PAT) is also why we've only just recently run out of IPv4 addresses. Without NAT/PAT, we'd have run out of IPv4 addresses more than a decade ago!

Types of Network Address Translation

NAT is available in the following three flavors:

Static NAT (one-to-one)   Static NAT is designed to allow one-to-one mapping between local and global addresses. Keep in mind that the static version requires you to have one real Internet IP address for every host on your network.

Dynamic NAT (many-to-many)   Dynamic NAT gives you the ability to map an unregistered IP address to a registered IP address from out of a pool of registered IP addresses. You don't have to statically configure your router to map each inside address to an individual outside address as you would using static NAT, but you do have to have enough real, bona fide IP addresses for everyone who's going to be sending packets to and receiving them from the Internet at the same time.

Overloading (one-to-many)   This is the most popular type of NAT configuration. Understand that overloading really is a form of dynamic NAT that maps multiple unregistered IP addresses to a single registered IP address (many-to-one) by using different source ports. Why is this so special? Well, because it's also known as *Port Address Translation (PAT)*, which is also commonly referred to as NAT Overload. Using PAT allows you to permit thousands of users to connect to the Internet using only one real global IP address—pretty slick, right? Seriously, NAT Overload is the real reason we haven't run out of valid IP addresses on the Internet. Really—I'm not joking!

NAT Names

The names we use to describe the addresses used with NAT are fairly straightforward. Addresses used after NAT translations are called *global addresses*. These are usually the public addresses used on the Internet, which you don't need if you aren't going on the Internet.

Local addresses are the ones we use before NAT translation. This means that the inside local address is actually the private address of the sending host that's attempting to get to the Internet. The outside local address would typically be the router interface connected to your ISP and is also usually a public address used as the packet begins its journey.

After translation, the inside local address is then called the *inside global address*, and the outside global address then becomes the address of the destination host. Check out Table 4.2, which lists all this terminology and offers a clear picture of the various names used with NAT. Keep in mind that these terms and their definitions can vary somewhat based on implementation. The table shows how they're used according to the Cisco exam objectives.

TABLE 4.2   NAT terms

Names	Meaning
Inside local	Source host inside address before translation—typically an RFC 1918 address.
Outside local	Address of an outside host as it appears to the inside network. This is usually the address of the router interface connected to ISP—the actual Internet address.
Inside global	Source host address used after translation to get onto the Internet. This is also the actual Internet address.
Outside global	Address of outside destination host and, again, the real Internet address.

How NAT Works

Okay, it's time to look at how this whole NAT thing works. I'm going to start by using Figure 4.2 to describe basic NAT translation.

You can see that host 10.1.1.1 is sending an Internet-bound packet to the border router configured with NAT. The router identifies the source IP address as an inside local IP address destined for an outside network, translates the source IP address in the packet, and documents the translation in the NAT table.

The packet is sent to the outside interface with the new translated source address. The external host returns the packet to the destination host, and the NAT router translates the inside global IP address back to the inside local IP address using the NAT table. This is as simple as it gets!

Let's take a look at a more complex configuration using overloading, also referred to as PAT. I'll use Figure 4.3 to demonstrate how PAT works by having an inside host HTTP to a server on the Internet.

With PAT, all inside hosts get translated to one single IP address, hence the term *overloading*. Again, the reason we haven't just run out of available global IP addresses on the Internet is because of overloading (PAT).

FIGURE 4.2   Basic NAT translation

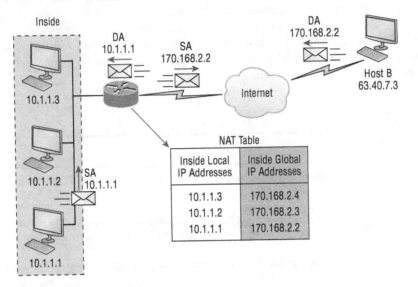

Take a look at the NAT table in Figure 4.3 again. In addition to the inside local IP address and inside global IP address, we now have port numbers. These port numbers help the router identify which host should receive the return traffic. The router uses the source port number from each host to differentiate the traffic from each of them. Understand that the packet has a destination port number of 80 when it leaves the router, and the HTTP server sends back the data with a destination port number of 1026, in this example. This allows the NAT translation router to differentiate between hosts in the NAT table and then translate the destination IP address back to the inside local address.

Port numbers are used at the Transport layer to identify the local host in this example. If we had to use real global IP addresses to identify the source hosts, that's called *static NAT*, and we would run out of addresses. PAT allows us to use the Transport layer to identify the hosts, which in turn allows us to theoretically use up to about 65,000 hosts with only one real IP address!

Why Do We Need IPv6?

Well, the short answer is because we need to communicate and our current system isn't really cutting it anymore. It's kind of like the Pony Express trying to compete with airmail! Consider how much time and effort we've been investing for years while we scratch our heads to resourcefully come up with slick new ways to conserve bandwidth and IP addresses. Sure, variable-length subnet masks (VLSMs) are wonderful and cool, but they're really just another invention to help us cope while we desperately struggle to overcome the worsening address drought.

FIGURE 4.3   NAT overloading example (PAT)

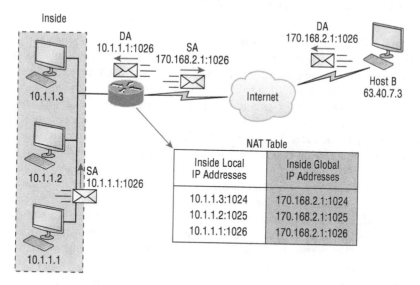

I'm not exaggerating about how dire things are getting; it's simply reality. The number of people and devices that connect to networks increases dramatically every day, which is not a bad thing. We're just finding new and exciting ways to communicate to more people, more often, which is good thing. And it's not likely to go away or even decrease in the littlest bit, because communicating and making connections are, in fact, basic human needs—they're in our very nature. But with our numbers increasing along with the rising tide of people joining the communications party increasing as well, the forecast for our current system isn't exactly clear skies and smooth sailing. IPv4, upon which our ability to do all this connecting and communicating is presently dependent, is quickly running out of addresses for us to use.

IPv4 has only about 4.3 billion addresses available—in theory—and we know that we don't even get to use most of those! Sure, the use of CIDR and NAT has helped to extend the inevitable dearth of addresses, but we will still run out of them, and it's going to happen within a few years. China is barely online, and we know there's a huge population of people and corporations there that surely want to be. There are myriad reports that give us all kinds of numbers, but all you really need think about to realize that I'm not just being an alarmist is this: There are about 7 billion people in the world today, and it's estimated that only just over 10 percent of that population is currently connected to the Internet. Wow!

That statistic is basically screaming at us the ugly truth that based on IPv4's capacity, every person can't even have a computer, let alone all the other IP devices we use with them! I have more than one computer, and it's pretty likely that you do too, and I'm not even including phones, laptops, game consoles, fax machines, routers, switches, and a mother lode of other devices we use every day! So I think I've made it pretty clear that we've got to do something before we run out of addresses and lose the ability to connect with each other as we know it. And that "something" just happens to be implementing IPv6.

The Benefits and Uses of IPv6

So what's so fabulous about IPv6? Is it really the answer to our coming dilemma? Is it really worth it to upgrade from IPv4? All good questions—you may even think of a few more. Of course, there's going to be that group of people with the time-tested "resistance to change syndrome," but don't listen to them. If we had done that years ago, we'd still be waiting weeks, even months, for our mail to arrive via horseback. Instead, just know that the answer is a resounding *yes*, it is really the answer, and it is worth the upgrade! Not only does IPv6 give us a lot of addresses (3.4×10^{38} = definitely enough), there are tons of other features built into this version that make it well worth the cost, time, and effort required to migrate to it.

Today's networks, as well as the Internet, have a ton of unforeseen requirements that simply weren't even considerations when IPv4 was created. We've tried to compensate with a collection of add-ons that can actually make implementing them more difficult than they would be if they were required by a standard. By default, IPv6 has improved upon and included many of those features as standard and mandatory. One of these sweet new standards is IPsec—a feature that provides end-to-end security.

But it's the efficiency features that are really going to rock the house! For starters, the headers in an IPv6 packet have half the fields, and they are aligned to 64 bits, which gives us some seriously souped-up processing speed. Compared to IPv4, lookups happen at light speed! Most of the information that used to be bound into the IPv4 header was taken out, and now you can choose to put it, or parts of it, back into the header in the form of optional extension headers that follow the basic header fields.

And of course there's that whole new universe of addresses—the 3.4×10^{38} I just mentioned—but where did we get them? Did some genie just suddenly arrive and make them magically appear? That huge proliferation of addresses had to come from somewhere! Well, it just so happens that IPv6 gives us a substantially larger address space, meaning the address itself is a whole lot bigger—four times bigger as a matter of fact! An IPv6 address is actually 128 bits in length, and no worries—I'm going to break down the address piece by piece and show you exactly what it looks like coming up in the section "IPv6 Addressing and Expressions." For now, let me just say that all that additional room permits more levels of hierarchy inside the address space and a more flexible addressing architecture. It also makes routing much more efficient and scalable because the addresses can be aggregated a lot more effectively. And IPv6 also allows multiple addresses for hosts and networks. This is especially important for enterprises veritably drooling for enhanced access and availability. Plus, the new version of IP now includes an expanded use of multicast communication—one device sending to many hosts or to a select group—that joins in to seriously boost efficiency on networks because communications will be more specific.

IPv4 uses broadcasts quite prolifically, causing a bunch of problems, the worst of which is, of course, the dreaded broadcast storm. This is that uncontrolled deluge of forwarded broadcast traffic that can bring an entire network to its knees and devour every last bit of bandwidth! Another nasty thing about broadcast traffic is that it interrupts each and every device on the network. When a broadcast is sent out, every machine has to stop what it's doing and respond to the traffic, whether the broadcast is relevant to it or not.

But smile assuredly, everyone. There's no such thing as a broadcast in IPv6, because it uses multicast traffic instead. And there are two other types of communications as well: unicast, which is the same as it is in IPv4, and a new type called *anycast*. Anycast communication allows the same address to be placed on more than one device so that when traffic is sent to the device service addressed in this way, it's routed to the nearest host that shares the same address. And this is just the beginning. I'll get into the various types of communication in the section "Address Types."

IPv6 Addressing and Expressions

Just as understanding how IP addresses are structured and used is critical with IPv4 addressing, it's also vital when it comes to IPv6. You've already read about the fact that at 128 bits, an IPv6 address is much larger than an IPv4 address. Because of this, as well as the new ways the addresses can be used, you've probably guessed that IPv6 will be more complicated to manage. But no worries! As I said, I'll break down the basics and show you what the address looks like and how you can write it as well as many of its common uses. It's going to be a little weird at first, but before you know it, you'll have it nailed!

Take a look at Figure 4.4, which shows a sample IPv6 address broken down into sections.

FIGURE 4.4   IPv6 address example

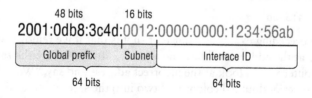

As you can clearly see, the address is definitely much larger. But what else is different? Well, first, notice that it has eight groups of numbers instead of four and that those groups are separated by colons instead of periods. And, hey, wait a second—there are letters in that address! Yep, the address is expressed in hexadecimal, just like a MAC address is, so you could say this address has eight 16-bit hexadecimal colon-delimited blocks. That's already quite a mouthful, and you probably haven't even tried to say the address out loud yet!

 There are four hexadecimal characters (16 bits) in each IPv6 field (with eight fields total), separated by colons.

Shortened Expression

The good news is there are a few tricks to help rescue us when writing these monster addresses. For one thing, you can actually leave out parts of the address to abbreviate it, but to get away with doing that you have to follow a couple of rules. First, you can drop any leading zeros in each of the individual blocks. After you do that, the sample address from earlier would then look like this:

```
2001:db8:3c4d:12:0:0:1234:56ab
```

That's a definite improvement—at least we don't have to write all of those extra zeros! But what about whole blocks that don't have anything in them except zeros? Well, we can kind of lose those too—at least some of them. Again referring to our sample address, we can remove the two consecutive blocks of zeros by replacing them with a doubled colon, like this:

```
2001:db8:3c4d:12::1234:56ab
```

Cool—we replaced the blocks of all zeros with a doubled colon. The rule you have to follow to get away with this is that you can replace only one contiguous block of such zeros in an address. So if my address has four blocks of zeros and each of them were separated, I just don't get to replace them all, because I can replace only one contiguous block with a doubled colon. Check out this example:

```
2001:0000:0000:0012:0000:0000:1234:56ab
```

And just know that you *can't* do this:

```
2001::12::1234:56ab
```

Instead, the best you can do is this:

```
2001::12:0:0:1234:56ab
```

The reason the preceding example is our best shot is that if we remove two sets of zeros, the device looking at the address will have no way of knowing where the zeros go back in. Basically, the router would look at the incorrect address and say, "Well, do I place two blocks into the first set of doubled colons and two into the second set, or do I place three blocks into the first set and one block into the second set?" And on and on it would go, because the information the router needs just isn't there.

Address Types

We're all familiar with IPv4's unicast, broadcast, and multicast addresses, which basically define who or at least how many other devices we're talking to. As I mentioned, however, IPv6 modifies that trio and introduces the anycast. Broadcasts, as we know them, have been eliminated in IPv6 because of their cumbersome inefficiency and basic tendency to drive us insane!

So let's find out what each of these types of IPv6 addressing and communication methods do for us:

Unicast Packets addressed to a unicast address are delivered to a single interface. For load balancing, multiple interfaces across several devices can use the same address, but we'll call that an anycast address. There are a few different types of unicast addresses, but we don't need to get further into that here.

Global Unicast Addresses (2000::/3) These are your typical publicly routable addresses, and they're the same as in IPv4. Global addresses start at 2000::/3. Figure 4.5 shows how a unicast address breaks down. The ISP can provide you with a minimum /48 network ID, which in turn provides you 16-bits to create a unique 64-bit router interface address. The last 64-bits are the unique host ID.

FIGURE 4.5 IPv6 global unicast addresses

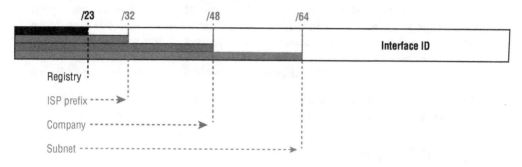

Link-local Addresses (FE80::/10) These are like the Automatic Private IP Address (APIPA) addresses that Microsoft uses to automatically provide addresses in IPv4, in that they're not meant to be routed. In IPv6 they start with FE80::/10, as shown in Figure 4.6. Think of these addresses as handy tools that give you the ability to throw a temporary LAN together for meetings or create a small LAN that's not going to be routed but still needs to share and access files and services locally.

FIGURE 4.6 IPv6 link local FE80::/10: The first 10 bits define the address type.

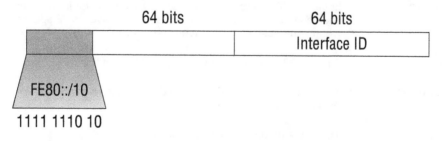

Unique Local Addresses (FC00::/7) These addresses are also intended for nonrouting purposes over the Internet, but they are nearly globally unique, so it's unlikely you'll ever have one of them overlap. Unique local addresses were designed to replace site-local addresses, so they basically do almost exactly what IPv4 private addresses do: allow communication throughout a site while being routable to multiple local networks. Site-local addresses were deprecated as of September 2004.

Multicast (FF00::/8)   Again, as in IPv4, packets addressed to a multicast address are delivered to all interfaces tuned into the multicast address. Sometimes people call them "one-to-many" addresses. It's really easy to spot a multicast address in IPv6 because it always starts with *FF*. I'll get deeper into multicast operation in the section "How IPv6 Works in an Internetwork."

Anycast   Like multicast addresses, an anycast address identifies multiple interfaces on multiple devices. But there's a big difference: The anycast packet is delivered to only one device—actually, to the closest one it finds defined in terms of routing distance. And again, this address is special because you can apply a single address to more than one host. These are referred to as *one-to-nearest addresses*. Anycast addresses are typically configured only on routers, never hosts, and a source address could never be an anycast address. Of note is that the IETF did reserve the top 128 addresses for each /64 for use with anycast addresses.

You're probably wondering if there are any special, reserved addresses in IPv6, because you know they're there in IPv4. Well, there are—plenty of them! Let's go over those now.

Special Addresses

Table 4.3 lists some of the addresses and address ranges that you should definitely make sure to remember, because you'll eventually use them. They're all special or reserved for a specific use, but unlike IPv4, IPv6 gives us a galaxy of addresses, so reserving a few here and there doesn't hurt at all!

TABLE 4.3   Special IPv6 addresses

Address	Meaning
0:0:0:0:0:0:0:0	Equals ::. This is the equivalent of IPv4's 0.0.0.0 and is typically the source address of a host before the host receives an IP address when you're using DHCP-driven stateful configuration.
0:0:0:0:0:0:0:1	Equals ::1. This is the equivalent of 127.0.0.1 in IPv4.
0:0:0:0:0:0:192.168.100.1	This is how an IPv4 address would be written in a mixed IPv6/IPv4 network environment.
2000::/3	This is the global unicast address range.
FC00::/7	This is the unique local unicast range.
FE80::/10	This is the link-local unicast range.
FF00::/8	This is the multicast range.

Address	Meaning
3FFF:FFFF::/32	This is reserved for examples and documentation.
2001:0DB8::/32	This is also reserved for examples and documentation.
2002::/16	This is used with 6-to-4 tunneling, which is an IPv4-to-IPv6 transition system. The structure allows IPv6 packets to be transmitted over an IPv4 network without the need to configure explicit tunnels.

When you run IPv4 and IPv6 on a router, you have what is called *dual-stack*.

How IPv6 Works in an Internetwork

It's time to explore the finer points of IPv6. A great place to start is by showing you how to address a host and what gives it the ability to find other hosts and resources on a network.

I'll also demonstrate a device's ability to automatically address itself—something called *stateless autoconfiguration*—plus another type of autoconfiguration known as *stateful*. Keep in mind that stateful autoconfiguration uses a DHCP server in a very similar way to how it's used in an IPv4 configuration. I'll also show you how Internet Control Message Protocol (ICMP) and multicasting works for us in an IPv6 network environment.

Manual Address Assignment

In order to enable IPv6 on a router, you have to use the ipv6 unicast-routing global configuration command:

```
Corp(config)#ipv6 unicast-routing
```

By default, IPv6 traffic forwarding is disabled, so using this command enables it. Also, as you've probably guessed, IPv6 isn't enabled by default on any interfaces either, so we have to go to each interface individually and enable it.

There are a few different ways to do this, but a really easy way is to just add an address to the interface. You use the interface configuration command
ipv6 address <*ipv6prefix*>/<*prefix-length*> [eui-64] to get this done.
Here's an example:

```
Corp(config-if)#ipv6 address 2001:db8:3c4d:1:0260:d6FF.FE73:1987/64
```

You can specify the entire 128-bit global IPv6 address as I just demonstrated with the preceding command, or you can use the EUI-64 option. Remember, the EUI-64 (extended unique identifier) format allows the device to use its MAC address and pad it to make the interface ID. Check it out:

```
Corp(config-if)#ipv6 address 2001:db8:3c4d:1::/64 eui-64
```

As an alternative to typing in an IPv6 address on a router, you can enable the interface instead to permit the application of an automatic link-local address.

To configure a router so that it uses only link-local addresses, use the `ipv6 enable` interface configuration command:

```
Corp(config-if)#ipv6 enable
```

 Remember, if you have only a link-local address, you will be able to communicate only on that local subnet.

Stateless Autoconfiguration (EUI-64)

Autoconfiguration is an especially useful solution because it allows devices on a network to address themselves with a link-local unicast address as well as with a global unicast address. This process happens through first learning the prefix information from the router and then appending the device's own interface address as the interface ID. But where does it get that interface ID? Well, you know every device on an Ethernet network has a physical MAC address, which is exactly what's used for the interface ID. But since the interface ID in an IPv6 address is 64 bits in length, and a MAC address is only 48 bits, where do the extra 16 bits come from? The MAC address is padded in the middle with the extra bits—it's padded with FFFE.

For example, let's say I have a device with a MAC address that looks like this: 0060:d673:1987. After it's been padded, it would look like this: 0260:d6FF:FE73:1987. Figure 4.7 illustrates what an EUI-64 address looks like.

FIGURE 4.7 EUI-64 interface ID assignment

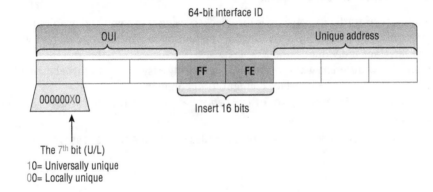

So where did that 2 in the beginning of the address come from? Another good question. You see that part of the process of padding, called *modified EUI-64 format*, changes a bit to specify if the address is locally unique or globally unique. And the bit that gets changed is the seventh bit in the address.

The reason for modifying the U/L bit is that, when using manually assigned addresses on an interface, it means you can simply assign the address 2001:db8:1:9::1/64 instead of the much longer 2001:db8:1:9:0200::1/64. Also, if you are going to manually assign a link-local address, you can assign the short address fe80::1 instead of the long fe80::0200:0:0:1 or fe80:0:0:0:0200::1. So, even though at first glance it seems the IETF made this harder for you to simply understand IPv6 addressing by flipping the seventh bit, in reality this made addressing much simpler. Also, since most people don't typically override the burned-in address, the U/L bit is a 0, which means that you'll see this inverted to a 1 most of the time. But because you're studying the Cisco exam objectives, you'll need to look at inverting it both ways.

Here are a few examples:

- **MAC address:** 0090:2716:fd0f

- **IPv6 EUI-64 address:** 2001:0db8:0:1:0290:27ff:fe16:fd0f

That one was easy! Too easy for the Cisco exam, so let's do another:

- **MAC address:** aa12:bcbc:1234

- **IPv6 EUI-64 address:** 2001:0db8:0:1:a812:bcff:febc:1234

10101010 represents the first 8 bits of the MAC address (aa), which when inverting the seventh bit becomes 10101000. The answer becomes A8.

Neighbor Discovery (NDP)

As with IPv4 and ICMP, IPv6 uses ICMPv6 to take over the task of finding the address of other devices on the local link. The Address Resolution Protocol is used to perform this function for IPv4, but that's been renamed neighbor discovery (ND) in ICMPv6. This process is now achieved via a multicast address called the solicited-node address, because all hosts join this multicast group upon connecting to the network.

Neighbor discovery enables these functions:

- Determining the MAC address of neighbors

- Router solicitation (RS) FF02::2 type code 133

- Router advertisements (RA) FF02::1 type code 134

- Neighbor solicitation (NS) type code 135

- Neighbor advertisement (NA) type code 136

- Duplicate address detection (DAD)

The part of the IPv6 address designated by the 24 bits farthest to the right is added to the end of the multicast address FF02:0:0:0:0:1:FF/104 prefix and is referred to as the *solicited-node address*. When this address is queried, the corresponding host will send back its layer 2 address.

Devices can find and keep track of other neighbor devices on the network in pretty much the same way. RA and RS messages use multicast traffic to request and send address information. That, too, is actually a function of ICMPv6—specifically, neighbor discovery.

In IPv4, the protocol Internet Group Management Protocol (IGMP) was used to allow a host device to tell its local router that it was joining a multicast group and would like to receive the traffic for that group. This IGMP function has been replaced by ICMPv6, and the process has been renamed *multicast listener discovery*.

With IPv4, our hosts could have only one default gateway configured, and if that router went down, we had to either fix the router, change the default gateway, or run some type of virtual default gateway with other protocols created as a solution for this inadequacy in IPv4. Figure 4.8 shows how IPv6 devices find their default gateways using neighbor discovery.

FIGURE 4.8 Router solicitation (RS) and router advertisement (RA)

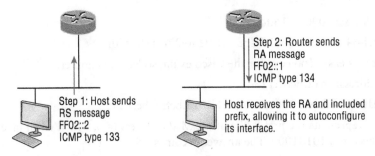

Step 2: Router sends RA message FF02::1 ICMP type 134

Step 1: Host sends RS message FF02::2 ICMP type 133

Host receives the RA and included prefix, allowing it to autoconfigure its interface.

IPv6 hosts send a router solicitation (RS) onto their data link asking for all routers to respond, and they use the multicast address FF02::2 to achieve this. Routers on the same link respond with a unicast to the requesting host or with a router advertisement (RA) using FF02::1.

But that's not all! Hosts also can send solicitations and advertisements between themselves using a neighbor solicitation (NS) and neighbor advertisement (NA), as shown in Figure 4.9. Remember that RA and RS gather or provide information about routers, and NS and NA gather information about hosts. Remember that a "neighbor" is a host on the same data link or VLAN.

Summary

This really was a fun chapter. Come on—admit it! You learned a lot about Network Address Translation (NAT) and how it's configured as static and dynamic as well as with Port Address Translation (PAT), also called NAT Overload.

FIGURE 4.9 Neighbor solicitation (NS) and neighbor advertisement (NA)

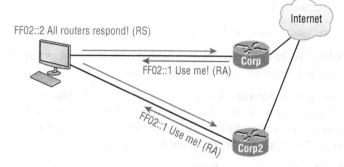

I also described how each flavor of NAT is used in a network as well as how each type is configured.

In addition, this chapter introduced you to some very key IPv6 structural elements as well as how to make IPv6 work within a Cisco internetwork. You now know that even when covering and configuring IPv6 basics, there's still a great deal to understand—and we just scratched the surface! But you're still well equipped with all you need to meet the Cisco exam objectives.

You learned the vital reasons why we need IPv6 and the benefits associated with it. I covered IPv6 addressing and the importance of using shortened expressions. As I covered addressing with IPv6, I also showed you the different address types, plus the special addresses reserved in IPv6.

Exam Essentials

Understand the term *NAT*.   This may come as news to you, because I didn't—okay, failed to—mention it earlier, but NAT has a few nicknames. In the industry, it's referred to as network masquerading, IP-masquerading, and (for those who are besieged with OCD and compelled to spell everything out) Network Address Translation. Whatever you want to dub it, basically, they all refer to the process of rewriting the source/destination addresses of IP packets when they go through a router or firewall. Just focus on the process that's occurring and your understanding of it (i.e., the important part), and you'll be on it for sure!

Remember the three methods of NAT.   The three methods are static, dynamic, and overloading; the latter is also called PAT.

Understand static NAT.   Static NAT is designed to allow one-to-one mapping between local and global addresses.

Understand dynamic NAT.   Dynamic NAT enables you to map a range of unregistered IP addresses to a registered IP address from out of a pool of registered IP addresses.

Understand overloading.   Overloading really is a form of dynamic NAT that maps multiple unregistered IP addresses to a single registered IP address (many-to-one) by using different ports. It's also known as *PAT*.

Understand why we need IPv6.   Without IPv6, the world would be depleted of IP addresses.

Understand link-local addresses.   Link-local addresses are like IPv4 private IP addresses, but they can't be routed at all, not even in your organization.

Understand unique local addresses.   Unique local addresses, like link-local addresses, are like private IP addresses in IPv4 and cannot be routed to the Internet. However, the difference between a link-local address and a unique local address is that a unique local address can be routed within your organization or company.

Remember IPv6 addressing.   IPv6 addressing is not like IPv4 addressing. IPv6 addressing has much more address space, is 128 bits long, and is represented in hexadecimal, unlike IPv4, which is only 32 bits long and represented in decimal.

Review Questions

 The following questions are designed to test your understanding of this chapter's material. For more information on how to get additional questions, please see www.lammle.com/ccst.

You can find the answers to these questions in Appendix, "Answers to Review Questions."

1. Which option is a valid IPv6 address?
   - **A.** 2001:0000:130F::099a::12a
   - **B.** 2002:7654:A1AD:61:81AF:CCC1
   - **C.** FEC0:ABCD:WXYZ:0067::2A4
   - **D.** 2004:1:25A4:886F::1

2. Which three statements about IPv6 prefixes are true? (Choose three.)
   - **A.** FF00::/8 is used for IPv6 multicast.
   - **B.** FE80::/10 is used for link-local unicast.
   - **C.** FC00::/7 is used in private networks.
   - **D.** 2001::1/127 is used for loopback addresses.
   - **E.** FE80::/8 is used for link-local unicast.
   - **F.** FEC0::/10 is used for IPv6 broadcast.

3. Which statements about IPv6 router advertisement messages are true? (Choose two.)
   - **A.** They use ICMPv6 type 134.
   - **B.** The advertised prefix length must be 64 bits.
   - **C.** The advertised prefix length must be 48 bits.
   - **D.** They are sourced from the configured IPv6 interface address.
   - **E.** Their destination is always the link-local address of the neighboring node.

4. Which of the following are true when describing an IPv6 anycast address? (Choose three.)
   - **A.** One-to-many communication model
   - **B.** One-to-nearest communication model
   - **C.** Any-to-many communications model
   - **D.** A unique IPv6 address for each device in the group
   - **E.** The same address for multiple devices in the group
   - **F.** Delivery of packets to the group interface that is closest to the sending device

5. You want to ping the loopback address of your IPv6 local host. What will you type?
   A. ping 127.0.0.1
   B. ping 0.0.0.0
   C. ping ::1
   D. trace 0.0.::1

6. Which of the following are features of the IPv6 protocol? (Choose three.)
   A. Optional IPsec
   B. Autoconfiguration
   C. No broadcasts
   D. Complicated header
   E. Plug-and-play
   F. Checksums

7. Which of the following statements describe characteristics of IPv6 unicast addressing? (Choose two.)
   A. Global addresses start with 2000::/3.
   B. Link-local addresses start with FE00:/12.
   C. Link-local addresses start with FF00::/10.
   D. There is only one loopback address, which is ::1.
   E. If a global address is assigned to an interface, then that is the only allowable address for the interface.

8. A host sends a router solicitation (RS) on the data link. What destination address is sent with this request?
   A. FF02::A
   B. FF02::9
   C. FF02::2
   D. FF02::1
   E. FF02::5

9. Which of the following are valid reasons for adopting IPv6 over IPv4? (Choose two.)
   A. No broadcast
   B. Change of source address in the IPv6 header
   C. Change of destination address in the IPv6 header
   D. No password required for Telnet access
   E. Autoconfiguration
   F. NAT

10. Which of the following is known as "one-to-nearest" addressing in IPv6?

   A. Global unicast

   B. Anycast

   C. Multicast

   D. Unspecified address

11. Which of the following statements about IPv6 addresses are true? (Choose two.)

   A. Leading zeros are required.

   B. Two colons (::) are used to represent successive hexadecimal fields of zeros.

   C. Two colons (::) are used to separate fields.

   D. A single interface will have multiple IPv6 addresses of different types.

12. Which of the following descriptions about IPv6 is correct?

   A. Addresses are not hierarchical and are assigned at random.

   B. Broadcasts have been eliminated and replaced with multicasts.

   C. There are 2.7 billion addresses.

   D. An interface can be configured with only one IPv6 address.

13. Which of the following are advantages of using NAT? (Choose three.)

   A. Translation introduces switching path delays.

   B. NAT conserves legally registered addresses.

   C. NAT causes loss of end-to-end IP traceability.

   D. NAT increases flexibility when connecting to the Internet.

   E. Certain applications will not function with NAT enabled.

   F. NAT remedies address overlap occurrence.

14. Port Address Translation is also called what?

   A. NAT Fast

   B. NAT Static

   C. NAT Overload

   D. Overloading Static

15. Which of the following is considered to be the inside host's address before translation?

   A. Inside local

   B. Outside local

   C. Inside global

   D. Outside global

16. Which of the following are methods of NAT? (Choose three.)

   A. Static

   B. IP NAT pool

   C. Dynamic

   D. NAT double-translation

   E. Overload

17. Which of the following are the disadvantages of using NAT? (Choose three.)

   A. Translation introduces switching path delays.

   B. NAT conserves legally registered addresses.

   C. NAT causes loss of end-to-end IP traceability.

   D. NAT increases flexibility when connecting to the Internet.

   E. Certain applications will not function with NAT enabled.

   F. NAT reduces address overlap occurrence.

IP Routing

THE CCST EXAM TOPICS COVERED IN THIS CHAPTER INCLUDE THE FOLLOWING:

✓ **4.0 Infrastructure**

- 4.4. Explain basic routing concepts.
  - Default gateway, layer 2 vs. layer 3 switches, local network vs. remote network

It's time now to turn our focus toward the core topic of the ubiquitous IP routing process. It's integral to networking because it pertains to all routers and configurations that use it, which is easily the lion's share. IP routing is basically the process of moving packets from one network to another network using routers.

The terms *router* and *layer 3 device* are interchangeable, so throughout this chapter when I use the term *router*, I am referring to any layer 3 device.

Before jumping into this chapter, I want to make sure you understand the difference between a *routing protocol* and a *routed protocol*. Routers use routing protocols to dynamically find all networks within the greater internetwork and to ensure that all routers have the same routing table. Routing protocols are also employed to determine the best path a packet should take through an internetwork to get to its destination most efficiently. RIP, RIPv2, EIGRP, and OSPF are great examples of the most common routing protocols.

Once all routers know about all networks, a routed protocol can be used to send user data (packets) through the established enterprise. Routed protocols are assigned to an interface and determine the method of packet delivery. Examples of routed protocols include IP and IPv6.

In this chapter, I'm going to show you how to understand IP routing with Cisco routers and guide you through the following two key topics:

- Routing basics
- The IP routing process

I want to start by nailing down the basics of how packets actually move through an internetwork, so let's get started!

To find up-to-the-minute updates for this chapter, please see www.lammle.com/ccst.

Routing Basics

Once you create an internetwork by connecting your WANs and LANs to a router, you'll need to configure logical network addresses, like IP addresses, to all hosts on that internetwork for them to communicate successfully throughout it.

The term *routing* refers to taking a packet from one device and sending it through the network to another device on a different network. Routers don't really care about hosts—they only care about networks and the best path to each one of them. The logical network address of the destination host is key to getting packets through a routed network. It's the hardware address of the host that's used to deliver the packet from a router and ensure it arrives at the correct destination host.

Routing is irrelevant if your network has no routers, because their job is to route traffic to all the networks in your internetwork, although this is rarely the case! So here's an important list of the minimum factors a router must know to be able to effectively route packets:

- Destination address

- Neighboring routers from which it can learn about remote networks

- Possible routes to all remote networks

- The best route to each remote network

- How to maintain and verify routing information

The router learns about remote networks from neighboring routers or from an administrator. The router then builds a routing table, which is basically a map of the internetwork; it describes how to find remote networks. If a network is directly connected, then the router already knows how to get to it.

But if a network isn't directly connected to the router, the router must use one of two ways to learn how to get to the remote network. The *static routing* method requires someone to hand-type all network locations into the routing table, which can be a pretty daunting task when used on all but the smallest of networks!

Conversely, when *dynamic routing* is used, a protocol on one router communicates with the same protocol running on neighboring routers. The routers then update each other about all the networks they know about and place this information into the routing table. If a change occurs in the network, the dynamic routing protocols automatically inform all routers about the event. If static routing is used, the administrator is responsible for updating all changes by hand onto all routers. Most people usually use a combination of dynamic and static routing to administer a large network.

Before jumping into the IP routing process, let's take a look at a very simple example that demonstrates how a router uses the routing table to route packets out of an interface.

I'll be going into a more detailed study of the process soon, but first I want to show you something called the *longest match rule*. With it, IP will scan a routing table to find the longest match as compared to the destination address of a packet. Take a look at Figure 5.1 to get a picture of this process.

Figure 5.1 shows a simple network. Lab_A has four interfaces. Can you see which interface will be used to forward an IP datagram to a host with a destination IP address of 10.10.10.30?

By using the command `show ip route` on a router, we can see the routing table (map of the internetwork) that Lab_A has used to make its forwarding decisions:

```
Lab_A#sh ip route
Codes: L - local, C - connected, S - static,
[output cut]
10.0.0.0/8 is variably subnetted, 6 subnets, 4 masks
C 10.0.0.0/8 is directly connected, FastEthernet0/3
L 10.0.0.1/32 is directly connected, FastEthernet0/3
C 10.10.0.0/16 is directly connected, FastEthernet0/2
L 10.10.0.1/32 is directly connected, FastEthernet0/2
C 10.10.10.0/24 is directly connected, FastEthernet0/1
L 10.10.10.1/32 is directly connected, FastEthernet0/1
S* 0.0.0.0/0 is directly connected, FastEthernet0/0
```

FIGURE 5.1 A simple routing example

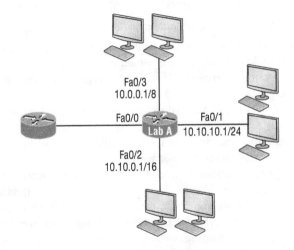

The C in the routing table output means that the networks listed are "directly connected," and until we add a routing protocol like RIPv2, OSPF, etc. to the routers in our internetwork, or enter static routes, only directly connected networks will show up in our routing table. But wait—what about that L in the routing table? That's new, isn't it? Yes, it is, because in the new Cisco IOS 15 code, Cisco defines a different route, called a *local host route*. Each local route has a /32 prefix, defining a route just for the one address. So, in this example, the router has relied upon these routes that list their own local IP addresses to more efficiently forward packets to the router itself.

But let's get back to the original question: By looking at Figure 5.1 and the output of the routing table, can you determine what IP will do with a received packet that has a destination IP address of 10.10.10.30? The answer is that the router will packet-switch the packet to interface FastEthernet 0/1, which will frame the packet and then send it out on the network segment. This is referred to as *frame rewrite*. Based upon the longest match rule, IP would look for 10.10.10.30, and if that isn't found in the table, then IP would search for 10.10.10.0, then 10.10.0.0, and so on, until a route is discovered.

Here's another example: Based on the output of the following routing table, which interface will a packet with a destination address of 10.10.10.14 be forwarded from?

```
Lab_A#sh ip route
[output cut]
Gateway of last resort is not set
C 10.10.10.16/28 is directly connected, FastEthernet0/0
L 10.10.10.17/32 is directly connected, FastEthernet0/0
C 10.10.10.8/29 is directly connected, FastEthernet0/1
L 10.10.10.9/32 is directly connected, FastEthernet0/1
C 10.10.10.4/30 is directly connected, FastEthernet0/2
L 10.10.10.5/32 is directly connected, FastEthernet0/2
C 10.10.10.0/30 is directly connected, Serial 0/0
L 10.10.10.1/32 is directly connected, Serial0/0
```

To figure this out, look closely at the output until you see that the network is subnetted and each interface has a different mask. And I have to tell you—you just can't answer this question if you can't subnet! 10.10.10.14 would be a host in the 10.10.10.8/29 subnet that's connected to the FastEthernet0/1 interface. Don't freak if you're struggling and don't get this! Instead, just go back and reread Chapter 3, "Easy Subnetting," until it becomes clear to you.

The IP Routing Process

The IP routing process is fairly simple and doesn't change, regardless of the size of your network. For a good example of this fact, I'll use Figure 5.2 to describe step-by-step what happens when Host A wants to communicate with Host B on a different network.

FIGURE 5.2 IP routing example using two hosts and one router

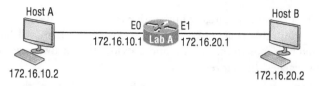

In Figure 5.2 a user on Host_A pinged Host_B's IP address. Routing doesn't get any simpler than this, but it still involves a lot of steps, so let's work through them now:

1. Internet Control Message Protocol (ICMP) creates an echo request payload, which is simply the alphabet in the data field.

2. ICMP hands that payload to Internet Protocol (IP), which then creates a packet. At a minimum, this packet contains an IP source address, an IP destination address, and a

Protocol field with 01h. Don't forget that Cisco likes to use *0x* in front of hex characters, so this could also look like 0x01. This tells the receiving host to whom it should hand the payload when the destination is reached—in this example, ICMP.

3. Once the packet is created, IP determines whether the destination IP address is on the local network or a remote network.

4. Since IP has determined that this is a remote request, the packet must be sent to the default gateway so that it can be routed to the remote network. The Registry in Windows is parsed to find the configured default gateway.

5. The default gateway of Host_A is configured to 172.16.10.1. In order for this packet to be sent to the default gateway, the hardware address of the router's interface Ethernet 0, which is configured with the IP address of 172.16.10.1, must be known. Why? So the packet can be handed down to the Data Link layer, framed, and sent to the router's interface that's connected to the 172.16.10.0 network. Because hosts communicate only via hardware addresses on the local LAN, it's important to recognize that in order for Host_A to communicate to Host_B, it has to send packets to the Media Access Control (MAC) address of the default gateway on the local network.

 MAC addresses are always local on the LAN and never go through and past a router.

6. Next, the Address Resolution Protocol (ARP) cache of the host is checked to see if the IP address of the default gateway has already been resolved to a hardware address.

    If it has, the packet is then free to be handed to the Data Link layer for framing. Remember that the hardware destination address is also handed down with that packet. To view the ARP cache on your host, use the following command:

```
C:\>arp -a
Interface: 172.16.10.2 --- 0x3
Internet Address Physical Address Type
172.16.10.1 00-15-05-06-31-b0 dynamic
```

    If the hardware address isn't already in the ARP cache of the host, an ARP broadcast will be sent out onto the local network to search for the 172.16.10.1 hardware address. The router then responds to the request and provides the hardware address of Ethernet 0, and the host caches this address.

7. Once the packet and destination hardware address are handed to the Data Link layer, the LAN driver is used to provide media access via the type of LAN being used, which is Ethernet in this case. A frame is then generated, encapsulating the packet with control information. Within that frame are the hardware destination and source addresses plus, in this case, an Ether-Type field, which identifies the specific Network layer protocol that handed the packet to the Data Link layer. In this instance, it's IP. At the end of the frame is something called a Frame Check Sequence (FCS) field that houses the result

of the cyclic redundancy check (CRC). The frame would look something like what I've detailed in Figure 5.3. It contains Host A's hardware (MAC) address and the destination hardware address of the default gateway. It does not include the remote host's MAC address—remember that!

FIGURE 5.3   Frame used from Host A to the Lab_A router when Host B is pinged

Destination MAC (router's E0 MAC address)	Source MAC (Host A MAC address)	Ether-Type field	Packet	FCS CRC

8. Once the frame is completed, it's handed down to the Physical layer to be put on the physical medium (in this example, twisted-pair wire) one bit at a time.

9. Every device in the collision domain receives these bits and builds the frame. They each run a CRC and check the answer in the FCS field. If the answers don't match, the frame is discarded.

    ■ If the CRC matches, then the hardware destination address is checked to see if it matches (which, in this example, is the router's interface Ethernet 0).

    ■ If it's a match, then the Ether-Type field is checked to find the protocol used at the Network layer.

10. The packet is pulled from the frame, and what is left of the frame is discarded. The packet is handed to the protocol listed in the Ether-Type field—it's given to IP.

11. IP receives the packet and checks the IP destination address. Since the packet's destination address doesn't match any of the addresses configured on the receiving router itself, the router will look up the destination IP network address in its routing table.

12. The routing table must have an entry for the network 172.16.20.0; otherwise, the packet will be discarded immediately, and an ICMP message will be sent back to the originating device with a destination network unreachable message.

13. If the router does find an entry for the destination network in its table, the packet is switched to the exit interface—in this example, interface Ethernet 1. The following output displays the Lab_A router's routing table. The C means "directly connected." No routing protocols are needed in this network since all networks (all two of them) are directly connected.

```
Lab_A>sh ip route
C 172.16.10.0 is directly connected, Ethernet0
L 172.16.10.1/32 is directly connected, Ethernet0
C 172.16.20.0 is directly connected, Ethernet1
L 172.16.20.1/32 is directly connected, Ethernet1
```

14. The router packet-switches the packet to the Ethernet 1 buffer.

15. The Ethernet 1 buffer needs to know the hardware address of the destination host and first checks the ARP cache.

▪ If the hardware address of Host_B has already been resolved and is in the router's ARP cache, then the packet and the hardware address will be handed down to the Data Link layer to be framed. Let's take a look at the ARP cache on the Lab_A router by using the show ip arp command:

```
Lab_A#sh ip arp
Protocol Address Age(min) Hardware Addr Type Interface
Internet 172.16.20.1 - 00d0.58ad.05f4 ARPA Ethernet1
Internet 172.16.20.2 3 0030.9492.a5dd ARPA Ethernet1
Internet 172.16.10.1 - 00d0.58ad.06aa ARPA Ethernet0
Internet 172.16.10.2 12 0030.9492.a4ac ARPA Ethernet0
```

The dash (-) signifies that this is the physical interface on the router. This output shows us that the router knows the 172.16.10.2 (Host_A) and 172.16.20.2 (Host_B) hardware addresses. Cisco routers will keep an entry in the ARP table for 4 hours.

▪ If the hardware address hasn't already been resolved, the router will send an ARP request out E1 looking for the 172.16.20.2 hardware address. Host_B responds with its hardware address, and the packet and destination hardware addresses are then both sent to the Data Link layer for framing.

16. The Data Link layer creates a frame with the destination and source hardware addresses, Ether-Type field, and FCS field at the end. The frame is then handed to the Physical layer to be sent out on the physical medium one bit at a time.

17. Host_B receives the frame and immediately runs a CRC. If the result matches the information in the FCS field, the hardware destination address will then be checked next. If the host finds a match, the Ether-Type field is then checked to determine the protocol that the packet should be handed to at the Network layer—in this example, IP.

18. At the Network layer, IP receives the packet and runs a CRC on the IP header. If that passes, IP then checks the destination address. Since a match has finally been made, the Protocol field is checked to find out to whom the payload should be given.

19. The payload is handed to ICMP, which understands that this is an echo request. ICMP responds to this by immediately discarding the packet and generating a new payload as an echo reply.

20. A packet is then created including the source and destination addresses, Protocol field, and payload. The destination device is now Host_A.

21. IP then checks to see whether the destination IP address is a device on the local LAN or on a remote network. Since the destination device is on a remote network, the packet needs to be sent to the default gateway.

22. The default gateway IP address is found in the Registry of the Windows device, and the ARP cache is checked to see if the hardware address has already been resolved from an IP address.

23. Once the hardware address of the default gateway is found, the packet and destination hardware addresses are handed down to the Data Link layer for framing.

24. The Data Link layer frames the packet of information and includes the following in the header:

- The destination and source hardware addresses
- The Ether-Type field with 0x0800 (IP) in it
- The FCS field with the CRC result in tow

25. The frame is now handed down to the Physical layer to be sent out over the network medium one bit at a time.

26. The router's Ethernet 1 interface receives the bits and builds a frame. The CRC is run, and the FCS field is checked to make sure the answers match.

27. Once the CRC is found to be okay, the hardware destination address is checked. Since the router's interface is a match, the packet is pulled from the frame and the Ether-Type field is checked to determine which protocol the packet should be delivered to at the Network layer.

28. The protocol is determined to be IP, so it gets the packet. IP runs a CRC check on the IP header first and then checks the destination IP address.

> IP does not run a complete CRC, as the Data Link layer does. It only checks the header for errors.

Since the IP destination address doesn't match any of the router's interfaces, the routing table is checked to see whether it has a route to 172.16.10.0. If it doesn't have a route over to the destination network, the packet will be discarded immediately. I want to take a minute to point out that this is exactly where the source of confusion begins for a lot of administrators because when a ping fails, most people think the packet never reached the destination host. But, as we see here, that's not *always* the case. All it takes for this to happen is for even just one of the remote routers to lack a route back to the originating host's network and—*poof!*—the packet is dropped on the *return trip*, not on its way to the host!

> Just a quick note to mention that when (and if) the packet is lost on the way back to the originating host, you will typically see a request timed-out message because it is an unknown error. If the error occurs because of a known issue, such as if a route is not in the routing table on the way to the destination device, you will see a destination unreachable message. This should help you determine if the problem occurred on the way to the destination or on the way back.

29. In this case, the router happens to know how to get to network 172.16.10.0—the exit interface is Ethernet 0—so the packet is switched to interface Ethernet 0.

30. The router then checks the ARP cache to determine whether the hardware address for 172.16.10.2 has already been resolved.

31. Since the hardware address to 172.16.10.2 is already cached from the originating trip to Host_B, the hardware address and packet are then handed to the Data Link layer.

32. The Data Link layer builds a frame with the destination hardware address and source hardware address and then puts IP in the Ether-Type field. A CRC is run on the frame and the result is placed in the FCS field.

33. The frame is then handed to the Physical layer to be sent out onto the local network one bit at a time.

34. The destination host receives the frame, runs a CRC, checks the destination hardware address, then looks into the Ether-Type field to find out to whom to hand the packet.

35. IP is the designated receiver, and after the packet is handed to IP at the Network layer, it checks the Protocol field for further direction. IP finds instructions to give the payload to ICMP, and ICMP determines the packet to be an ICMP echo reply.

36. ICMP acknowledges that it has received the reply by sending an exclamation point (!) to the user interface. ICMP then attempts to send four more echo requests to the destination host.

You've just experienced Todd's 36 easy steps to understanding IP routing. The key point here is that if you had a much larger network, the process would be the *same*. It's just that the larger the internetwork, the more hops the packet goes through before it finds the destination host.

It's super important to remember that when Host_A sends a packet to Host_B, the destination hardware address used is the default gateway's Ethernet interface. Why? Because frames can't be placed on remote networks—only on local networks. So, packets destined for remote networks must go through the default gateway.

Let's take a look at Host_A's ARP cache:

```
C:\ >arp -a
Interface: 172.16.10.2 --- 0x3
Internet Address Physical Address Type
172.16.10.1 00-15-05-06-31-b0 dynamic
172.16.20.1 00-15-05-06-31-b0 dynamic
```

Did you notice that the hardware (MAC) address that Host_A uses to get to Host_B is the Lab_A E0 interface? Hardware addresses are *always* local and *never* pass through a router's interface. Understanding this process is as important as air to you, so carve this into your memory!

Testing Your IP Routing Understanding

Since understanding IP routing is super important, it's time for that little test I talked about earlier on how well you've got the IP routing process down so far. I'm going to do that by having you look at a couple of figures and answer some very basic IP routing questions.

Figure 5.4 shows a LAN connected to RouterA, which is connected via a WAN link to RouterB. RouterB has a LAN connected with an HTTP server attached.

FIGURE 5.4   IP routing example 1

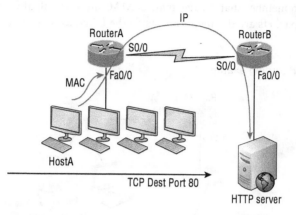

1. The critical information you want to obtain by looking at Figure 5.4 is exactly how IP routing will occur in this example. Let's determine the characteristics of a frame as it leaves HostA. Okay, we'll cheat a bit. I'll give you the answer, but then you should go back over the figure and see if you can answer example 2 without looking at my three-step answer!

2. The destination address of a frame from HostA would be the MAC address of Router A's Fa0/0 interface.

3. The destination address of a packet would be the IP address of the HTTP server's network interface card (NIC).

4. The destination port number in the segment header would be 80.

That was a pretty simple, straightforward scenario. One thing to remember is that when multiple hosts are communicating to a server using HTTP, they must all use a different source port number. The source and destination IP addresses and port numbers are how the server keeps the data separated at the Transport layer.

Let's complicate matters by adding another device into the network and then see if you can find the answers. Figure 5.5 shows a network with only one router but two switches.

The key thing to understand about the IP routing process in this scenario is what happens when HostA sends data to the HTTPS server? Here's your answer:

1. The destination address of a frame from HostA would be the MAC address of RouterA's Fa0/0 interface.

2. The destination address of a packet is the IP address of the HTTPS server's network interface card (NIC).

3. The destination port number in the segment header will have a value of 443.

Did you notice that the switches weren't used as either a default gateway or any other destination? That's because switches have nothing to do with routing. I wonder how many of you chose the switch as the default gateway (destination) MAC address for HostA? If you did, don't feel bad—just take another look to see where you went wrong and why. It's very important to remember that the destination MAC address will always be the router's interface—if your packets are destined for outside the LAN, as they were in these last two examples.

FIGURE 5.5 IP routing example 2

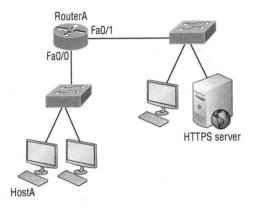

Before moving on into some of the more advanced aspects of IP routing, let's look at another issue. Take a look at the output of this router's routing table:

```
Corp#sh ip route
[output cut]
R 192.168.215.0 [120/2] via 192.168.20.2, 00:00:23, Serial0/0
R 192.168.115.0 [120/1] via 192.168.20.2, 00:00:23, Serial0/0
R 192.168.30.0 [120/1] via 192.168.20.2, 00:00:23, Serial0/0
C 192.168.20.0 is directly connected, Serial0/0
L 192.168.20.1/32 is directly connected, Serial0/0
C 192.168.214.0 is directly connected, FastEthernet0/0
L 192.168.214.1/32 is directly connected, FastEthernet0/0
```

What do we see here? If I were to tell you that the corporate router received an IP packet with a source IP address of 192.168.214.20 and a destination address of 192.168.22.3, what do you think the Corp router will do with this packet?

If you said, "The packet came in on the FastEthernet 0/0 interface, but because the routing table doesn't show a route to network 192.168.22.0 (or a default route), the router will discard the packet and send an ICMP destination unreachable message back out to interface FastEthernet 0/0," then you're a genius! The reason that's the correct answer is because that's the source LAN where the packet originated from.

Now let's talk about the frames and packets in detail. I'm not really going over anything new here; I'm just making sure you totally, completely, thoroughly, fully understand basic IP routing! It is the crux of this book and the topic the exam objectives are geared toward. It's all about IP routing, which means you need to be all over this stuff! We'll use Figure 5.6 for the next few scenarios.

FIGURE 5.6   Basic IP routing using MAC and IP addresses

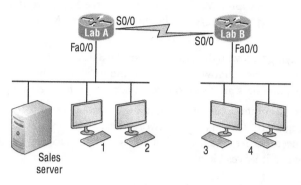

Referring to Figure 5.6, here's a list of all the answers to questions you need inscribed in your brain:

1. In order to begin communicating with the Sales server, Host 4 sends out an ARP request. How will the devices exhibited in the topology respond to this request?

2. Host 4 has received an ARP reply. Host 4 will now build a packet and place this packet in the frame. What information will be placed in the header of the packet that leaves Host 4 if Host 4 is going to communicate to the Sales server?

3. The Lab_A router has received the packet and will send it out Fa0/0 onto the LAN toward the server. What will the frame have in the header as the source and destination addresses?

4. Host 4 is displaying two web documents from the Sales server in two browser windows at the same time. How did the data find its way to the correct browser windows?

The following should probably be written in a teensy font and put upside down in another part of the book so that it would be really hard for you to cheat and peek, but since I'm not that mean and you really need to have this down, here are your answers, in the same order that the scenarios were just presented:

1. In order to begin communicating with the server, Host 4 sends out an ARP request. How will the devices exhibited in the topology respond to this request? Since MAC addresses must stay on the local network, the Lab_B router will respond with the MAC address of the Fa0/0 interface, and Host 4 will send all frames to the MAC address of the Lab_B Fa0/0 interface when sending packets to the Sales server.

2. Host 4 has received an ARP reply. Host 4 will now build a packet and place this packet in the frame. What information will be placed in the header of the packet that leaves

Host 4 if Host 4 is going to communicate to the Sales server? Since we're now talking about packets, not frames, the source address will be the IP address of Host 4, and the destination address will be the IP address of the Sales server.

3. Finally, the Lab_A router has received the packet and will send it out Fa0/0 onto the LAN toward the server. What will the frame have in the header as the source and destination addresses? The source MAC address will be the Lab_A router's Fa0/0 interface, and the destination MAC address will be the Sales server's MAC address, because all MAC addresses must be local on the LAN.

4. Host 4 is displaying two web documents from the Sales server in two different browser windows at the same time. How did the data find its way to the correct browser windows? TCP port numbers are used to direct the data to the correct application window.

Great! But we're not quite done yet. I've got a few more questions for you before you actually get to configure routing in a real network. Ready? Figure 5.7 shows a basic network, and Host 4 needs to get email. Which address will be placed in the destination address field of the frame when it leaves Host 4?

FIGURE 5.7   Testing basic routing knowledge

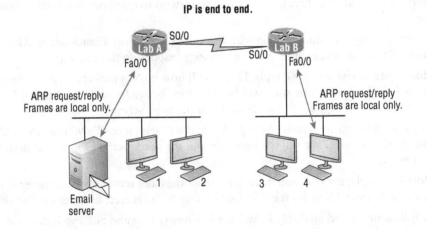

The answer is that Host 4 will use the destination MAC address of the Fa0/0 interface on the Lab_B router. You knew that, right? Look at Figure 5.7 again. What if Host 4 needs to communicate with Host 1—not the server, but with Host 1. Which OSI layer 3 source address will be found in the packet header when it reaches Host 1?

Hopefully you've got this: At layer 3, the source IP address will be Host 4, and the destination address in the packet will be the IP address of Host 1. Of course, the destination MAC address from Host 4 will always be the Fa0/0 address of the Lab_B router, right? And since we have more than one router, we'll need a routing protocol that communicates between both of them so that traffic can be forwarded in the right direction to reach the network that Host 1 is connected to.

Okay, one more scenario and you're on your way to being an IP routing machine! Again, using Figure 5.7, Host 4 is transferring a file to the email server connected to the Lab_A router. What would be the layer 2 destination address leaving Host 4? Yes, I've asked this question more than once. But not this one: What will be the source MAC address when the frame is received at the email server?

Hopefully, you answered that the layer 2 destination address leaving Host 4 is the MAC address of the Fa0/0 interface on the Lab_B router, and that the source layer 2 address that the email server will receive is the Fa0/0 interface of the Lab_A router.

If you did, you're ready to discover how IP routing is handled in a larger network environment!

Configuring IP Routing

Is our network really good to go? But how will our routers send packets to remote networks when they get their destination information by looking into their local tables that only include directions about directly connected networks? And routers promptly discard packets they receive with addresses for networks that aren't listed in their routing table!

So, we're not exactly ready to rock after all. But we will be soon, because there are several ways to configure the routing tables to include all the networks in our little internetwork so that packets will be properly forwarded. As usual, one size fits all rarely fits at all, and what's best for one network isn't necessarily what's best for another. That's why understanding the different types of routing will be really helpful when choosing the best solution for your specific environment and business requirements.

The next sections discuss the following three routing methods:

- Static routing
- Default routing
- Dynamic routing

I'm going to explain the first way using static routing on our network, because if you can implement static routing *and* make it work, you've demonstrated that you definitely have a solid understanding of the internetwork. Let's get started.

Static Routing

Static routing is the process that ensues when you manually add routes in each router's routing table. Predictably, there are pros and cons to static routing, but that's true for all routing approaches.

Here are the pros:

- There is no overhead on the router CPU, which means you could probably make do with a cheaper router than you would need for dynamic routing.

- There is no bandwidth usage between routers, saving you money on WAN links as well as minimizing overhead on the router since you're not using a routing protocol.
- It adds security because you, the administrator, can be very exclusive and choose to allow routing access to certain networks only.

And here are the cons:

- The administrator must have a vault-tight knowledge of the internetwork and how each router is connected in order to configure routes correctly. If you don't have a good, accurate map of your internetwork, things will get very messy quickly!
- If you add a network to the internetwork, you have to tediously add a route to it on all routers by hand, which only gets increasingly insane as the network grows.
- Due to the last point, it's just not feasible to use it in most large networks because maintaining it would be a full-time job in itself.

But that list of cons doesn't mean you get to skip learning all about it, mainly because of that first disadvantage I listed—the fact that you must have such a solid understanding of a network to configure it properly and that your administrative knowledge has to practically verge on the supernatural! So let's dive in and develop those skills. Starting at the beginning, here's the command syntax you use to add a static route to a routing table from global config:

```
ip route [destination_network] [mask] [next-hop_address or
exitinterface] [administrative_distance] [permanent]
```

This list describes each command in the string:

ip route   The command used to create the static route.

destination_network   The network you're placing in the routing table.

mask   The subnet mask being used on the network.

next-hop_address   This is the IP address of the next-hop router that will receive packets and forward them to the remote network, which must signify a router interface that's on a directly connected network. You must be able to successfully ping the router interface before you can add the route. Note that if you type in the wrong next-hop address or the interface to the correct router is down, the static route will show up in the router's configuration but not in the routing table.

exitinterface   Used in place of the next-hop address, if you want, and shows up as a directly connected route.

administrative_distance   By default, static routes have an administrative distance of 1 or 0 if you use an exit interface instead of a next-hop address. You can change the default value by adding an administrative weight at the end of the command.

I'll talk a lot more about this later in the chapter when we get to the section on dynamic routing.

permanent   If the interface is shut down or the router can't communicate to the next-hop router, the route will automatically be discarded from the routing table by default. Choosing the permanent option keeps the entry in the routing table no matter what happens.

Before I guide you through configuring static routes, let's take a look at a sample static route to see what we can find out about it:

```
Router(config)#ip route 172.16.3.0 255.255.255.0 192.168.2.4
```

- The ip route command tells us simply that it's a static route.
- 172.16.3.0 is the remote network we want to send packets to.
- 255.255.255.0 is the mask of the remote network.
- 192.168.2.4 is the next hop, or router, that packets will be sent to.

But what if the static route looked like this instead?

```
Router(config)#ip route 172.16.3.0 255.255.255.0 192.168.2.4 150
```

That 150 at the end changes the default administrative distance (AD) of 1 to 150. As I said, I'll talk much more about AD when we get into dynamic routing; for now, just remember that the AD is the trustworthiness of a route, where 0 is best and 255 is worst.

One more example:

```
Router(config)#ip route 172.16.3.0 255.255.255.0 s0/0/0
```

Instead of using a next-hop address, we can use an exit interface that will make the route show up as a directly connected network. Functionally, the next hop and exit interface work the same.

Default Routing

A *stub route* indicates that the networks in a network design have only one way out to reach all other networks, which means that instead of having to create multiple static routes, we can just use a single default route. This default route is used by IP to forward any packet with a destination not found in the routing table, which is why it is also called a gateway of last resort. Here's a sample default route configuration:

```
Router#config t
Router(config)#ip route 0.0.0.0 0.0.0.0 172.16.10.5
Router(config)#do show ip route
        [output cut]
Gateway of last resort is 172.16.10.5 to network 0.0.0.0
```

Dynamic Routing

Dynamic routing is when protocols are used to find networks and update routing tables on routers. This is whole lot easier than using static or default routing, but it will cost you in terms of router CPU processing and bandwidth on network links. A routing protocol defines the set of rules used by a router when it communicates routing information between neighboring routers.

The routing protocol I'm going to talk about in this chapter is Routing Information Protocol (RIP) versions 1 and 2.

Two types of routing protocols are used in internetworks: *interior gateway protocols (IGPs)* and *exterior gateway protocols (EGPs)*. IGPs are used to exchange routing information with routers in the same *autonomous system (AS)*. An AS is either a single network or a collection of networks under a common administrative domain, which basically means that all routers sharing the same routing-table information are in the same AS. EGPs are used to communicate between ASs. An example of an EGP is Border Gateway Protocol (BGP), which we're not going to bother with because it's beyond the scope of this book. BGP is the dynamic routing protocol the propagates routes for routing packets on the Internet.

Since routing protocols are so essential to dynamic routing, I'm going to give you the basic information you need to know about them next.

Routing Protocol Basics

There are some important things you should know about routing protocols before we get deeper into RIP routing—for example, administrative distances and the three different kinds of routing protocols. Let's take a look.

Administrative Distances

The *administrative distance (AD)* is used to rate the trustworthiness of routing information received on a router from a neighbor router. An administrative distance is an integer from 0 to 255, where 0 is the most trusted and 255 means no traffic will be passed via this route.

If a router receives two updates listing the same remote network, the first thing the router checks is the AD. If one of the advertised routes has a lower AD than the other, then the route with the lowest AD will be chosen and placed in the routing table.

If both advertised routes to the same network have the same AD, then routing protocol metrics like *hop count* and/or the bandwidth of the lines will be used to find the best path to the remote network. The advertised route with the lowest metric will be placed in the routing table, but if both advertised routes have the same AD as well as the same metrics, then the routing protocol will load-balance to the remote network, meaning the protocol will send data down each link.

Table 5.1 shows the default administrative distances that a Cisco router uses to decide which route to take to a remote network.

TABLE 5.1   Default administrative distances

Route Source	Default AD
Connected interface	0
Static route	1
External BGP	20
EIGRP	90
OSPF	110
RIP	120
External EIGRP	170
Internal BGP	200
Unknown	255 (This route will never be used.)

If a network is directly connected, the router will always use the interface connected to the network. If you configure a static route, the router will then believe that route over any other ones it learns about. You can change the administrative distance of static routes, but they have an AD of 1 by default. This AD allows us to configure routing protocols without having to remove the static routes, because it's nice to have them there for backup in case the routing protocol experiences some kind of failure.

If you have a static route, a RIP-advertised route, and an EIGRP-advertised route listing the same network, which route will the router go with? That's right—by default, the router will always use the static route unless you change its AD!

Routing Protocols

There are three classes of routing protocols:

Distance Vector   The distance-vector protocols in use today find the best path to a remote network by judging distance. In RIP routing, each instance where a packet goes through a router is called a hop, and the route with the least number of hops to the network will be chosen as the best one. The vector indicates the direction to the remote network. RIP is a distance-vector routing protocol and periodically sends out the entire routing table to directly connected neighbors.

Link State   In link-state protocols, also called shortest-path-first (SPF) protocols, each router creates three separate tables. One of the tables keeps track of directly attached neighbors; one table determines the topology of the entire internetwork; and one table is used as the routing table. Link-state routers know more about the internetwork than any distance-vector routing protocol ever could. OSPF is an IP routing protocol that's completely link-state. Link-state routing tables are not exchanged periodically; instead, triggered updates containing only specific link-state information are sent. Periodic keepalives that are small and efficient, in the form of hello messages, are exchanged between directly connected neighbors to establish and maintain neighbor relationships.

Advanced Distance Vector   Advanced distance-vector protocols use aspects of both distance-vector and link-state protocols, and EIGRP is a great example. EIGRP may act like a link-state routing protocol because it uses a Hello protocol to discover neighbors and form neighbor relationships and because only partial updates are sent when a change occurs. However, EIGRP is still based on the key distance-vector routing protocol principle that information about the rest of the network is learned from directly connected neighbors.

There's no set of rules to follow that dictate exactly how to broadly configure routing protocols for every situation. It's a task that really must be undertaken on a case-by-case basis, with an eye on the specific requirements of each one. If you understand how the different routing protocols work, you can make good decisions that will solidly meet the individual needs of any business!

Summary

This chapter covered IP routing in detail. Again, it's extremely important to fully understand the basics covered in this chapter because everything that's done on a Cisco router will typically have some kind of IP routing configured and running.

You learned how IP routing uses frames to transport packets between routers and to the destination host. From there, we configured static routing on our routers and discussed the administrative distance used by IP to determine the best route to a destination network.

You found out that if you have a stub network, you can configure default routing, which sets the gateway of last resort on a router.

Exam Essentials

Describe the basic IP routing process.   You need to remember that the frame changes at each hop, but that the packet is never changed or manipulated in any way until it reaches the destination device. (The TTL field in the IP header is decremented for each hop, but that's it!)

List the information required by a router to successfully route packets.   To be able to route packets, a router must know, at a minimum, the destination address, the location of neighboring routers through which it can reach remote networks, possible routes to all remote networks, the best route to each remote network, and how to maintain and verify routing information.

Describe how MAC addresses are used during the routing process.   A MAC (hardware) address will be used only on a local LAN. It will never pass a router's interface. A frame uses MAC (hardware) addresses to send a packet on a LAN. The frame will take the packet to either a host on the LAN or a router's interface (if the packet is destined for a remote network). As packets move from one router to another, the MAC addresses used will change, but normally the original source and destination IP addresses within the packet will not.

Differentiate the three types of routing.   The three types of routing are static (in which routes are manually configured at the CLI), dynamic (in which the routers share routing information via a routing protocol), and default routing (in which a special route is configured for all traffic without a more specific destination network found in the table).

Compare and contrast static and dynamic routing.   Static routing creates no routing update traffic and creates less overhead on the router and network links, but it must be configured manually and does not have the ability to react to link outages. Dynamic routing creates routing update traffic and uses more overhead on the router and network links.

Understand administrative distance and its role in the selection of the best route.   Administrative distance (AD) is used to rate the trustworthiness of routing information received on a router from a neighbor router. Administrative distance is an integer from 0 to 255, where 0 is the most trusted and 255 means no traffic will be passed via this route. All routing protocols are assigned a default AD, but it can be changed at the CLI.

Differentiate distance-vector and link-state   Distance-vector routing protocols make routing decisions based on hop count (think RIP), whereas link-state routing protocols are able to consider multiple factors such as bandwidth available and building a topology table.

Review Questions

The following questions are designed to test your understanding of this chapter's material. For more information on how to get additional questions, please see www.lammle.com/ccst.

You can find the answers to these questions in Appendix, "Answers to Review Questions."

1. Which command was used to generate the following output?
   ```
   Codes: L - local, C - connected, S - static,
   [output cut]
   10.0.0.0/8 is variably subnetted, 6 subnets, 4 masks
   C 10.0.0.0/8 is directly connected, FastEthernet0/3
   L 10.0.0.1/32 is directly connected, FastEthernet0/3
   C 10.10.0.0/16 is directly connected, FastEthernet0/2
   L 10.10.0.1/32 is directly connected, FastEthernet0/2
   C 10.10.10.0/24 is directly connected, FastEthernet0/1
   L 10.10.10.1/32 is directly connected, FastEthernet0/1
   S* 0.0.0.0/0 is directly connected, FastEthernet0/0
   ```
   A. show running-config
   B. show ip route
   C. show routing table
   D. show ip path

2. Which of the following statements are true regarding the command
   ip route 172.16.4.0 255.255.255.0 192.168.4.2? (Choose two.)
   A. The command is used to establish a static route.
   B. The default administrative distance is used.
   C. The command is used to configure the default route.
   D. The subnet mask for the source address is 255.255.255.0.
   E. The command is used to establish a stub network.

3. What destination addresses will be used by HostA to send data to the HTTPS server as shown in the following network? (Choose two.)

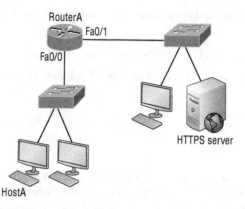

RouterA

Fa0/1

Fa0/0

HTTPS server

HostA

A. The IP address of the switch

B. The MAC address of the remote switch

C. The IP address of the HTTPS server

D. The MAC address of the HTTPS server

E. The IP address of RouterA's Fa0/0 interface

F. The MAC address of RouterA's Fa0/0 interface

4. Which of the following is called an advanced distance-vector routing protocol?

A. OSPF

B. EIGRP

C. BGP

D. RIP

5. When a packet is routed across a network, the _____ in the packet changes at every hop whereas the _____ does not.

A. MAC address, IP address

B. IP address, MAC address

C. Port number, IP address

D. IP address, port number

6. Which of the following statements regarding the distance-vector and link-state routing protocols are true? (Choose two.)

A. Link state sends its complete routing table out of all active interfaces at periodic time intervals.

B. Distance vector sends its complete routing table out of all active interfaces at periodic time intervals.

   C. Link state sends updates containing the state of its own links to all routers in the internetwork.

   D. Distance vector sends updates containing the state of its own links to all routers in the internetwork.

7. What does the 150 at the end of the following command mean?

   `Router(config)#ip route 172.16.3.0 255.255.255.0 192.168.2.4 150`

   A. Metric

   B. Administrative distance

   C. Hop count

   D. Cost

8 A network administrator views the output from the `show ip route` command. A network that is advertised by both RIP and EIGRP appears in the routing table flagged as an EIGRP route. Why is the RIP route to this network not used in the routing table?

   A. EIGRP has a faster update timer.

   B. EIGRP has a lower administrative distance.

   C. RIP has a higher metric value for that route.

   D. The EIGRP route has fewer hops.

   E. The RIP path has a routing loop.

9. Which of the following is *not* an advantage of static routing?

   A. Less overhead on the router CPU

   B. No bandwidth usage between routers

   C. Adds security

   D. Recovers automatically from lost routes

10. Which of the following are advantages of static routing? (Choose three.)

   A. Less overhead on the router CPU

   B. No bandwidth usage between routers

   C. Adds security

   D. Recovers automatically from lost routes

Chapter

6

Switching

THE CCST EXAM TOPICS COVERED IN THIS
CHAPTER INCLUDE THE FOLLOWING:

✓ **4.0 Infrastructure**

- 4.4. Explain basic routing concepts.

  - Default gateway, layer 2 vs. layer 3 switches, local
    network vs. remote network

- 4.5. Explain basic switching concepts.

  - MAC address tables, MAC address filtering, VLAN

When people at Cisco discuss switching in regard to the Cisco exam objectives, they're talking about layer 2 switching unless they say otherwise. Layer 2 switching is the process of using the hardware address of devices on a LAN to segment a network. Since you've got the basic idea of how that works nailed down by now, we're going to dive deeper into the particulars of layer 2 switching to ensure that your concept of how it works is solid and complete.

You already know that we rely on switching to break up large collision domains into smaller ones and that a collision domain is a network segment with two or more devices sharing the same bandwidth. A hub network is a typical example of this type of technology. But since each port on a switch is actually its own collision domain, we were able to create a much better Ethernet LAN network by simply replacing our hubs with switches!

Switches truly have changed the way networks are designed and implemented. If a pure switched design is properly implemented, it absolutely will result in a clean, cost-effective, and resilient internetwork. In this chapter, I'll survey and compare how networks were designed before and after switching technologies were introduced.

To find up-to-the-minute updates for this chapter, please see www.lammle.com/ccst.

Switching Services

Unlike old bridges, which used software to create and manage a content-addressable memory (CAM) filter table, newer, faster switches use application-specific integrated circuits (ASICs) to build and maintain their MAC filter tables. But it's still okay to think of a layer 2 switch as a multiport bridge because their basic reason for being is the same: to break up collision domains.

Layer 2 switches and bridges are faster than routers because they don't take up time looking at the Network layer header information. Instead, they look at the frame's hardware addresses before deciding to either forward, flood, or drop the frame.

Unlike hubs, switches create private, dedicated collision domains and provide independent bandwidth exclusive on each port.

Here's a list of four important advantages we gain when using layer 2 switching:

- Hardware-based bridging (ASICs)
- Wire speed

- Low latency
- Low cost

A big reason layer 2 switching is so efficient is that no modification to the data packet takes place. The device only reads the frame encapsulating the packet, which makes the switching process considerably faster and less error-prone than routing processes are.

And if you use layer 2 switching for both workgroup connectivity and network segmentation (breaking up collision domains), you can create more network segments than you can with traditional routed networks. Plus, layer 2 switching increases bandwidth for each user because, again, each connection, or interface into the switch, is its own, self-contained collision domain.

Three Switch Functions at Layer 2

Three distinct functions of layer 2 switching are vital for you to remember: *address learning*, *forward/filter decisions*, and *loop avoidance*.

Address Learning   Layer 2 switches remember the source hardware address of each frame received on an interface and enter this information into a MAC database called a forward/filter table.

Forward/Filter Decisions   When a frame is received on an interface, the switch looks at the destination hardware address, then chooses the appropriate exit interface for it in the MAC database. This way, the frame is only forwarded out of the correct destination port.

Loop Avoidance   If multiple connections between switches are created for redundancy purposes, network loops can occur. Spanning Tree Protocol (STP) is used to prevent network loops while still permitting redundancy.

Next, I'm going to talk about address learning and forward/filtering decisions.

Address Learning

When a switch is first powered on, the MAC forward/filter table (CAM) is empty, as shown in Figure 6.1.

FIGURE 6.1   An empty forward/filter table on a switch

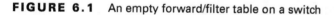
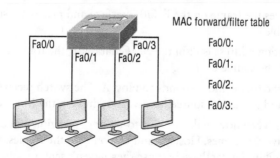

When a device transmits and an interface receives a frame, the switch places the frame's source address in the MAC forward/filter table, allowing it to refer to the precise interface the sending device is located on. The switch then has no choice but to flood the network with this frame out of every port except the source port because it has no idea where the destination device is actually located.

If a device answers this flooded frame and sends a frame back, then the switch will take the source address from that frame and place that MAC address in its database as well, associating this address with the interface that received the frame. Because the switch now has both of the relevant MAC addresses in its filtering table, the two devices can now make a point-to-point connection. The switch doesn't need to flood the frame as it did the first time because now the frames can and will only be forwarded between these two devices. This is exactly why layer 2 switches are so superior to hubs. In a hub network, all frames are forwarded out all ports every time—no matter what. Figure 6.2 shows the processes involved in building a MAC database.

FIGURE 6.2   How switches learn hosts' locations

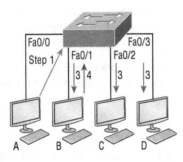

CAM/MAC forward/filter table

Fa0/0:   0000.8c01.000A   Step 2

Fa0/1:   0000.8c01.000B   Step 4

Fa0/2:

Fa0/3:

In this figure, you can see four hosts attached to a switch. When the switch is powered on, it has nothing in its MAC address forward/filter table, just as in Figure 6.1. But when the hosts start communicating, the switch places the source hardware address of each frame into the table along with the port that the frame's source address corresponds to.

Let me give you an example of how a forward/filter table is populated using Figure 6.2:

1. Host A sends a frame to Host B. Host A's MAC address is 0000.8c01.000A, and Host B's MAC address is 0000.8c01.000B.

2. The switch receives the frame on the Fa0/0 interface and places the source address in the MAC address table.

3. Since the destination address isn't in the MAC database, the frame is forwarded out all interfaces except the source port.

4. Host B receives the frame and responds to Host A. The switch receives this frame on interface Fa0/1 and places the source hardware address in the MAC database.

5. Host A and Host B can now make a point-to-point connection and only these specific devices will receive the frames. Hosts C and D won't see the frames, nor will their MAC addresses be found in the database because they haven't sent a frame to the switch yet.

If Host A and Host B don't communicate to the switch again within a certain time period, the switch will flush their entries from the database to keep it as current as possible.

Forward/Filter Decisions

When a frame arrives at a switch interface, the destination hardware address is compared to the forward/filter MAC database. If the destination hardware address is known and listed in the database, the frame is only sent out of the appropriate exit interface. The switch won't transmit the frame out any interface except for the destination interface, which preserves bandwidth on the other network segments. This process is called *frame filtering*.

But if the destination hardware address isn't listed in the MAC database, then the frame will be flooded out all active interfaces except the interface it was received on. If a device answers the flooded frame, the MAC database is then updated with the device's location—its correct interface.

If a host or server sends a broadcast on the LAN, by default, the switch will flood the frame out all active ports except the source port. Remember, the switch creates smaller collision domains, but it's always still one large broadcast domain by default.

In Figure 6.3, Host A sends a data frame to Host D. What do you think the switch will do when it receives the frame from Host A?

FIGURE 6.3   A forward/filter table

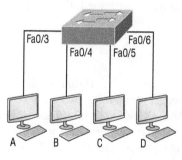

Switch# show mac address-table

VLAN	Mac Address	Ports
1	0005.dccb.d74b	Fa0/4
1	000a.f467.9e80	Fa0/5
1	000a.f467.9e8b	Fa0/6

Let's examine Figure 6.4 to find the answer.

FIGURE 6.4   A forward/filter table answer

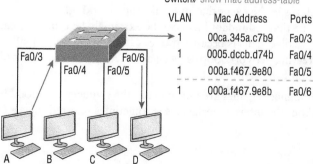

Switch# show mac address-table

VLAN	Mac Address	Ports
1	00ca.345a.c7b9	Fa0/3
1	0005.dccb.d74b	Fa0/4
1	000a.f467.9e80	Fa0/5
1	000a.f467.9e8b	Fa0/6

Since Host A's MAC address is not in the forward/filter table, the switch will add the source address and port to the MAC address table, then forward the frame to Host D. It's really important to remember that the source MAC is always checked first to make sure it's in the CAM table. After that, if Host D's MAC address weren't found in the forward/filter table, the switch would've flooded the frame out all ports except for port, Fa0/3 because that's the specific port the frame was received on.

Now let's take a look at the output that results from using a show mac address-table command:

```
Switch#sh mac address-table
Vlan Mac Address Type Ports]]>
---- ----------- -------- -----
1 0005.dccb.d74b DYNAMIC Fa0/1
1 000a.f467.9e80 DYNAMIC Fa0/3
1 000a.f467.9e8b DYNAMIC Fa0/4
1 000a.f467.9e8c DYNAMIC Fa0/3
1 0010.7b7f.c2b0 DYNAMIC Fa0/3
1 0030.80dc.460b DYNAMIC Fa0/3
1 0030.9492.a5dd DYNAMIC Fa0/1
1 00d0.58ad.05f4 DYNAMIC Fa0/1
```

But let's say the preceding switch received a frame with the following MAC addresses:

Source MAC: 0005.dccb.d74b

Destination MAC: 000a.f467.9e8c

How will the switch handle this frame? The right answer is that the destination MAC address will be found in the MAC address table, and the frame will only be forwarded out Fa0/3. Never forget that if the destination MAC address isn't found in the forward/filter table, the frame will be forwarded out all of the switch's ports except for the one on which it was originally received in an attempt to locate the destination device. Now that you can see the MAC address table and how switches add host addresses to the forward filter table, how do think we can secure it from unauthorized users?

Loop Avoidance

Redundant links between switches are important to have in place because they help prevent nasty network failures in the event that one link stops working.

But while it's true that redundant links can be extremely helpful, they can also cause more problems than they solve! This is because frames can be flooded down all redundant links simultaneously, creating network loops as well as other evils. Here's a list of some of the ugliest problems that can occur:

■   If no loop avoidance schemes are put in place, the switches will flood broadcasts endlessly throughout the internetwork. This is sometimes referred to as a *broadcast storm*.

Most of the time, they're referred to in very unprintable ways! Figure 6.5 illustrates how a broadcast can be propagated throughout the network. Observe how a frame is continually being flooded through the internetwork's physical network media.

- A device can receive multiple copies of the same frame because that frame can arrive from different segments at the same time. Figure 6.6 demonstrates how a whole bunch of frames can arrive from multiple segments simultaneously. The server in the figure sends a unicast frame to Router C. Because it's a unicast frame, Switch A forwards the frame and Switch B provides the same service—it forwards the unicast. This is bad because it means that Router C receives that unicast frame twice, causing additional overhead on the network.

- You may have thought of this one: The MAC address filter table could be totally confused about the source device's location because the switch can receive the frame from more than one link. Worse, the bewildered switch could get so caught up in constantly updating the MAC filter table with source hardware address locations that it will fail to forward a frame! This is called thrashing the MAC table.

- One of the vilest events is when multiple loops propagate throughout a network. Loops can occur within other loops, and if a broadcast storm were to occur simultaneously, the network wouldn't be able to perform frame switching—period!

FIGURE 6.5   A broadcast storm

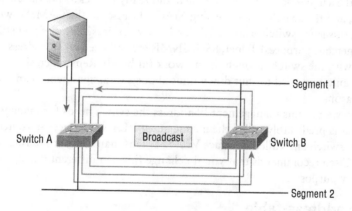

All of these problems spell disaster or close, and they're all evil situations that must be avoided or fixed somehow. That's where the Spanning Tree Protocol comes into play. It was actually developed to solve each and every one of the problems I just told you about!

Now that I've explained the issues that can occur when you have redundant links, or when you have links that are improperly implemented, I'm sure you understand how vital it is to prevent them. However, the best solutions are beyond the scope of this chapter and among the territory covered in the more advanced Cisco exam objectives. For now, let's focus on configuring some switching!

FIGURE 6.6   Multiple frame copies

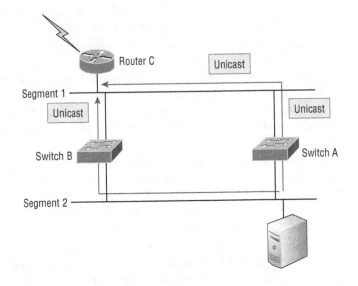

Do We Need to Put an IP Address on a Switch?

Absolutely not! Switches have all ports enabled and ready to rock. Take the switch out of the box, plug it in, and the switch starts learning MAC addresses in the CAM. So why would I need an IP address since switches are providing layer 2 services? Because you still need it for in-band management purposes! Telnet, SSH, SNMP, etc., all need an IP address in order to communicate with the switch through the network (in-band). Remember, since all ports are enabled by default, you need to shut down unused ports or assign them to an unused VLAN for security reasons.

So where do we put this management IP address the switch needs for management purposes? On what is predictably called the management VLAN interface—a routed interface on every Cisco switch and called interface VLAN 1. This management interface can be changed, and Cisco recommends that you do change this to a different management interface for security purposes.

show mac address-table

I'm sure you remember being shown this command earlier in the chapter. Using it displays the forward filter table, also called a content-addressable memory (CAM) table. Here's the output from the S1 switch:

```
S3#sh mac address-table
Mac Address Table]]>
-------------------------------------------

Vlan Mac Address Type Ports]]>
---- ----------- -------- -----

All 0100.0ccc.cccc STATIC CPU
[output cut]
```

```
1 000e.83b2.e34b DYNAMIC Fa0/1
1 0011.1191.556f DYNAMIC Fa0/1
1 0011.3206.25cb DYNAMIC Fa0/1
1 001a.2f55.c9e8 DYNAMIC Fa0/1
1 001a.4d55.2f7e DYNAMIC Fa0/1
1 001c.575e.c891 DYNAMIC Fa0/1
1 b414.89d9.1886 DYNAMIC Fa0/5
1 b414.89d9.1887 DYNAMIC Fa0/6
```

The switches use things called base MAC addresses, which are assigned to the CPU. The first one listed is the base MAC address of the switch. From the preceding output, you can see that we have six MAC addresses dynamically assigned to Fa0/1, meaning that port Fa0/1 is connected to another switch. Ports Fa0/5 and Fa0/6 only have one MAC address assigned, and all ports are assigned to VLAN 1.

Let's take a look at the S2 switch CAM and see what we can find out.

```
S2#sh mac address-table
Mac Address Table]]>
-----------------------------------------
Vlan Mac Address Type Ports]]>
---- ----------- -------- -----
All 0100.0ccc.cccc STATIC CPU
[output cut
1 000e.83b2.e34b DYNAMIC Fa0/5
1 0011.1191.556f DYNAMIC Fa0/5
1 0011.3206.25cb DYNAMIC Fa0/5
1 001a.4d55.2f7e DYNAMIC Fa0/5
1 581f.aaff.86b8 DYNAMIC Fa0/5
1 ecc8.8202.8286 DYNAMIC Fa0/5
1 ecc8.8202.82c0 DYNAMIC Fa0/5
Total Mac Addresses for this criterion: 27
S2#
```

This output tells us that we have seven MAC addresses assigned to Fa0/5, which is our connection to S3. But where's port 6? Since port 6 is a redundant link to S3, STP placed Fa0/6 into blocking mode.

VLAN Basics

Figure 6.7 illustrates the flat network architecture that used to be so typical for layer 2 switched networks. With this configuration, every broadcast packet transmitted is seen by every device on the network regardless of whether the device needs to receive that data or not.

By default, routers allow broadcasts to occur only within the originating network, whereas switches forward broadcasts to all segments. Oh, and by the way, the reason it's called a *flat network* is because it's one *broadcast domain*, not because the actual design is physically flat. In Figure 6.7 we see Host A sending out a broadcast and all ports on all switches forwarding it—all except the port that originally received it.

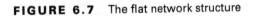

FIGURE 6.7   The flat network structure

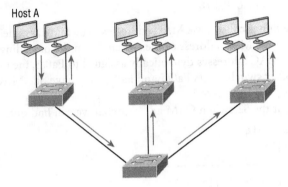

Now check out Figure 6.8. It pictures a switched network and shows Host A sending a frame with Host D as its destination. Clearly, the important factor here is that the frame is only forwarded out the port where Host D is located.

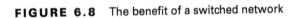

FIGURE 6.8   The benefit of a switched network

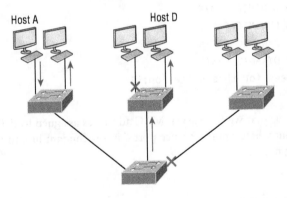

This is a huge improvement over the old hub networks, unless having one *collision domain* by default is what you really want for some reason!

Okay, you already know that the biggest benefit gained by having a layer 2 switched network is that it creates individual collision domain segments for each device plugged into each port on the switch. This scenario frees us from the old Ethernet density constraints and enables us to build larger networks. Too often, however, each new advance comes with new issues. For instance, the more users and devices that populate and use a network, the more broadcasts and packets each switch must handle.

And there's another big issue: security! This one is real trouble because within the typical layer 2 switched internetwork, all users can see all devices by default. And you can't stop devices from broadcasting, plus you can't stop users from trying to respond to broadcasts. This means your security options are dismally limited to placing passwords on your servers and other devices.

But wait—there's hope if you create a *virtual LAN (VLAN)*! You can solve many of the problems associated with layer 2 switching with VLANs, as you'll soon see.

VLANs work like this: Figure 6.9 shows all hosts in a very small company connected to one switch, meaning all hosts will receive all frames, which is the default behavior of all switches.

FIGURE 6.9   One switch, one LAN: Before VLANs, there were no separations between hosts.

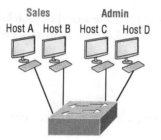

If we want to separate the host's data, we could either buy another switch or create virtual LANs, as shown in Figure 6.10.

In Figure 6.10, I configured the switch to be two separate LANs, two subnets, two broadcast domains, two VLANs—they all mean the same thing—without buying another switch. We can do this 1,000 times on most Cisco switches, which saves thousands of dollars and more!

Notice that even though the separation is virtual and the hosts are all still connected to the same switch, the LANs can't send data to each other by default. This is because they are still separate networks, but no worries—we'll get into inter-VLAN communication later in this chapter.

Here's a short list of ways VLANs simplify network management:

- Network adds, moves, and changes are achieved with ease by just configuring a port into the appropriate VLAN.

- A group of users who need an unusually high level of security can be put into its own VLAN so that users outside of that VLAN can't communicate with the group's users.

- As a logical grouping of users by function, VLANs can be considered independent from their physical or geographic locations.

- VLANs greatly enhance network security if implemented correctly.

- VLANs increase the number of broadcast domains while decreasing their size.

FIGURE 6.10 One switch, two virtual LANs (*logical* separation between hosts): Still physically one switch, but this switch acts as many separate devices.

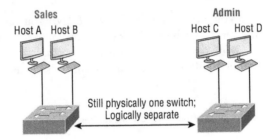

Coming up, we'll thoroughly explore the world of switching, and you learn exactly how and why switches provide us with much better network services than hubs can in our networks today.

Broadcast Control

Broadcasts occur in every protocol, but how often they occur depends on the following three things:

- The type of protocol

- The application(s) running on the internetwork

- How these services are used

Some older applications have been rewritten to reduce their bandwidth consumption, but there's a new generation of applications that are so bandwidth greedy they'll consume any and all they can find. These gluttons are the legion of multimedia applications that use both broadcasts and multicasts extensively. As if they weren't enough trouble, factors like faulty equipment, inadequate segmentation, and poorly designed firewalls can seriously compound the problems already caused by these broadcast-intensive applications. All of this has added a major new dimension to network design and presents a bunch of new challenges for an administrator. Ensuring that your network is properly segmented so that you can quickly isolate a single segment's problems to prevent them from propagating throughout your entire internetwork is now imperative. And the most effective way to do that is through strategic switching and routing!

Since switches have become more affordable, almost everyone has replaced their flat hub networks with pure switched network and VLAN environments. All devices within a VLAN are members of the same broadcast domain and receive all broadcasts relevant to it. By default, these broadcasts are filtered from all ports on a switch that aren't members of the same VLAN. This is great because you get all the benefits you would with a switched design without getting hit with all the problems you'd have if all your users were in the same broadcast domain. Sweet!

Security

But there's always a catch, right? Time to get back to those security issues. A flat internetwork's security used to be tackled by connecting hubs and switches together with routers. So it was basically the router's job to maintain security. This arrangement was pretty ineffective for several reasons. First, anyone connecting to the physical network could access the network resources located on that particular physical LAN. Second, all anyone had to do to observe any and all traffic traversing that network was to simply plug a network analyzer into the hub. And similar to that last, scary, fact, users could easily join a workgroup by just plugging their workstations into the existing hub. That's about as secure as a barrel of honey in a bear enclosure!

But that's exactly what makes VLANs so cool. If you build them and create multiple broadcast groups, you can still have total control over each port and user! So the days when anyone could just plug their workstations into any switch port and gain access to network resources are history because now you get to control each port and any resources it can access.

And that's not even all—VLANs can be created in harmony with a specific user's need for the network resources. Plus, switches can be configured to inform a network management station about unauthorized access to those vital network resources. And if you need inter-VLAN communication, you can implement restrictions on a router to make sure this all happens securely. You can also place restrictions on hardware addresses, protocols, and applications. *Now* we're talking security—our honey barrel is now sealed tightly, made of solid titanium and wrapped in razor wire!

Flexibility and Scalability

If you've been paying attention so far, you know that layer 2 switches only read frames for filtering because they don't look at the Network layer protocol. You also know that by default, switches forward broadcasts to all ports. But if you create and implement VLANs, you're essentially creating smaller broadcast domains at layer 2.

As a result, broadcasts sent out from a node in one VLAN won't be forwarded to ports configured to belong to a different VLAN. But if we assign switch ports or users to VLAN groups on a switch or on a group of connected switches, we gain the flexibility to exclusively add only the users we want to let into that broadcast domain regardless of their physical location. This setup can also work to block broadcast storms caused by a faulty network interface card (NIC) as well as prevent an intermediate device from propagating broadcast storms throughout the entire internetwork. Those evils can still happen on the VLAN where the problem originated, but the disease will be fully contained in that one ailing VLAN!

Another advantage is that when a VLAN gets too big, you can simply create more VLANs to keep the broadcasts from consuming too much bandwidth. The fewer users in a VLAN, the fewer users affected by broadcasts. This is all good, but you seriously need to keep network services in mind and understand how the users connect to these services when creating a VLAN. A good strategy is to try to keep all services, except for the email and Internet access that everyone needs, local to all users whenever possible.

Identifying VLANs

Switch ports are layer 2–only interfaces that are associated with a physical port that can belong to only one VLAN if it's an access port or all VLANs if it's a trunk port.

Switches are definitely pretty busy devices. As myriad frames are switched throughout the network, switches have to be able to keep track of all of them, plus understand what to do with them depending on their associated hardware addresses. And remember—frames are handled differently according to the type of link they're traversing.

There are two different types of ports in a switched environment. Let's take a look at the first type in Figure 6.11.

FIGURE 6.11   Access ports

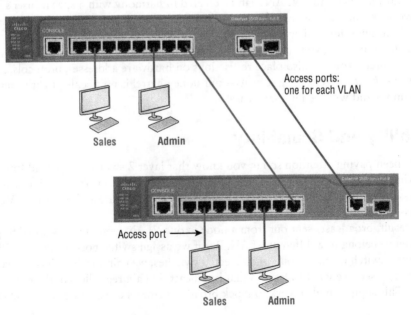

Notice there are access ports for each host and an access port between switches—one for each VLAN.

Access Ports   An *access port* belongs to and carries the traffic of only one VLAN. Traffic is both received and sent in native formats with no VLAN information (tagging) whatsoever. Anything arriving on an access port is simply assumed to belong to the VLAN assigned to the port. Because an access port doesn't look at the source address, tagged traffic—a frame with added VLAN information—can be correctly forwarded and received only on trunk ports.

With an access link, this can be referred to as the *configured VLAN* of the port. Any device attached to an *access link* is unaware of a VLAN membership—the device just assumes it's part of some broadcast domain. But it doesn't have the big picture, so it doesn't understand the physical network topology at all.

Another good bit of information to know is that switches remove any VLAN information from the frame before it"s forwarded out to an access-link device. Remember that access-link devices can't communicate with devices outside their VLAN unless the packet is routed. Also, you can only create a switch port to be either an access port or a trunk port, not both. So you've got to choose one or the other and know that if you make it an access port, that port can be assigned to one VLAN only. In Figure 6.12, only the hosts in the Sales VLAN can talk to other hosts in the same VLAN. This is the same with the Admin VLAN, and they can both communicate to hosts on the other switch because of an access link for each VLAN configured between switches.

Voice Access Ports   Not to confuse you, but all that I just said about the fact that an access port can be assigned to only one VLAN is really only sort of true. Nowadays, most switches will allow you to add a second VLAN to an access port on a switch port for your voice traffic, called the voice VLAN. The voice VLAN used to be called the auxiliary VLAN, which allowed it to be overlaid on top of the data VLAN, enabling both types of traffic to travel through the same port. Even though this is technically considered to be a different type of link, it's still just an access port that can be configured for both data and voice VLANs. This allows you to connect both a phone and a PC device to one switch port but still have each device in a separate VLAN.

Trunk Ports   Believe it or not, the term *trunk port* was inspired by the telephone system trunks, which carry multiple telephone conversations at a time. So it follows that trunk ports can similarly carry multiple VLANs at a time as well.

A *trunk link* is a 100, 1,000, or 10,000 Mbps point-to-point link between two switches, between a switch and router, or even between a switch and server, and it carries the traffic of multiple VLANs—from 1 to 4,094 VLANs at a time. But the amount is really only up to 1,001 unless you're going with something called extended VLANs.

Instead of an access link for each VLAN between switches, we'll create a trunk link, demonstrated in Figure 6.12.

FIGURE 6.12   VLANs can span across multiple switches by using trunk links, which carry traffic for multiple VLANs.

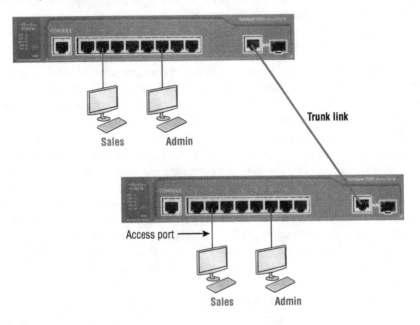

Trunking can be a real advantage because with it, you get to make a single port part of a whole bunch of different VLANs at the same time. This is a great feature because you can actually set up ports to have a server in two separate broadcast domains simultaneously, so your users won't have to cross a layer 3 device (router) to log in and access it. Another benefit to trunking comes into play when you're connecting switches. Trunk links can carry the frames of various VLANs across them, but by default, if the links between your switches aren't trunked, only information from the configured access VLAN will be switched across that link.

Okay, it's finally time to tell you about frame tagging and the VLAN identification methods used in it across our trunk links.

Assigning Switch Ports to VLANs

You configure a port to belong to a VLAN by assigning a membership mode that specifies the kind of traffic the port carries plus the number of VLANs it can belong to. You can also configure each port on a switch to be in a specific VLAN (access port) by using the interface `switchport` command. You can even configure multiple ports at the same time with the `interface range` command.

In the next example, I'll configure interface Fa0/3 to VLAN 3. This is the connection from the S3 switch to the host device:

```
S3#config t
S3(config)#int fa0/3
S3(config-if)#switchport mode ?
access Set trunking mode to ACCESS unconditionally
dot1q-tunnel set trunking mode to TUNNEL unconditionally
dynamic Set trunking mode to dynamically negotiate access or trunk mode
private-vlan Set private-vlan mode
trunk Set trunking mode to TRUNK unconditionally
S3(config-if)#switchport mode access
S3(config-if)#switchport access vlan 3
S3(config-if)#switchport voice vlan 5
```

By starting with the `switchport mode access` command, you're telling the switch that this is a nontrunking layer 2 port. You can then assign a VLAN to the port with the `switchport access` command, as well as configure the same port to be a member of a different type of VLAN, called the voice VLAN.

Let's take a look at our VLANs now:

```
S3#show vlan
VLAN Name Status Ports
---- ------------------------ --------- -------------------------------
1 default active Fa0/4, Fa0/5, Fa0/6, Fa0/7
Fa0/8, Fa0/9, Fa0/10, Fa0/11,
Fa0/12, Fa0/13, Fa0/14, Fa0/19,
Fa0/20, Fa0/21, Fa0/22, Fa0/23,
Gi0/1 ,Gi0/2
2 Sales active
3 Marketing active Fa0/3
5 Voice active Fa0/3
```

Notice that port Fa0/3 is now a member of VLAN 3 and VLAN 5—two different types of VLANs. But, can you tell me where ports 1 and 2 are? And why aren't they showing up in the output of show vlan? That's right, because they are trunk ports!

We can also see this with the show `interfaces interface switchport` command:

```
S3#sh int fa0/3 switchport
Name: Fa0/3
Switchport: Enabled
Administrative Mode: static access
Operational Mode: static access
Administrative Trunking Encapsulation: negotiate
Negotiation of Trunking: Off
```

```
Access Mode VLAN: 3 (Marketing) Trunking Native Mode VLAN: 1 (default)
Administrative Native VLAN tagging: enabled Voice VLAN: 5 (Voice)
```

The output shows that Fa0/3 is an access port and a member of VLAN 3 (Marketing), as well as a member of the Voice VLAN 5.

That's it. Well, sort of. If you plug devices into each VLAN port, they can only talk to other devices in the same VLAN. But as soon as you learn more about trunking, we will enable inter-VLAN communication!

Routing Between VLANs

Hosts in a VLAN live in their own broadcast domain and can communicate freely. VLANs create network partitioning and traffic separation at layer 2 of the OSI, and, as I said when I told you why we still need routers, if you want hosts or any other IP-addressable device to communicate between VLANs, you must have a layer 3 device to provide routing.

For this, you can use a router that has an interface for each VLAN or a router that supports the Cisco Inter-Switch Link (ISL) or the IEEE 802.1Q trunking protocol for routing. ISL and 802.1Q are considered a type of frame tagging. *Frame tagging* refers to VLAN identification; this is what switches use to keep track of all those frames as they're traversing a switch fabric. It's how switches identify which frames belong to which VLANs over trunk links.

Anyway, as shown in Figure 6.13, if you had two or three VLANs, you could get by with a router equipped with two or three FastEthernet connections. And 10Base-T is okay for home study purposes, and I mean only for your studies, but for anything else I'd highly recommend Gigabit interfaces for real power under the hood!

What we see in Figure 6.13 is that each router interface is plugged into an access link. This means that each of the routers' interface IP addresses would then become the default gateway address for each host in each respective VLAN.

FIGURE 6.13   A router connecting three VLANs together for inter-VLAN communication—one router interface for each VLAN

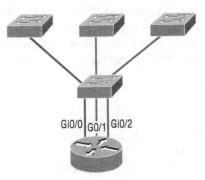

If you have more VLANs available than router interfaces, you can configure trunking on one FastEthernet interface or buy a layer 3 switch, like the old and now cheap 3560 or a higher-end switch like a 3850. You could even opt for a 6800 if you've got money to burn!

Instead of using a router interface for each VLAN, you can use one FastEthernet interface and run ISL or 802.1Q frame tagging on a trunk link. Figure 6.14 shows how a FastEthernet interface on a router will look when configured with ISL or 802.1Q trunking. This allows all VLANs to communicate through one interface. Cisco calls this a router on a stick (ROAS).

FIGURE 6.14   Router on a stick: a single router interface connecting all three VLANs together for inter-VLAN communication

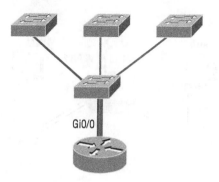

I really want to point out that this creates a potential bottleneck, as well as a single point of failure, so your host/VLAN count is limited. To how many? Well, that depends on your traffic level. To really make things right, you'd be better off using a higher-end switch and routing on the backplane. But if you just happen to have a router sitting around, configuring this method is free, right?

Figure 6.15 shows how we would create a router on a stick using a router's physical interface by creating logical interfaces—one for each VLAN.

FIGURE 6.15   A router creates logical interfaces.

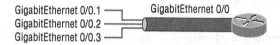

Here we see one physical interface divided into multiple subinterfaces, with one subnet assigned per VLAN, each subinterface being the default gateway address for each VLAN/subnet. An encapsulation identifier must be assigned to each subinterface to define the VLAN ID of that subinterface.

But wait, there's still one more way to go about routing! Instead of using an external router interface for each VLAN, or an external router on a stick, we can configure logical interfaces on the backplane of the layer 3 switch. This is called inter-VLAN routing (IVR), and it's configured with a switched virtual interface (SVI). Figure 6.16 shows how hosts see these virtual interfaces.

In Figure 6.16, it appears there's a router present, but there is no physical router present, as when we used a router on a stick. The IVR process takes little effort and is easy to implement, which makes it very cool! Plus, it's a lot more efficient for inter-VLAN routing than an external router is.

FIGURE 6.16   With IVR, routing runs on the backplane of the switch, and it appears to the hosts that a router is present.

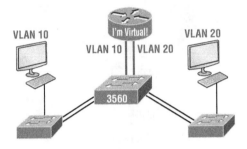

Summary

In this chapter, I talked about the differences between switches and bridges and how they both work at layer 2. They create MAC address forward/filter tables in order to make decisions on whether to forward or flood a frame.

I also covered some problems that can occur if you have multiple links between bridges (switches).

Exam Essentials

Remember the three switch functions.   Address learning, forward/filter decisions, and loop avoidance are the functions of a switch.

Remember the command *show mac address-table*.   The command
`show mac address-table` will show you the forward/filter table used on the LAN switch.

Understand the term *frame tagging*.   *Frame tagging* refers to VLAN identification; this is what switches use to keep track of all those frames as they're traversing a switch fabric. It's how switches identify which frames belong to which VLANs.

Remember to check a switch port's VLAN assignment when plugging in a new host. If you plug a new host into a switch, then you must verify the VLAN membership of that port. If the membership is different from what is needed for that host, the host will not be able to reach the needed network services, such as a workgroup server or printer.

Remember how to create a Cisco router on a stick to provide inter-VLAN communication. You can use a Cisco FastEthernet or Gigabit Ethernet interface to provide inter-VLAN routing. The switch port connected to the router must be a trunk port; then you must create virtual interfaces (subinterfaces) on the router port for each VLAN connecting to it. The hosts in each VLAN will use this subinterface address as their default gateway address.

Review Questions

The following questions are designed to test your understanding of this chapter's material. For more information on how to get additional questions, please see www.lammle.com/ccst.

You can find the answers to these questions in Appendix, "Answers to Review Questions."

1. Which of the following statements regarding VLANs is true?

    A. VLANs greatly reduce network security.

    B. VLANs increase the number of collision domains while decreasing their size.

    C. VLANs decrease the number of broadcast domains while decreasing their size.

    D. Network adds, moves, and changes are achieved with ease by just configuring a port into the appropriate VLAN.

2. Which of the following statements regarding layer 2 switching is *not* true?

    A. Layer 2 switches and bridges are faster than routers because they don't take up time looking at the Data Link layer header information.

    B. Layer 2 switches and bridges look at the frame's hardware addresses before deciding to either forward, flood, or drop the frame.

    C. Switches create private, dedicated collision domains and provide independent bandwidth on each port.

    D. Switches use application-specific integrated circuits (ASICs) to build and maintain their MAC filter tables.

3. Write the command that generated the following output.

```
Vlan Mac Address Type Ports]]>
---- ----------- -------- -----
All 0100.0ccc.cccc STATIC CPU
[output cut]
1 000e.83b2.e34b DYNAMIC Fa0/1
1 0011.1191.556f DYNAMIC Fa0/1
1 0011.3206.25cb DYNAMIC Fa0/1
1 001a.2f55.c9e8 DYNAMIC Fa0/1
1 001a.4d55.2f7e DYNAMIC Fa0/1
1 001c.575e.c891 DYNAMIC Fa0/1
1 b414.89d9.1886 DYNAMIC Fa0/5
1 b414.89d9.1887 DYNAMIC Fa0/6
```

4. Which of the following is *not* an issue addressed by STP?

    A. Broadcast storms

    B. Gateway redundancy

    C. A device receiving multiple copies of the same frame

    D. Constant updating of the MAC filter table

5. Write the command that must be present on any switch that you need to manage from a different subnet.

6. _____ is the loop avoidance mechanism used by switches.

7. What is the purpose of frame tagging in virtual LAN (VLAN) configurations?

    A. Inter-VLAN routing

    B. Encryption of network packets

    C. Frame identification over trunk links

    D. Frame identification over access links

8. On which default interface do you configure an IP address for a switch?

    A. int fa0/0

    B. int vty 0 15

    C. int vlan 1

    D. int s/0/0

9. Which command will show you the VLAN port assignments?

    A. `show port-assignments`

    B. `show vlan`

    C. `show vlan-ports`

    D. `show database`

10. Which of the following are the basic layer 2 switch functions? (Choose three.)

    A. Address learning

    B. Forward/filter decision

    C. IP management

    D. Loop avoidance

Chapter

7

Cables and Connectors

THE CCST EXAM TOPICS COVERED IN THIS CHAPTER INCLUDE THE FOLLOWING:

✓ **1.0 Standards and Concepts**

- 1.3. Differentiate between LAN, WAN, MAN, CAN, PAN, and WLAN.
  - Identify and illustrate common physical and logical network topologies.

✓ **3.0 Endpoints and Media Types**

- 3.1. Identity cables and connectors commonly used in local area networks.
  - Cable types: fiber, copper, twisted pair; Connector types: coax, RJ-45, RJ-11, fiber connector types

You'd have to work pretty hard these days to find someone who would argue when we say that our computers have become invaluable to us personally and professionally. Our society has become highly dependent on the resources they offer and on sharing them with each other. The ability to communicate with others—whether they're in the same building or in some faraway land—completely hinges on our capacity to create and maintain solid, dependable networks.

And those vitally important networks come in all shapes and sizes, from small and simple to humongous and super complicated. But whatever their flavor, they all need to be maintained properly, and to do that well, you have to understand networking basics. The various types of devices and technologies that are used to create networks, as well as how they work together, is what this book is about, and I'll go through this critical information one step at a time with you.

Understanding all this will not only equip you with a rock-solid base to build on as you gain IT knowledge and grow in your career, it will also arm you with what you'll need to ace the CCST certification exam!

To find up-to-the-minute updates for this chapter, please see www.lammle.com/ccst.

The Basic Network Topologies

The dictionary defines the word *network* as "a group or system of interconnected people or things." Similarly, in the computer world, the term *network* means two or more connected computers that can share resources such as data and applications, office machines, an Internet connection, or some combination of these, as shown in Figure 7.1.

FIGURE 7.1 A basic network

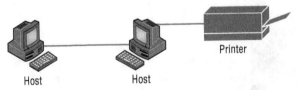

Host   Host   Printer

Figure 7.1 shows a really basic network made up of only two host computers connected; they share resources such as files and even a printer hooked up to one of the hosts. These two hosts "talk" to each other using a computer language called *binary code*, which consists of a lot of 1s and 0s in a specific order that describes exactly what they want to "say."

Next, I'm going to tell you about local area networks, how they work, and even how we can connect LANs together. Then, later in this chapter, I'll describe how to connect remote LANs together through something known as a wide area network (WAN).

Local Area Networks

Just as the name implies, a *local area network (LAN)* is usually restricted to spanning a particular geographic location such as an office building, a single department within a corporate office, or even a home office.

Back in the day, you couldn't put more than 30 workstations on a LAN, and you had to cope with strict limitations on how far those machines could actually be from each other. Because of technological advances, all that's changed now, and we're not nearly as restricted in regard to both a LAN's size and the distance a LAN can span. Even so, it's still best to split a big LAN into smaller logical zones known as *workgroups* to make administration easier.

The meaning of the term *workgroup* in this context is slightly different from when the term is used in contrast to domains. In that context, a workgroup is a set of devices with no security association with one another (whereas in a domain they do have that association). In this context, we simply mean they physically are in the same network segment.

In a typical business environment, it's a good idea to arrange your LAN's workgroups along department divisions; for instance, you would create a workgroup for Accounting, another for Sales, and maybe another for Marketing—you get the idea. Figure 7.2 shows two separate LANs, each as its own workgroup.

FIGURE 7.2　Two separate LANs (workgroups)

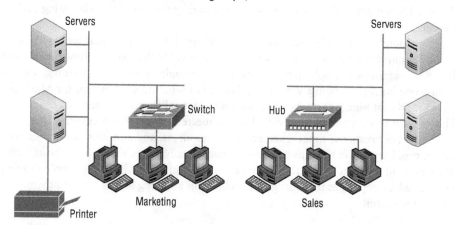

Don't stress about the devices labeled *hub* and *switch*—these are just connectivity devices that allow hosts to physically connect to resources on a LAN.

Anyway, back to Figure 7.2. Notice that there's a Marketing workgroup and a Sales workgroup. These are LANs in their most basic form. Any device that connects to the Marketing LAN can access the resources of the Marketing LAN—in this case, the servers and printer.

There are two problems with this:

- You must be physically connected to a workgroup's LAN to get the resources from it.
- You can't get from one LAN to the other LAN and use its server data and printing resources remotely.

This is a typical network issue that's easily resolved by using a cool device called a *router* to connect the two LANs, as shown in Figure 7.3.

FIGURE 7.3   A router connects LANs.

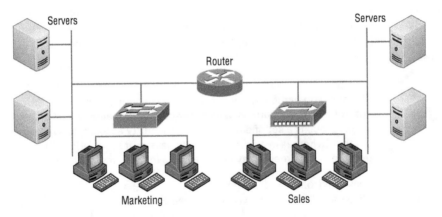

Nice—problem solved! Even though you can use routers for more than just connecting LANs, the router shown in Figure 7.3 is a great solution because the host computers from the Sales LAN can get to the resources (server data and printers) of the Marketing LAN, and vice versa.

Now, you might be thinking that we really don't need the router—that we could just physically connect the two workgroups with a type of cable that would allow the Marketing and Sales workgroups to hook up somehow. Well, we could do that, but if we did, we would have only one big, cumbersome workgroup instead of separate workgroups for Marketing and Sales, and that kind of arrangement just isn't practical for today's networks.

This is because with smaller, individual-yet-connected groups, the users on each LAN enjoy much faster response times when accessing resources, and administrative tasks are a lot easier, too. Larger workgroups run more slowly because there's a legion of hosts within them that are all trying to get to the same resources simultaneously. So the router shown in Figure 7.3, which separates the workgroups while still allowing access between them, is a really great solution!

Wide Area Networks

There are legions of people who, if asked to define a *wide area network (WAN)*, just couldn't do it. Yet most of them use the big dog of all WANs—the Internet—every day! With that in mind, you can imagine that WAN networks are what we use to span large geographic areas and truly go the distance. Like the Internet, WANs usually employ both routers and public links, so that's generally the criteria used to define them.

Here's a list of some of the important ways that WANs are different from LANs:

- WANs usually need a router port or ports.

- WANs span larger geographic areas and/or can link disparate locations.

- WANs are usually slower.

- We can choose when and how long we connect to a WAN. A LAN is all or nothing—our workstation is connected to it either permanently or not at all, although most of us have dedicated WAN links now.

- WANs can utilize either private or public data transport media such as phone lines.

We get the word *Internet* from the term *internetwork*. An internetwork is a type of LAN and/or WAN that connects a bunch of networks, or *intranets*. In an internetwork, hosts still use hardware addresses to communicate with other hosts on the LAN. However, they use logical addresses (IP addresses) to communicate with hosts on a different LAN (other side of the router).

And *routers* are the devices that make this possible. Each connection into a router is a different logical network. Figure 7.4 demonstrates how routers are employed to create an internetwork and how they enable our LANs to access WAN resources.

FIGURE 7.4   An internetwork

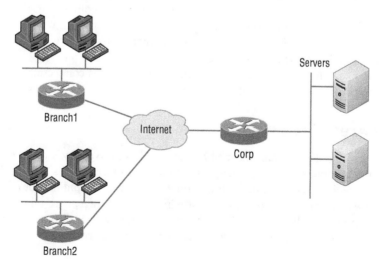

The Internet is a prime example of what's known as a *distributed* WAN—an internetwork that's made up of a lot of interconnected computers located in a lot of different places. There's another kind of WAN, referred to as *centralized*, that's composed of a main, centrally located computer or location that remote computers and devices can connect to. A good example is remote office branches that connect to a main corporate office, as shown in Figure 7.4.

Metropolitan Area Networks

A metropolitan area network (MAN) is just as it sounds: a network covering a metropolitan area used to interconnect various buildings and facilities usually over a carrier provided network. Think of a MAN as a concentrated WAN and you've got it. MANs typically offer high-speed interconnections using in-ground fiber optics and can be very cost effective for high-speed interconnects.

Campus Area Networks

A campus area network (CAN) covers a limited geographical network such as a college or corporate campus. A CAN typically interconnects LANs in various buildings and offers a Wi-Fi component for roaming users.

A CAN is between a LAN and WAN in scope. It is larger than a LAN but smaller than a MAN or WAN.

Most CANs offer Internet connectivity as well as access to data center resources.

Personal Area Networks

For close proximity connections, there are personal area networks (PANs). These are seen with smartphones and laptops in a conference room where local connections are used for collaboration and sending data between devices. While a PAN can use a wired connection such as Ethernet, firewire, or USB, it is more common that short-distance wireless connections are used using Bluetooth, infrared or Zigbee.

PANs are intended for close proximity between devices, such as connecting to a projector, printer, or a coworker's computer, and are extended usually only a few meters.

Storage Area Networks

Storage area networks (SANs) are designed for, and used exclusively by, storage systems. SANs interconnect servers to storage arrays containing centralized banks of hard drive or similar storage media. SANs are usually found only in data centers and do not mix traffic with other LANs. The protocols are designed specifically for storage, with Fibre Channel being the most prevalent along with iSCSI. The network hardware is different from LAN switches and routers, and is designed specifically to carry storage traffic.

Physical Network Topologies

Just as a topographical map is a type of map that shows the shape of the terrain, the *physical topology* of a network is also a type of map. It defines the specific characteristics of a network, such as where all the workstations and other devices are located and the precise arrangement of all the physical media such as cables. Logical topologies, however, delineate exactly how data moves through the network. Now, even though these two topologies are usually a lot alike, a particular network can actually have physical and logical topologies that are very different. Basically, what you want to remember is that a network's physical topology gives you the lay of the land, and the logical topology shows how a digital signal or data navigates through that layout.

Here's a list of the topologies you're most likely to run into these days:

- Bus
- Star/hub-and-spoke
- Ring
- Mesh
- Point-to-point
- Point-to-multipoint
- Hybrid

Bus Topology

This type of topology is the most basic one of the bunch, and it really does sort of resemble a bus, but more like one that's been in a wreck! Anyway, the *bus topology* consists of two distinct and terminated ends, with each of its computers connecting to one unbroken cable running its entire length. Back in the day, we used to attach computers to that main cable with wire taps, but this didn't work all that well, so we began using drop cables in their place. If we were dealing with 10Base2 Ethernet, we would slip a "T" into the main cable anywhere we wanted to connect a device to it instead of using drop cables.

Figure 7.5 depicts what a typical bus network's physical topology looks like.

Even though all the computers on this kind of network see all the data flowing through the cable, only the one computer, which the data is specifically addressed to, actually *gets* the data. Some of the benefits of using a bus topology are that it's easy to install and not very expensive, partly because it doesn't require as much cable as the other types of physical topologies. But it also has some drawbacks: For instance, it's hard to troubleshoot, change, or move, and it really doesn't offer much in the way of fault tolerance because everything is connected to that single cable. This means that any fault in the cable would basically bring down the whole network!

FIGURE 7.5 A typical bus network's physical topology

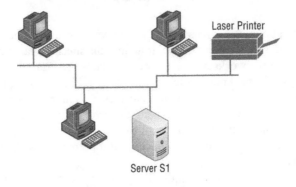

Laser Printer

Server S1

 By the way, *fault tolerance* is the capability of a computer or a network system to respond to a condition automatically, often resolving it, which reduces the impact on the system. If fault-tolerance measures have been implemented correctly on a network, it's highly unlikely that any of that network's users will know that a problem ever existed at all.

Star Topology

A star (*hub-and-spoke*) topology's computers are connected to a central point with their own individual cables or wireless connections. You'll often find that central spot inhabited by a device like a hub, a switch, or an access point.

Star topology offers a lot of advantages over bus topology, making it more widely used even though it obviously requires more physical media. One of its best features is that because each computer or network segment is connected to the central device individually, if the cable fails, it only brings down the machine or network segment related to the point of failure. This makes the network much more fault tolerant as well as a lot easier to troubleshoot. Another great thing about a star topology is that it's a lot more scalable—all you have to do if you want to add to it is run a new cable and connect to the machine at the core of the star. In Figure 7.6, you'll find a great example of a typical star topology.

Although it is called a *star* (hub-and-spoke) topology, it also looks a lot like a bike wheel, with spokes connecting to the hub in the middle of the wheel and extending outward to connect to the rim. And just as with that bike wheel, it's the hub device at the center of a star topology network that can give you the most grief if something goes wrong with it. If that central hub happens to fail, down comes the whole network, so it's a very good thing hubs don't fail often!

Just as it is with pretty much everything, a star topology has its pros and cons. But the good news far outweighs the bad, which is why people often opt for a star topology. Here's a list of benefits you gain by going with it:

- New stations can be added or moved easily and quickly.

- A single cable failure won't bring down the entire network.

- It's relatively easy to troubleshoot.

FIGURE 7.6   Typical star topology with a hub

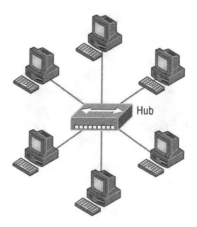

Hub

And here are the disadvantages to using a star topology:

- The total installation cost can be higher because of the larger number of cables, even though prices are becoming more competitive.

- It has a single point of failure—the hub or other central device.

There are two more sophisticated implementations of a star topology. The first is called a *point-to-point link*, where you have not only the device in the center of the spoke acting as a hub but also the device on the other end, which extends the network. This is still a star-wired topology, but as I'm sure you can imagine, it gives you a lot more scalability!

Another refined version is the wireless version, but to understand this variety well, you've got to have a solid grasp of all the capabilities and features of any devices populating the wireless star topology.

For now, it's good enough for you to know that access points are pretty much just wireless hubs or switches that behave like their wired counterparts. Basically, they create a point-by-point connection to endpoints and other wireless access points.

Ring Topology

In this type of topology, each computer is directly connected to other computers within the same network. Looking at Figure 7.7, you can see that the network's data flows from computer to computer back to the source, with the network's primary cable forming a ring. The problem is, the *ring topology* has a lot in common with the bus topology because if you want to add to the network, you have no choice but to break the cable ring, which is likely to bring down the entire network!

This is one big reason that ring topology isn't very popular—you just won't run into it a lot, as I did in the 1980s and early 1990s. It's also pricey because you need several cables to connect each computer, it's really hard to reconfigure, and, as you've probably guessed, it's not fault tolerant.

FIGURE 7.7 A typical ring topology

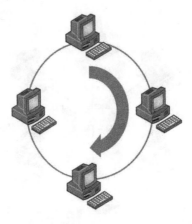

But even with all that being said, if you work at an ISP, you may still find a physical ring topology in use for a technology called SONET or some other WAN technology. However, you just won't find any LANs in physical rings anymore.

Mesh Topology

In this type of topology, you'll find that there's a path from every machine to every other one in the network. That's a lot of connections—in fact, the *mesh topology* wins the prize for the most physical connections per device! You won't find it used in LANs very often, if ever, these days, but you will find a modified version of it known as a *hybrid mesh* used in a restrained manner on WANs, including the Internet.

Often, hybrid mesh topology networks will have quite a few connections between certain places to create redundancy (backup). Other types of topologies can sometimes be found in the mix too, which is another reason it's dubbed *hybrid*. Just remember that it isn't a full-on mesh topology if there isn't a connection between all devices in the network. And understand that it's fairly complicated. Figure 7.8 gives you a great picture of just how much only four connections can complicate things!

FIGURE 7.8 A typical mesh topology

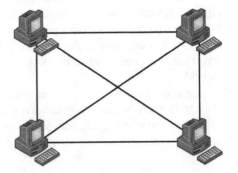

You can clearly see that everything gets more and more complex as both the wiring and the connections multiply. For each *n* locations or hosts, you end up with *n*(*n*–1)/2 connections. This means that in a network consisting of only four computers, you have 4(4–1)/2, or 6 connections. And if that little network grows to, say, a population of 10 computers, you'll then have a whopping 45 connections to cope with! That's a huge amount of overhead, so only small networks can really use this topology and manage it well. On the bright side, you get a really nice level of fault tolerance, but mesh still isn't used in corporate LANs anymore because it is so complicated to manage.

A full mesh physical topology is least likely to have a collision, which happens when the data from two hosts trying to communicate simultaneously "collides" and gets lost.

This is also the reason you'll usually find the hybrid version in today's WANs. In fact, the mesh topology is actually pretty rare now, but it's still used because of the robust fault tolerance it offers. Because you have a multitude of connections, if one goes on the blink, computers and other network devices can simply switch to one of the many redundant connections that are up and running. Clearly, all that cabling in the mesh topology makes it a very pricey implementation. Plus, you can make your network management much less insane than it is with mesh by using what's known as a *partial mesh topology* solution instead, so why not go that way? You may lose a little fault tolerance, but if you go the partial mesh route, you still get to use the same technology between all the network's devices. Just remember that with partial mesh, not all devices will be interconnected, so it's very important to choose the ones that will be very wisely.

Point-to-Point Topology

As its name implies, in a *point-to-point* topology you have a direct connection between two routers or switches, giving you one communication path. The routers in a point-to-point topology can be linked by a serial cable, making it a physical network, or if they're located far apart and connected only via a circuit within a Frame Relay or MPLS network, it's a logical network instead.

Figure 7.9 illustrates three examples of a typical T1, or WAN, point-to-point connection.

What you see here is a lightning bolt and a couple of round things with a bunch of arrows projecting from them, right? Well, the two round things radiating arrows represent our network's two routers, and that lightning bolt represents a WAN link. (A T1 is an old example, but they are still out there! We just don't see serial links all that much anymore since broadband is so prevalent.) These symbols are industry standard, and I'll be using them throughout this book, so it's a good idea to get used to them!

Okay, so part two of the diagram shows two computers connected by a cable—a point-to-point link. By the way, this should remind you of something we just went over. Remember peer-to-peer networks? Good! I hope you also remember that a big drawback to peer-to-peer network sharing is that it's not very scalable. You probably won't be all that surprised that even if both machines have a wireless point-to-point connection, this network still won't be very scalable.

FIGURE 7.9   Three point-to-point connections

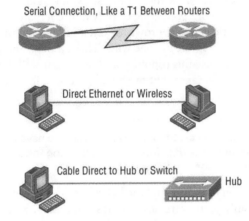

You'll usually find point-to-point networks within many of today's WANs, and, as shown in part three of Figure 7.9, a link from a computer to a hub or switch is also a valid point-to-point connection. A common version of this setup consists of a direct wireless link between two wireless bridges that's used to connect computers in two different buildings.

Point-to-Multipoint Topology

Again, as the name suggests, a *point-to-multipoint* topology consists of a succession of connections between an interface on one router and multiple destination routers—one point of connection to multiple points of connection. Each of the routers and every one of their interfaces involved in the point-to-multipoint connection are part of the same network.

Figure 7.10 shows a WAN and demonstrates a point-to-multipoint network. You can clearly see a single, corporate router connecting to multiple branches.

FIGURE 7.10   A point-to-multipoint network, example 1

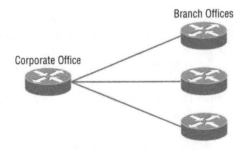

Figure 7.11 shows another prime example of a point-to-multipoint network: a college or corporate campus.

FIGURE 7.11   A point-to-multipoint network, example 2

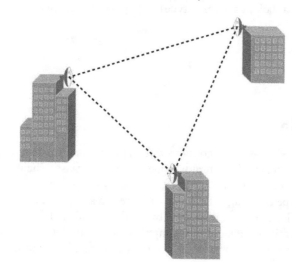

Hybrid Topology

I know I just talked about the hybrid network topology in the section about mesh topology, but I didn't give you a mental picture of it in the form of a figure. I also want to point out that *hybrid topology* means just that—a combination of two or more types of physical or logical network topologies working together within the same network.

Figure 7.12 depicts a simple hybrid network topology; it shows a LAN switch or hub in a star topology configuration that connects to its hosts via a bus topology.

FIGURE 7.12   A simple hybrid network

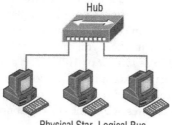

Hub

Physical Star, Logical Bus

Physical Media

A lot of us rely on wireless networking methods that work using technologies like radio frequency and infrared, but even wireless depends on a physical media backbone in place somewhere. And the majority of installed LANs today communicate via some kind of cabling, so let's take a look at the three types of popular cables used in modern networking designs:

- Coaxial
- Twisted-pair
- Fiber optic

Coaxial Cable

Coaxial cable, referred to as *coax*, contains a center conductor made of copper that's surrounded by a plastic jacket with a braided shield over it. A plastic such as polyvinyl chloride (PVC) or fluoroethylenepropylene (FEP, commonly known as Teflon) covers this metal shield. The Teflon-type covering is frequently referred to as a *plenum-rated coating*, and it's definitely expensive but often mandated by local or municipal fire code when cable is hidden in walls and ceilings. Plenum rating applies to all types of cabling and is an approved replacement for all other compositions of cable sheathing and insulation like PVC-based assemblies.

The difference between plenum and non-plenum cable comes down to how each is constructed and where you can use it. Many large multistory buildings are designed to circulate air through the spaces between the ceiling of one story and the floor of the next; this space between floors is referred to as the *plenum*. And it just happens to be a perfect spot to run all the cables that connect the legions of computers that live in the building. Unless there's a fire—if that happens, the non-plenum cable becomes a serious hazard because its insulation gives off poisonous smoke that gets circulated throughout the whole building. Plus, non-plenum cables can actually become "wicks" for the fire, helping it quickly spread from room to room and floor to floor—yikes!

Because it's a great goal to prevent towering infernos, the National Fire Protection Association (NFPA) demands that cables run within the plenum have been tested and guaranteed as safe. They must be fire retardant and create little or no smoke and poisonous gas when burned. This means you absolutely can't use a non-plenum-type cable in the plenum, but it doesn't mean you can't use it in other places where it's safe. And because it's a lot cheaper, you definitely want to use it where you can.

Thin Ethernet, also referred to as *thinnet* or 10Base2, is a thin coaxial cable. It is basically the same as thick coaxial cable except it's only about 5 mm, or 2/10", diameter coaxial cable. Thin Ethernet coaxial cable is Radio Grade 58, or just RG-58. Figure 7.13 shows an example of thinnet. This connector resembles the coaxial connector used for cable TV, which is called an *F-type connector*.

Oh, by the way, if you use thinnet cable, you've got to use *BNC* connectors to attach stations to the network, as shown in Figure 7.14, and you have to use 50-ohm terminating resistors at each end of the cable in order to achieve the proper performance. Today, this is mostly used for closed-circuit television (CCTV), which is a TV system where signals are transmitted and monitored primarily for video surveillance and security use cases.

You can attach a BNC connector to the cable with a crimper, which looks like a weird pair of pliers and has a die to crimp the connector. A simple squeeze crimps the connector to the cable. You can also use a screw-on connector, but I avoid doing that because it's not very reliable.

FIGURE 7.13   A stripped-back thinnet cable

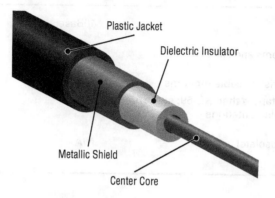

Plastic Jacket

Dielectric Insulator

Metallic Shield

Center Core

FIGURE 7.14   Male and female BNC connectors

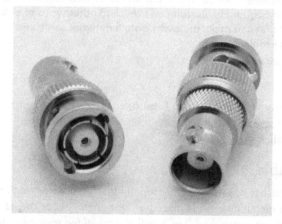

You can use a BNC coupler to connect two male connectors together or two female connectors together.

Table 7.1 lists some specifications for the different types of coaxial cable.

TABLE 7.1   Coaxial cable specifications

RG Rating	Popular Name	Ethernet Implementation	Type of Cable
RG-58 U	N/A	None	Solid copper
RG-58 A/U	Thinnet	10Base2	Stranded copper

TABLE 7.1   Coaxial cable specifications *(continued)*

RG Rating	Popular Name	Ethernet Implementation	Type of Cable
RG-8	Thicknet	10Base5	Solid copper
RG-59	CCTV systems and HD over coax	N/A	Solid copper
RG-6	Cable television, cable modems Longer distances than RG-59; some power implementations	N/A	Solid copper
RG-62	ARCnet (obsolete)	N/A	Solid/ stranded

An advantage of using coax cable is the braided shielding that provides resistance to electronic pollution like *electromagnetic interference (EMI)*, *radio frequency interference (RFI)*, and other types of stray electronic signals that can make their way onto a network cable and cause communication problems.

F-type

The F connector, or F-type connector, is a form of coaxial connector that is used for cable TV. It has an end that screws to tighten the connector to the interface. It resembles the RG-58 mentioned earlier in this section.

Twisted-Pair Cable

Twisted-pair cable consists of multiple individually insulated wires that are twisted together in pairs. Sometimes a metallic shield is placed around them, hence the name *shielded twisted-pair (STP)*. Cable without outer shielding is called *unshielded twisted-pair (UTP)*, and it's used in twisted-pair Ethernet (10BaseT, 100BaseTX, 1000BaseTX) networks.

Ethernet Cable Descriptions

Ethernet cable types are described using a code that follows this format: N *<Signaling>* X. The N refers to the signaling rate in megabits per second; *<Signaling>* refers to the signaling type (either baseband or broadband); and the X is a unique identifier for a specific Ethernet cabling scheme.

Here's a common example: 100BaseX. The 100 tells us that the transmission speed is 100 Mb, or 100 megabits. The X value can mean several different things; for example, a T is short for *twisted-pair*. This is the standard for running 100-megabit Ethernet over two pairs (four wires) of Category 5, 5e, or 6 UTP.

So why are the wires in this cable type twisted? Because when electromagnetic signals are conducted on copper wires in close proximity—like inside a cable—it causes interference called *crosstalk*. Twisting two wires together as a pair minimizes interference and even protects against interference from outside sources. This cable type is the most common today for the following reasons:

- It's cheaper than other types of cabling.
- It's easy to work with.
- It allows transmission rates that were impossible 10 years ago.

UTP cable is rated in the following categories:

Category 1   Category 1 cable consists of two twisted wire pairs (four wires). It's the oldest type and is only voice grade—it isn't rated for data communication. People refer to it as plain old telephone service (POTS). Before 1983, this was the standard cable used throughout the North American telephone system. POTS cable still exists in parts of the public switched telephone network (PSTN) and supports signals limited to the 1 MHz frequency range.

Category is often shortened to *Cat*. Today, any cable installed should be a minimum of Cat 5e because some cable is now certified to carry bandwidth signals of 350 MHz or beyond (The MHz is a certification in which the cable is tested at a specific frequency.) This allows unshielded twisted-pair cables to exceed speeds of 1 Gbps—fast enough to carry broadcast-quality video over a network.

Category 2   Cat 2 cable consists of four twisted wire pairs (eight wires). It handles up to 4 Mbps, with a frequency limitation of 10 MHz, and is now obsolete.

Category 3   Cat 3 cable comprises four twisted wire pairs (eight wires), with three twists per foot. This type can handle transmissions up to 16 MHz. It was popular in the mid-1980s for up to 10 Mbps Ethernet, but it's now limited to telecommunication equipment and, again, is obsolete for networks.

Category 4   Cat 4 cable consists of four twisted wire pairs (eight wires), is rated for 20 MHz, and is also obsolete.

Category 5   Cat 4 cable comprises four twisted wire pairs (eight wires), is used for 100BaseTX (two pair wiring), and is rated for 100 MHz. But why use Cat 5 when you can use Cat 5e for the same price? I am not sure you can even buy plain Cat 5 anymore!

Category 5e (Enhanced)   Cat 5e cable consists of four twisted wire pairs (eight wires), is recommended for 1000BaseT (four pair wiring), and is rated for 100 MHz, although it is capable of handling the disturbance on each pair that's caused by transmitting on all four pairs at the same time—a feature that's needed for Gigabit Ethernet. Any category below 5e shouldn't be used in today's network environments.

Figure 7.15 shows a basic Cat 5e cable with the four wire pairs twisted to reduce crosstalk.

FIGURE 7.15   Cat 5e UTP cable

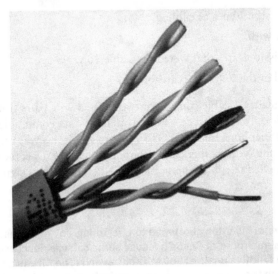

Category 6   Cat 6 cable consists of four twisted wire pairs (eight wires), is used for 1000BaseTX (two pair wiring), and is rated for 250 MHz. Cat 6 became a standard in June 2002. You would usually use it as riser cable to connect floors together. If you're installing a new network in a new building, there's no reason to use anything but Category 6 UTP cabling and to run fiber between floors.

Category 6A (Augmented)   Basic Category 6 cable has a reduced maximum length when used for 10GBaseT; however, Category 6A cable, or Augmented Category 6, is characterized to 500 MHz and has improved crosstalk characteristics, which allows 10GBaseT to be run for up to 100 meters. The most important point is a performance difference between Electronic Industries Alliance and Telecommunications Industry Association (EIA/TIA) component specifications for the NEXT (near-end crosstalk) transmission parameter. Running at a frequency of 500 MHz, an ISO/IEC Cat 6A connector provides double the power (3dB) of a Cat 6A connector that conforms with the EIA/TIA specification. Note that 3 dB equals a 100 percent increase of a near-end crosstalk noise reduction. This is our future cable indeed!

Category 7   Cat 7 cable allows 10 Gigabit Ethernet over 100 m of copper cabling. The cable contains four twisted copper wire pairs, just like the earlier standards.

Category 8   Cat 8 cable was developed to address the ever-increasing speed of Ethernet and added support for 25G and 40G transmission with a distance of 30 meters, which is perfect for data center deployments.

Connecting UTP

BNC connectors won't fit very well on UTP cable, so you need to use a *registered jack (RJ)* connector, which you're familiar with because most telephones connect with them. The connector used with UTP cable is called RJ-11 for phones that use four wires; RJ-45 has four pairs (eight wires), as shown in Figure 7.16.

FIGURE 7.16   RJ-11 and RJ-45 connectors

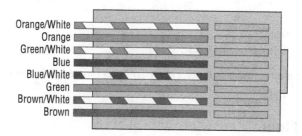

Figure 7.17 shows the pinouts used in a typical RJ-45 connector. Looking from the bottom of the connector, pin 1 would be on the left.

FIGURE 7.17   The pinouts in an RJ-45 connector, T568B standard

Orange/White
Orange
Green/White
Blue
Blue/White
Green
Brown/White
Brown

Most of the time, UTP uses RJ connectors, and you use a crimper to attach them to a cable, just as you would with BNC connectors. The only difference is that the die that holds the connector is a different shape. Higher-quality crimping tools have interchangeable dies for both types of cables. We don't use RJ-11 for local area networks (LANs), but we do use them for our home digital subscriber line (DSL) connections.

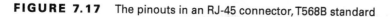

NOTE   RJ-11 uses two wire pairs, and RJ-45 uses four wire pairs.

There's one other type of copper connector, called the RJ-48c, which looks exactly like an RJ-45 connector. This plug is very similar to the RJ-45 in that it has four wire pairs, but they are wired differently and used for different circumstances.

RJ-45 is mainly used in LANs with short distances (typically up to 100 meters), whereas the RJ-48c wiring type would be used with a T1 connection, which is a long-distance wide area network (WAN). In addition, to protect the signal in an RJ-48c, the wires are typically shielded, whereas the RJ-45 uses unshielded wiring.

Fiber-Optic Cable

Because fiber-optic cable transmits digital signals using light impulses rather than electricity, it's immune to EMI and RFI. Anyone who's seen a network's UTP cable run down an elevator shaft would definitely appreciate this fiber feature. Fiber cable allows light impulses to be carried on either a glass or a plastic core. Glass can carry the signal a greater distance, but plastic costs less. Whichever the type of core, it's surrounded by a glass or plastic cladding with a different refraction index that reflects the light back into the core. Around this is a layer of flexible plastic buffer that can be wrapped in an armor coating that's usually Kevlar, which is then sheathed in PVC or plenum.

The cable itself comes in either single-mode fiber (SMF) or multimode fiber (MMF); the difference between them is in the number of light rays (the number of signals) they can carry. Multimode fiber is most often used for shorter-distance applications and single-mode fiber for spanning longer distances.

Although fiber-optic cable may sound like the solution to many problems, it has its pros and cons, just like the other cable types.

Here are the pros:

- It's completely immune to EMI and RFI.
- It can transmit up to 40 kilometers (about 25 miles).

And here are the cons:

- It's difficult to install.
- It's more expensive than twisted-pair.
- Troubleshooting equipment is more expensive than twisted-pair test equipment.
- It's harder to troubleshoot.

Single-Mode Fiber

Single-mode fiber-optic cable (SMF) is a very high-speed, long-distance media that consists of a single strand—sometimes two strands—of glass fiber that carries the signals. Light-emitting diodes (LEDs) and laser are the light sources used with SMF. The light source is transmitted from end to end and pulsed to create communication. This is the type of fiber cable employed to span really long distances because it can transmit data 50 times farther than multimode fiber at a faster rate.

Clearly, because the transmission media is glass, the installation of SMF can be a bit tricky. Yes, there are outer layers protecting the glass core, but the cable still shouldn't be crimped or pinched around any tight corners.

Multimode Fiber

Multimode fiber-optic cable (MMF) also uses light to communicate a signal, but with it, the light is dispersed on numerous paths as it travels through the core and is reflected back. A special material called *cladding* is used to line the core and focus the light back onto it. MMF provides high bandwidth at high speeds over medium distances (up to about 3,000 feet), but beyond that it can be really inconsistent. This is why MMF is most often used within a smaller area of one building; SMF can be used between buildings.

MMF is available in glass or in a plastic version that makes installation a lot easier and increases the installation's flexibility.

Fiber-Optic Connectors

A whole bunch of different types of connectors are available to use with fiber-optic cables, but the two most popular are the *straight tip (ST)* and the *subscriber (or square) connector (SC)*. The ST fiber-optic connector (developed by AT&T) is one of the most widely used fiber-optic connectors; it uses a BNC attachment mechanism similar to RG-59 that makes connections and disconnections fairly frustration-free. In fact, this is the feature that makes this connector so popular. Figure 7.18 shows an example of an ST connector. Notice the BNC attachment mechanism.

FIGURE 7.18   An example of an ST connector

The SC connector is another type of fiber-optic connector. As you can see in Figure 7.19, SC connectors are *latched*—a mechanism holds the connector in securely and prevents it from falling out.

FIGURE 7.19   A sample SC connector

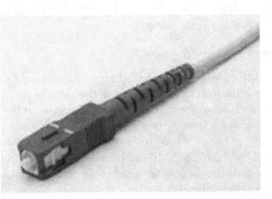

SC connectors work with both single-mode and multimode optical fibers and will last for around 1,000 matings. They're being used more now but still aren't nearly as popular as ST connectors for LAN connections.

Another type of connector I want to mention is the FC connector, or field assembly connector, also called the ferrule connector, which isn't very popular. It's still used in telecommunications and measurement equipment with single-mode lasers, but the SC is a way more popular fiber end. The only reason I mention it here is that it is an exam objective; other than that, you probably won't ever see it in production. FC connectors look identical to ST connectors.

You can also get a fiber coupler in order to connect an ST to an SC connector, for example, but you will lose a lot of your power (dB) if you do so.

Fiber Distribution Panel

Fiber distribution panels (FDP) are termination and distribution systems for fiber-optic cable facilities. This consists of a cable management tray and a splice drawer. FDPs are designed for central offices, remote offices, and LANs using fiber-optic facilities.

Small Form Factor Fiber-Optic Connectors

Another cool fiber-optic connector is the *small form factor (SFF)* connector, which allows more fiber-optic terminations in the same amount of space than its standard-sized counterparts. The two most popular versions are the *mechanical transfer registered jack (MT-RJ or MTRJ)*, designed by AMP, and the *local connector (LC)*, designed by Lucent.

The MT-RJ fiber-optic connector was the first small form factor fiber-optic connector to be widely used, and it's only one-third the size of the SC and ST connectors it most often replaces. It offers the following benefits:

- Small size
- TX and RX strands in one connector
- Keyed for single polarity

- Pre-terminated ends that require no polishing or epoxy
- Easy to use

Figure 7.20 shows an example of an MT-RJ fiber-optic connector.

FIGURE 7.20 An MT-RJ fiber-optic connector

LC is a newer style of SFF fiber-optic connector that's pulling ahead of the MT-RJ. It's especially popular for use with Fibre-Channel adapters (FCs) and is a standard used for fast storage area networks and Gigabit Ethernet adapters. Figure 7.21 depicts an example of the LC connector.

FIGURE 7.21 An LC fiber-optic connector

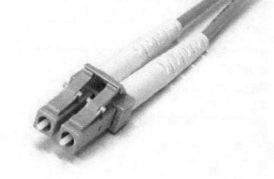

LC connectors have similar advantages to MT-RJ and other SFF-type connectors but are easier to terminate. They use a ceramic insert, just as standard-sized fiber-optic connectors do.

Summary

This chapter provided a solid foundation on which to build your networking knowledge as you go through this book.

You learned what, exactly, a network is, and you got an introduction to some of the components involved in building one.

You also learned that the components required to build a network aren't all you need. Understanding the various types of network connection methods, like coax, twisted pair, and fiber, is all-so-important!

Exam Essentials

Know the network topologies.   Know the names and descriptions of the network topologies. Be aware of the difference between physical networks (what humans see) and logical networks (what the equipment "sees").

Know the advantages and disadvantages of the network topologies.   It is important to know what each topology brings to the table. Knowing the various characteristics of each topology comes in handy during troubleshooting.

Understand the terms *LAN* and *WAN*.   You need to understand when you would use a LAN and when you would use a WAN. A LAN is used to connect a group of hosts together, and a WAN is used to connect various LANs together.

Understand the various types of cables used in today's networks.   Coaxial is rarely used (other than for cable modems), but twisted-pair and fiber-optic cable are very common in today's networks.

Review Questions

The following questions are designed to test your understanding of this chapter's material. For more information on how to get additional questions, please see www.lammle.com/ccst.

You can find the answers to these questions in Appendix, "Answers to Review Questions."

1. Why would a network administrator use plenum-rated cable during an installation? (Choose two.)

    A. It has a low combustion temperature.

    B. It has a high combustion temperature.

    C. It reduces toxic gas released during a fire.

    D. It is not susceptible to any interference.

2. Which of the following Ethernet unshielded twisted-pair cabling types is/are commonly used?

    A. 10BaseT

    B. 100BaseTX

    C. 1000BaseTX

    D. All of the above

3. In which of the following categories is UTP cable not rated?

    A. Category 2

    B. Category 3

    C. Category 5e

    D. Category 9

4. What type of connector does UTP cable typically use?

    A. BNC

    B. ST

    C. RJ-45

    D. SC

5. Which of the following provides the longest cable run distance?

    A. Single-mode fiber

    B. Multimode fiber

    C. Category 3 UTP

    D. Coax

6. In a physical star topology, what happens when a workstation loses its physical connection to another device?

   A. The ring is broken, so no devices can communicate.

   B. Only that workstation loses its ability to communicate.

   C. That workstation and the device it's connected to lose communication with the rest of the network.

   D. No devices can communicate because there are now two unterminated network segments.

7. Why is fiber-optic cable immune to electromagnetic interference (EMI) and radio frequency interference (RFI)?

   A. Because it transmits analog signals using electricity

   B. Because it transmits analog signals using light impulses

   C. Because it transmits digital signals using light impulses

   D. Because it transmits digital signals using electricity

8. What type of cable transmits lights from end to end?

   A. Coax

   B. Fiber-optic

   C. UTP

   D. Category 2

9. What is the main difference between single-mode fiber (SMF) and multimode fiber (MMF)?

   A. Electrical signals.

   B. Number of light rays.

   C. Number of digital signals.

   D. That signal-mode can be run a shorter distance.

10. What type of cable should be used if you need to make a cable run longer than 100 meters?

    A. Category 5e

    B. Category 6

    C. Fiber-optic

    D. Coaxial

11. What is a logical grouping of network users and resources called?

    A. WAN

    B. LAN

    C. MPLS

    D. Host

12. You have a network with multiple LANs and want to keep them separate but still connect them together so they can all get to the Internet. Which of the following is the best solution?

   A. Use static IP addresses.

   B. Add more hubs.

   C. Implement more switches.

   D. Install a router.

13. What is a difference between a LAN and a WAN?

   A. A WAN requires a router.

   B. A WAN covers larger geographical areas.

   C. A WAN can utilize either private or public data transport.

   D. All of the above.

14. Which of the following is an example of a LAN?

   A. Ten buildings interconnected by Ethernet connections over fiber-optic cabling

   B. Ten routers interconnected by MPLS circuits

   C. Two routers interconnected with a Serial circuit

   D. A computer connected to another computer so they can share resources

Chapter

8

Wireless Technologies

THE CCST EXAM TOPICS COVERED IN THIS CHAPTER INCLUDE THE FOLLOWING:

✓ **3.0 Endpoints and Media Types**

- 3.2. Differentiate between Wi-Fi, cellular, and wired network technologies.

  - Copper, including sources of interference; fiber; wireless, including 802.11 (unlicensed, 2.4GHz, 5GHz, 6GHz), cellular (licensed), sources of interference

- 3.4. Demonstrate how to set up and check network connectivity on Windows, Linux, Mac OS, Android, and Apple iOS.

  - Networking utilities on Windows, Linux, Android, and Apple operating systems; how to run troubleshooting commands; wireless client settings (SSID, authentication, WPA mode)

✓ **6.0 Security**

- 6.3. Configure basic wireless security on a home router (WPAx).

  - WPA, WPA2, WPA3; choosing between Personal and Enterprise; wireless security concepts

Wireless connectivity is everywhere these days, so to really get away, I recently vacationed to a beautiful spot with no cell or Internet service on purpose! I know—crazy, right? While it's true that I definitely chilled out, most of the time I wouldn't even think of checking in anywhere that doesn't offer these things!

Clearly, those of us already in or wishing to enter the IT field better have our chops down on wireless network components and installation factors, which brings us to a great starting point: If you want to understand the basic wireless LANs (WLANs) used today, just think Ethernet connectivity with hubs—except the wireless devices we connect to are called access points (APs). This means that our WLANs run half-duplex communication—everyone is sharing the same bandwidth, with only one device communicating at a time per channel. This isn't necessarily bad; it's just not good enough. Not only do we want it fast, but we also want it secure!

I know you've crushed all the previous chapters, so you're ready to dive into this one! If that's not exactly you, just know that Chapter 6, "Switching," provides a really nice review on switching and VLANs.

Why do you need a strong background in switching and VLANs? If you think about it for a minute, you come to the important realization that APs must connect to something. If not, how else would all those hosts hanging around in a wireless network area be able to connect to your wired resources or to the Internet?

You also might be surprised to hear that wireless security is basically nonexistent on access points and clients by default. That's because the original 802.11 committee just didn't foresee that wireless hosts would one day outnumber bounded media hosts. Same thing with the IPv4 routed protocol—unfortunately, engineers and scientists just didn't include wireless security standards robust enough to work in a corporate environment. These factors leave us to face this problem with proprietary solution add-ons to create a secure wireless network. The good news is that some of the standards actually do provide some solid wireless security. And they're also pretty easy to implement, with a little practice.

Let's start this chapter by defining a basic wireless network as well as basic wireless principles. I'll talk about different types of wireless networks, the minimum devices required to create a simple wireless network, as well as some basic wireless topologies. After that, I'll get into basic security by covering WPA, WPA2, and WPA3.

To find your included bonus material, as well as Todd Lammle videos, practice questions & hands-on labs, please see www.lammle.com/ccst.

Wireless Networks

Wireless networks come in many forms, cover various distances, and provide a wide range of bandwidth capacities depending on the type that's been installed. The typical wireless network today is an extension of an Ethernet LAN, with wireless hosts utilizing Media Access Control (MAC) addresses, IP addresses, and so forth, just like they would on a wired LAN.

Figure 8.1 shows a simple, typical WLAN.

FIGURE 8.1   Wireless LANs are an extension of our existing LANs.

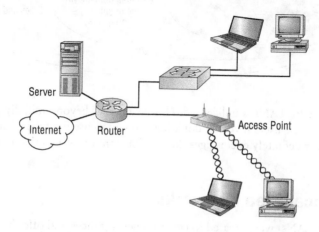

Wireless networks are more than just run-of-the-mill LANs—because they're wireless, of course. They cover a range of distances, from short-range personal area networks (PANs) to wide area networks (WANs) that really go the distance.

Figure 8.2 illustrates how different types of wireless networks look and the related distances they'll provide coverage for in today's world.

Now that you've got a mental picture, let's explore each of these networks in more detail.

Wireless Personal Area Networks

A wireless personal area network (PAN) works in a very small area and connects devices like mice, keyboards, PDAs, headsets, and cell phones to our computers. This conveniently eliminates the cabling clutter of the past. If you're thinking Bluetooth, you've got it, because it's by far the most popular type of PAN around.

PANs are low power, cover short distances, and they're small. You can stretch one of these to cover about 30 feet max, but most devices on a PAN have a short reach, making them popular for small and/or home offices. Bigger isn't always better—you don't want your

PAN's devices interfering with your other wireless networks, or someone else's. Plus, you've got the usual security concerns to manage. So, remember that PANs are the perfect solution for small devices you want to connect to your PC.

FIGURE 8.2   Today's wireless networks

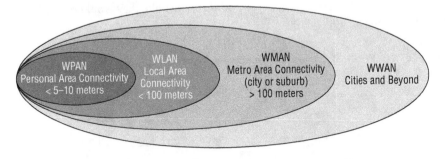

The standard use for PANs is unlicensed. This means that beyond initially purchasing PAN-typical devices, the users involved don't have to pay to use the type of devices in this network. This factor definitely encourages the development of devices that can use PAN frequencies.

Wireless Local Area Networks

Wireless LANs (WLANs) were created to cover longer distances and offer higher bandwidth than PANs. They're the most popular type of wireless networks in use today.

The first WLAN had a data rate up to 2 Mbps, could stretch about 200–300 feet, depending on the area, and was called 802.11. The typical rates in use today are higher: 11 Mbps for IEEE 802.11b and 54 Mbps for 802.11g/a.

The ideal for a WLAN is to have many users connect to the network simultaneously, but this can cause interference and collisions because the network's users are all competing for the same bandwidth.

Like PANs, WLANs use an unlicensed frequency band, which means you don't have to pay for the frequency band in order to transmit. And, again, this attribute has resulted in an explosion of new development in the WLAN arena.

Wireless Metro Area Networks

Wireless metro area networks (WMANs) cover a fairly large geographic area like a city or small suburb. They're becoming increasingly common as more and more products are introduced into the WLAN sector, causing the price tag to drop.

You can think of WMANs as low-budget, bridging networks. They'll save you some real cash compared to shelling out for much more costly leased lines, but there's a catch: In order to get your discount long-distance wireless network to work, you've got to have a line of sight between each hub or building.

Fiber connections are ideal to build an ultra-solid network backbone with, so go with them if they're available in your area. If your ISP doesn't offer the fiber option, or you just don't have the cash for it, a WMAN is a perfectly fine and economical alternative for covering something like a campus or another large area, so long as you've got that vital line of sight factor in check!

Wireless Wide Area Networks

So far, it's very rare to come across a wireless wide area network (WWAN) that can provide you with WLAN speeds, but there sure is a lot of chatter about them. A good example of a WWAN would be the latest cellular networks, which can transmit data at a pretty good clip. But even though WWANs can certainly cover plenty of area, they're still not speedy enough to replace our ubiquitous WLANs.

Some people—especially those shilling stuff on TV—claim to adore their infallible, turbo-charged cellular networks. These terminally happy people are usually watching high-speed video while uploading images and gaming on their smart phones, but I don't know anyone who lives outside the TV who actually gets that kind of speed. And as for that "coverage anywhere" schtick? Off the set, dead zones, and frozen phones are just reality for now.

It's possible that we'll see more efficiency and growth for WWANs soon, but since WWANs are used to provide connectivity over a really large geographic area, it follows that implementing one will separate your cell service provider from a large quantity of cash. So it's going to come to motivation; as more people demand this type of service and are willing to pay for it, cellular companies will gain the resources to expand and improve upon these exciting networks.

Another set of positives in favor of WWAN growth and development: They meet a lot of business requirements, and technology is growing in a direction that the need for this type of long-distance wireless network is getting stronger. So it's a fairly good bet connectivity between a WLAN and a WWAN will be critical to many things in our future. For instance, when we have more IPv6 networks, the "pass-off" between these two types of networks may be seamless.

Basic Wireless Devices

Though it might not seem this way to you right now, *simple* wireless networks (WLANs) are less complex than their wired cousins because they require fewer components. To make a basic wireless network work properly, all you need are two main devices: a wireless AP and a wireless network interface card (NIC). This also makes it a lot easier to install a wireless network, because basically you just need an understanding of these two components in order to make it happen.

Wireless Access Points

You'll find a central component like a hub or switch in the vast majority of wired networks, which is there to connect hosts together and allow them to communicate. Wireless technologies also has a component that connects all wireless devices together, only that device is known as a wireless *access point* (AP). Wireless APs have at least one antenna. Usually there are two for better reception (referred to as diversity) and a port to connect them to a wired network.

Figure 8.3 shows an example of a Cisco wireless AP, which just happens to be one of my personal favorites.

FIGURE 8.3 A wireless access point

APs have the following characteristics:

- APs function as a central junction point for the wireless stations much like a switch or hub does within a wired network. Due to the half-duplex nature of wireless networking, the hub comparison is more accurate, even though hubs are rarely found in the wired world anymore.

- APs have at least one antenna—most likely two.

- APs function as a bridge to the wired network, giving the wireless station access to the wired network and/or the Internet.

- SoHo APs come in two flavors: the stand-alone AP and the wireless router. They can and usually do include functions like network address translation (NAT) and Dynamic Host Configuration Protocol (DHCP).

Even though it's not a perfect analogy, you can compare an AP to a hub because it doesn't create collision domains for each port like a switch does. But APs are definitely smarter than hubs. An AP is a portal device that can either direct network traffic to the wired backbone or back out into the wireless realm. If you look at Figure 8.1 again, understand that the connection back to the wired network is called the distribution system (DS), and it also maintains MAC address information within the 802.11 frames. What's more, these frames are capable of holding as many as four MAC addresses, but only when a wireless DS is in use.

An AP also maintains an association table that you can view from the web-based software used to manage the AP. What's an association table? It's basically a list of all workstations currently connected to or associated with the AP, which are listed by their MAC addresses. Another nice AP feature is that wireless routers can function as NAT routers, and they can carry out DHCP addressing for workstations as well.

In the Cisco world, there are two types of APs: autonomous and lightweight. An autonomous AP is one that's configured, managed, and maintained in isolation with regard to all the other APs that exist in the network. A lightweight AP gets its configuration from a central device called a wireless controller. In this scenario, the APs are functioning as antennas, and all information is sent back to the wireless LAN controller (WLC). There are a bunch of advantages to this, like the capacity for centralized management and more seamless roaming. You'll learn all about using WLC and lightweight APs throughout this book.

You can think of an AP as a bridge between the wireless clients and the wired network. And, depending on the settings, you can even use an AP as a wireless bridge for bridging two, wired network segments together.

In addition to the stand-alone AP, there's another type of AP that includes a built-in router, which you can use to connect both wired and wireless clients to the Internet. These devices are usually employed as NAT routers and are the type shown in Figure 8.3.

Wireless Network Interface Card

Every host you want to connect to a wireless network needs a wireless *network interface card* (NIC) to do so. Basically, a wireless NIC does the same job as a traditional NIC, only instead of having a socket/port to plug a cable into, the wireless NIC has a radio antenna.

Figure 8.4 gives you a picture of a wireless NIC.

FIGURE 8.4   A wireless NIC

The wireless card shown in Figure 8.4 is used in a laptop or desktop computer, and pretty much all laptops have wireless cards plugged into or built into the motherboard.

These days it's pretty rare to use an external wireless client card because all laptops come with them built in, and desktops can be ordered with them too. But it's good to know that you can still buy the client card shown in Figure 8.4. Typically, you would use cards like the ones shown in the figure for areas of poor reception or for use with a network analyzer because they can have better range, depending on the antenna you use.

Wireless Antennas

Wireless antennas work with both transmitters and receivers. Two broad classes of antennas are on the market today: *omnidirectional* (or point-to-multipoint) and *directional* (or point-to-point). Refer to Figure 8.3 for an example of omnidirectional antennas attached to the Cisco 800 AP.

Yagi antennas usually provide greater range than omnidirectional antennas of equivalent gain. Why? Because Yagi antennas focus all their power in a single direction. Omnidirectional antennas must disperse the same amount of power in all directions at the same time, like a large donut.

A downside to using a directional antenna is that you have to be much more precise when aligning communication points. It's also why most APs use omnidirectional antennas— because clients and other APs often can be located in any direction at any given moment.

To get a picture of this, think of the antenna on your car. Yes, it's a non-networking example, but it's still a good one because it clarifies the fact that your car's particular orientation doesn't affect the signal reception of whatever radio station you happen to be listening to. Well, most of the time, anyway. If you're in the boonies, you're out of range and out of luck—something that also applies to the networking version of omnidirectional antennas.

Wireless Principles

Next up, I'm going to cover different types of networks you'll run into and/or design and implement as your wireless networks grow:

- IBSS
- BSS
- SSID
- ESS

Independent Basic Service Set (Ad Hoc)

This is the easiest way to install wireless 802.11 devices. In this mode, the wireless NICs (or other devices) can communicate directly without the need for an AP. A good example of this is two laptops with wireless NICs installed. If both cards were set up to operate in ad hoc mode, they could connect and transfer files as long as the other network settings, like protocols, were set up to enable this as well. We'll also call this an *independent basic service* set *(IBSS),* which is born as soon as two wireless devices communicate.

To create an ad hoc network, all you need is two or more wireless-capable devices. Once you've placed them within a range of 20–40 meters of each other, they'll "see" each other and be able to connect—assuming they share some basic configuration parameters. One computer may be able to share the Internet connection with the rest of them in your group.

Figure 8.5 shows an example of an ad hoc wireless network. Notice that there's no access point!

FIGURE 8.5   A wireless network in ad hoc mode

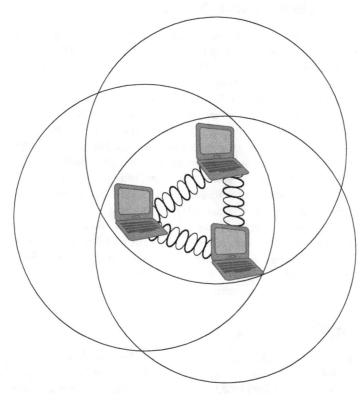

An ad hoc network, also known as peer to peer, doesn't scale well, and I wouldn't recommend it due to collision and organization issues in today's corporate networks. With the low cost of APs, you don't need this kind of network anymore anyway, except for maybe in your home—and probably not even there.

Another con is that ad hoc networks are pretty insecure, so you really want to have the AdHoc setting turned off before connecting to your wired network.

Basic Service Set

A basic service set (BSS) is the area, or cell, defined by the wireless signal served by the AP. It can also be called a basic service area (BSA); the two terms, BSS and BSA, are interchangeable. Even so, BSS is the most common term that's used to define the cell area. Figure 8.6 shows an AP providing a BSS for hosts in the area and the basic service area (cell) that's covered by the AP.

The AP isn't connected to a wired network in this example, but it provides for the management of wireless frames so the hosts can communicate. Unlike an ad hoc network, this network will scale better, and more hosts can communicate because the AP manages all network connections.

Infrastructure Basic Service Set

In infrastructure mode, wireless NICs communicate only with an access point instead of directly with each other, like they do when they're in ad hoc mode. All communication between hosts, as well as any wired portion of the network, must go through the access point. Remember this important fact: In infrastructure mode, wireless clients appear to the rest of the network as though they are standard, wired hosts.

Figure 8.6 shows a typical infrastructure mode wireless network. Pay special attention to the access point and the fact that it's also connected to the wired network. This connection from the access point to the wired network is called the *distribution system (DS)* and is how the APs communicate to each other about hosts in the BSA. Basic stand-alone APs don't communicate with each other via the wireless network, only through the DS.

Before you configure a client to operate in wireless infrastructure mode, you need to understand SSIDs. The *service set identifier (SSID)* is the unique 32-character identifier that represents a particular wireless network and defines the BSS. And, just so you know, a lot of people use the terms SSID and BSS interchangeably, so don't let that confuse you! All devices involved in a particular wireless network can be configured with the same SSID. Sometimes access points even have multiple SSIDs.

Let's talk about that a little more now.

Service Set ID

Technically, *service set ID* (SSID) is a basic name that defines the basic service area (BSA) transmitted from the AP. A good example of this is "Linksys" or "Netgear." You've probably seen that name pop up on our host when looking for a wireless network. This is the name the AP transmits out to identify which WLAN the client station can associate with.

The SSID can be up to 32 characters long. It normally consists of human-readable ASCII characters, but the standard doesn't require this. The SSID is defined as a sequence of 1–32 octets, each of which may take any value.

The SSID is configured on the AP and can be either broadcasted to the outside world or hidden. If the SSID is broadcasted, when wireless stations use their client software to scan for wireless networks, the network will appear in a list identified by its SSID. But if the SSID is hidden, either it won't appear in the list at all or it will show up as "unknown network," depending on the client's operating system.

FIGURE 8.6   Basic service set/basic service area

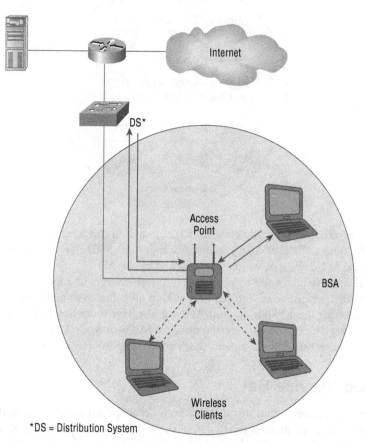

*DS = Distribution System

Either way, a hidden SSID requires the client station be configured with a wireless profile, including the SSID, in order to connect. And this requirement is above and beyond any other normal authentication steps or security essentials.

The AP associates a MAC address to this SSID. It can be the MAC address for the radio interface itself—called the basic service set identifier (BSSID)—or it can be derived from the MAC address of the radio interface if multiple SSIDs are used. The latter is sometimes called a virtual MAC address, and also referred to as a multiple basic service set identifier (MBSSID), as shown in Figure 8.7.

FIGURE 8.7   A network with MBSSIDs configured on an AP

There are two things you really want to make note of in this figure: First, there's a "Contractor BSSID" and a "Sales BSSID"; second, each of these SSID names is associated with a separate virtual MAC address, which was assigned by the AP.

These SSIDs are virtual, and implementing things this way won't improve your wireless network's or AP's performance. You're not breaking up collision domains or broadcast domains by creating more SSIDs on your AP; you just have more hosts sharing the same half-duplex radio. The reason for creating multiple SSIDs on your AP is so that you can set different levels of security for each client that's connecting to your AP(s).

Extended Service Set

A good to thing to know is that if you set all your access points to the same SSID, mobile wireless clients can roam around freely within the same network. This is the most common wireless network design you'll find in today's corporate settings.

Doing this creates something called an *extended service set (ESS)*, which provides more coverage than a single access point and allows users to roam from one AP to another without having their host disconnected from the network. This design gives us the ability to move fairly seamlessly from one AP to another.

Figure 8.8 shows two APs configured with the same SSIDs in an office, thereby creating an ESS network.

For users to be able to roam throughout the wireless network—from AP to AP without losing their connection to the network—all APs must overlap by 20 percent of their signal or more to their neighbor's cells. To make this happen, be sure the channels (frequency) on each AP are set differently.

FIGURE 8.8   An extended service set (ESS) network

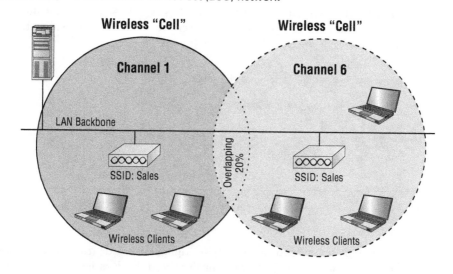

Nonoverlapping Wi-Fi channels

In both the 2.4 GHz and the 5 GHz frequency band, channels are defined by the standards. 802.11, 802.11b, and 802.11g use the 2.4 GHz band, also known as the industrial, scientific, and medical (ISM) band. 802.11a uses the 5 GHz band. When two access points are operating in the same area on the same channel or even an adjacent channel, they will interfere with each other. Interference lowers the throughput. Therefore, channel management to avoid interference is critical to ensure reliable operation. This section examines issues that impact channel management.

2.4 GHz Band

Within the 2.4 GHz (ISM) band are 11 channels approved for use in the United States, 13 in Europe, and 14 in Japan. Each channel is defined by its center frequency, but remember, that signal is spread across 22 MHz. There's 11 MHz on one side of the center frequency and 11 MHz on the other side, so each channel encroaches on the channel next to it—even others farther from it to a lesser extent.

Take a look at Figure 8.9.

Consequently, within the United States, only channels 1, 6, and 11 are considered non-overlapping. So, when you have two APs in the same area that are operating on overlapping channels, the effect depends on whether they're on the same channel or on adjacent channels. Let's examine each scenario.

When APs are on the same channel, they will hear each other and defer to one another when transmitting. This is due to information sent in the header of each wireless packet that instructs all stations in the area (including any APs) to refrain from transmitting until the current transmission is received. The APs perform this duty based partially on the duration field. The end result is that both networks will be slower because they'll be dividing their transmission into windows of opportunity to transmit between them.

FIGURE 8.9 2.4 GHz band 22 MHz-wide channels

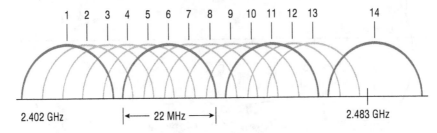

When the APs are only one or two channels apart, things get a little tricky, because in this case they may not be able to hear each clearly enough to read the duration field. The ugly result of this is that they'll transmit at the same time, causing collisions that cause retransmissions and can seriously slow down your throughput. Ugh! Therefore, although the two behaviors are different within these two scenarios, the end result is the same: greatly lowered throughput.

5 GHz Band (802.11ac)

802.11a uses the 5 GHz frequency, which is divided into three unlicensed bands called the Unlicensed National Information Infrastructure (UNII) bands. Two bands are adjacent to each other, but there is a frequency gap between the second and third. These bands are known as UNII-1, UNII-2, and UNII-3—the lower, middle, and upper UNII bands, respectively. Each of these bands hosts discrete channels, as in the ISM.

The 802.11a amendment specifies the location of the center point of each frequency, as well as the distance that must exist between the center point frequencies, but it failed to specify the exact width of each frequency. The good news is that the channels only overlap with the next adjacent channel, so it's easier to find nonoverlapping channels in 802.11a.

In the lower UNII band, the center points are 10 MHz apart, and in the other two, the center frequencies are 20 MHz apart. Figure 8.10 illustrates the overlap of the UNII bands (top and bottom), compared to the 2.4 GHz band (middle).

The channel numbers in the lower UNII are 36, 40, 44, and 48. In the middle UNII, the channels are 52, 56, 60, and 64. The channels in UNII-3 are 149, 153, 157, and 161.

2.4 GHz / 5GHz (802.11n)

802.11n builds on previous 802.11 standards by adding *multiple-input multiple-output (MIMO)*, which uses multiple transmitters and receiver antennas to increase data throughput and range. 802.11n can allow up to eight antennas, but most of today's APs use only four to six. This setup permits considerably higher data rates than 802.11a/b/g does.

FIGURE 8.10   5 GHz band 20 MHz-wide channels

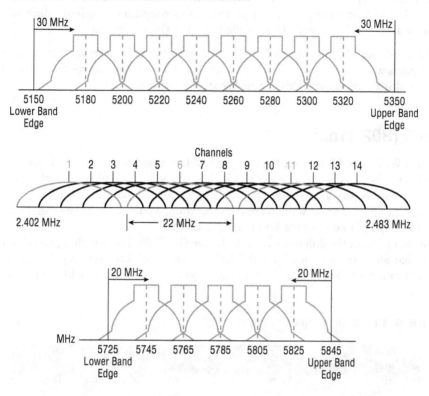

The following three vital items are combined in 802.11n to enhance performance:

- At the Physical layer, the way a signal is sent is changed, enabling reflections and interferences to become an advantage instead of a source of degradation.
- Two 20 MHz-wide channels are combined to increase throughput.
- At the MAC layer, a different way of managing packet transmission is used.

It's important to know that 802.11n isn't truly compatible with 802.11b, 802.11g, or even 802.11a, but it is designed to be backward compatible with them. 802.11n achieves backward compatibility by changing the way frames are sent so they can be understood by 802.11a/b/g.

Here's a list of some of the primary components of 802.11n that together sum up why people claim 802.11n is more reliable and predictable:

40 MHz Channels   802.11g and 802.11a use 20 MHz channels and employ tones on the sides of each channel that are not used in order to protect the main carrier. This means that 11 Mbps go unused and are basically wasted. 802.11n aggregates two carriers to double the speed from 54 Mbps to more than 108. Add in those wasted 11 Mbps rescued from the side tones, and you get a grand total of 119 Mbps!

MAC Efficiency   802.11 protocols require acknowledgment of each and every frame. 802.11n can pass many packets before an acknowledgment is required, which saves you a huge amount of overhead. This is called *block acknowledgment*.

Multiple-Input Multiple-Output   Several frames are sent by several antennae over several paths and are then recombined by another set of antennae to optimize throughput and multipath resistance. This is called *spatial multiplexing*.

Wi-Fi 6 (802.11ax)

So, what is Wi-Fi 6 and is it faster than Wi-Fi 5? Well, I would hope so, since it is one number greater than 5, but that is only because this is the sixth generation of Wi-Fi with enough changes to possibly give us twice the speed, but only time will tell if that is true.

To say that 802.11ax and Wi-Fi 6 are the same thing would definitely be true, and it's great marketing right now for the Wi-Fi manufacturers.

Figure 8.11 shows the difference from 802.11ac (Wi-Fi 5). The first thing you should notice is that 802.1ax uses both 2.4 and 5 GHz, whereas 802.1ac uses only 5 GHz, and 802.1ax has more OFDM symbols and a higher modulation, which provides superior data rates.

FIGURE 8.11   Comparing Wi-Fi 5 to Wi-Fi 6

	802.11ac	802.11ax
BANDS	5 GHz	**2.4 GHz** and 5 GHz
CHANNEL BANDWIDTH	20 MHz, 40 MHz, 80 MHz, 80+80 MHz & 160 MHz	20 MHz, 40 MHz, 80 MHz, 80+80 MHz & 160 MHz
FFT SIZES	64, 128, 256, 512	256, 512, 1024, 2048
SUBCARRIER SPACING	312.5 kHz	**78.125 kHz**
OFDM SYMBOL DURATION	3.2 us + 0.8/0.4 us CP	**12.8 us + 0.8/1.6/3.2 us CP**
HIGHEST MODULATION	256-QAM	**1024-QAM**
DATA RATES	433 Mbps (80 MHz, 1 SS)	600.4 Mbps (80 MHz, 1 SS)
	6933 Mbps (160 MHz, 8 SS)	9607.8 Mbps (160 MHz, 8 SS)

Some benefits of this newer Wi-Fi 6 technology include the following:

- Denser modulation using 1024 quadrature amplitude modulation (QAM), enabling a more than 35 percent speed burst

- Orthogonal frequency-division multiple access (OFDMA)-based scheduling, to reduce overhead and latency

- Robust high-efficiency signaling for better operation at a significantly lower received signal strength indication (RSSI)

- Better scheduling and longer device battery life with target wake time (TWT)

Interference

One factor that affects wireless performance is outside interference. Because 802.11 wireless protocols operate in the 900 MHz, 2.4 GHz, and 5 GHz ranges, interference can come from many sources. These include wireless devices like Bluetooth, cordless telephones, cell phones, other wireless LANs, and any other device that transmits a radio frequency (RF) near the frequency bands that 802.11 protocols use. Even microwave ovens—a huge adversary of 802.11b and 802.11g—can be serious culprits!

Range and Speed Comparisons

Table 8.1 delimits the range comparisons of each 802.11 standard and shows these different ranges using an indoor open-office environment as a factor. (We'll be using default power settings.)

TABLE 8.1   Range and speed comparisons

Standard	802.11b	802.11a	802.11g	802.11n	802.11ac	802.11ax
Speed	11 Mbps	54 Mbps	54 Mbps	300 Mbps	1 Gbps	3.5+ Gbps
Frequency	2.4 GHz	5 GHz	2.4 GHz	2.4/5 GHz	5 GHz	2.4/5/6 GHz
Range (in feet)	100–150	25–75	100–150	>230	>230	Unknown

Cellular Technologies

As part of implementing the appropriate cellular and mobile wireless technologies and configurations, consider the following options.

GSM   The Global System for Mobile Communications (GSM) is a type of cellphone that contains a Subscriber Identity Module (SIM) chip. These chips contain all the information about the subscriber and must be present in the phone in order for it to function. One of the dangers with these phones is cell phone cloning, a process where copies of the SIM chip are made, allowing another user to make calls as the original user. Secret key cryptography is used (using a common secret key) when authentication is performed between the phone and the network.

FDMA   Frequency-division multiple access (FDMA) is one of the modulation techniques used in cellular wireless networks. FDMA divides the frequency range into bands and assigns a band to each subscriber. This was used in 1G cellular networks.

TDMA   Time-division multiple access (TDMA) increases the speed over FDMA by dividing the channels into time slots and assigning slots to calls. This also helps to prevent eavesdropping in calls.

CDMA   Code-division multiple access (CDMA) assigns a unique code to each call or transmission and spreads the data across the spectrum, allowing a call to make use of all frequencies.

3G   This third generation (3G) of cellular data networks was really a game changer over 1G and 2G and allowed the basics to get smartphones working and achieving usable data speeds (kinda), but 2 Mbps was a lot of bandwidth in the 1990s and really provided the start of smartphone apps, which lead to more research and technologies, and, of course, the plethora of apps we have now.

2G networks handled phone calls, basic text messaging, and small amounts of data over a protocol called MMS. When 3G connectivity arrived, a number of larger data formats became much more accessible, such as HTML pages, videos, and music—and there was no going back!

4G   This is the fourth generation speed and connection standard for cellular data networks. The speeds really helped push smartphones to customers, as it provided 100 Mbps up to 1 Gbps, but you'd have to be in a 4G mobile hotspot to achieve the maximum speed.

LTE   Most of 4G networks were called Long-Term Evolution (LTE) or 4G LTE. Although 5G has taken over and 6G is here to stay, LTE is still prevalent in many markets. In the 2000s, your phone would display 4G, but it didn't really mean it, because it just couldn't provide what the standard mandated.

When the cellular standards bodies set the minimum speeds for 4G, they could never reach those speeds even though cell carriers spend millions trying to get them. Because of this, the regulating body decided that LTE (which really was just the pursuit of the 4G standard) could be labeled as 4G as long as it provided an improvement over the 3G technology speeds.

5G   5G, which stands for the "fifth generation" of cellular technology, is a standard for mobile telecommunications service that is significantly faster than today's 4G technology—up to 100 times faster.

Since this technology has been out for years, you know that you can upload or download videos and use data-intensive or other applications much more quickly and smoothly than with 3G and 4G.

This is because 5G technology utilizes a higher-frequency band of the wireless spectrum, called the millimeter wave, that allows data to be transferred much more rapidly than the lower-frequency band dedicated to 4G.

However, the millimeter wave signals don't travel as far, so you need more antennas spaced closer together than the previous wireless 3G and 4G.

Table 8.2 shows the comparisons between 3G, 4G and 5G.

TABLE 8.2   Cellular comparisons

Technology	3G	4G	5G
Deployment	1990	2000	2014
Bandwidth	2 Mbps	200–1000 Mbps	1–10 Gbps
Standards	WCDMA, CDMA-2000	CDMA, LTE, WiMAX	OFDM, MIMO, nm Waves
Technology	CDMA/IP	Unified IP, LAN/WAN	Unified IP, LAN/WAN

Technologies That Facilitate the Internet of Things

The Internet of Things (IoT), the newest buzzword in IT, introduced all sorts of devices to the network (and Internet) that were not formerly there. Refrigerators, alarm systems, building service systems, elevators, and power systems are now equipped with networked sensors that allow us to monitor and control these systems from the Internet.

These systems depend on several technologies to facilitate their operations, including the following:

Z-Wave   Z-Wave is a wireless protocol used for home automation. It uses a mesh network using low-energy radio waves to communicate from appliance to appliance. Residential appliances and other devices such as lighting controls, security systems, thermostats, windows, locks, swimming pools and garage door openers can use this system.

Ant+   ANT+ is another wireless protocol for monitoring sensor data such as a person's heart rate or a bicycle's tire pressure, as well as the control of systems like indoor lighting or a television set. ANT+ is designed and maintained by the ANT+ Alliance, which is owned by Garmin.

Bluetooth   Some systems use Bluetooth, which is considered a personal area network (PAN). Bluetooth operates in the 2.4 GHz range, so while it can cause some interference with 802.11b/g, it's really low power.

The idea of a PAN is to allow personal items such as keyboards, mice, and phones to communicate to our PC/laptop/display/TV wirelessly instead of having to use any wires at all—over short distances of up to 30 feet, of course. The wireless office hasn't quite come to fruition completely yet (but its close); however, you have to admit that Bluetooth really has helped us out tremendously in our offices and especially in our cars!

NFC   Some systems use near-field communication (NFC). In order for NFC to work, the actual antenna must be smaller than the wavelength on both the transmitter and receiver. For instance, if you look at a 2.4 GHz or 5 GHz antenna, they are the exact length of one wavelength for that specific frequency. With NFC, the antenna is about one-quarter the size of the wavelength, which means that the antenna can create either an electric field or a magnetic field, but not an electromagnet field.

NFC can be used for wireless communication between devices like smartphones and/or tablets, but you need to be near the device transmitting the RF to pick up the signal— really close. A solid example would be when you're swiping your phone over a QR code.

IR   Some systems use infrared (IR). We can use IR to communicate short range with our devices, like Bluetooth-enabled devices, but it isn't really as popular as Bluetooth to use within network infrastructures. Unlike Wi-Fi and Bluetooth, the infrared wireless signals cannot penetrate walls and only work line-of-sight. Finally, the rates are super slow, and most transfers are only 115 Kbps—up to 4 Mbps on a really good day!

RFID   While RFID may be most known for asset tracking, it can also be used in IoT. Objects are given an RFID tag so that they are uniquely identifiable. Also, an RFID tag allows the object to wirelessly communicate certain types of information.

Truly smart objects will be embedded with both an RFID tag and a sensor to measure data. The sensor may capture fluctuations in the surrounding temperature, changes in quantity, or other types of information.

802.11   Finally, 802.11 can also be used for this communication. 802.11 was discussed previously in this chapter.

Wireless Security

Now that we've covered the very basics of wireless devices used in today's networks, let's move on to wireless security.

At the foundational level, authentication uniquely identifies the user and/or machine. The encryption process protects the data or the authentication process by scrambling the information enough that it becomes unreadable by anyone trying to capture the raw frames.

Authentication and Encryption

Two types of authentications were specified by the IEEE 802.11 committee: open and shared-key authentication. Open authentication involves little more than supplying the right SSID, but it's the most common method in use today.

With shared-key authentication, the access point sends the client device a challenge-text packet, which the client must then encrypt with the correct Wired Equivalent Privacy (WEP) key and return to the access point. Without the correct key, authentication will fail and the client won't be allowed to associate with the access point.

Figure 8.12 shows shared-key authentication.

FIGURE 8.12   Shared-key authentication

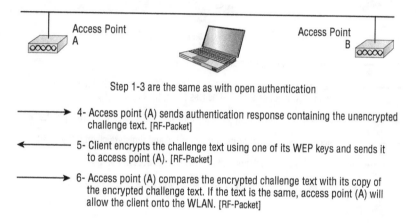

Step 1-3 are the same as with open authentication

4- Access point (A) sends authentication response containing the unencrypted challenge text. [RF-Packet]

5- Client encrypts the challenge text using one of its WEP keys and sends it to access point (A). [RF-Packet]

6- Access point (A) compares the encrypted challenge text with its copy of the encrypted challenge text. If the text is the same, access point (A) will allow the client onto the WLAN. [RF-Packet]

Shared-key authentication is still not considered secure because all a bad guy has to do to get around it is to detect both the clear text challenge, the same challenge encrypted with a WEP key, and then decipher the WEP key. It's no surprise that shared-key authentication isn't used in today's WLANs.

All Wi-Fi-certified wireless LAN products are shipped in "open access" mode, with their security features turned off. Although open access or no security sounds scary, it's totally acceptable for places like public hot spots. But it's definitely not an option for an enterprise organization, and it's not a good idea for your private home network either!

Figure 8.13 shows the open access process.

You can see that an authentication request has been sent and "validated" by the AP. But when open authentication is used or set to "none" in the wireless controller, the request is pretty much guaranteed not to be denied. For now, understand that this authentication is done at the MAC layer (layer 2), so don't confuse this with the higher-layer authentication we'll cover later, which occurs after the client is associated to the access point.

WEP

With open authentication, even if a client can complete authentication and associate with an access point, the use of WEP prevents the client from sending and receiving data from an access point unless the client has the correct WEP key.

A WEP key is composed of either 40 or 128 bits and, in its basic form, is usually statically defined by the network administrator on the access point, and on all clients that communicate with that access point. When static WEP keys are used, a network administrator must perform the tedious task of entering the same keys on every device in the WLAN.

FIGURE 8.13 Open access process

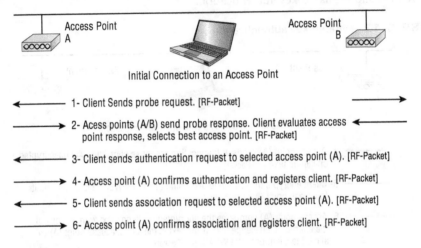

Initial Connection to an Access Point

1- Client Sends probe request. [RF-Packet]

2- Acess points (A/B) send probe response. Client evaluates access point response, selects best access point. [RF-Packet]

3- Client sends authentication request to selected access point (A). [RF-Packet]

4- Access point (A) confirms authentication and registers client. [RF-Packet]

5- Client sends association request to selected access point (A). [RF-Packet]

6- Access point (A) confirms association and registers client. [RF-Packet]

Clearly, we now have fixes for this because tackling this manually would be administratively impossible in today's huge corporate wireless networks!

WPA and WPA2: An Overview

Wi-Fi Protected Access (WPA) and WPA2 were created in response to the shortcomings of WEP. WPA was a stopgap measure taken by the Wi-Fi Alliance to provide better security until the IEEE finalized the 802.11i standard. When 802.11i was ratified, WPA2 incorporated its improvements, so there are some significant differences between WPA and WPA2.

These are each essentially another form of basic security that is really just an add-on to the specifications. Even though you can totally lock the vault, WPA/WPA2 pre-shared key (PSK) is a better form of wireless security than any other basic wireless security method I've talked about so far. Still, keep in mind that I did say basic!

WPA is a standard developed by the Wi-Fi Alliance and provides a standard for authentication and encryption of WLANs that's intended to solve known security problems. The standard takes into account the well-publicized AirSnort and man-in-the-middle WLAN attacks. So, of course, we use WPA2 to help us with today's security issues because we can use Advanced Encryption Standard (AES) encryption, which provides for better key caching than WPA does. WPA is only a software update, whereas WPA2 requires a hardware update, but you'd be hard-pressed to find a laptop or any PC today that doesn't have built-in WPA2 support.

The PSK verifies users via a password or identifying code, often called a passphrase, on both the client machine and the access point. A client gains access to the network only if its password matches the access point's password. The PSK also provides keying material that Temporal Key Integrity Protocol (TKIP) or AES uses to generate an encryption key for each packet of transmitted data.

Wi-Fi Protected Access

WPA was designed to offer two methods of authentication in implementation. The first, called WPA Personal or WPA (PSK), was designed to work using a passphrase for authentication, but it improves the level of protection for authentication and data encryption too. WPA PSK uses the exact same encryption as WPA Enterprise—the PSK just replaces the check to a RADIUS server for the authentication portion.

The only known weakness of WPA PSK lies in the complexity of the password or key used on the AP and the stations. If it happens to be one that's easily guessed, it could be susceptible to something known as a dictionary attack. This type of attack uses a dictionary file that tries out a huge number of passwords until the correct match is found. Consequently, this is very time-consuming for the hacker. WPA3's big difference is how it can prevent a dictionary attack.

Because of this, WPA PSK should mainly be used in a small office, home office (SOHO) environment, and in an enterprise environment only when device restrictions, such as voice over IP (VoIP) phones, don't support RADIUS authentication.

WPA2 Enterprise

Regardless of whether WPA or WPA2 is used during the initial connection between the station and the AP, the two agree on common security requirements. Following that agreement, the following series of important key-related activities occur (in this specific order):

1. The authentication server derives a key called the Pairwise Master Key (PMK). This key will remain the same for the entire session. The same key is derived on the station. The server moves the PMK to the AP where it's needed.

2. The next step is called the four-way handshake. Its purpose is to derive another key called the Pairwise-Transient-Key (PTK). This step occurs between the AP and the station and requires the following four steps:

   a. The AP sends a random number known as a nonce to the station.

   b. Using this value along with the PMK, the station creates a key used to encrypt a nonce that's called the snonce, which is then sent to the AP. It includes a reaffirmation of the security parameters that were negotiated earlier. It also protects the integrity of this frame with a MIC. This bidirectional exchange of nonces is a critical part of the key-generation process.

   c. Now that the AP has the client nonce, it will generate a key for unicast transmission with the station. It sends the nonce back to the station along with a group key commonly called a group transient key, as well as a confirmation of security parameters.

d. The fourth message simply confirms to the AP that the temporal keys (TKs) are in place.

One final function performed by this four-way handshake is to confirm that the two peers are still "alive."

802.11i

Although WPA2 was built with the 802.11i standard in mind, the following features were added when the standard was ratified:

- A list of EAP methods that can be used with the standard.

- AES-CCMP for encryption instead of RC4.

- Better key management; the master key can be cached, permitting a faster reconnect time for the station.

But wait, there's more! There is a new sheriff in town, and its name is WPA3.

WPA3

In 2018 the Wi-Fi Alliance announced the new WPA3, a Wi-Fi security standard to replace WPA2. The WPA2 standard has served us well, but it's been around since 2004! WPA3 will improve on the WPA2 protocol with more security features, just like WPA2 was designed to fix WPA.

What's fun about WPA3 is the naming used to define the handshake as well as the exploits—yes, exploits are already out there! First, remember that WPA2 uses a PSK, but WPA3 has been upgraded to 128-bit encryption and uses a system called Simultaneous Authentication of Equals (SAE). This is referred to as the Dragonfly handshake. It forces network interaction on a login so that hackers can't deploy a dictionary attack by downloading its cryptographic hash and then running cracking software to break it.

Even more fun, the known exploits of WPA3 are called Dragonblood. The reason these Dragonblood exploits are already out is because the protections in WPA2 haven't really changed that much in WPA3—at least not yet. Worse, WPA3 is backward compatible, meaning that if someone wants to attack you, they can just use WPA2 in an attack to effectively downgrade your WPA3-compatible system back to WPA2!

Like WPA2, the Wi-Fi Protected Access security includes solutions for personal and enterprise networks. But WPA3 offers some very cool new goodies that pave the way for more powerful authentication and enhanced cryptographic clout. It also helps to protect vital networks by preserving resiliency and offers a cleaner approach to security.

Here's a list of characteristics shared by all WPA3 networks:

- They use the latest security methods.

- They don't allow outdated legacy protocols.

- They require the use of Protected Management Frames (PMF).

Like us, our Wi-Fi networks have different levels of risk tolerance according to type and function. For the non-public, home, or enterprise -variety, WPA3 gives us some cool tools to shut down password-guessing attacks. WPA3 also works with superior security protocols for networks that require or want a higher degree of protection.

As mentioned, WPA3 is backwards compatible and provides interoperability with WPA2 devices, but this is really only an option for companies developing certified devices. I'm sure that it will become a required piece over time as market adoption grows.

WPA3-Personal

How does being able to seriously protect your individual users sound? WPA3-Personal provides that capability by offering powerful password-based authentication via Simultaneous Authentication of Equals (SAE). This is a big upgrade from WPA2's pre-shared key (PSK) and works really well even when users choose simple, easy to crack passwords!

Like I said, WPA3 also frustrates a hacker's attempts to crack passwords via dictionary attacks. Some additional perks include the following :

- *Natural password selection*: WPA3 allows users to choose passwords that are easier to remember.

- *Ease of use*: WPA3 delivers enhanced protections with no change to the way users connect to a network.

- *Forward secrecy*: WPA3 protects data traffic even if a password is compromised after the data was transmitted.

WPA3-Enterprise

Basically, wireless networks of all kinds gain a lot of security with WPA3, but those with sensitive data on them, like networks belonging to financial institutions, governments, and even enterprises, really get a boost! WPA3-Enterprise improves everything WPA2 offers, plus it really streamlines how security protocols are applied throughout our networks.

WPA3-Enterprise even gives us the option to use 192-bit, minimum-strength security protocols, plus some very cool cryptographic tools to lock things down tight!

Here's a list of the ways WPA3 beefs up security:

- *Sweet feature alert*: WPA3 uses a system called Wi-Fi Device Provisioning Protocol (DPP) that allows users to utilize NFC tags or QR codes to allow devices on the network. Sweet!

- *Authenticated encryption*: 256-bit Galois/Counter Mode protocol (GCMP-256).

- *Key derivation and confirmation*: 384-bit Hashed Message Authentication Mode (HMAC) with Secure Hash Algorithm (HMAC-SHA384).

- *Key establishment and authentication*: Elliptic Curve Diffie-Hellman (ECDH) exchange and Elliptic Curve Digital Signature Algorithm (ECDSA) using a 384-bit elliptic curve.

- *Robust management frame protection*: 256-bit Broadcast/Multicast Integrity Protocol Galois Message Authentication Code (BIP-GMAC-256).

- The 192-bit security mode offered by WPA3-Enterprise ensures that the right combination of cryptographic tools are used and sets a consistent baseline of security within a WPA3 network.

WPA3 has also improved upon 802.11's open authentication support by giving us something called Opportunistic Wireless Encryption (OWE). The idea behind the OWE enhancement option is to offer encryption communication for networks without passwords. It works by giving every device on the network its own unique key.

This implements something called Individualized Data Protection (IDP), which happens to come in handy for password-protected networks too because even if an attacker gets a hold of the network password, they still can't access any other encrypted data!

All good—we've got WPA, WPA2, and now WPA3 covered. But how do they compare? Table 8.3 breaks them down.

TABLE 8.3   WPA, WPA2, and WPA3 compared

Security Type	WPA	WPA2	WPA3
Enterprise Mode: Business, education, government	Authentication: IEEE 802.1X/EAP	Authentication: IEEE 802.1X/EAP	Authentication: IEEE 802.1X/EAP
	Encryption: TKIP/MIC	Encryption: AES-CCMP	Encryption: GCMP-256
Personal Mode: SOHO, home, and personal	Authentication: PSK	Authentication: PSK	Authentication: SAE
	Encryption: TKIP/MIC	Encryption: AES-CCMP	Encryption: AES-CCMP
	128-bit RC4 w/TKIP encryption	128-bit AES encryption	128-bit AES encryption
	Ad hoc not supported	Ad hoc not supported	Ad hoc not supported

Network Host Utilities

Modern operating systems try to make using wireless as easy as possible, but if everything always worked, then we would have to find a new career! Most devices have a bunch of tools built-in that can help you troubleshoot most issues that can stop you from getting online.

Let's have a look at some of the more common ways to get connected and troubleshoot some simple issues. One thing to keep in mind is that while the host utilities are neat, they might not always solve the problem if the issue is outside of the computer, like the AP is on fire.

Windows

Windows tends to hide the more complicated side of wireless unless you need to see it. To connect a wireless network, simply do the following (I'm using Windows 11):

1. Click the Network and Internet Settings icon in the taskbar.

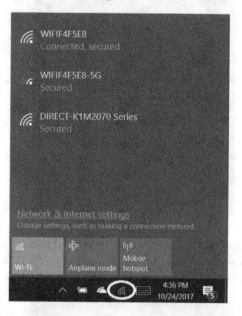

2. Click the ➤ icon is the wireless section of the menu that just popped up.

3. Select your wireless network (in my case, I'm joining the LAMMLE SSID), and then click Connect.

4. If your SSID is configured to use security, you will need to enter your password for the WLAN. It will be masked as you type, but you can click the little eyeball on the right of the field if you want to see what you're typing. Once you're done, click Next.

5. In a perfect world, you should be connected! If you want to see more information, you can click the information circle on the right.

6. This page shows a ton of useful information, such as the IPv4 and IPv6 addresses, the wireless adapter model, your expected speed, and even what protocol and security your wireless connection is using.

Network & internet › **Wi-Fi** › **LAMMLE**

☑ Connect automatically when in range

Metered connection
Some apps might work differently to reduce data usage when you're connected to this network   Off ⬤

Set a data limit to help control data usage on this network

Random hardware addresses
Help protect your privacy by making it harder for people to track your device location when you connect to   Off ∨
this network. The setting takes effect the next time you connect to this network.

IP assignment:	Automatic (DHCP)	Edit
DNS server assignment:	Automatic (DHCP)	Edit
SSID:	LAMMLE	Copy
Protocol:	Wi-Fi 6 (802.11ax)	
Security type:	WPA3-Personal	
Manufacturer:	Intel Corporation	
Description:	Intel(R) Wi-Fi 6 AX201 160MHz	
Driver version:	22.220.0.4	
Network band (channel):	5 GHz (108)	
Aggregated link speed (Receive/ Transmit):	138/103 (Mbps)	
IPv6 address:	2001:56a:7793:1305:2d29:976f:7804:b9d6	
Link-local IPv6 address:	fe80::aa83:d2e5:5569:b208%37	
IPv6 default gateway:	fe80::667c:e8ff:feb5:a330%37	
IPv4 address:	10.30.21.121	
IPv4 DNS servers:	10.30.11.10 (Unencrypted) 10.30.12.10 (Unencrypted)	
Physical address (MAC):	A8-64-F1-E5-C7-61	

It's worth pointing out that Windows has several different ways of connecting to a wireless network. For example, instead of using the taskbar icon, you can search for Wi-Fi settings. Once there, you can select your wireless network and connect to it, just like before.

A more old-school way of getting on wireless is through Network Connections. You can get there by searching for *view network connections* or by directly typing **ncpa.cpl** in the search bar. This shows you all the network adapters in the computer, and it's useful for doing more advanced things like setting up a static IP address. To connect to a wireless network, just right-click your wireless adapter and click Connect.

Verification

Now that I have shown you how to connect to a wireless network, let's see what kind of information you can get about your connection. You already looked at one of the windows in the previous step 6, but you can also get a bunch of good info by double-clicking the adapter in Network Connections. This method provides a lot of good networking information, such as whether DHCP is being used and the address information, including the IP address, subnet mask, default gateway, and DNS servers.

Windows also has several CLI commands that you can use to verify your connection. You can access the Windows CLI by opening Command Prompt. Windows has a few other options, such as PowerShell, but we don't need to get into them at this level.

One command you'll be using all the time is `ipconfig`; it shows the basic IP information on all interfaces:

```
C:\Users\drobb>ipconfig

Windows IP Configuration

Wireless LAN adapter Wi-Fi:

   Connection-specific DNS Suffix  . : tpt-lab.com
   IPv6 Address. . . . . . . . . . . : 2001:56a:7793:1305:2d29:976f:7804:b9d6
   Temporary IPv6 Address. . . . . . : 2001:56a:7793:1305:5dbd:809b:a99:482f
   Link-local IPv6 Address . . . . . : fe80::aa83:d2e5:5569:b208%37
   IPv4 Address. . . . . . . . . . . : 10.30.21.121
   Subnet Mask . . . . . . . . . . . : 255.255.255.0
   Default Gateway . . . . . . . . . : fe80::667c:e8ff:feb5:a330%37
```

If you need to see more information, such as the DNS servers, then you can use `ipconfig /all` instead:

```
C:\Users\drobb>ipconfig /all

Windows IP Configuration
Wireless LAN adapter Wi-Fi:
    Connection-specific DNS Suffix  . : tpt-lab.com
    Description . . . . . . . . . . . : Intel(R) Wi-Fi 6 AX201 160MHz
    Physical Address. . . . . . . . . : A8-64-F1-E5-C7-61
    DHCP Enabled. . . . . . . . . . . : Yes
    Autoconfiguration Enabled . . . . : Yes
    IPv6 Address. . . . . . . . . . . : 2001:56a:7793:1305:2d29:976f:7804:b9d6(
Preferred)
    Temporary IPv6 Address. . . . . . : 2001:56a:7793:1305:5dbd:809b:a99:482f(
Preferred)
    Link-local IPv6 Address . . . . . : fe80::aa83:d2e5:5569:b208%37(Preferred)
    IPv4 Address. . . . . . . . . . . : 10.30.21.121(Preferred)
    Subnet Mask . . . . . . . . . . . : 255.255.255.0
    Lease Obtained. . . . . . . . . . : Monday, May 8, 2023 12:43:13 AM
    Lease Expires . . . . . . . . . . : Tuesday, April 1, 2025 12:23:45 PM
    Default Gateway . . . . . . . . . : fe80::667c:e8ff:feb5:a330%37
                                        10.30.21.1
    DHCP Server . . . . . . . . . . . : 10.30.21.1
    DHCPv6 IAID . . . . . . . . . . . : 413689073
    DHCPv6 Client DUID. . . . . . . . :
00-01-00-01-2B-D3-4A-7D-A8-64-F1-E5-C7-61
    DNS Servers . . . . . . . . . . . : 10.30.11.10
                                        10.30.12.10
    NetBIOS over Tcpip. . . . . . . . : Enabled
```

Troubleshooting

Our attempt to connect to a wireless network was successful, but let's look at some things to try if it's not. The first thing to check when your wireless isn't working is to see if it is turned on! You may think that is obvious, but everyone has been burned by that one way or another.

Your laptop may have a button on your keyboard or a switch on the side that physically enables the adapter. Also, it's possible to disable the adapter inside of Windows. You can enable it again from the taskbar or from Wi-Fi settings.

You can disable the adapter as part of troubleshooting. Turning it "off and on" again is a classic IT troubleshooting step because it helps refresh everything, as the adapter will need to go through the DHCP process again on the way back up.

Sometimes you need to set a static IP on your wireless adapter, particularly when you're studying wireless and are playing around with wireless equipment in a lab. Or sometimes you are simply having problems with your DHCP server and need to get on the network to fix it. To set an IP address, go to Network Connections, right-click the adapter, and then select Properties. From there double-click Internet Protocol Version 4, select Use The Following IP Address, and enter the IP info. You can do this with the CLI as well, but that is out of scope for this book.

If you need to go back to DHCP, simply go back to the same spot and click Obtain An IP Address Automatically instead.

Sometimes it's useful to have Windows simply forget the wireless network. This can come up if the wireless network changes its settings such as the encryption type or the password, or if you're in a hotel where the wireless can have a hard time keeping track of you. To clear your wireless:

1. Go back to Wi-Fi Settings and click Manage Known Networks.

2. Inside Known Networks, click Forget next to the wireless network. Afterwards you will have to connect again from the beginning.

If you need to test network connectivity, a good choice is the ping command:

```
C:\Users\drobb>ping www.google.com

Pinging www.google.com [142.251.33.68] with 32 bytes of data:
Reply from 142.251.33.68: bytes=32 time=19ms TTL=119
Reply from 142.251.33.68: bytes=32 time=18ms TTL=119
Reply from 142.251.33.68: bytes=32 time=18ms TTL=119
Reply from 142.251.33.68: bytes=32 time=19ms TTL=119

Ping statistics for 142.251.33.68:
    Packets: Sent = 4, Received = 4, Lost = 0 (0% loss),
Approximate round trip times in milli-seconds:
    Minimum = 18ms, Maximum = 19ms, Average = 18ms

C:\Users\drobb>ping 10.255.255.111

Pinging 10.255.255.111 with 32 bytes of data:
Request timed out.
Request timed out.
Request timed out.
Request timed out.

Ping statistics for 10.255.255.111:
    Packets: Sent = 4, Received = 0, Lost = 4 (100% loss),
```

You can also test the network path with the `tracert` tool:

```
C:\Users\drobb>tracert www.google.com

Tracing route to www.google.com [142.251.33.68]
over a maximum of 30 hops:

  1    <1 ms    <1 ms    <1 ms  10.30.10.1
  2     2 ms     2 ms     2 ms  50.99.126.65
  3    19 ms    20 ms    20 ms  154.11.12.217
  4    22 ms    22 ms    23 ms  74.125.50.110
  5    21 ms    20 ms    21 ms  142.251.229.135
  6    18 ms    19 ms    18 ms  142.251.50.243
  7    19 ms    18 ms    19 ms  sea09s28-in-f4.1e100.net [142.251.33.68]

Trace complete.
```

MacOS

MacOS is like Windows in the sense that it tries to make life easy for wireless users. To connect to a wireless network, you can use the wireless icon on the top right or go to Network from inside System Settings. From there simply select the wireless network and then click Connect.

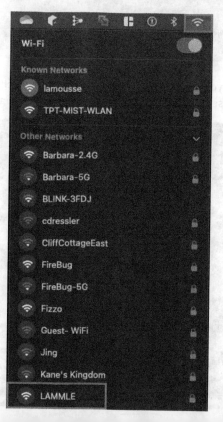

If the wireless network requires a password, you will need to enter it. You can choose to show what you're typing if you prefer.

Verification

To see the connection info, click Details in the Wi-Fi section.

Just like with Windows, you can see all kinds of information, such as the IP information, though it is a bit easier to use because this page is also where you change settings.

MacOS also has a lot of CLI tools that you can use. The main one for checking your IP is `ifconfig`. Wireless adapters in Macs tend to be called *en0*, so you can view your adapter by typing **ifconfig en0**.

```
> ifconfig en0
en0: flags=8863<UP,BROADCAST,SMART,RUNNING,SIMPLEX,MULTICAST> mtu 1500
        options=50b<RXCSUM,TXCSUM,VLAN_HWTAGGING,AV,CHANNEL_IO>
        ether 14:98:77:33:f4:72
        inet6 fe80::10b5:96ff:7399:dc56%en0 prefixlen 64 secured scopeid 0x6
        inet 10.30.10.115 netmask 0xffffff00 broadcast 10.30.10.255
        inet6 2001:56a:7793:1300:14c9:1d7c:89b1:f752 prefixlen 64 autoconf
secured
        inet6 2001:56a:7793:1300:38fc:93da:27fa:6cb9 prefixlen 64 deprecated
autoconf temporary
        inet6 2001:56a:7793:1300:7113:9dd8:2507:dc60 prefixlen 64 deprecated
autoconf temporary
        inet6 2001:56a:7793:1300:2c5f:abc8:106:e780 prefixlen 64 deprecated
autoconf temporary
        inet6 2001:56a:7793:1300:5124:c2dc:3970:1819 prefixlen 64 deprecated
autoconf temporary
        inet6 2001:56a:7793:1300:615b:cb24:895a:99d5 prefixlen 64 deprecated
autoconf temporary
        inet6 2001:56a:7793:1300:cc3c:19af:91b0:53e6 prefixlen 64 autoconf
temporary
        nd6 options=201<PERFORMNUD,DAD>
        media: autoselect (1000baseT <full-duplex>)
        status: active
```

By the way, if you are wondering why my Mac has so many IPv6 addresses, it's because Windows and Macs change their wireless MAC addresses by default as a privacy feature since IPv6 addresses are based on your interface MAC.

Troubleshooting

Troubleshooting is straightforward on a Mac, if you need to disable wireless, simply click the toggle in the Wi-Fi section.

If you need to set a static IP, click TCP/IP inside the Wi-Fi details, change Configure IPv4 to Manually, and then enter the IP information. The DNS servers are configured in the DNS tab.

One gotcha is that when you move back to DHCP, you will still need to remove any static DNS servers that are configured; otherwise, you may find that your DNS stops working when you take your laptop to another location.

Finally, if you need to forget a network, simply click the Forget This Network button.

MacOS also has the `ping` and `traceroute` commands, though they work a bit differently from Windows. The `ping` command runs forever by default until you manually stop it by pressing Ctrl+C:

```
> ping www.google.com
PING www.google.com (142.250.217.68): 56 data bytes
64 bytes from 142.250.217.68: icmp_seq=0 ttl=119 time=17.218 ms
64 bytes from 142.250.217.68: icmp_seq=1 ttl=119 time=17.809 ms
64 bytes from 142.250.217.68: icmp_seq=2 ttl=119 time=16.746 ms
^C
--- www.google.com ping statistics ---
3 packets transmitted, 3 packets received, 0.0% packet loss
round-trip min/avg/max/stddev = 16.746/17.258/17.809/0.435 ms
```

Cisco uses the `traceroute` command instead of `tracert` like Microsoft does:

```
> traceroute www.google.com
traceroute to www.google.com (142.250.217.68), 64 hops max, 52 byte packets
 1  10.30.10.1 (10.30.10.1)  3.113 ms  24.709 ms  0.555 ms
 2  50.99.126.65 (50.99.126.65)  2.239 ms  2.002 ms  2.383 ms
 3  154.11.12.217 (154.11.12.217)  41.522 ms  40.493 ms
    154.11.12.219 (154.11.12.219)  26.131 ms
 4  74.125.50.110 (74.125.50.110)  21.517 ms  21.248 ms  20.963 ms
 5  * * *
 6  209.85.254.236 (209.85.254.236)  19.677 ms
    142.251.48.212 (142.251.48.212)  19.358 ms
    142.251.50.244 (142.251.50.244)  19.352 ms
 7  74.125.243.189 (74.125.243.189)  18.759 ms  17.883 ms  17.866 ms
 8  sea09s29-in-f4.1e100.net (142.250.217.68)  18.389 ms  18.621 ms  17.222 ms
~
```

Linux

Linux is a lot harder to talk about because endless distributions are available. For the purposes of this book, I'll just focus on the latest version of Ubuntu at the time of writing, which is 23.04 (though the steps would be similar in Red Hat-based distributions). The first thing to know about Linux is that, unlike Windows or Mac, the GUI is entirely optional, and in fact isn't even installed when Linux is used on a server. Because of that we'll have to cover both the GUI and CLI for completeness.

Assuming you are using the default desktop that comes with Ubuntu, you can connect to Wi-Fi as follows:

1. Click the network icon on the top right, then click the > next to Wi-Fi.

2. Select the wireless SSID that you want to connect to.

3. Enter the password, if one is required. Again, you can choose to show what you type if you need to.

If you don't have a GUI installed, then you will need to use the Linux CLI to configure the Wi-Fi connection. To configure the wireless connection, perform the following steps:

1. Verify the wireless adapter is recognized by Network Manager by typing **nmcli device**. In this case, the wireless adapter in my system is called "wlx1cbfcef803c0" because I'm using a USB adapter, so it has a terribly long hardware name.

```
the-packet-thrower@ubdesktop31:~$ nmcli device
DEVICE            TYPE       STATE                  CONNECTION
ens33             ethernet   connected              Wired connection 1
lo                loopback   connected (externally) lo
wlx1cbfcef803c0   wifi       disconnected           --
```

2. You can list all the available SSIDs that the adapter can see by using `nmcli device wifi list`:

```
the-packet-thrower@ubdesktop31:~$ nmcli device wifi list
IN-USE  BSSID              SSID        MODE   CHAN  RATE       SIGNAL
BARS    SECURITY
        72:A7:41:BC:A6:E6  --          Infra  149   270 Mbit/s  89
   ▂▄▆  WPA2
        72:A7:41:9C:A6:E6  lamousse    Infra  149   270 Mbit/s  89
   ▂▄▆  WPA2
        A8:53:7D:68:12:13  LAMMLE      Infra  44    540 Mbit/s  87
   ▂▄▆  WPA3
```

3. Finally, you can connect with the `nmcli device wifi connect <SSID> password <password>` command, where the `<SSID>` is your wireless network and `<PASSWORD>` is the wireless password:

```
the-packet-thrower@ubdesktop31:~$ sudo nmcli device wifi connect LAMMLE
password Lammle1234
Device 'wlx1cbfcef803c0' successfully activated with '29dd1a45-e82b-4df9-b295-
a3679094d1d6'.
```

Verification

Once wireless is connected, you can view the connection details by going to Settings ➤ Wi-Fi.

You can also verify the connection with the CLI. The nmcli device command should now show that wireless is connected:

```
the-packet-thrower@ubdesktop31:~$ nmcli device
DEVICE           TYPE       STATE                  CONNECTION
ens33            ethernet   connected              Wired connection 1
wlx1cbfcef803c0  wifi       connected              LAMMLE
lo               loopback   connected (externally) lo
```

If you need more info, you can use the iwconfig command, which provides details about the wireless connection:

```
the-packet-thrower@ubdesktop31:~$ iwconfig wlx1cbfcef803c0
wlx1cbfcef803c0  IEEE 802.11  ESSID:"LAMMLE"
          Mode:Managed  Frequency:5.22 GHz  Access Point: A8:53:7D:68:12:13
          Bit Rate=200 Mb/s   Tx-Power=20 dBm
```

```
Retry short limit:7   RTS thr:off   Fragment thr:off
Power Management:on
Link Quality=62/70  Signal level=-48 dBm
Rx invalid nwid:0  Rx invalid crypt:0  Rx invalid frag:0
Tx excessive retries:0  Invalid misc:1   Missed beacon:0
```

Lastly, you can verify the IP info with the `ip addr` command:

```
the-packet-thrower@ubdesktop31:~$ ip addr show wlx1cbfcef803c0
4: wlx1cbfcef803c0: <BROADCAST,MULTICAST,UP,LOWER_UP> mtu 1500 qdisc noqueue
state UP group default qlen 1000
    link/ether 1c:bf:ce:f8:03:c0 brd ff:ff:ff:ff:ff:ff
    inet 10.30.21.148/24 brd 10.30.21.255 scope global dynamic noprefixroute
wlx1cbfcef803c0
       valid_lft 59999909sec preferred_lft 59999909sec
    inet6 2001:56a:7793:1305:44d5:bebe:65f8:514a/64 scope global temporary
dynamic
       valid_lft 14612sec preferred_lft 14312sec
    inet6 2001:56a:7793:1305:248f:48c3:d920:bb9a/64 scope global dynamic
mngtmpaddr noprefixroute
       valid_lft 14612sec preferred_lft 14312sec
    inet6 fe80::f1c9:a65f:898:ddb0/64 scope link noprefixroute
       valid_lft forever preferred_lft forever
```

Troubleshooting

If the device shows as unavailable, then the adapter is probably turned off in Ubuntu. You can turn it back on from the GUI or by using the `sudo nmcli radio wifi on` command:

```
the-packet-thrower@ubdesktop31:~$ nmcli device
DEVICE            TYPE       STATE                    CONNECTION
ens33             ethernet   connected                Wired connection 1
lo                loopback   connected (externally)   lo
wlx1cbfcef803c0   wifi       unavailable              --
the-packet-thrower@ubdesktop31:~$ sudo nmcli radio wifi on
the-packet-thrower@ubdesktop31:~$ nmcli device
DEVICE            TYPE       STATE                    CONNECTION
ens33             ethernet   connected                Wired connection 1
lo                loopback   connected (externally)   lo
wlx1cbfcef803c0   wifi       disconnected             --
```

If you need to forget the wireless connection, you can use the wireless details page shown earlier or the `nmcli connection delete <SSID>` command:

```
the-packet-thrower@ubdesktop31:~$ sudo nmcli connection delete LAMMLE
Connection 'LAMMLE' (29dd1a45-e82b-4df9-b295-a3679094d1d6) successfully
deleted.
```

Linux operates similarly to MacOS in regards to troubleshooting tools such as `ping` or `traceroute`. This is because of MacOS's Unix background, so many basic utilities are common between the two. In fact, the brew project allows you to install a large number of Linux solutions on your Mac.

Apple

If you have a cell phone or a tablet, there is a good chance it is an Apple device. Even if you don't own one, it is very likely you will encounter one through your work or family, so it's a good idea to know how to get them online!

Mobile devices are much more locked down than desktop operating systems, so they don't tend to have options like the native CLI utilities mentioned previously. This makes learning how to do wireless configurations easy because both Apple and Android have everything in their Settings app under Wireless.

Simply click the wireless network and then enter a password if the SSID requires it. Unlike the other examples, you cannot see the full password; however, it does briefly show you the character you just typed before it gets masked.

Once you're connected, you should see the SSID on top with a Wi-Fi icon next to it.

Verification

To see more info about your connection, click the info icon shown earlier. This page will give you useful information like your IP address.

If you need to set a static IP address, click Configure IP in the network's details.

Then enter the info.

If you need to change the DNS servers, go back to the network details and click DNS.

Troubleshooting

If you travel a lot, you might find yourself putting your phone or tablet in airplane mode for several reasons. Airplane mode is a feature that disables your wireless and cell antenna. In Apple devices, the toggle is right above Wi-Fi in Settings. You can also turn off wireless like you can with the other devices we looked at from the Wi-Fi tab.

If you need to forget a wireless network, go into the wireless details and click Forget This Network.

Unlike the desktop operating systems discussed previously, utilities like ping are not built-in, but you can install third-party apps that provide that functionality. For example, here is a utility I use called Mocha Ping. The app provides a number of tools such as `ping` and `traceroute`.

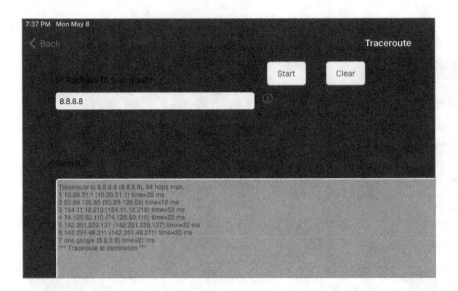

Android

If you don't use an Apple device, you are probably using an Android device. Compared to Apple, Android is less streamlined but tends to offer more knobs that you can tinker with. The downside is that Android has many different distributors, and they all like to tinker with the OS a bit. That said, it's still pretty easy to get it connected.

To connect to a wireless network, follow these steps:

1.   Go to Settings, select Connections, and click Wi-Fi.

2. Click the wireless network you want to connect to.

3. Enter the password if one is required. You can show what you're typing if you need to.

If everything worked okay, you should see that the network is connected.

Verification

To see more wireless information, click the wireless network. From here you can see the IP address, what wireless security is being used, and the wireless speed.

If you need to set a static IP address, click Advanced from the network details.

Then enter the IP info as needed. Unlike as with Apple, you can change the DNS servers directly instead of having to go to another section.

Troubleshooting

If you need to enable/disable Wi-Fi or flight mode (Android's version of airplane mode), you can do so from the connections page.

To forget a network, simply go to the Wi-Fi page that lists all the SSIDs and hold your finger on the network you want to forget. A menu will pop up that says Forget Network.

Just like with Apple devices, there are no real native tools for troubleshooting network connectivity aside from the built-in diagnostics. If you want a tool that provides pings, etc., you will need to get an app.

Summary

This chapter really packed a punch! Like rock 'n' roll, wireless technologies are here to stay, and for those of us who have come to depend on wireless technologies, it's actually pretty hard to imagine a world without wireless networks. What did we do before cell phones?

This chapter began by exploring the essentials and fundamentals of how wireless networks function.

Springing off that foundation, I then introduced you to the basics of wireless RF and the IEEE standards. I discussed 802.11, from its inception through its evolution to current and near-future standards, and talked about the subcommittees that create them.

All of this led to a discussion of wireless security—or rather, non-security for the most part—which logically directed us toward the WPA, WPA2, and WPA3 standards.

Finally, the chapter finished by looking at how to connect to and troubleshoot wireless networks for various endpoint devices.

Exam Essentials

Understand the IEEE 802.11a specification. 802.11a runs in the 5 GHz spectrum, and if you use the 802.11h extensions, you have 23 nonoverlapping channels. 802.11a can run up to 54 Mbps, but only if you are less than 50 feet from an access point.

Understand the IEEE 802.11b specification. IEEE 802.11b runs in the 2.4 GHz range and has three nonoverlapping channels. It can handle long distances, but only with a maximum data rate of up to 11 Mbps.

Understand the IEEE 802.11g specification. IEEE 802.11g is 802.11b's big brother and runs in the same 2.4 GHz range, but it has a higher data rate of 54 Mbps if you are less than 100 feet from an access point.

Understand the IEEE 802.11n components. 802.11n uses 40 MHz-wide channels to provide more bandwidth, provides MAC efficiency with block acknowledgments, and uses MIMO to allow better throughput and distance at high speeds.

Understand the difference between WPA3-Personal and WPA3-Enterprise. WPA3-Personal gives us the ability to offer password-based authentication via Simultaneous Authentication of Equals (SAE). This is a big upgrade from WPA2's pre-shared key (PSK). WPA3-Enterprise even provides the option to use 192-bit minimum-strength security protocols, as well as cryptographic tools.

Understand how to configure the various operating systems for wireless connectivity and security. Know how to configure Windows, MacOS, Linux, Apple, and Android operating systems for wireless connectivity as well as wireless security.

Review Questions

The following questions are designed to test your understanding of this chapter's material. For more information on how to get additional questions, please see www.lammle.com/ccst.

You can find the answers to these questions in Appendix, "Answers to Review Questions."

1. Which encryption type does enterprise WPA3 use?

   A. AES-CCMP

   B. GCMP-256

   C. PSK

   D. TKIP/MIC

2. What is the frequency range of the IEEE 802.11b standard?

   A. 2.4 Gbps

   B. 5 Gbps

   C. 2.4 GHz

   D. 5 GHz

3. What is the frequency range of the IEEE 802.11a standard?

   A. 2.4 Gbps

   B. 5 Gbps

   C. 2.4 GHz

   D. 5 GHz

4. What is the frequency range of the IEEE 802.11g standard?

   A. 2.4 Gbps

   B. 5 Gbps

   C. 2.4 GHz

   D. 5 GHz

5. You've finished physically installing an access point on the ceiling of your office. At a minimum, which parameter must be configured on the access point in order to allow a wireless client to operate on it?

   A. AES

   B. PSK

   C. SSID

   D. TKIP

   E. WEP

   F. 802.11i

6. Which encryption type does WPA2 use?

    A. AES-CCMP

    B. PPK via IV

    C. PSK

    D. TKIP/MIC

7. How many nonoverlapping channels are available with 802.11b?

    A. 3

    B. 12

    C. 23

    D. 40

8. Which of the following has built-in resistance to dictionary attacks?

    A. WPA

    B. WPA2

    C. WPA3

    D. AES

    E. TKIP

9. What is the maximum data rate for the 802.11a standard?

    A. 6 Mbps

    B. 11 Mbps

    C. 22 Mbps

    D. 54 Mbps

10. What is the maximum data rate for the 802.11g standard?

    A. 6 Mbps

    B. 11 Mbps

    C. 22 Mbps

    D. 54 Mbps

11. What's the maximum data rate for the 802.11b standard?

    A. 6 Mbps

    B. 11 Mbps

    C. 22 Mbps

    D. 54 Mbps

12. WPA3 replaced the default open authentication with which of the following enhancements?

A. AES

B. OWL

C. OWE

D. TKIP

13. A wireless client can't connect to an 802.11b/g BSS with a b/g wireless card, and the client section of the access point doesn't list any active WLAN clients. What's a possible reason for this?

A. The incorrect channel is configured on the client.

B. The client's IP address is on the wrong subnet.

C. The client has an incorrect pre-shared key.

D. The SSID is configured incorrectly on the client.

14. Which features did WPA add to address the inherent weaknesses found in WEP? (Choose two.)

A. A stronger encryption algorithm

B. Key mixing using temporal keys

C. Shared key authentication

D. A shorter initialization vector

E. Per frame sequence counter

15. Which of the following wireless encryption methods are based on the RC4 encryption algorithm? (Choose two.)

A. WEP

B. CCKM

C. AES

D. TKIP

E. CCMP

16. Two workers have established wireless communication directly between their wireless laptops. Which type of wireless topology has been created by these two employees?

A. BSS

B. SSID

C. IBSS

D. ESS

17. Which of the following statements describe the wireless security standard that WPA defines? (Choose two.)

A. It specifies the use of dynamic encryption keys that change throughout the users connection time.

B. It requires that all devices use the same encryption key.

C. It can use PSK authentication.

D. Static keys must be used.

18. Which wireless LAN design ensures that a mobile wireless client will not lose connectivity when moving from one access point to another?

A. Using adapters and access points manufactured by the same company

B. Overlapping the wireless cell coverage by at least 15 percent

C. Configuring all access points to use the same channel

D. Utilizing MAC address filtering to allow the client MAC address to authenticate with the surrounding APs

19. You're connecting your access point and it's set to root. What does extended service set ID mean?

A. That you have more than one access point and they are in the same SSID connected by a distribution system

B. That you have more than one access point and they are in separate SSIDs connected by a distribution system

C. That you have multiple access points but they are placed physically in different buildings

D. That you have multiple access points but one is a repeater access point

20. What of the following are basic parameters to configure on a wireless access point? (Choose three.)

A. Authentication method

B. RF channel

C. RTS/CTS

D. SSID

E. Microwave interference resistance

Cisco Devices

THE CCST EXAM TOPICS COVERED IN THIS CHAPTER INCLUDE THE FOLLOWING:

✓ **4.0 Infrastructure**

- 4.1. Identify the status lights on a Cisco device when given instruction by an engineer.

    - Link light color and status (blinking or solid)

- 4.2. Use a network diagram provided by an engineer to attach the appropriate cables.

    - Patch cables, switches, and routers, small topologies, power, rack layout

- 4.3. Identify the various ports on network devices.

    - Console port, serial port, fiber port, Ethernet ports, SFPs, USB port, PoE

✓ **5.0 Diagnosing Problems**

- 5.4. Differentiate between different ways to access and collect data about network devices.

    - Remote access (RDP, SSH, telnet), VPN, terminal emulators, Console, Network Management Systems, cloud-managed network (Meraki), scripts

- 5.5. Run basic show commands on a Cisco network device.

    - show run, show cdp neighbors, show ip interface brief, show ip route, show version, show inventory, show switch, show mac-address-table, show interface, show interface x, show interface status; privilege levels; command help and auto-complete

This chapter covers network infrastructure and how to diagnose problems. For the CCST Networking exam, you need to be able to look at a basic Cisco device and understand some simple lights and their meaning, as well as be able to understand various type of cables and how they are used to connect to devices using different types of ports.

From there I'll discuss different ways to connect and access local and remote network devices, and talk about some basic Cisco IOS commands that can help you find and diagnose problems.

To find up-to-the-minute updates for this chapter, please see www.lammle.com/ccst.

Status Lights

I want you to be familiar with the boot process of Cisco switches, so let's go through a typical Cisco switch and understand the lights. Figure 9.1 shows a Cisco Catalyst switch.

FIGURE 9.1 A typical Cisco Catalyst switch

The first thing I want to point out is that the console port for Catalyst switches is typically found on the back of the switch. On a smaller switch, like the older 3560 shown in Figure 9.1, the console is right in the front to make it easier to use. The eight-port 2960 looks the same. I mention older because they are end-of-life, but there are a lot of these out there still! I have dozens in my own networks. These switches are inexpensive and work great.

When the switch is booting, the top light will be blinking. When the POST completes successfully, the system LED turns solid green, but if the POST fails, it will turn an amber color. That amber glow is an ominous thing—typically fatal.

The bottom button is used to indicate which lights are providing Power over Ethernet (PoE). You can see this by pressing the Mode button. The PoE is a very cool feature because it allows you to power you access point or phone by just connecting them to the switch with an Ethernet cable. Sweet!

Connecting to a Cisco Device

You can connect to a Cisco router or switch in various ways in order to configure it, verify its configuration, and check statistics. Typically, the first place you would connect to is the console port.

The *console port* is usually an RJ-45 (8-pin modular) connection located on the back of the router. A password may or may not be set by default.

You can also connect to a Cisco router through an *auxiliary port*, which is really the same thing as a console port, so it follows that you can use it as one. But an auxiliary port also allows you to configure modem commands so that a modem can be connected to the router. This is a cool feature—it lets you dial up a remote router and attach to the auxiliary port if the router is down and you need to configure it *out-of-band* (meaning from outside of the network).

The third way to connect to a Cisco router is in-band, through a terminal emulation program with Secure Shell (SSH), and you can still use *Telnet*, although it's not recommended because it's insecure. (*In-band* means configuring the router through the network, the opposite of *out-of-band*.) Telnet is a terminal emulation program that acts as though it's a dumb terminal. You can use Telnet to connect to any active interface on a router, such as an Ethernet or serial port. I'll discuss something called Secure Shell (SSH) later in this chapter, which is a more secure way to connect in-band—meaning through the network.

Figure 9.2 shows a Cisco series modular router. Pay close attention to all the different kinds of interfaces and connections.

FIGURE 9.2   A Cisco modular router

This router has one console and one auxiliary connection via RJ-45 connectors.

Another router I want to talk about is the newer 1000 series (see Figure 9.3). This router has replaced the 2900 series router and is referred to as an integrated services router (ISR) because of the built-in security services. Multiple types of modules are available for the newer 1000 series routers.

FIGURE 9.3   A Cisco 1000 router with 6G

These routers provide built-in SD-WAN, Gigabit LAN and WAN ports, PoE, LTE, 6G, Wi-Fi 6, and more!

You get some serious bang for your buck with the 1000—unless you start adding a lot of extra interfaces and options to it. You have to pay for each one of those little beauties, and things can really start to add up fast!

Before you can start adding cables such as patch cables and power cables to a device, you need to consider the placement of the router and/or switch. Typically, you would use a rack in a server room or data center for the devices or devices, but in smaller topologies, the rack layout may not be needed, and the devices could be mounted on the wall or on a shelf in a network closet. Figure 9.4 shows an illustration of adding a Cisco device into a rack found in a closet or data center.

Let's talk about connecting to the various ports on a Cisco device.

FIGURE 9.4   Adding a device into a rack

Physical Ports and Cables

Cisco routers and switches have a combination of console, serial, fiber, Ethernet, small form-factor pluggable (SFP), universal serial bus (USB), and Power over Ethernet (PoE) ports. Let's start with the most used port, the console port.

Console Port

You connect to a Cisco device to configure it, verify its configuration, and check statistics. Although there are different approaches to this, the first place you would usually connect to is the console port. This is considered an *out-of-band* port because you do not get to this port by going through the network; rather, you must plug directly into the device to get to this port.

Rolled Cable

Although *rolled cable* isn't used for Ethernet connections, you can use a rolled Ethernet cable to connect a host EIA-TIA 232 interface to a router console serial communication (COM) port. Some EIA-TIA 232 connectors are wired, which allows you to use a common Ethernet cable to connect to the host.

If you have a Cisco router or switch, you will use a rolled cable to connect your PC, Mac, or a device like an iPad to the Cisco hardware. A rolled cable uses eight wires to connect serial devices, although not all eight are used to send information, just as in Ethernet networking. Figure 9.5 shows the eight wires used in a rolled cable.

FIGURE 9.5   A rolled Ethernet cable

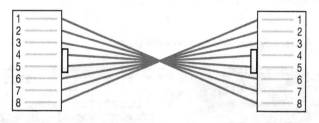

Rolled cables are probably the easiest cables to make because you just cut the end off on one side of a straight-through cable, turn it over, and put it back on—with a new connector, of course.

Okay, once you have the correct cable connected from your PC to the Cisco router or switch console port, you can start an emulation program such as PuTTY or SecureCRT to create a console connection and configure the device. Set the configuration as shown in Figure 9.6.

FIGURE 9.6   Configuring your console emulation program

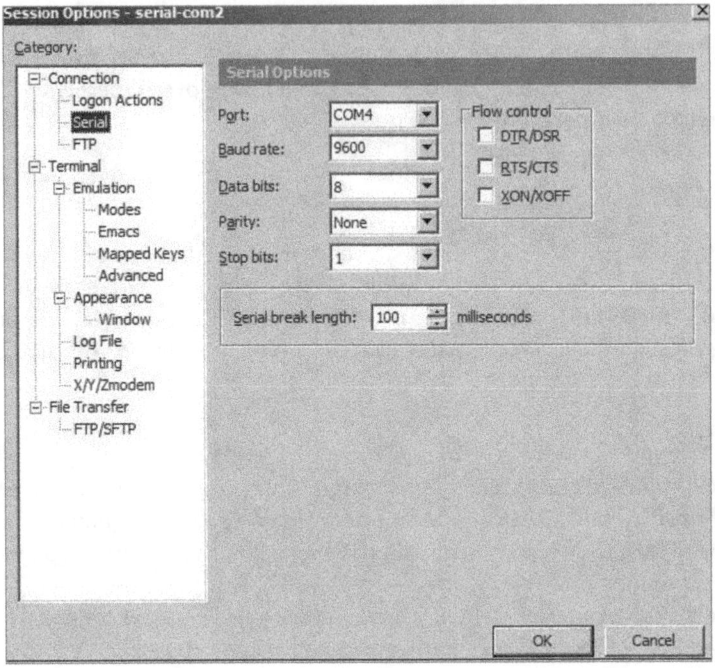

Notice that Baud Rate is set to 9600, Data Bits to 8, Parity to None, and that no Flow Control options are set. At this point, when you click Connect and press the Enter key, you should be connected to your Cisco device console port.

Figure 9.7 shows a switch with two console ports.

FIGURE 9.7   A Cisco switch with two console ports

Notice that this switch has two console connections: a typical original RJ-45 connection and the newer mini type-B USB console. Remember that the new USB port supersedes the RJ-45 port if you just happen to plug into both at the same time, and the USB port can have speeds up to 115,200 Kbps, which is awesome if you have to use Xmodem to update an IOS. I've even seen some cables that allow iPhones and iPads to connect to these mini USB ports!

The *console port* is usually an RJ-45, 8-pin modular connection located on either the front or back of the device, and there may or may not be a password set on it by default.

Serial Port

In network communications, *serial* means that one bit after another is sent out onto the wire or fiber and interpreted by a network card or other type of interface on the other end. By that definition, you can now surmise that we don't use these ports anymore.

Each 1 or 0 was read separately and then combined with others to form data. This is very different from parallel communication, where bits are sent in groups and must be read together to make sense of the message they represent. A good example of a parallel cable is an old printer cable, which has been replaced by USB, as I'll get to in a minute.

Serial ports were all the rage in the 1990s and into the 2000s, but just aren't used anymore—or just rarely.

Figure 9.8 shows an old Cisco 2500 router with two serial ports and a 10 Mbps Ethernet port. This was a very popular router for more than 10 years! The old, simple router allows you to use a serial connection (a T1, for example). Other configurations were also available with this router.

FIGURE 9.8   A Cisco 2500 router with serial ports

That other port is an attachment unit interface (AUI) port that allows you to attach to a 10 Mbps Ethernet coax network, and then eventually, we could use a transceiver that allowed us to connect to a twisted-pair RJ-45. Talk about some old history!

Universal Serial Bus

Universal serial bus (USB) is now the built-in serial bus du jour of most motherboards. You usually get a maximum of four external USB interfaces, but add-on adapters can increase that to as many as 16 serial interfaces.

USB can actually connect a maximum of 127 external devices, and it's a much more flexible peripheral bus than either serial or parallel.

USB is used to connect printers, scanners, and a host of other input devices like keyboards, joysticks, and mice. When connecting USB peripherals, you have to connect them either directly to one of the USB ports on the PC or to a USB hub that is connected to one of those USB ports. Figure 9.9 shows a USB connector.

Hubs can be chained together to provide multiple USB connections, but even though you can connect up to 127 devices, it's really not practical to do so. Each device has a USB plug, as shown in Figure 9.10.

FIGURE 9.9   A USB connector

FIGURE 9.10   A USB plug

Fiber Port

Because fiber-optic cable transmits digital signals using light impulses rather than electricity, it's immune to electromagnetic interference (EMI) and radio frequency interference (RFI). Anyone who's seen a network's unshielded twisted-pair (UTP) cable run down an elevator shaft would appreciate this feature. Fiber cable allows light impulses to be carried on either a glass or a plastic core.

Fiber-optic cabling has been around for a long time and provides some solid advantages. The cable allows for very fast transmission of data, is made of glass (even plastic), is very thin, and works as a waveguide to transmit light between two ends of the fiber. Fiber-optic cabling has been used to go very long distances, as in intercontinental connections, but it's becoming more and more popular in Ethernet LAN networks due to the fast speeds available. Also, unlike UTP, it's immune to interference like crosstalk.

The main components of fiber-optic cabling are the core and the cladding. The core holds the light, and the cladding confines the light to the core. Remember, the tighter the cladding, the smaller the core; the smaller the core, the less light sent through it, but it can go faster and farther.

Single-Mode Fiber

Single-mode fiber (SMF) is a very high-speed, long-distance cable that consists of a single strand—sometimes two strands—of glass fiber that carries the signals. Light-emitting diodes (LEDs) and laser are the light sources used with SMF. The light source is transmitted from end to end and pulsed to create communication. This is the type of fiber cable employed to span really long distances because it can transmit data 50 times farther than multimode fiber (MMF) at a faster rate.

Clearly, because the transmission media is glass, the installation of SMF can be a bit tricky. Yes, there are outer layers protecting the glass core, but the cable still shouldn't be crimped or pinched around any tight corners.

Multimode Fiber

Multimode fiber-optic cable (MMF) also uses light to communicate a signal, but the light is dispersed on numerous paths as it travels through the core and is reflected back. A special material called *cladding* is used to line the core and focus the light back onto it. MMF provides high bandwidth at high speeds over medium distances (up to about 3,000 feet), but beyond that it can be really inconsistent. This is why MMF is most often used within a smaller area of one building, whereas SMF can be used between buildings.

MMF is available in glass or in a plastic version that makes installation a lot easier and increases the installation's flexibility.

There are about 70 different connectors for fiber, and Cisco uses just a few of them, as well as proprietary connectors. To use these, you'll need an SFP.

SFPs

SFP stands for small form-factor pluggable, also known as mini-gbic (gigabit interface converter). An SFP module is simply a small modular transceiver that plugs into an SFP port on a network switch or server.

The SFP ports on a switch with the SFP modules enable the switch/router to connect to fiber and Ethernet cables of different types and speeds.

Figure 9.11 shows a Cisco GLC-T 1000BaseT Gigabit RJ-45 SFP transceiver, which you can use with Ethernet.

Figure 9.12 shows a Cisco GLC-LH-SMD 1000BaseLX/LH SFP fiber transceiver.

Ethernet Ports

You'll find an Ethernet port on pretty much any type of networking equipment worldwide, on every type of manufactures' equipment.

A discussion about Ethernet cabling is an important one, especially if you are planning on taking the Cisco exams. You need to really understand the following three types of cables:

- Straight-through cable

- Crossover cable

- Rolled cable (covered previously in the "Console Port" section)

FIGURE 9.11   A Cisco GLC-T 1000BaseT transceiver

FIGURE 9.12   A Cisco GLC-LH-SMD transceiver

The following sections discuss each type of cable, but first let's take a look at the most common Ethernet cable used today, the category 5 enhanced unshielded twisted-pair (UTP), as shown in Figure 9.13.

FIGURE 9.13 Category 5 enhanced UTP cable

Category 5 can be an old term for a cable type that's been around for a long time, but enhanced UTP cat 5 is still what most people use because it's the easiest to install.

Category 5 enhanced UTP cable can handle speeds up to a gigabit, with a distance of up to 100 meters. Typically, you'd use this cable for 100 Mbps and category 6 for a gigabit, but category 5 enhanced is rated for gigabit speeds, and category 6 is rated for 10 Gbps! However, cat 6 can have some distance limitations.

Straight-Through Cable

Straight-through cable is used to connect the following devices:

- Host to switch or hub

- Router to switch or hub

Four wires are used in straight-through cable to connect Ethernet devices. It's relatively simple to create this type. Figure 9.14 shows the four wires (two-pairs) used in a straight-through Ethernet cable.

FIGURE 9.14 A straight-through Ethernet cable

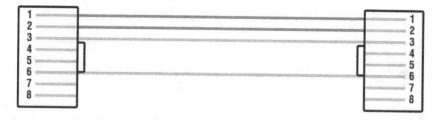

Notice that only pins 1, 2, 3, and 6 are used. Just connect 1 to 1, 2 to 2, 3 to 3, and 6 to 6, and you'll be up and networking in no time. However, remember that this would be a 10/100 Mbps Ethernet-only cable and wouldn't work with gigabit, voice, or other LAN or WAN technologies, so this was for illustration only at this point, as you'd always have all 8 pins (four-pairs) connected together.

Crossover Cable

Crossover cable can be used to connect the following devices:

- Switch to switch
- Hub to hub
- Host to host
- Hub to switch
- Router direct to host
- Router to router

The same wires used in the straight-through cable are used in a crossover cable—you just connect different pins together. Figure 9.15 shows how the wires are used in a crossover Ethernet cable.

FIGURE 9.15 A crossover Ethernet cable

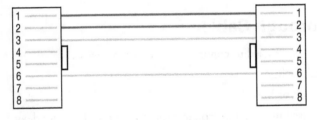

Notice that instead of connecting 1 to 1, 2 to 2, and so on, here we connect pins 1 to 3 and 2 to 6 on each side of the cable. Figure 9.16 shows some typical uses of straight-through and crossover cables.

FIGURE 9.16 Typical uses for straight-through and cross-over Ethernet cables

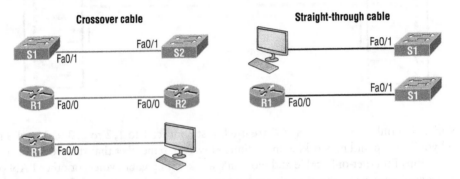

The crossover examples in Figure 9.16 are switch port to switch port, router Ethernet port to router Ethernet port, and router Ethernet port to PC Ethernet port. For the straight-through examples, I used PC Ethernet to switch port and router Ethernet port to switch port.

> It's possible to connect a straight-through cable between two switches. It will start working because of an autodetect mechanism called *automatic medium-dependent interface-crossover (Auto-MDIX)*.

UTP Gigabit Wiring (1000Base-T)

In the previous examples of 10Base-T and 100Base-T UTP wiring, only two wire pairs were used, but that is not good enough for gigabit ethernet UTP transmission.

1000Base-T UTP wiring (Figure 9.17) requires four wire pairs and uses more advanced electronics so that each and every pair in the cable can transmit simultaneously. Even so, gigabit wiring is almost identical to my earlier 10/100 example, except that the other two pairs in the cable are used.

FIGURE 9.17   UTP Gigabit crossover Ethernet cable

For a straight-through cable, it's still 1 to 1, 2 to 2, and so on, up to pin 8. And when creating the gigabit crossover cable, you would still cross 1 to 3 and 2 to 6, but you would add 4 to 7 and 5 to 8—pretty straightforward!

PoE

Power over Ethernet (PoE and PoE+) technology describes a system for transmitting electrical power, along with data, to remote devices over standard twisted-pair cable in an Ethernet network. This technology is useful for powering IP phones (Voice over IP, or VoIP), wireless LAN access points, network cameras, remote network switches, embedded computers, and other appliances. These are all situations where it would be inconvenient, expensive, and possibly not even feasible to supply power separately. A big reason for this is because the main wiring must be installed by qualified, licensed electricians in order to meet legal and/or insurance mandates.

The IEEE has created a standard for PoE called 802.3af. For PoE+ it's referred to as 802.3at. These standards describe precisely how a powered device is detected as well as two methods of delivering Power over Ethernet to a given powered device. Keep in mind that the PoE+ standard, 802.3at, delivers more power than 802.3af, which is compatible with Gigabit Ethernet with four-wire pairs at 30w.

This process happens in one of two ways: either by receiving the power from an Ethernet port on a switch (or other capable device) or via a power injector. Note that you can't use both approaches to get the job done. And be careful here because doing this wrong can lead to serious trouble! Be sure before connecting.

Figure 9.18 shows an example of a Cisco next-generation firewall (NGFW). It has eight ports, which can be routed or switched ports, and ports 7 and 8 are listed as PoE ports at 0.6A.

FIGURE 9.18   NGFW ports provide PoE

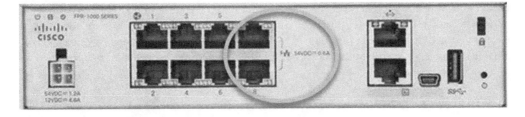

This is an excellent new NGFW that I personally use in my office. Note that if you don't have a switch with PoE, you can use a power injector.

Remote Access

This section covers how to remotely connect to your devices. I'll describe terminal emulators, remote desktop connections, Telnet, Secure Shell (SSH), VPNs, NMS stations, and Meraki. I'll also discuss how to use scripts for remote access.

Terminal Emulators

Terminal emulators replicate the functionality of a traditional computer terminal to provide users with access to a local or distant host. The emulator presents a terminal window to appear as though it is directly connected to the client.

Most terminal emulators are designed for specific uses and function only with specific operating systems. Companies use these tools to access data and programs on remote devices, servers, or mainframes.

Personally, I like SecureCRT, and I know a lot of people who also like and use PuTTY, but there literally are hundreds of terminal emulators to choose from.

Remote Desktop Gateway/Remote Desktop Protocol

There are times when you need to make a remote connection to a machine to perform troubleshooting but you are miles away. Connectivity software is designed to allow you to make a connection to a machine, see the desktop, and perform any action you could perform if you were sitting in front of it.

Remote Desktop Gateway (RDG or RD Gateway) is a Windows Server role that provides a secure encrypted connection to the server via RDP.

Remote Desktop Protocol (RDP) is a proprietary protocol developed by Microsoft. It allows you to connect to another computer and run programs, which is somewhat like what Telnet was created for, except instead of getting a command-line interface prompt, as you do with Telnet, you get the actual graphical user interface (GUI) of the remote computer.

You need to have an RDP gateway and an RDP client. Microsoft renamed their Terminal Services to Remote Desktop Services. Microsoft's official client name is Remote Desktop Connection, which was called Terminal Services Client. RDP uses TCP port 3389, so make sure to open this port on your firewall if needed.

After establishing a connection, the user sees a terminal window that's basically a precon-figured window that looks like a Windows desktop or another operating system's desktop. From there, the user on the client computer can access applications and files available to them by using the remote desktop.

As an example of how I use this protocol, I use an RDP client for my students in my various Cisco classes so they can get to a remote computer running an RDP Gateway in my data center. From there, they can configure the pod of gear used for the classroom labs.

Telnet

Telnet was one of the first Internet standards, developed in 1969, and is the chameleon of protocols—its specialty is terminal emulation. It allows a user on a remote client machine, called the Telnet client, to access the resources of another machine, the Telnet server, in order to access a command-line interface. Telnet achieves this by pulling a fast one on the Telnet server and making the client machine appear as though it were a terminal directly attached to the local network. This projection is actually a software image—a virtual terminal that can interact with the chosen remote host. A major drawback is that no encryption tech-niques are available within the Telnet protocol, so everything must be sent in clear text, including passwords!

Figure 9.19 shows an example of a Telnet client trying to connect to a Telnet server.

FIGURE 9.19 Telnet

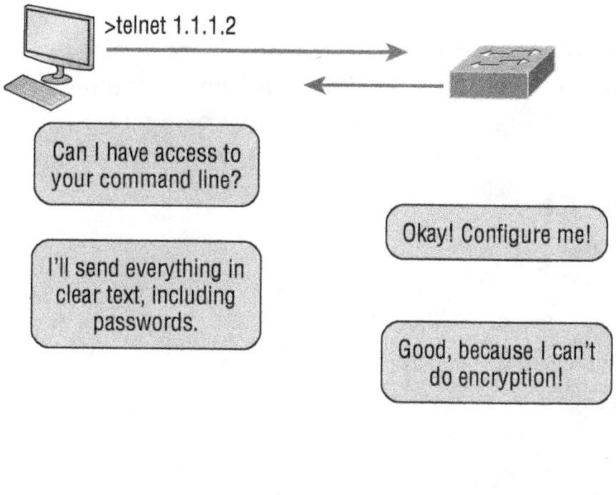

These emulated terminals are of the text-mode type and can execute defined procedures such as displaying menus that give users the opportunity to choose options and access the applications on the duped server. Users begin a Telnet session by running the Telnet client software and then logging into the Telnet server. Telnet uses an 8-bit, byte-oriented data connection over TCP port 23, which makes it very thorough. It's still in use today because it is easy to use and has very low overhead, but again, with everything sent in clear text, it's not recommended in production.

As part of the TCP/IP protocol suite, *Telnet* is a virtual terminal protocol that allows you to make connections to remote devices, gather information, and run programs.

After your routers and switches are configured, you can use the Telnet program to reconfigure and/or check up on them without using a console cable. You run the Telnet program by typing **telnet** from any command prompt (Windows or Cisco), but you need to have VTY passwords set on the IOS devices in order for this to work.

You can issue the `telnet` command from any router or switch prompt. In the following code, I'm trying to telnet from switch 1 to switch 3 located at the destination IP address of 10.100.128.8:

```
SW-1#telnet 10.100.128.8
Trying 10.100.128.8 ... Open

Password required, but none set

[Connection to 10.100.128.8 closed by foreign host]
```

Oops! Clearly, I didn't set my passwords—how embarrassing! Remember that the VTY ports are configured by default as `login`, meaning that we have to either set the VTY passwords or use the no `login` command.

 If you can't telnet into a device, it could be that the password on the remote device hasn't been set. It's also quite possible that an access control list is filtering the Telnet session.

Telnet Password

To set the user-mode password for Telnet access into the router or switch, use the `line vty` command. IOS switches typically have 15 lines, but routers running the Enterprise edition have considerably more. The best way to find out how many lines you have is to use a question mark, as follows:

```
Todd(config)#line vty 0 ?
<1-15> Last Line number
<cr>
Todd(config)#line vty 0 15
Todd(config-line)#password telnet
Todd(config-line)#login
```

What will happen if you try to telnet into a device that doesn't have a VTY password set? You'll receive an error saying the connection has been refused because the password isn't set. So, if you try to Telnet into a switch and receive a message like the following, which I got from Switch B, it means the switch doesn't have the VTY password set:

```
Todd#telnet SwitchB
Trying SwitchB (10.0.0.1)...Open
Password required, but none set
[Connection to SwitchB closed by foreign host]
Todd#
```

However, you can still get around this and tell the switch to allow Telnet connections without a password by using the no login command:

```
SwitchB(config-line)#line vty 0 15
SwitchB(config-line)#no login
```

 I definitely do *not* recommend using the no login command to allow Telnet connections without a password, unless you're in a testing or classroom environment. In a production network, always set your VTY password!

After your IOS devices are configured with an IP address, you can use the Telnet program to configure and check your routers instead of having to use a console cable. You can use the Telnet program by typing **telnet** from any command prompt (DOS or Cisco).

If you want to view the connections from your router or switch to a remote device, just use the show sessions command. In this case, I've telnetted into both the SW-3 (IP address 10.100.128.8) and SW-2 (IP address 10.100.128.9) switches from SW1:

```
SW-1#sh sessions
Conn Host Address Byte Idle Conn Name
1 10.100.128.9 10.100.128.9 0 10.100.128.9
* 2 10.100.128.8 10.100.128.8 0 10.100.128.8
SW-1#
```

See that asterisk (*) next to connection 2? It means that session 2 was the last session I connected to. You can return to your last session by pressing Enter twice. You can also return to any session by typing the number of the connection and then pressing Enter.

Secure Shell

The *Secure Shell (SSH)* protocol sets up a secure session that's similar to Telnet over a standard TCP/IP connection and is employed for doing things like logging into systems, running programs on remote systems, and moving files from one system to another. And it does all of this while maintaining an encrypted connection.

Figure 9.20 shows a SSH client trying to connect to a SSH server. The client must send the data encrypted.

FIGURE 9.20   Secure Shell

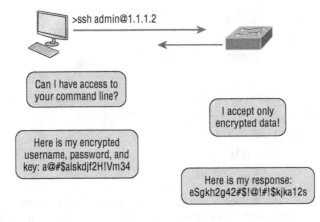

You can think of SSH as the new-generation protocol that's now used in place of the antiquated and very unused `rsh` and `rlogin`—even Telnet.

I strongly recommend using Secure Shell (SSH) instead of Telnet because it creates a more secure session. The Telnet application uses an unencrypted data stream, but SSH uses encryption keys to send data so your username and password aren't sent in the clear and vulnerable to anyone lurking around!

Here are the steps for setting up SSH:

1. Set your hostname:

```
Router(config)#hostname Todd
```

2. Set the domain name. Both the hostname and domain name are required for the encryption keys to be generated:

```
Todd(config)#ip domain-name Lammle.com
```

3. Set the username to allow SSH client access:

```
Todd(config)#username Todd password Lammle
```

4. Generate the encryption keys for securing the session:

```
Todd(config)#crypto key generate rsa
The name for the keys will be: Todd.Lammle.com
Choose the size of the key modulus in the range of 350 to
5095 for your General Purpose Keys. Choosing a key modulus
Greater than 512 may take a few minutes.
How many bits in the modulus [512]: 1025
```

```
% Generating 1025 bit RSA keys, keys will be non-exportable...
[OK] (elapsed time was 5 seconds)
Todd(config)#
1d15h: %SSH-5-ENABLED: SSH 1.99 has been enabled*June 25
19:25:30.035: %SSH-5-ENABLED: SSH 1.99 has been enabled
```

5. Enable SSH version 2 on the device—not mandatory, but strongly suggested:

    Todd(config)#**ip ssh version 2**

6. Connect to the VTY lines of the switch or router:

    Todd(config)#**line vty 0 15**

7. Tell the lines to use the local database for password:

    Todd(config-line)#**login local**

8. Configure your access protocols:

    ```
    Todd(config-line)#transport input ?
    all All protocols
    none No protocols
    ssh TCP/IP SSH protocol
    telnet TCP/IP Telnet protocol
    ```

Beware of the following line and never use it in production because it's a horrendous security risk:

```
Todd(config-line)#transport input all
```

Instead, I recommend using the following line to secure your VTY lines with SSH:

```
Todd(config-line)#transport input ssh ?
telnet TCP/IP Telnet protocol
<cr>
```

I actually do use Telnet once in a while when a situation arises that specifically calls for it. It just doesn't happen very often. But if you want to go with SSH and Telnet, here's how you do that:

```
Todd(config-line)#transport input ssh telnet
```

Note that if you don't use the keyword telnet at the end of the command string, then only SSH will work on the device. You can go with either, just so long as you understand that SSH is much more secure than Telnet.

Virtual Private Networks

Of course, you've heard the term *VPN* before and probably have a pretty good idea of what one is, but just in case: A *virtual private network (VPN)* allows the creation of private networks across the Internet, providing privacy and the tunneling of non-TCP/IP protocols.

VPNs are used daily to give remote users and disparate networks connectivity over a public medium like the Internet instead of using more expensive, permanent means.

VPNs are actually pretty easy to understand. A VPN fits somewhere between a LAN and WAN, with the WAN often simulating a LAN link. Basically, your computer on one LAN connects to a different, remote LAN and uses its resources remotely. The challenge when using VPNs is a big one—security! This may sound a lot like connecting a LAN (or virtual LAN [VLAN]) to a WAN, but a VPN is so much more.

Here's the key difference: A typical WAN connects two or more remote LANs together using a router and someone else's network, like your Internet service provider's. Your local host and router see these networks as remote networks, not local networks or local resources.

A VPN actually makes your local host part of the remote network by using the WAN link that connects you to the remote LAN. The VPN will make your host appear as though it's actually local on the remote network. This means you gain access to the remote LAN's resources, and that access is also very secure.

Figure 9.21 shows my host using a VPN connection from Colorado to Texas. This allows me to access the remote network services and servers as if my host were right there on the same VLAN.

FIGURE 9.21   An example of using a VPN

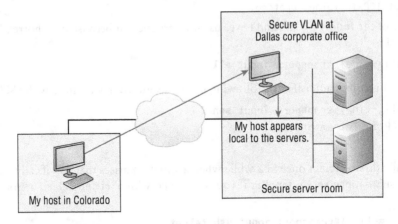

Why is this so important? If you answered, "Because my servers in Texas are secure, and only the hosts on the same VLAN are allowed to connect to them and use the resources of these servers," you nailed it!

A VPN allows me to connect to these resources by locally attaching to the VLAN through a VPN across the WAN. My other option is to open my network and servers to everyone on the Internet, so clearly it's vital for me to have a VPN!

Network Management Systems

Although the *Simple Network Management Protocol (SNMP)* certainly isn't the oldest protocol, it's still pretty old, considering it was created way back in 1988 (RFC 1065).

SNMP is an Application layer protocol that provides a message format for agents on a variety of devices to communicate with network management stations (NMSs). Examples include Cisco Prime and HP OpenView. Agents send messages to the NMS station, which then reads the information from a database stored on the NMS called a Management Information Base (MIB).

NMS periodically queries or polls the SNMP agent on a device to gather and analyze statistics via GET messages. End devices running SNMP agents will send an SNMP TRAP message to the NMS if a problem occurs (see Figure 9.22).

FIGURE 9.22   SNMP GET and TRAP messages

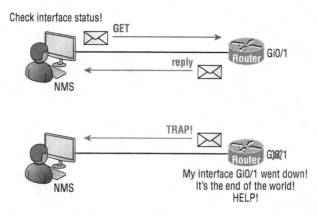

You can also use SNMP to provide agents with SET messages. In addition to polling for statistics, SNMP can analyze information and compile it into a report or even a graph. When thresholds are exceeded, a process is triggered alerting about the event. Graphing tools are used to monitor the CPU statistics of Cisco devices, such as core routers. The CPU should be monitored continuously, and the NMS can graph the statistics. Notifications are sent when any threshold you've set is exceeded.

Cloud-Managed Network (Meraki)

The new kid in town is the ability to manage network devices from a cloud. The benefit of this management method is that instead of using a CLI to configure the device, the device registers itself to the cloud portal.

Once the device is registered, you do all the configuration from the cloud portal using a web browser or with scripts—but I'll talk about that later. In fact, cloud-managed solutions like Cisco Meraki don't have a CLI at all!

Figure 9.23 shows a switch port configuration in Meraki. You can see that many of the concepts discussed in this book, such as VLANs or trunks, are still there, but you configure them by filling out the text boxes or selecting the proper button. You still need to understand what the features do; you just configure them differently than you have done up till now.

FIGURE 9.23   A Meraki switch configuration

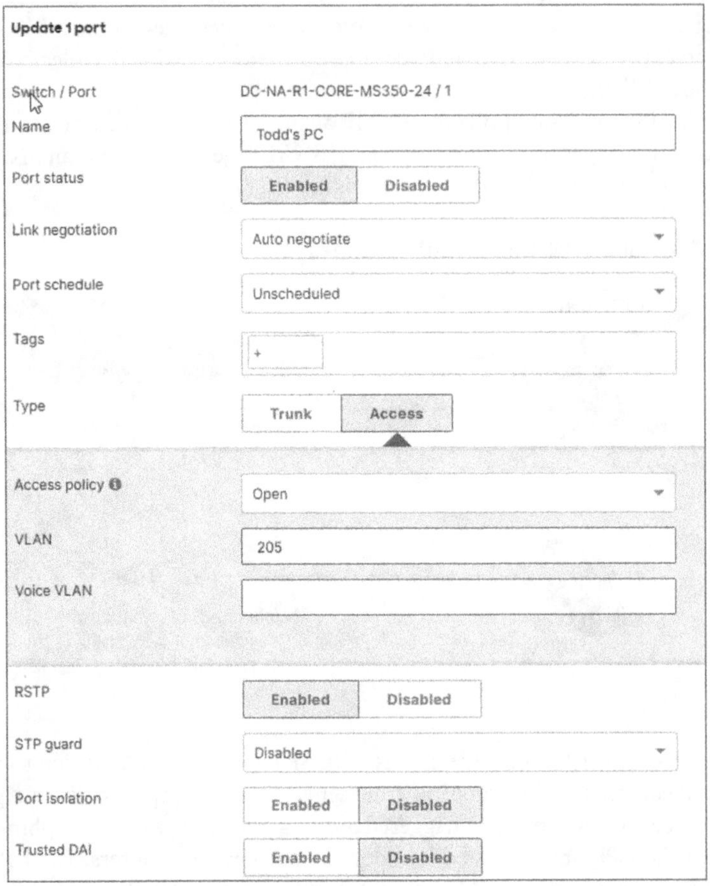

Cisco's Meraki product line offers a wide range of solutions, including switches, firewalls, and even security cameras. Meraki configuration is a lot more streamlined than with its big brother, Cisco.

Scripts

Automation is a hot topic right now because manually configuring network devices eventually becomes tedious after you configured a switch virtual interface (SVI) on a switch a couple thousand times over your career. More importantly, manual configuration can be risky because every line you type in a router has the possibility of you accidentally messing something up that ends up creating problems. Maybe you mess up the ACL you're making and block access to everything; maybe you shut down the wrong interface; or maybe you log into the wrong device and paste in configuration for another device entirely.

Scripts can help both the tedium and errors by letting you push configuration to many devices at once; however, if you mess up your script, you'll just end up breaking all devices instead of the one you were manually configuring! Scripting itself is a massive topic with endless options. There are scripting/programming languages such as Python, network controllers such as Cisco's DNA Center, and configuration-management solutions such as Ansible—all of which are covered in more detail in the *CCNA Study Guide*.

For reference, the upcoming longer code is an example of a Python script that connects to three routers and shows the output from the following command, which shows all the interfaces with IP addresses assigned:

```
show ip interface brief | exclude unass
```

It's important to note that the CCST exam requires you only to know that scripting exists; Cisco isn't going to want to see if you can write a script or anything like that.

So, you don't need to know how the following script works at this technical level, but if this piques your interest, then consider looking at the DevNet Associate when you get more experience:

```
from netmiko import ConnectHandler

username = "admin"
password = "CiscoIsFun"

r01 = {
          'device_type': 'cisco_ios',
          'host': 'r01.tpt-lab.com',
          'username': username,
          'password': password,
          'secret': password
}

r02 = {
          'device_type': 'cisco_ios',
          'host': 'r02.tpt-lab.com',
          'username': username,
          'password': password,
          'secret': password
}

r03 = {
          'device_type': 'cisco_ios',
          'host': 'r03.tpt-lab.com',
          'username': username,
          'password': password,
          'secret': password
```

```
}

all_routers = [r01, r02, r03]

for device in all_routers:
    net_connect = ConnectHandler(**device)
    net_connect.enable()
    net_connect.send_command("terminal width 0")
    print("*****" * 20)
    print(device['host'])
    print("*****" * 20 + "\n")
    print(net_connect.send_command("show ip interface brief | exclude un"))
```

The result from this script shows the device name followed by the output from the show ip interface brief command:

```
************************************************************************************
*********************
r01.tpt-lab.com
************************************************************************************
*********************

Interface              IP-Address      OK? Method Status
Protocol
GigabitEthernet1       10.30.10.81     YES NVRAM  up                          up
GigabitEthernet2.12    10.1.2.1        YES NVRAM  up                          up
GigabitEthernet2.13    10.1.3.1        YES NVRAM  up                          up
GigabitEthernet2.14    10.1.4.1        YES NVRAM  up                          up
Loopback0              192.168.255.1   YES NVRAM  up                          up


************************************************************************************
*********************
r02.tpt-lab.com
************************************************************************************
*********************

Interface              IP-Address      OK? Method Status
Protocol
GigabitEthernet1       10.30.10.82     YES NVRAM  up                          up
GigabitEthernet2.12    10.1.2.2        YES NVRAM  up                          up
GigabitEthernet2.23    10.2.3.2        YES NVRAM  up                          up
GigabitEthernet2.24    10.2.4.2        YES NVRAM  up                          up
```

```
Loopback0              192.168.255.2   YES NVRAM  up                    up

**********************************************************************
**********************
r03.tpt-lab.com
**********************************************************************
**********************

Interface              IP-Address      OK? Method Status
Protocol
GigabitEthernet1       10.30.10.83     YES NVRAM  up                    up
GigabitEthernet2.13    10.1.3.3        YES NVRAM  up                    up
GigabitEthernet2.23    10.2.3.3        YES NVRAM  up                    up
GigabitEthernet2.34    10.3.4.3        YES NVRAM  up                    up
Loopback0              192.168.255.3   YES NVRAM  up                    up


Process finished with exit code 0
```

Cisco Device *show* Commands

In this section, I'll run through some basic and very common Cisco router and switch commands. Let's get started with the common Cisco CLI command, show running-config.

show running-config (show run)

To verify the configuration in dynamic RAM (DRAM), use the show running-config command (sh run for short), which provides the current configuration the device is using:

```
Router#show running-config
Building configuration...
Current configuration : 877 bytes
!
version 15.0
```

Next, you should check the configuration stored in non-volatile RAM (NVRAM), which is basically RAM that is not deleted when the device is either turned off or rebooted. To see this, use the show startup-config command (sh start for short):

```
Router#sh start
Using 877 out of 724288 bytes
!
! Last configuration change at 04:49:14 UTC Fri Mar 7 2019
!
version 15.0
```

As shown in the following output, by copying running-config to NVRAM as a backup, you ensure that your running-config file will always be reloaded if the router gets rebooted. Starting in the 12.0 IOS, you'll be prompted for the filename you want to use.

```
Router#copy running-config startup-config
Destination filename [startup-config]?[enter]
Building configuration...
[OK]
```

To delete the startup-config file on a Cisco router or switch, use the command erase startup-config:

```
Todd#erase startup-config
Erasing the nvram filesystem will remove all configuration files!
Continue? [confirm][enter]
[OK]
Erase of nvram: complete
*Mar 7 17:55:20.405: %SYS-7-NV_BLOCK_INIT: Initialized the geometry of nvram
Todd#reload
System configuration has been modified. Save? [yes/no]:n
Proceed with reload? [confirm][enter]
*Mar 7 17:55:31.079: %SYS-5-RELOAD: Reload requested by console.
Reload Reason: Reload Command.
```

This command deletes the contents of NVRAM on the switch and router. If you type reload while in privileged mode and say no to saving changes, the switch or router will reload and come up into setup mode since you no longer have a configuration on the device.

show cdp neighbors

The show cdp neighbors command (sh cdp nei for short) delivers information about directly connected devices. It's important to remember that CDP packets aren't passed through a Cisco switch and that you see only what's directly attached. This means that if your router is connected to a switch, you won't see any of the Cisco devices connected to that switch!

The following output shows the show cdp neighbors command:

```
SW-3#sh cdp neighbors
Capability Codes: R - Router, T - Trans Bridge, B - Source Route Bridge
S - Switch, H - Host, I - IGMP, r - Repeater, P - Phone,
D - Remote, C - CVTA, M - Two-port Mac Relay Device ID Local Intrfce Holdtme
Capability Platform Port ID
SW-1 Fas 0/1 150 S I WS-C3560- Fas 0/15
SW-1 Fas 0/2 150 S I WS-C3560- Fas 0/16
SW-2 Fas 0/5 162 S I WS-C3560- Fas 0/5
SW-2 Fas 0/6 162 S I WS-C3560- Fas 0/6
```

You can see that SW-3 is directly connected with a console cable to the SW-3 switch, and that SW-3 is directly connected to two other switches. CDP allows me to see who my directly connected neighbors are and gather information about them. From the SW-3 switch, you can see that there are two connections to SW-1 and two connections to SW-2. SW-3 connects to SW-1 with ports Fas 0/1 and Fas 0/2, and there are connections to SW-2 with local interfaces Fas 0/5 and Fas 0/6. Both the SW-1 and SW-2 switches are 3650 switches. SW-1 is using ports Fas 0/15 and Fas 0/16 to connect to SW-3. SW-2 is using ports Fas 0/5 and Fas 0/6.

To summarize, the device ID shows the configured hostname of the connected device, that the local interface is our interface, and that the port ID is the remote device's directly connected interface. Remember that all you get to view are directly connected devices!

Table 9.1 summarizes the information displayed by the show cdp neighbors command for each device.

TABLE 9.1 Output of the show cdp neighbors command

Field	Description
Device ID	The hostname of the device directly connected.
Local Interface	The port or interface that CDP packets are received on.
Holdtime	The amount of time the router will hold the information before discarding it if no more CDP packets are received.
Capability	The capability of the neighbor—the router, switch, or repeater. The capability codes are listed at the top of the command output.
Platform	The type of Cisco device directly connected. In the previous output, the SW-3 shows that it's directly connected to two 3560 switches.
Port ID	The neighbor device's port or interface that CDP packets are multicast from.

Another command that will deliver the goods on neighbor information is the show cdp neighbors detail command (show cdp nei de for short).

The show cdp neighbors detail command can be run on both routers and switches. It displays detailed information about each device connected to the device you're running the command on. Check out the router output:

```
SW-3#sh cdp neighbors detail
-------------------------
Device ID: SW-1
Device ID: SW-1
Entry address(es):
  IP address: 10.100.128.10
```

```
Platform: cisco WS-C3560-24TS,  Capabilities: Switch IGMP
Interface: FastEthernet0/1,  Port ID (outgoing port): FastEthernet0/15
Holdtime : 135 sec

Version :
Cisco IOS Software, C3560 Software (C3560-IPSERVICESK9-M), Version 12.2(55)
SE5, RELEASE SOFTWARE (fc1)
Technical Support: http://www.cisco.com/techsupport
Copyright (c) 1986-2013 by Cisco Systems, Inc.
Compiled Mon 28-Jan-13 10:10 by prod_rel_team

advertisement version: 2
Protocol Hello:  OUI=0x00000C, Protocol ID=0x0112; payload len=25, value=
00000000FFFFFFFF010221FF000000000000001C555EC880Fc00f000
VTP Management Domain: 'NULL'
Native VLAN: 1
Duplex: full
Power Available TLV:

    Power request id: 0, Power management id: 1, Power available: 0, Power
management level: -1
Management address(es):
  IP address: 10.100.128.10
------------------------

[output cut]

------------------------

Device ID: SW-2
Entry address(es):
  IP address: 10.100.128.9
Platform: cisco WS-C3560-8PC,  Capabilities: Switch IGMP
Interface: FastEthernet0/5,  Port ID (outgoing port): FastEthernet0/5
Holdtime : 129 sec

Version :
Cisco IOS Software, C3560 Software (C3560-IPBASE-M), Version 12.2(35)SE5,
RELEASE SOFTWARE (fc1)
Copyright (c) 1986-2005 by Cisco Systems, Inc.
Compiled Thu 19-Jul-05 18:15 by nachen

advertisement version: 2
Protocol Hello:  OUI=0x00000C, Protocol ID=0x0112; payload len=25, value=
00000000FFFFFFFF010221FF000000000000B41489D91880Fc00f000
```

```
VTP Management Domain: 'NULL'
Native VLAN: 1
Duplex: full
Power Available TLV:

    Power request id: 0, Power management id: 1, Power available: 0, Power
management level: -1
Management address(es):
  IP address: 10.100.128.9
[output cut]
```

So what do we see here? We've been given the hostname and IP address of all directly connected devices. In addition to the same information displayed by the show cdp neighbors command, the show cdp neighbors detail command tells us the IOS version and IP address of the neighbor device. Nice!

Documenting a Network Topology Using CDP

As the title of this section implies, I'm now going to show you how to document a sample network by using CDP. You'll learn to determine the appropriate router types, interface types, and IP addresses of various interfaces using only CDP commands and the show running-config command. And you can only console into the Lab_A router to document the network. You'll have to assign any remote routers the next IP address in each range. You will use Figure 9.24 to complete the documentation.

FIGURE 9.24 Documenting a network topology using CDP

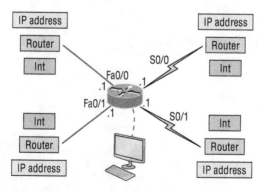

In this output, you can see that you have a router with four interfaces: two Fast Ethernet interfaces and two serial interfaces. First, determine the IP addresses of each interface by using the show running-config command:

Lab_A#**sh running-config**

```
Building configuration...

Current configuration : 960 bytes
!
version 12.2
service timestamps debug uptime
service timestamps log uptime
no service password-encryption
!
hostname Lab_A
!
ip subnet-zero
!
!
interface FastEthernet0/0
 ip address 192.168.21.1 255.255.255.0
 duplex auto
!
interface FastEthernet0/1
 ip address 192.168.18.1 255.255.255.0
 duplex auto
!
interface Serial0/0
ip address 192.168.23.1 255.255.255.0
 !
interface Serial0/1
ip address 192.168.28.1 255.255.255.0
 !
ip classless
!
line con 0
line aux 0
line vty 0 4
!
end
```

With this step completed, you can now write down the IP addresses of the Lab_A router's four interfaces. Next, you need to determine the type of device on the other end of each of these interfaces. It's easy to do this—just use the show cdp neighbors command:

```
Lab_A#sh cdp neighbors
Capability Codes: R - Router, T - Trans Bridge, B - Source Route Bridge
S - Switch, H - Host, I - IGMP, r - Repeater
Device ID   Local Intrfce    Holdtme    Capability Platform  Port ID
Lab_B       Fas 0/0          178        R          2501      E0
```

Lab_C	Fas 0/1	137	R	2621	Fa0/0
Lab_D	Ser 0/0	178	R	2514	S1
Lab_E	Ser 0/1	137	R	2620	S0/1
Lab_A#					

You have a good deal of information now! By using both the show running-config and show cdp neighbors commands, you know about all the IP addresses of the Lab_A router plus the types of routers connected to each of the Lab_A router's links and all the interfaces of the remote routers.

And by using all the information gathered from show running-config and show cdp neighbors, you can now create the topology shown in Figure 9.25.

FIGURE 9.25   Network topology documented

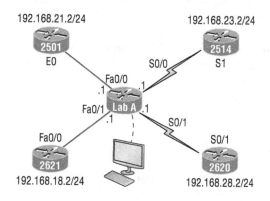

If necessary, you could have also used the show cdp neighbors detail command to view the neighbor's IP addresses.

Link Layer Discovery Protocol

Before moving away from CDP, I need to discuss a nonproprietary discovery protocol that provides much of the same information as CDP but works in multivendor networks.

The IEEE created a new standardized discovery protocol called 802.1AB for Station and Media Access Control Connectivity Discovery. We'll just call it the Link Layer Discovery Protocol (LLDP).

LLDP defines basic discovery capabilities, but it was also enhanced to specifically address the voice application, and this version is called LLDP-MED (Media Endpoint Discovery). LLDP and LLDP-MED are not compatible.

show ip route

By using the command show ip route on a router, you can see the routing table (map of the internetwork) that the following router output used to make its forwarding decisions:

Lab_A#**sh ip route**

```
Codes: L - local, C - connected, S - static,
[output cut]
10.0.0.0/8 is variably subnetted, 6 subnets, 4 masks
C 10.0.0.0/8 is directly connected, FastEthernet0/3
L 10.0.0.1/32 is directly connected, FastEthernet0/3
C 10.10.0.0/16 is directly connected, FastEthernet0/2
L 10.10.0.1/32 is directly connected, FastEthernet0/2
C 10.10.10.0/24 is directly connected, FastEthernet0/1
L 10.10.10.1/32 is directly connected, FastEthernet0/1
S* 0.0.0.0/0 is directly connected, FastEthernet0/0
```

The C in the routing table output means that the networks listed are directly connected. Until you add a dynamic routing protocol like RIPv2, OSPF, etc., to the routers in your internetwork, or enter static routes, only directly connected networks will show up in our routing table.

But what about that L in the routing table? That's new, isn't it? Yes! In the new Cisco IOS 15 code, Cisco defines a different route, called a local host route. Each local route has a /32 prefix, defining a route just for the one address.

So, in this example, the router relied on these routes, which list their own local IP addresses, to more efficiently forward packets to the router itself.

show version

You can see the current value of the configuration register by using the show version command (sh version or show ver for short), as follows:

```
Router#show version
[output cut]
System returned to ROM by power-on
System image file is "flash:c2600nm-advsecurityk9-mz.151-4.M6.bin"
[output cut]
Cisco 2611 (revision 1.0) with 249656K/12266K bytes of memory.
Processor board ID FTX1049A1AB
2 FastEthernet interfaces
2 Serial(sync/async) interfaces
1 Virtual Private Network (VPN) Module
DRAM configuration is 64 bits wide with parity enabled.
239K bytes of non-volatile configuration memory.
62820K bytes of ATA CompactFlash (Read/Write)
Configuration register is 0x2102
```

Notice that the show version command provides the IOS version. In the preceding example, it shows the IOS version as 15.1(4)M6. This output also shows the RAM, NVRAM, and flash size.

The last information given from this command is the value of the configuration register. In this example, the value is 0x2102—the default setting. The configuration register setting of 0x2102 tells the router to look in NVRAM for the boot sequence.

> The show version command displays system hardware configuration information, the software version, and the names of the boot images on a router.

To change the configuration register, use the config-register command from global configuration mode:

```
Router(config)#config-register 0x2142
Router(config)#do sh ver
[output cut]
Configuration register is 0x2102 (will be 0x2142 at next reload)
```

Be careful when setting the configuration register!

show inventory

The show inventory command displays a list of the specified components in the chassis. If no components are specified when you run the command, all components are listed.

This command also retrieves and displays inventory information about each Cisco product in the form of a universal device identifier (UDI). The UDI is a combination of three separate data elements: a product identifier (PID), a version identifier (VID), and the serial number (SN).

The PID is the name by which the product can be ordered; it has been historically called the *Product Name* or *Part Number*. This is the number that you would use to order a replacement part.

Here is the show inventory command run on a Cisco Firepower 1010 series device. The command provides useful information about that device, such as the number and types of ports and the serial number of the device:

```
firepower# show inventory
Name: "module 0", DESCR: "Firepower 1010 Appliance, Desktop, 8 GE, 1 MGMT"
PID: FPR-1010          , VID: V01     , SN: JMX2539X06S
```

Here is the same command on the Cisco 12008 switch. It shows the cards in each slot, their capability, and the S/N.

```
Router# show inventory
NAME: "Chassis", DESCR: "12008/GRP chassis"
PID: GSR8/40           , VID: V01,  SN: 63915640

NAME: "slot 0", DESCR: "GRP"
```

```
PID: GRP-B              , VID: V01,  SN: CAB021300R5

NAME: "slot 1", DESCR: "4 port ATM OC3 multimode"
PID: 40C3/ATM-MM-SC     , VID: V01,  SN: CAB04036GT1

NAME: "slot 3", DESCR: "4 port 0C3 POS multimode"
PID: LC-40C3/POS-MM     , VID: V01,  SN: CAB014900GU

NAME: "slot 5", DESCR: "1 port Gigabit Ethernet"
PID: GE-GBIC-SC-B       , VID: V01,  SN: CAB034251NX

NAME: "slot 7", DESCR: "GRP"
PID: GRP-B              , VID: V01,  SN: CAB0428AN40
```

show switch

A typical access closet contains one of more access switches placed next to each other in the same rack and uses high-speed redundant links with copper, or more typically fiber, to the distribution layer switches.

Here are three big drawbacks to a typical switch topology:

- There is an overhead of management.
- STP will block half of the uplinks.
- There is no direct communication between switches.

Cisco StackWise technology connects switches that are mounted in the same rack so that they basically become one larger switch. By doing this, you can add more access ports for each closet while avoiding the cost of upgrading to a bigger switch.

So, you're adding ports as you grow your company, instead of front-loading the investment into a pricier, larger switch all at once. And since these stacks are managed as a single unit, it reduces the management of your network.

All switches in a stack share configuration and routing information, so you can easily add or remove switches at any time without disrupting your network or affecting its performance.

The show switch command provides information about switch stacks. The following options are available with the show switch command:

```
3560-New#show switch ?
   <1-8>        Switch Number
   detail       show detailed information about the stack ring
   hstack-ports show the status of the horizontal stack ports
   neighbors    show each switch's neighbors
   stack-ports  show the status of the stack ports
   stack-ring   show stack ring
   |            Output modifiers
   <cr>
```

I ran the command on my Master switch. The following output shows the base MAC address, the priority to become Master, the version, and the state of the switch:

```
3560-New#show switch
Switch/Stack Mac Address : 4ca6.4d28.2380
                                       H/W   Current
Switch#  Role   Mac Address    Priority Version State
-------------------------------------------------------
*1       Master 4ca6.4d28.2380   1      4       Ready
```

show mac-address-table

When a frame arrives at a switch interface, the destination hardware address is compared to the forward/filter MAC database. If the destination hardware address is known and listed in the database, the frame is only sent out of the appropriate exit interface. The switch won't transmit the frame out any interface except for the destination interface, which preserves bandwidth on the other network segments. This process is called *frame filtering*.

But if the destination hardware address isn't listed in the MAC database, also known as the content addressable memory (CAM) table, then the frame will be flooded out all active interfaces except the interface it was received on. If a device answers the flooded frame, the MAC database is then updated with the device's location—its correct interface.

If a host or server sends a broadcast on the LAN, by default, the switch will flood the frame out all active ports except the source port. Remember, the switch creates smaller collision domains, but it's always still one large broadcast domain by default.

Figure 9.26 shows Host A sending a data frame to Host D. What do you think the switch will do when it receives the frame from Host A?

FIGURE 9.26   Forward/filter table

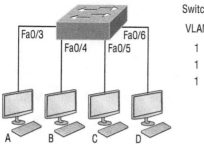

VLAN	Mac Address	Ports
1	0005.dccb.d74b	Fa0/4
1	000a.f467.9e80	Fa0/5
1	000a.f467.9e8b	Fa0/6

Switch# show mac address-table

Let's examine Figure 9.27 to find the answer.

Since Host A's MAC address is not in the forward/filter table, the switch will add the source address and port to the MAC address table, then forward the frame to Host D.

It's important to remember that the source MAC is always checked first to make sure it's in the CAM table. After that, if Host D's MAC address wasn't found in the forward/filter table, the switch would've flooded the frame out all ports except for port Fa0/3 because that's the specific port the frame was received on.

FIGURE 9.27   Forward/filter table answer

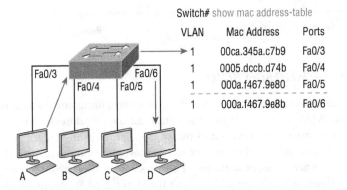

Now let's take a look at the output that results from using a `show mac address-table` command:

```
Switch#sh mac address-table
Vlan Mac Address Type Ports]]>
---- ----------- -------- -----
1 0005.dccb.d74b DYNAMIC Fa0/1
1 000a.f467.9e80 DYNAMIC Fa0/3
1 000a.f467.9e8b DYNAMIC Fa0/4
1 000a.f467.9e8c DYNAMIC Fa0/3
1 0010.7b7f.c2b0 DYNAMIC Fa0/3
1 0030.80dc.460b DYNAMIC Fa0/3
1 0030.9492.a5dd DYNAMIC Fa0/1
1 00d0.58ad.05f4 DYNAMIC Fa0/1
```

Let's say the preceding switch received a frame with the following MAC addresses:

Source MAC: 0005.dccb.d74b
Destination MAC: 000a.f467.9e8c

How will the switch handle this frame? The right answer is that the destination MAC address will be found in the MAC address table and the frame will only be forwarded out Fa0/3. Never forget that if the destination MAC address isn't found in the forward/filter table, the frame will be forwarded out all of the switch's ports except for the one on which it was originally received in an attempt to locate the destination device.

show interface

The command `show interface` x reveals the hardware address, logical address, and encapsulation method as well as statistics on collisions, as shown here:

```
Router#sh int f0/0
FastEthernet0/0 is up, line protocol is up
  Hardware is MV96340 Ethernet, address is 001a.2f55.c9e8 (bia 001a.2f55.c9e8)
  Internet address is 192.168.1.33/27
MTU 1500 bytes, BW 100000 Kbit, DLY 100 usec,
    reliability 255/255, txload 1/255, rxload 1/255
  Encapsulation ARPA, loopback not set
  Keepalive set (10 sec)
  Auto-duplex, Auto Speed, 100BaseTX/FX
  ARP type: ARPA, ARP Timeout 04:00:00
  Last input never, output 00:02:07, output hang never
  Last clearing of "show interface" counters never
  Input queue: 0/75/0/0 (size/max/drops/flushes); Total output drops: 0
  Queueing strategy: fifo
  Output queue: 0/40 (size/max)
  5 minute input rate 0 bits/sec, 0 packets/sec
  5 minute output rate 0 bits/sec, 0 packets/sec
```

> The show interfaces command, *plural*, displays the configurable parameters and statistics of all interfaces on a router.

The preceding interface is working and looks to be in good shape. The `show interfaces` command will show you if you're receiving errors on the interface, and it will also show you the maximum transmission unit (MTU). MTU is the maximum packet size allowed to transmit on that interface, bandwidth (BW) is for use with routing protocols, and 255/255 means that reliability is perfect! The load is 1/255, meaning no load.

Continuing through the output, can you figure out the bandwidth of the interface? Well, other than the easy giveaway of the interface being called a "FastEthernet" interface, you can see that the bandwidth is 100,000 Kbit, which is 100,000,000. Kbit means to add three zeros, which is 100 Mbits per second, or Fast Ethernet. Gigabit would be 1,000,000 Kbits per second.

Be sure that you don't miss the output errors and collisions, which show 0 in my output. If these numbers are increasing, then you have some sort of Physical or Data Link layer issue. Check your duplex! If you have one side as half-duplex and one as full-duplex, your interface will work, albeit really slow, and those numbers will be increasing fast!

The most important statistic of the `show interface` command is the output of the line and Data Link protocol status.

If the output reveals that FastEthernet 0/0 is up and the line protocol is up, then the interface is up and running at layers 1 and 2:

```
Router#sh int fa0/0
FastEthernet0/0 is up, line protocol is up
```

Troubleshooting with the *show interfaces* Command

Let's take a look at the output of the show interfaces command one more time, as there are some important statistics in this output:

```
275496 packets input, 35226811 bytes, 0 no buffer
   Received 69748 broadcasts (58822 multicasts)
   0 runts, 0 giants, 0 throttles
   0 input errors, 0 CRC, 0 frame, 0 overrun, 0 ignored
   0 watchdog, 58822 multicast, 0 pause input
   0 input packets with dribble condition detected
   2392529 packets output, 337933522 bytes, 0 underruns
   0 output errors, 0 collisions, 1 interface resets
   0 babbles, 0 late collision, 0 deferred
   0 lost carrier, 0 no carrier, 0 PAUSE output
   0 output buffer failures, 0 output buffers swapped out
```

Knowing where to start when troubleshooting an interface can be difficult, but you should look right away for the number of input errors and CRCs. Typically, you would see those statistics increase with a duplex error, but it could be another Physical layer issue such as the cable might be receiving excessive interference or the network interface cards might have a failure. Typically, you can tell if it is interference when the CRC and input errors output grow but the collision counters do not.

Let's take a look at some of the output:

No Buffer   This isn't a number you want to see incrementing. This means you don't have any buffer room left for incoming packets. Any packets received once the buffers are full are discarded. You can see how many packets are dropped with the ignored output.

Ignored   If the packet buffers are full, packets will be dropped. You see this increment along with the no buffer output. Typically, if the no buffer and ignored outputs are incrementing, you have some sort of broadcast storm on your LAN. This can be caused by a bad NIC or even a bad network design.

Runts   Runts are frames that did not meet the minimum frame size requirement of 64 bytes. Typically caused by collisions.

Giants   Giants are frames received that are larger than 1,518 bytes.

Input Errors   This is the total of many counters: runts, giants, no buffer, CRC, frame, overrun, and ignored counts.

CRC   At the end of each frame is a frame check sequence (FCS) field that holds the answer to a cyclic redundancy check (CRC). If the receiving host's answer to the CRC does not match the sending host's answer, then a CRC error will occur.

Frame   This output increments when the frames received are of an illegal format or not complete. Typically, the output is incremented when a collision occurs.

Packets Output   This is the total number of packets (frames) forwarded out the interface.

Output Errors   This is the total number of packets (frames) that the switch port tried to transmit but for which some problem occurred.

Collisions   When transmitting a frame in half-duplex, the NIC listens on the receiving pair of the cable for another signal. If a signal is transmitted from another host, a collision has occurred. This output should not increment if you are running full-duplex.

Late Collisions   If all Ethernet specifications are followed during the cable installation, all collisions should occur by the 64th byte of the frame. If a collision occurs after 64 bytes, the late collisions counter increments. This counter will increment on a duplex mismatched interface.

show ip interface brief

The show ip interface brief command is probably one of the best commands that you can ever use on a Cisco router or switch. This command provides a quick overview of the devices interfaces, including the logical address and interface status at layers 1 and 2:

```
Router#sh ip int brief
Interface          IP-Address      OK? Method Status                Protocol
FastEthernet0/0    unassigned      YES unset  up                    up
FastEthernet0/1    unassigned      YES unset  up                    up
Serial0/0/0        unassigned      YES unset  up                    down
Serial0/0/1        unassigned      YES unset  administratively down down
Serial0/1/0        unassigned      YES unset  administratively down down
Serial0/2/0        unassigned      YES unset  administratively down down
```

Remember, *administratively down* means that you need to type **no shutdown** in order to enable the interface. Notice that Serial0/0/0 is up/down, which means that the Physical layer is good and carrier detect is sensed but no keepalives are being received from the remote end. In a nonproduction network, like the one I am working with, this tells us the clock rate hasn't been set.

Verifying with the *show ip interface* Command

The show ip interface command provides you with information regarding the layer 3 configurations of a router's interfaces:

```
Router#sh ip interface
```

```
FastEthernet0/0 is up, line protocol is up
  Internet address is 1.1.1.1/24
  Broadcast address is 255.255.255.255
  Address determined by setup command
  MTU is 1500 bytes
  Helper address is not set
  Directed broadcast forwarding is disabled
  Outgoing access list is not set
  Inbound  access list is not set
  Proxy ARP is enabled
  Security level is default
  Split horizon is enabled
[output cut]
```

The status of the interface, the IP address and mask, information on whether an access list is set on the interface, and basic IP information are all included in this output.

Privilege Level

Privilege levels are used to help you define which commands users can issue after they have logged into a network device. There are three default privilege levels in the Cisco IOS:

Level 0   Zero-level access allows you to run only five commands: `logout`, `enable`, `disable`, `help`, and `exit`.

Level 1   User-level access provides very limited read-only access to the router.

Level 15   Privilege-level access provides complete control over the router.

Cisco IOS devices use privilege levels for more granular security and what is called role-based access control (RBAC), in addition to usernames and passwords. In total, there are 16 privilege levels of admins access (0–15) on a Cisco router or switch that you can configure, with 0 being the lowest level and 15 being the highest privileged.

Cisco Privilege-Level Configuration

To assign the specific privilege levels, you use a number when indicating the username and password of the user to assign the privilege:

```
Router(config)#username todd privilege 0 secret ccst-network
Router(config)#username don privilege 15 secret ccst-devnet
Router(config)#username lammle secret ccst-video-series
```

Let's try to verify the output of our configuration by logging in to each user. Enter the username and the corresponding password, starting with `todd`:

```
User Access Verification

Username: todd
```

```
Password:
Router>?
Exec commands:
disable  Turn off privileged commands
enable   Turn on privileged commands
exit     Exit from the EXEC
help     Description of the interactive help system
logout   Exit from the EXEC

Router>
```

Notice in the previous output that the user todd is under User Exec mode and has only five commands: logout, enable, disable, help, and exit. Now, let's log in as don:

```
User Access Verification

Username: don
Password:
Router#show privilege
current privilege level is 15

Router#
```

The previous output shows that the user don is currently in level 15, and we verified that by typing the show privilege command on the CLI. Notice also that we are in Privileged Exec mode.

Lastly, let's log in as lammle:

```
User Access Verification

Username: lammle
Password:
Router>show privilege
current privilege level is 1

Router>
```

The show privilege command shows that lammle received the default privilege level of 1 by default since it wasn't specified in the configuration of the user.

The Help Command

The Cisco advanced editing features can also help you configure your router. If you type in a question mark (?) at any prompt, you'll be given a list of all the commands available from that prompt:

```
Switch#?
Exec commands:
```

```
access-enable Create a temporary Access-List entry
access-template Create a temporary Access-List entry
archive manage archive files
cd Change current directory
clear Reset functions
clock Manage the system clock
cns CNS agents
configure Enter configuration mode
connect Open a terminal connection
copy Copy from one file to another
debug Debugging functions (see also 'undebug')
delete Delete a file
diagnostic Diagnostic commands
dir List files on a filesystem
disable Turn off privileged commands
disconnect Disconnect an existing network connection
dot1x IEEE 802.1X Exec Commands
enable Turn on privileged commands
eou EAPoUDP
erase Erase a filesystem
exit Exit from the EXEC
--More-- ?
Press RETURN for another line, SPACE for another page, anything else to quit.
```

And if this is not enough information for you, you can press the spacebar to get another whole page of information, or you can press Enter to go one command at a time. You can also press Q—or any other key, for that matter—to quit and return to the prompt. Notice that I typed a question mark (?) at the More prompt, and it told me what my options were from that prompt.

Here's a shortcut: To find commands that start with a certain letter, use the letter and the question mark with no space between them, as follows:

```
Switch#c?
cd clear clock cns configure
connect copy
Switch#c
```

Okay, see that? By typing **c?**, I got a response listing all the commands that start with *c*. Also notice that the Switch#c prompt reappears after the list of commands is displayed. This can be really helpful when you happen to be working with long commands but you're short on patience and still need the next possible one. It would get old fast if you actually had to retype the entire command every time you used a question mark!

So, with that, let's find the next command in a string by typing the first command and then a question mark:

```
Switch#clock ?
```

```
set Set the time and date
Switch#clock set ?
hh:mm:ss Current Time
Switch#clock set 2:35 ?
% Unrecognized command
Switch#clock set 2:35:01 ?
<1-31> Day of the month
MONTH Month of the year
Switch#clock set 2:35:01 21 july ?
<1993-2035> Year
Switch#clock set 2:35:01 21 august 2013
Switch#
00:19:55: %SYS-5-CLOCKUPDATE: System clock has been updated from 00:19:55
UTC Mon Mar 1 1993 to 02:35:01 UTC Wed Aug 21 2013, configured from console
by console.
```

I entered the **clock ?** command and got a list of the next possible parameters plus what they do. Note that you can just keep typing a command, a space, and then a question mark until <cr> (carriage return) is your only option left.

And if you're typing commands and receive the following, no worries; this is only telling you that the command string simply isn't complete quite yet:

```
Switch#clock set 11:15:11
% Incomplete command.
```

All you need to do is to press the up arrow key to redisplay the last command entered and then continue with the command by using a question mark.

But if you get the following error, all is not well; it means that you entered a command incorrectly:

```
Switch(config)#access-list 100 permit host 1.1.1.1 host 2.2.2.2
^
% Invalid input detected at '^' marker.
```

See that little caret—the ^? It's a very helpful tool that marks the exact point where you blew it and made a mess.

Auto-Complete

Auto-complete is a helpful feature that you can use to finish typing a command for you. Auto-complete is as simple as pressing the Tab key; the command-line options will fill in automatically.

If more than one option is available, you can press the Tab key twice to display all possible choices, and you can continue typing until there is only one matching choice left.

If somehow the auto-complete is disabled, press Ctrl+Shift+Space.

Summary

This chapter covered network infrastructure and how to diagnose problems. You learned how to look at a basic Cisco device and understand some simple lights and their meaning, as well as be able to understand various type of cables and how they will be used for connecting to devices using different types of ports.

The chapter also discussed different ways to connect and access network devices, and you learned some basic Cisco IOS commands that provide helpful information when you are trying to find and diagnose problems.

Exam Essentials

Differentiate the types of Ethernet cabling and identify their proper application. The three types of cables that can be created from an Ethernet cable are straight-through (to connect a PC's or router's Ethernet interface to a hub or switch), crossover (to connect hub to hub, hub to switch, switch to switch, or PC to PC), and rolled (for a console connection from a PC to a router or switch).

Understand how to connect a console cable from a PC to a router and switch. Connect a rolled cable from the COM port of the host to the console port of the router. Start your emulation program, such as PuTTY or SecureCRT, and set the bits per second to 9600, parity 8-bits wide, and a flow control to None.

Know how to document a network topology using CDP. Using the various show cdp commands and their outputs, you can both draw out your network and get information about all directly connected devices, including interfaces connected, IOS version, IP address, and more. This is a very useful command for troubleshooting problems.

Understand how to use remote access to connect to devices. You can connect remotely to your devices by using terminal emulators, remote desktop connections, Telnet, Secure Shell (SSH), VPNs, NMS stations, Meraki, and scripts.

Be familiar with the various *show* commands. You should be familiar with the following commands: show running-config, show cdp neighbor, show switch, show interfaces, show ip interface brief, show mac address-table, show version, and show route.

Review Questions

You can find the answers to these questions in Appendix, "Answers to Review Questions."

1. Which command can you use to determine the IP address of a directly connected neighbor?

    A. show cdp

    B. show cdp neighbors

    C. show cdp neighbors detail

    D. show neighbor detail

2. Which of the following is a network protocol that is designed as a secure alternative to command-based utilities such as Telnet?

    A. SSL

    B. SSH

    C. STP

    D. STFP

3. Which of the following commands provides a quick overview of all a device's interfaces, including the logical address and interface status at layers 1 and 2?

    A. show running-config

    B. show processes

    C. show ip interface brief

    D. show mac address-table

    E. show interfaces

4. Between which systems could you use a cable that uses the pinout pattern shown here?

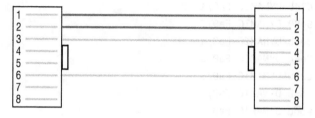

    A. With a connection from a switch to a switch

    B. With a connection from a router to a router

    C. With a connection from a host to a host

    D. With a connection from a host to a switch

5.   Which type of cable uses the pinout shown here?

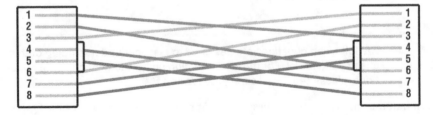

A.   Fiber-optic

B.   Crossover Gigabit Ethernet

C.   Straight-through Fast Ethernet

D.   Coaxial

6.   Which cable type uses the pinout arrangement shown here?

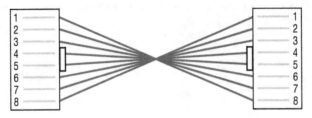

A.   Fiber-optic

B.   Rolled

C.   Straight-through

D.   Crossover

7.   Which of the following commands provide this output?

```
Switch#show _____
Vlan Mac Address Type Ports]]
1 0005.dccb.d74b DYNAMIC Fa0/1
1 000a.f467.9e80 DYNAMIC Fa0/3
1 000a.f467.9e8b DYNAMIC Fa0/4
1 000a.f467.9e8c DYNAMIC Fa0/3
1 0010.7b7f.c2b0 DYNAMIC Fa0/3
1 0030.80dc.460b DYNAMIC Fa0/3
1 0030.9492.a5dd DYNAMIC Fa0/1
      1    00d0.58ad.05f4 DYNAMIC Fa0/1
```

A.   show interfaces

B.   show mac address-table

C.   show ip interface brief

D.   show switch

8. Which of the following commands provides this output?

```
Switch#show _____
Capability Codes: R - Router, T - Trans Bridge, B - Source Route Bridge
S - Switch, H - Host, I - IGMP, r - Repeater, P - Phone,
D - Remote, C - CVTA, M - Two-port Mac Relay Device ID Local Intrfce
Holdtme Capability Platform Port ID
SW-1 Fas 0/1 150 S I WS-C3560- Fas 0/15
SW-1 Fas 0/2 150 S I WS-C3560- Fas 0/16
SW-2 Fas 0/5 162 S I WS-C3560- Fas 0/5
SW-2 Fas 0/6 162 S I WS-C3560- Fas 0/6
```

A. show interfaces

B. show mac address-table

C. show ip interface brief

D. show cdp neighbors

E. show ip route

9. Which of the following remote access technologies allows you to connect to a remote location and have your host appear as though it is local on that network?

A. Meraki

B. SSH

C. Virtual private network

D. Telnet

10. Which command will you run in the following output to show the switch stack's base MAC address, priority to become Master, version, and the state of the switch?

```
3560-New#show _____
Switch/Stack Mac Address : 4ca6.4d28.2380
                                    H/W   Current
Switch#  Role   Mac Address    Priority Version State
-----------------------------------------------------------
*1       Master 4ca6.4d28.2380    1       4      Ready
```

A. show interfaces

B. show mac address-table

C. show ip interface brief

D. show switch

Security

THE CCST EXAM TOPICS COVERED IN THIS CHAPTER INCLUDE THE FOLLOWING:

✓ **6.0 Security**

- 6.1. Describe how firewalls operate to filter traffic.

  - Firewalls (blocked ports and protocols); rules deny or permit access

- 6.2. Describe foundational security concepts.

  - Confidentiality, integrity, and availability (CIA); authentication, authorization, and accounting (AAA); Multifactor Authentication (MFA); encryption, certificates, and password complexity; identity stores/databases (Active Directory); threats and vulnerabilities; spam, phishing, malware, and denial of service

Network security has grown from consideration into a critically important essential. In an age of increasing use and dependence on the Internet, nearly everyone—from individuals and small businesses to huge corporations, institutions, and worldwide organizations—is now a potential victim of hackers and e-crime. And although our defense techniques continue to improve with time, so do the sophistication and weaponry used by the bad guys.

Today's tightest security will be laughably transparent three years from now, making it absolutely necessary for administrators to stay up with the industry's quickly evolving security trends.

Among additional important technologies, this chapter will cover authentication, authorization, and accounting (AAA). AAA is a technology that gives us substantial control over users and what they're permitted to do inside our networks. That's just the beginning—there are more tools in the box! RADIUS and TACACS+ and security servers, like Identity Services Engine (ISE), help us implement a centralized security plan by recording network events to the security server, or to a syslog server via logging.

Solid security hasn't just become imperative; it's also becoming increasingly complex. Cisco continues to develop and extend its features to meet these demands by providing us with a whole suite of hardware and software solutions.

Identity Services Engine, Cisco Prime, Tetration, Application Centric Infrastructure (ACI), and other powerful tools—like Cisco's next-generation girewall (NGFW), also called Cisco Firepower, and Firepower Threat Defense (FTD)—will be covered in depth in my new CCNP security books.

For now, let's get started on firewalls and access control lists!

To find up-to-the-minute updates for this chapter, please see www.lammle.com/ccst.

Firewalls

So what, exactly, is a *firewall*? Basically, firewalls are your network's security guards, and to be real, they're probably the most important thing to implement on your network. That's because today's networks are almost always connected to the Internet—a situation that makes security crucial!

A firewall protects your LAN resources from invaders who prowl the Internet for unprotected networks while simultaneously preventing all or some of your LAN's computers from accessing certain services on the Internet. You can employ them to filter packets based on rules that you or the network administrator create and configure to strictly delimit the type of information allowed to flow in and out of the network's Internet connection. Firewalls operate at multiple layers of the OSI model. Some firewalls can operate up to the Application layer.

Cisco's newer next-generation firewall (NGFW) provides layer 7 protection and is called Cisco Secure Firewall, or Firepower.

A firewall can be either a stand-alone "black box" or a software implementation placed on a server or router. Either way, the firewall will have at least two network connections: one to the Internet (known as the *public* side) and one to the network (known as the *private* side). Sometimes, there is a second firewall, as shown in Figure 10.1. This firewall is used to connect servers and equipment that can be considered both public and private (like web and email servers). This intermediary network is known as a *demilitarized zone (DMZ)* or *screened-subnet*.

FIGURE 10.1   Firewalls with a DMZ

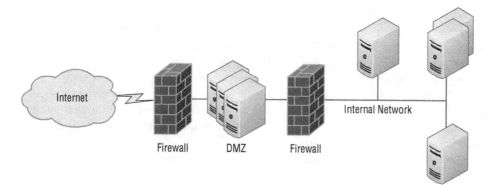

Firewalls are the first line of defense for an Internet-connected network. Without them in place, any network that's connected to the Internet is essentially wide open to anyone with a little technical savvy who seeks to exploit LAN resources and/or access your network's sensitive information.

Controlling Network Access

How do we know who's really at the other end of our connections? The answer to that may seem simple enough because the computer or person on the other end must identify him/her/itself, right? Wrong! That's just not good enough because people—especially hackers—lie, so it's totally naïve to assume that the person or computer on the other end of the line is who they're claiming to be. Sad but true: Hackers use the many tools out there today with the precise goal of convincing us they're someone else, and way too many of us have been, or know of someone who has been, a victim of identity theft thanks to bad guys with the right spoofing software in hand.

This means it's imperative to control who or what can get into our network by identifying the specific computers and individuals who have the right to gain access to it and its resources. But how do we do this? Well, for starters, I'm going to cover some basic ways to safely allow the computers you want to have access into your network plus ways to keep out the ones you don't.

The first line of defense is something called *security filtering*, which broadly refers to ways to let people securely access your resources by using an access-list. This process is twofold and includes ensuring (hopefully) that only authorized computers get to enter your network and making sure data you're sending back and forth between networks is secured so it can't be intercepted and translated by bad guys.

Access Control Lists

It's rare to find a network these days that isn't connected to the Internet. The Internet is clearly a public internetwork that anyone can connect to, but your company's or personal network is—and definitely should be—a private one. The catch here is that every time you connect to the Internet (where everyone is welcome) from a private network, you're instantly vulnerable to security break-ins. This is where something we call a *firewall* comes into play. Firewalls are basically tools that you can implement to prevent any unauthorized users roaming around on public networks from gaining access to your private network.

Access control lists (ACLs) typically reside on routers to determine which packets are allowed to route through them based on the requesting device's source or destination Internet Protocol (IP) address. Oh, and just so you know, ACLs have been around for decades and have other uses apart from firewalls.

Figure 10.2 demonstrates how ACLs prevent users on Network B from accessing Network A.

FIGURE 10.2   Two networks with an ACL-enabled router

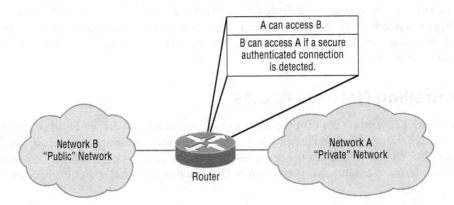

Okay, what we see here is that users in Network A can pass through the router into Network B. This means that an IP spoofing attack, when someone pretends to have a network address on the inside of a firewall to gain network access, can still happen if a user in Network B pretends to be located in Network A.

You can create a wide array of ACLs, from the very simple to the highly complex, depending on exactly what you want to have them do for you. One example is placing separate inbound and outbound ACLs on a router to ensure that the data that's leaving your network comes from a different source than the data that's coming into it.

When configuring ACLs between the Internet and your private network to mitigate security problems, it's a good idea to include the following four conditions:

- Deny any addresses from your internal networks.
- Deny any local host addresses (127.0.0.0/8).
- Deny any reserved private addresses.
- Deny any addresses in the IP multicast address range (224.0.0.0/4).

None of these addresses should ever be allowed to enter your internetwork. Interestingly enough, because of the way in-public IP addresses are issued, with some research, you can create a filter that blocks a country, state, or even locale based on IP addresses!

Port Filtering

ACLs can also be used to filter based on port numbers as well as IP addresses. In fact, most firewalls default to allowing only the open ports that you specify. This is another version of the implicit deny (anything not allowed specifically is denied).

When managing a firewall, it's important to know the port numbers of all traffic that needs to be allowed through it. This means that for some of your applications, you will need to read and learn the port numbers being used.

This also explains why it's a big deal to know the port numbers of security protocols like SSL and IPSec. Successful firewall management involves being aware of and allowing *only* the ports to keep things running.

Next Generation Firewalls

Next-generation firewalls (NGFWs) are a category of devices that attempt to address traffic inspection and application awareness shortcomings of a traditional stateful firewall, without hampering the performance. These provide an ACL, but on steroids. The ACL goes through layer 7 and provides deep packet inspection (DPI) using security intelligence, intrusion prevention systems, file and malware protection, and more.

NGFWs are application aware, which means they can distinguish between specific applications instead of allowing all traffic coming in via typical web ports. Moreover, they examine packets only once during the deep packet inspection phase (which is required to detect malware and anomalies).

Confidentiality, Integrity, Availability

The three fundamentals of security are confidentiality, integrity, and availability (CIA), often referred to as the CIA triad. Most security issues result in a violation of at least one facet of the CIA triad. Understanding these three security principles will help ensure that the security controls and mechanisms implemented protect at least one of these principles.

Confidentiality

To ensure confidentiality, you must prevent the disclosure of data or information to unauthorized entities. As part of confidentiality, the sensitivity level of data must be determined before putting any access controls in place. Data with a higher sensitivity level will have more access controls in place than data at a lower sensitivity level. Identification, authentication, authorization, and encryption can be used to maintain data confidentiality.

Integrity

Integrity, the second part of the CIA triad, ensures that data is protected from unauthorized modification or data corruption. The goal of integrity is to preserve the consistency of data, including data stored in files, databases, systems, and networks.

Availability

Availability means ensuring that data is accessible when and where it is needed. Only individuals who need access to data should be allowed access to that data. The two main areas where availability is affected are (1) when attacks are carried out that disable or cripple a system and (2) when service loss occurs during and after disasters. Technologies that provide fault tolerance, such as RAID or redundant sites, are examples of controls that help to improve availability.

Authentication Methods

A whole bunch of authentication schemes are used today, and although it's important to know about the different schemes and how they work, all that knowledge doesn't equal power if your network's users aren't schooled on how to manage their account names and passwords correctly. In the following sections, you'll learn about authentication systems and techniques.

Multifactor

Multifactor authentication is designed to add an additional level of security to the authentication process by verifying more than one characteristic of a user before allowing access to a resource.

Users can be identified in one of five ways:

- By something they know (password)
- By something they are (retinas, fingerprint, facial recognition)
- By something they possess (smart card)
- By somewhere they are (location)
- By something they do (behavior)

Two-factor authentication is when two of the preceding factors are being tested, whereas multifactor authentication is when more than two of the preceding factors are being tested. An example of two-factor authentication would be requiring both a smart card and a PIN to log into the network. The possession of either by itself would not be sufficient to authenticate. This protects against the loss and theft of the card as well as the loss of the password. An example of multifactor authentication would be when three items are required, such as a smart card, a PIN, and a username and password.

This process can get as involved as the security requires. In an extremely high-security situation, you might require a smart card, a password, a retina scan, and a fingerprint scan. The trade-off to all the increased security is an inconvenient authentication process for the user and the high cost of biometric authentication devices.

Biometrics

For high security scenarios that warrant the additional cost and administrative effort involved, biometrics is a viable option. Biometric devices use physical characteristics to identify the user. Such devices are becoming more common in the business environment.

Biometric systems include hand scanners, retinal scanners, and soon, possibly, DNA scanners. To gain access to resources, you must pass a physical screening process. In the case of a hand scanner, this may include identifying fingerprints, scars, and markings on your hand. Retinal scanners compare your eye's retinal pattern, which are as unique as fingerprints, to a stored retinal pattern to verify your identity. DNA scanners will examine a unique portion of your DNA structure to verify that you are who you say you are.

With the passing of time, the definition of *biometric* is expanding from simply identifying physical attributes about a person to being able to describe patterns in their behavior. Recent advances have been made in the ability to authenticate someone based on the key pattern they use when entering their password (how long they pause between each key, the amount of time each key is held down, and so forth). A company adopting biometric technologies needs to consider the controversy they may face. (Some authentication methods are considered more intrusive than others.) It also needs to consider the error rate and that errors can include both false positives and false negatives.

Authentication, Authorization, and Accounting

In computer security speak, AAA (triple A, like the auto club) refers to authentication, authorization, and accounting. AAAA is a more robust version that adds auditing into the mix.

AAA and AAAA aren't really protocols; instead, they're systematized, conceptual models for managing network security through one central location.

Two common implementations of AAA are RADIUS and TACACS+.

Remote Authentication Dial-In User Service

Although its name implies it, the *Remote Authentication Dial-In User Service (RADIUS)* is not a dial-up server. Like pretty much everything else, it originated that way, but it's evolved into more of a verification service. Today, RADIUS is an authentication and accounting service that's used for verifying users over various types of links, including dial-up. Many ISPs use a RADIUS server to store the usernames and passwords of their clients in a central spot through which connections are configured to pass authentication requests. RADIUS servers are client-server-based authentication and encryption services maintaining user profiles in a central database.

RADIUS is also used in conjunction with firewalls, in which case a user must provide a username and a password when they want to access a particular TCP/IP port. The firewall then contacts the RADIUS server to verify the credentials given. If the verification is successful, the user is granted access to that port.

 RADIUS is an authentication server that allows for domain-level authentication on both wired and wireless networks.

Terminal Access Controller Access-Control System Plus

The *Terminal Access Controller Access-Control System Plus (TACACS+)* protocol is also a AAA method and an alternative to RADIUS. Like RADIUS, it is capable of performing authentication on behalf of multiple wireless APs, RAS servers, or even LAN switches that are 802.1X capable. Based on its name, you would think it's an extension of the TACACS protocol (and in some ways it is), but the two definitely are not compatible.

Here are two major differences between TACACS+ and RADIUS:

- RADIUS combines user authentication and authorization into one profile, whereas TACACS+ separates the two.
- TACACS+ uses the connection-based TCP, but RADIUS uses UDP instead.

Even though both are commonly used today, because of these two reasons TACACS+ is considered more stable and secure than RADIUS.

Just to clarify things, in the IT world, accounting has nothing to do with money. Here's what I mean: When a TACACS+ session is closed, the information in the following list is logged, or accounted for. This isn't a complete list; it's just meant to give you an idea of the type of accounting information TACACS+ gathers:

- Connection start time and stop time
- The number of bytes sent and received by the user
- The number of packets sent and received by the user
- The reason for the disconnection

The only time the accounting feature has anything to do with money is if your service provider is charging you based on the amount of time you've spent logged in or for the amount of data sent and received.

Encryption

Sometimes, like it or not, sending out corporate financial and other types of sensitive data over the Internet just can't be avoided. This is why being able to hide or encode that data with encryption technologies is so vital for shielding it from the prying eyes of a company's competitors, identity thieves—anyone who wants to take a look. Without encryption, our sensitive files and information are essentially being paraded on full display as the data courses over the Internet.

Encryption works by running the data (which when encoded is represented as numbers) through a special encryption formula called a *key* that the designated sending and receiving devices both "know." When encrypted data arrives at its specified destination, the receiving device uses that key to decode the data back into its original form.

Back in 1979, the National Security Agency (NSA) classified encryption tools and their associated formulas as munitions, and the NSA has overseen their regulation ever since. The dangerous possibility that hostile nations, terrorists, and criminals may use encrypted communications to plan crimes and go undetected is the compelling reason for doing so. It's also the reason that we're only allowed to export weak encryption methods.

This brings up an important question: Exactly how do we measure an encryption algorithm's strength? One way to do that is to measure its bit strength. Until 1998, only software with 40-bit strength or less could be exported, but today, the bar has been raised to 64-bit strength. And by the way, exporting any software with a key length greater than 64 bits is subject to review by the Export Administration Regulations (EAR) required by the US Department of Commerce's Bureau of Industry and Security. This doesn't include exporting to every country because some—like most of those in Western Europe plus Canada, Australia, and Japan—are countries we trust with the technology. But if you happen to be curious or just want to be really careful, check out the current regulations at `www.bis.doc.gov/index.php/regulations#ear`. Remember, these regulations aren't there to make life a hassle; they're in place to protect us. The greater the number of bits that are encrypted, the tougher it is to crack the code.

Clearly, the security of monetary transfers is extremely important. The NSA does allow US banks to use more secure encryption methods for this reason and to ensure that they communicate very securely with their overseas branches, customers, and affiliates.

Encrypting passwords being sent from a workstation to a server at login is the most basic need for internal networks, and it's done automatically by most network operating systems today. But legacy utilities like File Transfer Protocol (FTP) and Telnet don't have the ability to encrypt passwords. Most email systems also give users the option to encrypt individual (or all) email messages, and third-party software packages like Pretty Good Privacy (PGP) are used by email systems that don't come with encryption abilities of their own. And you already know how critical encryption is for data transmission over VPNs. Last but not least, encryption capability is clearly very important for e-commerce transactions, online banking, and investing.

I mentioned a key earlier, but I didn't tell you exactly what it is: An encryption key is essentially a random string of characters that is used in conjunction with the encryption algorithm. The algorithm is the same for all transactions, but the key is unique to each transaction. Encryption keys come in two flavors: symmetrical and asymmetrical.

Symmetrical Encryption Keys

Using symmetrical key encryption, both the sender and receiver have the same key and use it to encrypt and decrypt all messages. The downside of this technique is that it becomes hard to maintain the security of the key. When the keys at each end are different, it is called an asymmetrical or public key. I'll talk about that right after discussing some encryption standards.

The Data Encryption Standard

Kudos go to IBM for coming up with one of the most widely used standards: *Data Encryption Standard (DES)*. It was made a standard back in 1977 by the US government. If you want, you can look it up in the Federal Information Processing Standards Publication 46-2 (FIPS 46-2).

Basically, DES uses lookup and table functions, and it actually works much faster than more complex systems. It uses 56-bit keys. RSA Data Systems once issued a challenge to see if anyone could break the key. A group of Internet users worked together to attempt the task, with each member dealing with a portion of the 72 quadrillion possible combinations. They succeeded and cracked the key in June 1997, after searching only 18 quadrillion keys. Their prize? Knowing they had succeeded when they read a plain-text message that said, "Strong cryptography makes the world a safer place."

Back in the day, DES was a great security standard, but its 56-bit key length has proved to be too short. As I said, the key was first cracked in June 1997. A year later, one was cracked in just 56 hours, and in January 1999, a DES key was broken in a blazing 22 hours and 15 minutes! Not exactly secure, right? We definitely needed something stronger.

The Triple Data Encryption Standard

That's when the *Triple Data Encryption Standard (3DES*, also referred to as *TDES)* came into its glory. Originally developed in the late 1970s, it became the recommended method of implementing DES encryption in 1999. As its name implies, 3DES is essentially three DES encryption methods combined into one.

So 3DES encrypts three times, and it allows us to use one, two, or three separate keys. Clearly, going with only one key is the most unsecure, and opting to use all three keys gives you the highest level of security. Three-key TDES has a key length of 168 bits (56 × 3), but due to a complex type of attack known as *meet-in-the-middle*, it really provides only 112 bits of security. It gets worse further down the food chain—even though the two-key version has a key size of 112 bits, it actually arms you with only 80 bits of effective security.

Another problem with 3DES is that it's slow. No one likes that, so the National Institute of Standards and Technology (NIST) believes that 3DES will be an effective encryption standard only until sometime around 2030. Even now, it's being phased out in favor of faster methods like AES.

The Advanced Encryption Standard

The *Advanced Encryption Standard (AES,* also known as Rijndael) has been the "official" encryption standard in the United States since 2002. It specifies key lengths of 128, 192, and 256 bits.

The US government has determined that 128-bit security is adequate for things like secure transactions and all materials deemed Secret, but all Top Secret information must be encoded using 192- or 256-bit keys.

The good news is that the AES standard has proven amazingly difficult to crack. Those who try use a popular method involving something known as a *side-channel attack.* This means that instead of going after the cipher directly, they attempt to gather the information they want from the physical implementation of a security system. Hackers attempt to use power consumption, electromagnetic leaks, or timing information (like the number of processor cycles taken to complete the encryption process) to give them critical clues about how to break the AES system. Although it's true that attacks like these are possible to pull off, they're not really practical to clinch over the Internet.

Certificates

A digital certificate provides an entity, usually a user, with the credentials to prove its identity and associates that identity with a public key. At minimum, a digital certification must provide the serial number, the issuer, the subject (owner), and the public key.

An X.509 certificate complies with the X.509 standard. An X.509 certificate contains the following fields:

- Version
- Serial Number
- Algorithm ID
- Issuer
- Validity
- Subject
- Subject Public Key Info
  - Public Key Algorithm
  - Subject Public Key
- Issuer Unique Identifier (optional)
- Subject Unique Identifier (optional)
- Extensions (optional)

VeriSign first introduced the following digital certificate classes:

- **Class 1:** For individuals and intended for email. These certificates get saved by web browsers.

- **Class 2:** For organizations that must provide proof of identity.
- **Class 3:** For servers and software signing in which independent verification and identity and authority checking is done by the issuing CA.

Hashes

Hashing is a cryptographic process that uses an algorithm to derive a value from a set of clear text to verify that the information came from where it says and that it has not changed. Therefore, we say hashes are used to provide data integrity and origin authentication. Two of the most well-known hashing algorithms, MD5 and SHA, are discussed in the following sections.

MD5

The MD5 message-digest algorithm was designed by Ron Rivest, and although it has been shown to have some flaws that cause many to prefer SHA (described in the next section), those flaws are not considered fatal and it is still widely used to ensure the integrity of transmission. As is the case with most hashing processes, the hash is created from the clear text and then sent along with the clear-text message. At the other end, a second hash of the clear text data is created using the same algorithm, and if the two hashes match, the data is deemed to be unchanged.

SHA

Secure Hash Algorithm (SHA) is a family of algorithm versions, much like MD5, which had multiple versions on its way to becoming MD5. Published by NIST as a US Federal Information Processing Standard (FIPS), SHA operates as any hash does and is considered to be superior to MD5.

Active Directory (Identity)

You may have wondered why the makers of Xbox are used in virtually all businesses around the world despite Microsoft always being featured in those pesky security advisories. One of the answers is that Active Directory (AD) is great at helping you manage your users and systems!

Active Directory is a solution where your company computers register to a special DNS domain hosted on a Windows Server. The server is called a *domain controller*, or *DC*, and its main job is to manage all the users, groups, and computers in the AD domain, as well as handle all authentication.

Many books and courses cover how Active Directory works in-depth, but this book isn't about a Microsoft certification, so we can just focus on the "need to know" stuff.

Once you have a working Active Directory domain, the first thing you need to do is create a user, as shown in Figure 10.3. Here you set the username and password as well as provide some extra information like the user's real name and, optionally, some contact information.

FIGURE 10.3   Adding a new AD user

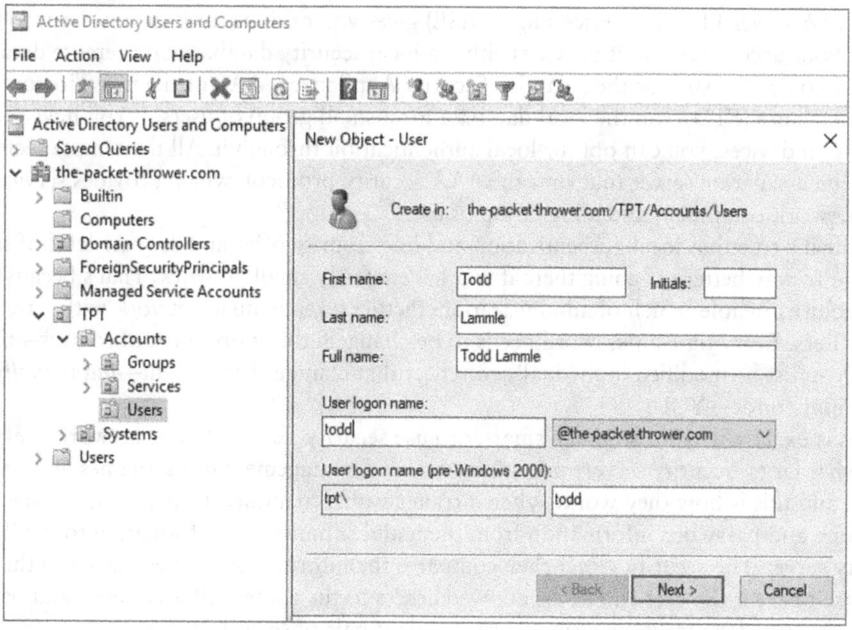

Having a user is great, but it can't really do much until you add it to a group. There are many built-in groups in Active Directory that permit various levels of access to resources, ranging from the bare minimum with the Domain Users group to the whole "keys to the kingdom" with the Domain Admins group; However, you typically will create a new group that you can use to log into your network devices. Figure 10.4 shows adding a user to a group.

FIGURE 10.4   Adding a user to an AD group

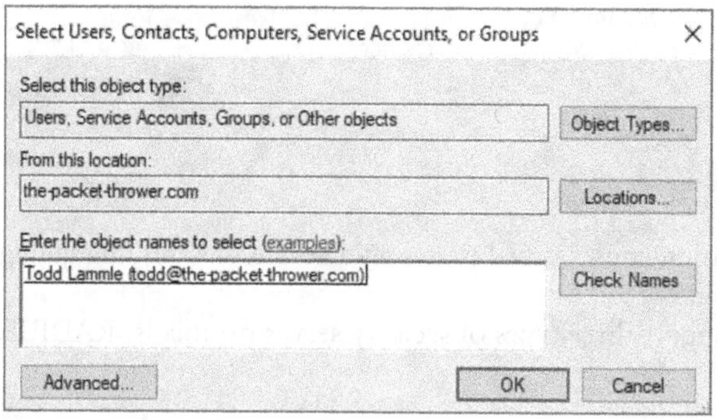

You can now configure your network devices to directly talk to AD for authentication, or you can use a AAA server like Cisco's Identity Service Engine (ISE) to query AD for you.

Identity Service Engine Authentication

Cisco AAA server Identity Service Engine (ISE) gives you options for how you want to handle your access control; it provides either a local security database or a remote database. Your Cisco devices such as the Adaptive Security Appliance (ASA), or the new Firepower Threat Defense (FTD), run the local database for a small group of users. If you have only one or two devices, you can opt for local authentication through it. All the remote security data is on a separate server that runs the AAA security protocol, which provides services for both network equipment and a big group of users.

While it's true that local authentication and line security offer an adequate level of security, you're way better off going there if you have a fairly small network. That's because they require a whole bunch of administration. Picture a really huge network with, say, 300 routers. Every time a password needs to be changed, the entire roost of routers—that's all 300—must be modified individually to reflect that change. That's right—*individually* by the administrator—YOU!

This is exactly why it's so much smarter to use security servers if your network is even somewhat large. Security servers provide centralized management of usernames and passwords, and this is how they work: When a router wants to authenticate a user, it collects the username and password information from them and submits that information to the ISE security server. The security server then compares the information it's been given to the user database to see if the user should be allowed access to the router. All usernames and passwords are stored centrally on a single or redundant pair of security servers.

Figure 10.5 illustrates the four-step AAA process.

FIGURE 10.5   External authentication options

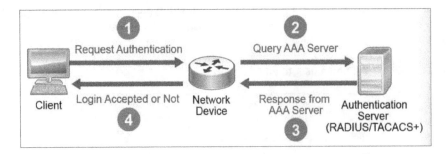

With administration consolidated on a single device like this, managing millions of users is a day at the beach!

Cisco routers support three types of security server protocols: RADIUS, TACACS+, and Kerberos.

Password Complexity

Strong passwords should be at least 8 characters (the more, the merrier), but they shouldn't be any longer than 15 characters to make them easier to remember. You absolutely must specify a minimum length for passwords because a short password is easily cracked—after all, there are only so many combinations of three characters, right? The upper limit depends on the capabilities of your operating system and the ability of your users to remember complex passwords. Here's what I call "The Weak List" for passwords—never use them!

- The word *password* (Not kidding—people actually do this!)
- Proper names
- Your pet's name
- Your spouse's name
- Your children's names
- Any word in the dictionary
- A license plate number
- Birth dates
- Anniversary dates
- Your username
- The word *server*
- Any text or label on the PC or monitor
- Your company's name
- Your occupation
- Your favorite color
- Any of the above with a leading number
- Any of the above with a trailing number
- Any of the above spelled backward

There are more, but you get the idea, and these really are the most commonly used brainless passwords. Figure 10.6 shows the Password Policy settings on a Windows machine.

Using Characters to Make a Strong Password

The good news is that solid passwords don't have to be in ancient Mayan to be hard to crack. They just need to include a combination of numbers, letters, and special characters—that's it. Special characters aren't letters or numbers but symbols like $ % ^ # @). Here's an example of a strong password: tqbf4#jotld. Looks like gibberish, but remember that famous sentence, "The quick brown fox jumped over the lazy dog"? Well, this particular password uses the first letter of each word in that sentence with a 4# thrown in the middle of it.

Sweet—solid and easy to remember. You can do this with favorite quotes, song lyrics, and so on, with a couple of numbers and symbols stuck in the middle. Just make sure you don't sing the song or quote Shakespeare every time you log in!

If you want to test the strength of passwords to make sure they're nice and tight, you can use auditing tools like crack programs that try to guess passwords. Clearly, if that program has a really tough time or even fails to crack the password, you have a good one. By the way, don't just use a regular word preceded by or ending with a special character because good crack programs strip off the leading and trailing characters during decryption attempts.

FIGURE 10.6 Password Policy settings

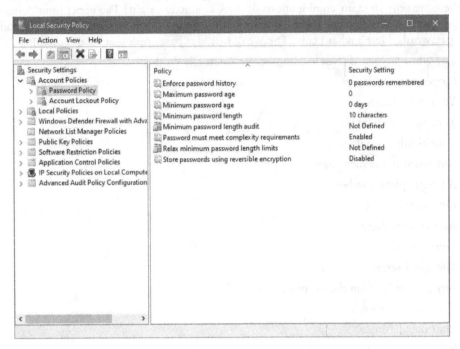

Threats

The first line of defense in providing CIA is to know about the types of threats out there because you can't do anything to protect yourself from something you don't know about. But once you understand the threats, you can begin to design defenses to combat bad guys lurking in the depths of cyberspace just waiting for an opportunity to strike.

There are four primary threats to network security you must be familiar with, in addition to being able to define the type of attacker:

Unstructured Threats These are threats typically originated by curious people who have downloaded information from the Internet and want to feel the sense of power this provides them. Sure, some of these types called script kiddies can be pretty nasty, but most of them are just doing it for the rush, thrills, and bragging rights. They're not talented, experienced hackers.

Structured Threats This kind of hacker is much more sophisticated, technically competent, and calculating. They're dedicated to their work, usually understanding network design and how to exploit routing and network vulnerabilities. They can create hacking scripts that allow them to penetrate deep into the network's systems, and they tend to be repeat offenders. Both structured and unstructured threats typically come from the Internet.

External Threats   These typically come from people on the Internet or from someone who has found a hole in your network from the outside. These serious threats have become ubiquitous now that all companies have an Internet presence. External threats generally make their way into your network via the Internet.

Internal Threats   These come from users on your network, typically employees. These are probably the scariest of all threats because they're really hard to catch and stop. Worse, since these hackers are authorized to be on the network, they can do some serious damage in less time because they're already in and know their way around. Add that to the profile of an angry, disgruntled employee or contractor out for revenge, and you've got a real problem! We all know doing this is illegal, but some of us also know it's pretty easy to cause a lot of damage really fast, and the odds aren't bad that they'll get away with it!

Vulnerabilities

A vulnerability is the absence of a countermeasure or a weakness in a countermeasure that is in place. Vulnerabilities can occur in software, hardware, or personnel.

An example of a vulnerability is unrestricted access to a folder on a computer. Most organizations implement a vulnerability assessment to identify vulnerabilities.

Common Vulnerabilities and Exposures

The *Common Vulnerability Scoring System (CVSS)* is a system of ranking vulnerabilities that are discovered based on predefined metrics. This system ensures that the most critical vulnerabilities can be easily identified and addressed after a vulnerability test is met.

The output of using this classification system is a database of known vulnerabilities called *Common Vulnerabilities and Exposures (CVE)*. The MITRE Corporation oversees CVE, and each entry describes a vulnerability in detail, using a number and letter system to describe what the vulnerability endangers, the environment it requires to be successful, and, in many cases, the proper mitigation. This system is used by security professionals to share and inform one another as new CVEs are discovered.

Zero-Day

Antivirus software uses definition files that identify known malware. These files must be updated frequently, but the update process can usually be automated so that it requires no help from the user.

If a new virus is created that has not yet been identified in the list, you will not be protected until the virus definition is added and the new definition file is downloaded.

Zero-day is named because the attack is found on the first day the virus has been released; therefore, no known fix exists. This term may also be applied to an operating system bug that has not been corrected.

Exploits

An exploit occurs when a threat agent takes advantage of a vulnerability and uses it to advance an attack. When a network attack takes advantage of a vulnerability, it is somewhat of an indictment of the network team, as most vulnerabilities can be identified and mitigated.

A good example of an exploited vulnerability is the unpatched Apache server that was compromised and led to the Equifax breach.

Social Engineering

Hackers are more sophisticated today than they were 10 years ago, but then again, so are network administrators. Because most of today's sys admins have secured their networks well enough to make it pretty tough for an outsider to gain access, hackers decided to try an easier route to gain information: They just asked the network's users for it.

Social engineering attacks occur when attackers use believable language and user gullibility to obtain user credentials or some other confidential information. The best countermeasure against social engineering threats is to provide user security awareness training. This training should be required and must occur on a regular basis because social engineering techniques evolve constantly.

Phishing

Phishing is a social engineering attack in which attackers try to learn personal information, including credit card information and financial data. This type of attack is usually carried out by implementing a fake website that is nearly identical to a legitimate website. Users are led there by fake emails that appear to come from a trusted source.

Users enter data, including credentials, on the fake website, allowing the attackers to capture any information entered. Spear phishing is a phishing attack carried out against a specific target by learning about the target's habits and likes. The best defense is security awareness training for the users.

Malware

Malicious software (or *malware*) is a term that describes any software that harms a computer, deletes data, or takes actions the user did not authorize. There is a wide array of malware types, including ones you have probably heard of, like viruses. Some types of malware require the assistance of a user to spread, whereas others do not.

A worm is a type of malware that can spread without the assistance of the user. A worm is a small program that, like a virus, is used to deliver a payload. One way to help mitigate the effects of worms is to place limits on sharing, writing, and executing programs.

However, the real solution is to deploy antivirus and antimalware software to all devices in the network. This software is designed to identify viruses, trojans, and worms and delete them, or at least quarantine them until they can be removed.

Viruses

Viruses with catchy names like Chernobyl, Michelangelo, Melissa, I Love You, and Love Bug are probably the best-known threats to your computer's security because they get a lot of media coverage as they proliferate and cause tons of damage to legions of people. In their simplest form, viruses are basically little programs that cause a variety of very bad things to happen on your computer, ranging from merely annoying to totally devastating. They can display a message, delete files, or even send huge amounts of meaningless data over a network to block legitimate messages. A key trait of viruses is that they can't replicate themselves to other computers or systems without a user doing something like opening an executable attachment in an email to propagate them.

Figure 10.7 shows how fast a virus can spread through an email system.

FIGURE 10.7 An email virus spreading rapidly

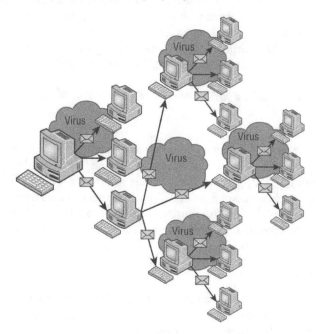

There are several different kinds of viruses, but the most popular ones are file viruses, macro (data file) viruses, and boot-sector viruses. Each type differs slightly in the way it works and how it infects your system. Predictably, many viruses attack popular applications like Microsoft Word, Excel, and PowerPoint because those programs are easy to use, so it's easy to create a virus for them. Unlike with denial-of-service (DoS) attacks, writing a unique virus is considered a programming challenge, so the scoundrel who's able to come up with it not only gains respect from the hacking community but also gets to bask in the glow of the media frenzy that results from their creation and relish their 15 minutes of fame. This is also a big reason viruses are becoming more and more complex and harder to eliminate.

Denial of Service/Distributed Denial of Service

A denial-of-service (DoS) attack does exactly what it sounds like it would do—it prevents users from accessing the network and/or its resources. Today, DoS attacks are commonly launched against a major company's intranet and especially its websites. "Joe the Hacker" (formerly a plumber) thinks that if he can make a mess of, say, Microsoft's or Amazon's website, he's done that company some serious damage. And you know what?

He's right!

Even though DoS attacks are nasty, strangely, hackers don't respect other hackers who execute them, because they're really easy to deploy. It's true—even a pesky little 10-year-old can execute one and bring you to your knees. (That's just wrong!) This means that "real" bad guys have no respect for someone who uses DoS attacks, and they usually employ much more sophisticated methods of wreaking havoc on you instead. I guess it comes down to that "honor among thieves" thing. Still, know that even though a DoS-type attack won't gain the guilty party any esteemed status among "real" hackers, it's still not exactly a day at the beach to deal with.

Worse, DoS attacks come in a variety of flavors. Let's talk about some of them now.

The Ping of Death

Ping is primarily used to see whether a computer is responding to IP requests. Usually, when you ping a remote host, what you're really doing is sending four normal-sized Internet Control Message Protocol (ICMP) packets to the remote host to see if it's available. But during a ping of death attack, a humongous ICMP packet is sent to the remote host victim, totally flooding the victim's buffer and causing the system to reboot or helplessly hang there, drowning. It's good to know that patches are available for most operating systems to prevent a ping of death attack from working.

Distributed DoS

Denial-of-service (DoS) attacks can be made more effective if the attacker can amplify them by recruiting helpers in the attack process. The following sections explain some terms and concepts that apply to a distributed denial-of-service (DDos) attack.

Botnet/Command and Control

A botnet is a group of programs connected on the Internet for the purpose of performing a task in a coordinated manner. Some botnets, such as those created to maintain control of Internet Relay Chat (IRC) channels, are legal, whereas others are created illegally to foist a DDoS. An attacker can recruit and build a botnet to help amplify a DoS attack, as illustrated in Figure 10.8.

FIGURE 10.8 A botnet

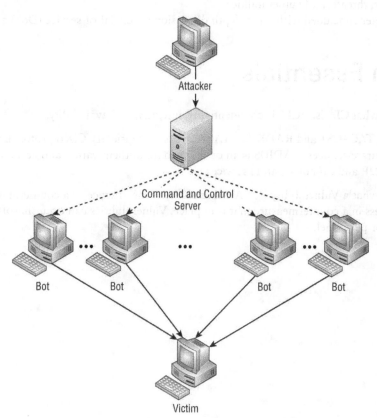

The steps in the process of building a botnet are as follows:

1. A botnet operator sends out viruses or worms whose payloads are malicious applications, the bots, infecting ordinary users' computers.

2. The bots on the infected PCs log into a server called a command-and-control (C&C) server under the control of the attacker.

3. At the appropriate time, the attacker, through the C&C server, sends a command to all bots to attack the victim at the same time, thereby significantly amplifying the effect of the attack.

Summary

In this chapter, I discussed how important network security is and how it has grown considerably over the last decade.

The chapter started with the three fundamentals of security: confidentiality, integrity, and availability (CIA), often referred to as the CIA triad.

You also learned about AAA, Radius, TACACS+, authentication, encryption, password complexities, threats, and vulnerabilities.

The chapter concluded with an in-depth discussion on denial-of-service (DoS) attacks.

Exam Essentials

Remember what CIA is.   CIA is confidentiality, integrity, and availability.

Understand TACACS+ and RADIUS.   TACACS+ is a proprietary Cisco protocol, uses TCP, and can separate services. RADIUS is an open-standard authentication and accounting service, uses UDP, and cannot separate services.

Remember what a Vulnerability is.   A vulnerability is the absence of a countermeasure or a weakness in a countermeasure that is in place. Vulnerabilities can occur in software, hardware, or personnel.

Review Questions

 The following questions are designed to test your understanding of this chapter's material. For more information on how to get additional questions, please see www.lammle.com/ccst.

You can find the answers to these questions in Appendix, "Answers to Review Questions."

1. Which of the following are true about TACACS+? (Choose two.)

   A. TACACS+ is a Cisco proprietary security mechanism.

   B. TACACS+ uses UDP.

   C. TACACS+ combines authentication and authorization services as a single process—after users are authenticated, they are also authorized.

   D. TACACS+ offers multiprotocol support.

2. Which of the following is *not* true about RADIUS?

   A. RADIUS is an open standard protocol.

   B. RADIUS separates AAA services.

   C. RADIUS uses UDP.

   D. RADIUS encrypts only the password in the access-request packet, from the client to the server. The remainder of the packet is unencrypted.

3. Which of the following is *not* a password alternative?

   A. Multifactor authentication (MFA)

   B. Malware lookups

   C. Biometrics

   D. Certificates

4. Which of the following are common denial-of-service attacks? (Choose two.)

   A. CnC

   B. DDos

   C. MFA

   D. Ping of death

5. Which of the following are listed threats that you need to be aware of as the first line of defense in providing CIA? (Choose four.)

   A. Structured threats

   B. External threats

   C. Internal threats

   D. Malware threats

   E. Unstructured threats

6. Which types of security server protocols are supported by Cisco routers? (Choose three.)

   A. RADIUS

   B. Kerberos

   C. DIA

   D. TACACS+

7. Which of the following describes an exploit?

   A. An exploit is when antivirus software uses definition files that identify known malware.

   B. An exploit is a system of ranking vulnerabilities that are discovered based on predefined metrics.

   C. An exploit is when a hacker confuses an internal user and gets them to turn over their credentials.

   D. An exploit is when a threat agent takes advantage of a vulnerability and uses it to advance an attack.

8. Multifactor authentication is designed to add an additional level of security to the authentication process by verifying more than one characteristic of a user before allowing access to a resource. Users can be identified in one of five ways. Which of the following can be part of multifactor authentication? (Choose three.)

   A. Something a user eats

   B. Something a user knows

   C. Something a user is

   D. Something a user possesses

9. What of the following statements about ACLs is true?

   A. They typically reside on routers to determine which packets are allowed to route through them based on the requesting device's source or destination Internet Protocol (IP) addresses.

   B. They run only on layer 2 switches.

   C. They run only on layers 3/4 and work only on Cisco's new NGFW.

   D. They use MAC addresses only to filter packets.

10. Which of the following statements best describes a firewall?

   A. A firewall provides full access to your internal network from the Internet so that, for example, accounting can update the spreadsheets used for payroll.

   B. A firewall blocks all traffic so that people cannot get out of the internal network without a written and signed document from the CTO.

   C. A firewall protects your inside networks from someone on the Internet, while at the same time inspecting traffic going to the Internet.

   D. A firewall provides biometrics for all data going from inside the network to outside the network.

Chapter

11

Cloud & IoT

THE CCST EXAM TOPICS COVERED IN THIS CHAPTER INCLUDE THE FOLLOWING:

✓ **1.0 Standards and Concepts**

- 1.4. Compare and contrast cloud and on-premises applications and services.

  - Public, private, hybrid, SaaS, PaaS, IaaS, remote work/hybrid work

✓ **3.0 Endpoints and Media Types**

- 3.3. Describe endpoint devices.

  - Internet of Things (IoT) devices, computers, mobile devices, IP Phone, printer, server

Cloud computing is by far one of the hottest topics in today's IT world. Basically, cloud computing can provide virtualized processing, storage, and computing resources to users remotely, making the resources transparently available regardless of the user connection. To put it simply, some people refer to the cloud as "someone else's hard drive." This is true, of course, but the cloud is much more than just storage.

Speaking of more than just storage, the term IoT, or Internet of Things, brings together a network of connected devices and the technology that basically provides communication between endpoint devices and the cloud, but don't forget that a lot of IoT devices communicate between themselves as well. Pretty much anything that has a sensor attached to it and that can transmit data from one object to another, to another sensor, or even to people through the Internet, is known as an IoT device. If you've heard of Apple AirTags (just one of a billion examples, really), then you get a general idea.

So, let's get started by discussing cloud computing, then move into cloud concepts, and, finally, to IoT endpoints.

To find up-to-the-minute updates for this chapter, please see www.lammle.com/ccst.

Cloud Computing and Its Effect on the Enterprise Network

The history of the consolidation and virtualization of our servers tells us that this has become the de facto way of implementing servers because of basic resource efficiency. Two physical servers will use twice the amount of electricity as one server, but through virtualization, one physical server can host two virtual machines, hence the main thrust toward virtualization. With it, network components can simply be shared more efficiently.

Users connecting to a cloud provider's network, whether it be for storage or applications, really don't care about the underlying infrastructure, because, as computing becomes a service rather than a product, it's then considered an on-demand resource, as illustrated in Figure 11.1.

FIGURE 11.1 Cloud computing is on demand.

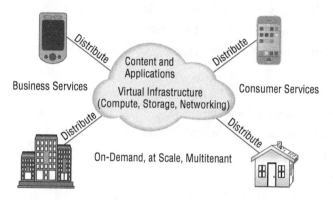

Centralization/consolidation of resources, automation of services, virtualization, and standardization are just a few of the big benefits cloud services offer (see Figure 11.2).

FIGURE 11.2 Advantages of cloud computing

Cloud computing has several advantages over the traditional use of computer resources. Here are the advantages to a cloud service builder or provider:

- Cost reduction, standardization, and automation
- High utilization through virtualized, shared resources
- Easier administration
- Fall-in-place operations model

Here are the advantages to cloud users:

- On-demand, self-service resource provisioning
- Fast deployment cycles
- Cost-effective
- Centralized appearance of resources
- Highly available, horizontally scaled application architectures
- No local backups

Having centralized resources is critical for today's workforce. For example, if you have your documents stored locally on your laptop and your laptop gets stolen, you're pretty much screwed, unless you're doing constant local backups. That is so 2005!

After I lost my laptop and all the files for the book I was writing at the time, I swore (yes, I did that too) to never have my files stored locally again. I started using only Google Drive, OneDrive, and Dropbox for all my files, and they became my best backup friends. If I lose my laptop now, I just need to log in from any computer from anywhere to my service provider's logical drives and, presto, I have all my files again. This is clearly a simple example of using cloud computing, specifically SaaS (which is discussed next), and it's wonderful!

So cloud computing provides for the sharing of resources, lower cost operations passed to the cloud consumer, computing scaling, and the ability to dynamically add new servers without going through the procurement and deployment process.

Cloud Concepts

Often you hear the terms *public cloud* and *private cloud*. *Clouds* can be thought of as virtual computing environments where virtual servers and desktops live and can be accessed by users. A private cloud is one in which this environment is provided to the enterprise by a third party for a fee. On the one hand, this is a good solution for a company that has neither the expertise nor the resources to manage its own cloud yet would like to take advantage of the benefits that cloud computing offers:

- Increased performance
- Increased fault tolerance

- Constant availability
- Access from anywhere

These types of clouds might be considered off-site or public clouds. On the other hand, for the organization that has the expertise and resources, a private or on-site solution might be better and might be more secure. This approach will enjoy the same benefits as a public cloud and may offer more precise control and more options to the organization.

Cloud storage locates the data on a central server, but unlike with an internal data center in the LAN, the data is accessible from anywhere and in many cases from a variety of device types. Moreover, cloud solutions typically provide fault tolerance and dynamic computer resource (CPU, memory, network) provisioning.

Cloud deployments can differ in the following two ways:

- The entity that manages the solution
- The percentage of the total solution provided by the vendor

Let's look at the options relative to the entity that manages the solution:

- **Private cloud:** This is a solution owned and managed by one company solely for that company's use.

- **Public cloud:** This is a solution provided by a third party. It offloads the details to the third party but gives up some control and can introduce security issues.

- **Hybrid cloud:** This is some combination of private and public. For example, perhaps you only use the facilities of the provider but still manage the data yourself.

- **Community cloud:** This is a solution owned and managed by a group of organizations that create the cloud for a common purpose.

Service Models

Cloud providers can offer you different available resources based on your needs and budget. You can choose just a vitalized network platform or go all in with the network, OS, and application resources.

Figure 11.3 shows the three service models available, depending on the type of service you choose to get from a cloud.

You can see that infrastructure as a service (IaaS) allows the customer to manage most of the network, whereas software as a service (SaaS) doesn't allow any management by the customer, and platform as a service (PaaS) is somewhere in the middle of the two. Clearly, choices can be cost driven, so the most important thing is that the customer pays only for the services or infrastructure they use.

Let's take a look at each service:

IaaS: Provides only the network.   IaaS delivers the computer infrastructure—a platform virtualization environment—where the customer has the most control and management capability. The vendor provides the hardware platform or data center, and the company installs and manages its own operating systems and application systems.

FIGURE 11.3   Cloud computing services

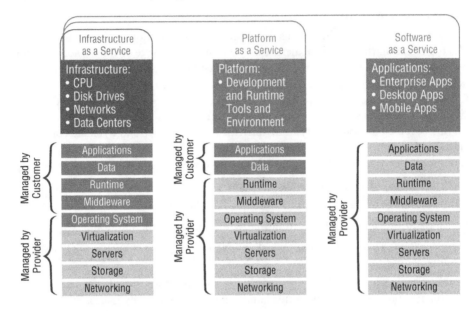

PaaS: Provides the operating system and the network.   The vendor provides the hardware platform or data center and the software running on the platform, allowing customers to develop, run, and manage applications without the complexity of building and maintaining the infrastructure typically associated with developing and launching an application. An example is Windows Azure.

SaaS: Provides the required software, operating system, and network.   The vendor provides the entire solution. This includes the operating system, infrastructure software, and the application. SaaS consists of common application software such as databases, web servers, and email software that's hosted by the SaaS vendor. The customer accesses this software over the Internet. Instead of having users install software on their computers or servers, the SaaS vendor owns the software and runs it on computers in its data center. Microsoft Office 365 and many Amazon Web Services (AWS) offerings are perfect examples of SaaS.

So, depending on your business requirements and budget, cloud service providers market a very broad offering of cloud computing products, from highly specialized offerings to a large selection of services.

What's nice here is that you're offered a fixed price for each service that you use, which allows you to easily budget wisely for the future. It's true—at first, you'll have to spend a little cash on staff training, but with automation you can do more with less staff because administration will be easier and less complex. All of this works to free up the company resources to work on new business requirements and allows the company to be more agile and innovative in the long run.

Connectivity Methods

When connecting to a virtual server that is in a cloud environment, there are several ways to make this connection:

- **Virtual private network (VPN) connections:** This is the most direct way to connect. An example is the Amazon Web Services (AWS) Virtual Private Cloud (VPC), which will set up a VPN connection between your entire enterprise network and its cloud.

- **Remote Desktop:** Whereas a VPN connection connects you to the virtual network, an RDP connection can be directly to a server. If the server is Windows, then you will use the Remote Desktop client. If the server is Linux, then the connection will most likely be an SSH connection to the command line.

- **File Transfer Protocol (FTP):** The FTP server will need to be enabled on the server, and then you can use the FTP client or work at the command line. This is best when performing bulk data downloads.

- **VMware remote console:** This allows you to mount a local DVD drive to the virtual server. This is handy for uploading ISO or installation disks to the cloud server.

Security Implications/Considerations

While an entire book could be written on the security implications of the cloud, there are some concerns that stand above the others. Among them are the following:

- While clouds increasingly contain valuable data, they are just as susceptible to attacks as on-premises environments. Cases such as the `Salesforce.com` incident, in which a technician fell for a phishing attack that compromised customer passwords, remind us of this.

- Customers are failing to ensure that the provider keeps their data safe in multitenant environments. They are failing to ensure that passwords are assigned, protected, and changed with the same attention to detail the customer might desire.

- No specific standard has been developed to guide providers with respect to data privacy.

- Data security varies greatly from country to country, and customers have no idea where their data is located at any point in time.

Relationship Between Local and Cloud Resources

When comparing the advantages of local and cloud environments and the resources that reside in each, several things stand out:

- A cloud environment requires very little infrastructure investment on the part of the customer, whereas a local environment requires an investment in both the equipment and the personnel to set it up and manage it.

- A cloud environment can be extremely scalable and change at a moment's notice while scaling a local environment up or out requires an investment in both equipment and personnel.

- Investments in cloud environments involve monthly fees rather than capital expenditures, as would be required in a local environment.

- While a local environment provides total control for the organization, a cloud takes away some of that control.

- While you always know where your data is in a local environment, that may not be the case in a cloud, and the location may change rapidly.

- Remote work/hybrid work is something that every company needs to be aware of, and on how to provide security between local resources and cloud resources. Mixed work locations are now the norm and are not going away. Without the mixture of both local and cloud resources, including the bring your own device (BYOD) security, this never would have been possible.

Cloud Endpoints

The Internet of Things (IoT) is our life now and is never going away. There literally are billions of real-world IOT applications in use right now. The estimated total is over 12.3 billion in 2023. The same source suggests that that number will grow by 22 percent annually between now and 2025, resulting in close to 27.1 billion connected things by that time. These are used for consumer, enterprise, manufacturing, and industrial (IIoT) companies.

Just about any business can benefit from IoT, as it brings process automation, analysis and insight, fleet and asset management, labor reduction, and performance monitoring to any enterprise; for many organizations, it's become a key milestone on the path to complete digital transformation. IoT continues to gain traction in manufacturing, transportation, and utilities, where sensors and other IoT devices help manage fleets and other hard assets. Figure 11.4 shows a hardened industrial switch.

So why is IoT the rage now? Because everything become more efficient and provides large-scale implementations in vertical markets, including agriculture, airline energy, health care, medical, logistics, telecommunications, and even large parks such as Disneyland, where they can now track and follow visitors. It's hard to think of any business that cannot benefit from IoT.

Now, if you're thinking about security and privacy right now, that is spot on! Since the doorbell of your home is probably some type of IoT device, supposedly the police or other three-letter agencies can tap into these at any time, so privacy should be a concern. Home security is key to IoT now, as well as activity trackers such as your home video cameras. Don't forget about motion detection and augmented reality glasses.

This list goes on and on in your home: dishwashers, refrigerators, washers/dryers, bathtubs, smart TVs, smart watches, cars and trucks, heating and cooling systems, fitness machines and trackers, smart fire alarms, smart door locks, and smart bicycles are examples of IoT-enabled products with which you may already have personal experience. All of this is both great and concerning at the same time.

FIGURE 11.4 A hardened industrial switch

If a company has a fleet of cars, or if you want to track your teenager when they are driving, for example, IoT is for you. IoT can track any vehicle so that you can know exactly where that vehicle is at any time, the mileage, service dates, as well as the speed of the car/truck.

 Some of the general benefits of IoT include reduced costs, better time management, workflow changes that improve employees' quality of life, as well as paperless workflow.

VoIP-IoT Applications

VoIP and IoT will share the same enterprise or home network infrastructure, namely an IP network, which means that they can be seamlessly integrated into each other's operations.

Figure 11.5 shows an IoT VoIP phone.

There are various integrations of VoIP and IoT applications, the most useful of which are as follows:

Building Management Integration Understanding building management is an important task for enterprise companies and can include security, surveillance, fire alarms and door/window monitoring, communication, and environmental monitoring. Sensors provide temperature readings, motion detection, and even sound detection. VoIP is an important part of building management, and IoT was truly built for something like this.

FIGURE 11.5   An IoT VoIP phone

User Status Integration   Maybe one of the most useful integrations for VoIP and IoT is the status of other users, which will inform other users of the status of the person they are trying to reach. This status provides information about either their availability or even willingness to communicate with a call, email, or cell phone, which can introduce more granularity and automation to the presentation of presence information. An example could be a user out of the office or not at their desk, in which case the IoT can let other users know that the person cannot be reached via their desk phone.

VoIP and IoT Data Integration   Taking off from building management as well as user status, what is really most important is data accumulated and stored over time.

In a business environment, where inventory, manufacturing status, and supply chains are vital for the health of a business, having that information at your fingertips is important, especially for contact center agents. IoT can provide this information to agents in real time, allowing them to respond appropriately to customers and partners alike. CRM, helpdesk, contact center statistics, and IoT data can together form a richer set of accumulated data that can be interrelated and interpolated to deliver richer information for more responsible decision-making.

Summary

This chapter went into great detail about cloud computing, which continues to evolve and take on more and more of IT workloads. You learned about the most common service models, including infrastructure as a service (IaaS), platform as a service (PaaS), and software as a service (SaaS).

Cloud computing provides virtualized processing, storage, and computing resources to users remotely, making the resources transparently available regardless of the user connection.

I also defined the term IoT, or Internet of Things. IoT brings together a network of connected devices and the technology that basically provides communication between end-point devices and the cloud.

Lastly, I discussed IoT devices and how they can both help and affect your everyday life. Remember that pretty much anything that has a sensor attached to it and that can transmit data from one object to another, to another sensor, or even to people through the Internet, is known as an IoT device.

Exam Essentials

Compare and contrast cloud technologies.   Understand the differences between IaaS, SaaS, and PaaS.

Know the basic cloud architectures.   Having many different customers or groups all sharing the same cloud provider's data centers is called multitenancy. Understand that elasticity is the ability to scale your resources up and down on demand, and scalability is the ability to reliably grow your cloud deployment based on demand. The public cloud relies on the Internet for access; however, private direct connections can be deployed for secure, reliable, low-latency connections from your data center to your cloud operations.

Understand the useful reasons for IoT and VoIP   Building management integration, user status integration, and VoIP and IoT data integration are the three useful IoT and VoIP integrations.

Remember the options of cloud deployments.

> **Private cloud:** This is a solution owned and managed by one company solely for that company's use.
>
> **Public cloud:** This is a solution provided by a third party. It offloads the details to the third party but gives up some control and can introduce security issues.
>
> **Hybrid cloud:** This is some combination of private and public. For example, perhaps you only use the facilities of the provider but still manage the data yourself.
>
> **Community cloud:** This is a solution owned and managed by a group of organizations that create the cloud for a common purpose.

Review Questions

The following questions are designed to test your understanding of this chapter's material. For more information on how to get additional questions, please see www.lammle.com/ccst.

You can find the answers to these questions in Appendix, "Answers to Review Questions."

1. When the vendor provides the hardware platform or data center, and the company installs and manages its own operating systems and application systems, which service type is being used?

   A. Software as a service

   B. Infrastructure as a service

   C. Platform as a service

   D. Desktop as a service

2. Which of the following devices would probably never be an IoT endpoint?

   A. Bathtub

   B. Convertible car

   C. Electric weed trimmer

   D. Outdoor lighting of your home/office

3. Which three of the following are the benefits of using cloud computing?

   A. Faster document updates

   B. Increased fault tolerance

   C. Constant availability

   D. Access from anywhere

4. Which of the following are advantages to a cloud service builder or provider?

   A. On-premise backups needed

   B. Cost-effective/cost-reduction

   C. Decentralized resources

   D. Centralized resources

   E. Faster deployment

5. Which three of the following are advantages to cloud users?

   A. On-demand, self-service resource provisioning

   B. Faster deployment cycles

   C. No local backups

   D. More expensive but worth it

6. Which one of the following is most useful for integrations of VoIP and IoT?

   A. Remote auto phones through IoT cell clouds

   B. Building management integration

   C. User status integration

   D. VoIP and IoT data integration

7. Which of the following provides only the network infrastructure?

   A. IaaS

   B. PaaS

   C. SaaS

   D. DaaS

8. Which of the following provides the operating system and the network infrastructure?

   A. IaaS

   B. PaaS

   C. SaaS

   D. DaaS

9. Which of the following provides the required software, operating system, and network?

   A. IaaS

   B. PaaS

   C. SaaS

   D. DaaS

10. Which of the following is some combination of private and public cloud?

   A. Private cloud

   B. Public cloud

   C. Hybrid cloud

   D. Community cloud

Chapter

12

Troubleshooting

THE CCST EXAM TOPICS COVERED IN THIS CHAPTER INCLUDE THE FOLLOWING:

✓ **1.0 Standards and Concepts**

- 1.2. Differentiate between bandwidth and throughput.

  - Latency, delay, speed test vs. Iperf

✓ **5.0 Diagnosing Problems**

- 5.1. Demonstrate effective troubleshooting methodologies and help desk best practices, including ticketing, documentation, and information gathering.

  - Policies and procedures, accurate and complete documentation, prioritization

- 5.2. Perform a packet capture with Wireshark and save it to a file.

  - Purpose of using a packet analyzer, saving and opening a .pcap file

- 5.3. Run basic diagnostic commands and interpret the results.

  - ping, ipconfig/ifconfig/ip, tracert/traceroute, nslookup; recognize how firewalls can influence the result

This chapter starts by discussing the help desk, what the purpose is, policies and procedures, ticketing, documentation and information gathering. Understanding documentation and how to maintain updated documents is a large part of working a help desk.

We'll also show you the Cisco Seven Step Troubleshooting for helping help desk personnel find and solve problems.

We'll then introduce you to Wireshark and its purpose as a network analyzer, how to use it, as well as saving and opening a file.

I'll wrap up the chapter by guiding you through some important Cisco basic IP and network troubleshooting techniques to ensure that you're well equipped with these key skills.

To find up-to-the-minute updates for this chapter, please see www.lammle.com/ccst.

Help Desk

Every company should have a help desk, even a small one. Setting up a help desk with ticketing is not an easy task if you want it to be efficient and organized with a central point of contact for your team or customers.

To run a help desk, you must understand the business you are trying to manage in order to help maintain the network, applications, and devices. Once you determine and write down the business requirements for the help desk, you need to be able to get issues resolved in an orderly fashion. This is cumbersome and not easy at times, so organization is key.

If your company does not have self-service tech support (i.e., it is outsourced), the cost for a single average trouble ticket, according to Informa Tech, is from $22 to $1015 dollars, depending on the vendor support you need. So, building a help desk in-house may be the best solution for your company. If you just got a job as a help desk administrator, congratulations! Just get a list of their procedures so that you can start helping right away!

Using a self-portal that people can go to when they have an issue is super helpful! The software or application may have a self-service web page for customers/users to submit tickets, to look up current known problems, and get the status of their tickets. Phone and chat support is pretty typical as well.

Take a look at Figure 12.1, which shows a sample flowchart that can assist a help desk engineer solve an issue.

FIGURE 12.1   A sample help desk flowchart

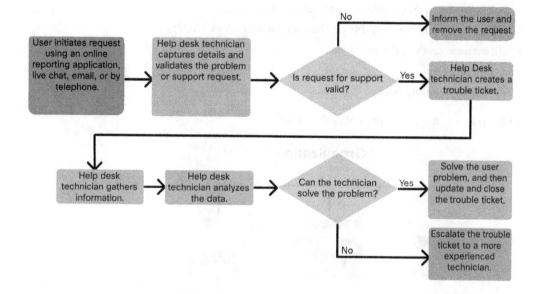

There is always more information that needs to be gathered, or so it seems. When you start questioning users or employees about their issues, you need to listen carefully to the answer. You might even need to go investigate physically or connect remotely to a device.

Once the help desk or technician receives a ticket, they should do one of the following:

- **Update the ticket:** Once the user problem has been addressed, the technician should update and close the trouble ticket. Updating the ticket solution is important because it can populate the ticketing system database. Therefore, if the same problem is reported by another user, the responding technician can search the database to quickly resolve the problem. In addition, administrators can analyze the tickets to identify common issues and their causes in order to globally eliminate the problem, if possible.

- **Escalate the ticket:** Some problems are more complex or require access to devices that the technician has no credentials for. In these cases, the technician must escalate (i.e., forward) the trouble ticket to a more experienced technician. It is important that all documentation captured from the user is clear, concise, and accurate.

Note that this information and process will vary for every company.

The Security Policy

A security policy is a must for all corporations. It must be a well-defined policy that can be created only by looking at network traffic and application flow.

To help protect both a company's technology and data, the security policy should be distributed to all employees and staff.

As shown in Figure 12.2, an organization's security policy should cover the following:

- How users are identified and authenticated
- Password length, complexity, and refresh interval
- What behavior is acceptable on the corporate network (AUP)
- Remote access requirements, etc.
- Maintenance
- Incident handling policy

FIGURE 12.2   A security policy flowchart

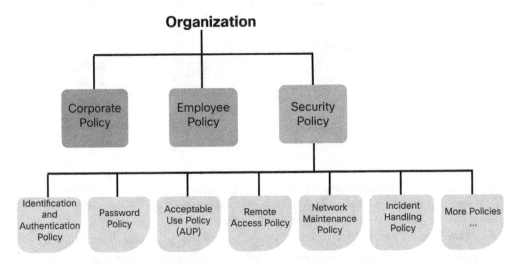

The security policy is fluid—constantly changing and evolving. Because of new attacks and found vulnerabilities, the security policy must be kept updated—even daily, if necessary.

To keep the network up and running, as well as secure, the help desk team and network staff must understand the following:

- **Standard operating procedures (SOP):** These define step-by-step actions that must be completed for any given task in order to comply with a policy. There are SOPs to follow when installing servers and other network gear, replacing or upgrading network devices, installing (or uninstalling) applications, onboarding new employees, terminating existing employees, and more.

- **Guidelines:** These cover the areas where no SOPs are defined.

The help desk must have the SOP and guidelines with them at all times when talking on the phone or interacting with a customer.

Let's take a look at ticketing now.

Ticketing

First, what is a ticket, also called a trouble ticket? I've also heard it called a support ticket at times. When a customer or employee has a problem, they will call, go online, or email. They can provide information on the issue they are reporting.

Tickets are designed to help you manage user problems, requests, and other issues. This process helps users get the support they need promptly, as well as hopefully helping tickets not get lost. Typically, a shared email address will be used to receive trouble tickets, but a portal on a server is even more efficient.

Figure 12.3, which shows a sample trouble ticket, is designed to help you understand what information a help desk ticket should cover. This is from a company called Spiceworks, which provides free trouble ticket help desk software.

FIGURE 12.3   A sample help desk ticket

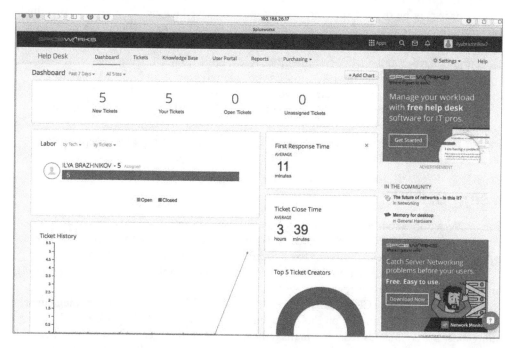

Typically, trouble tickets are customized within a company to help with proprietary applications. The customized fields could be the OS, platform, network address, browser version, and other useful fields.

Lastly, it's important to be a good listener. The only way you'll understand the problem reported by the user or customer is to practice active listening skills. Make sure you allow the customer to tell the whole story when they are reporting an issue.

Commands for gathering troubleshooting information are covered in Chapter 9, "Cisco Devices," and more commands are listed later in this chapter.

Information Gathering Using Network Documentation

I'll admit it: Creating network documentation is one of my least favorite tasks in network administration. It just isn't as exciting to me as learning about the coolest new technology or tackling and solving a challenging problem.

Part of it may be that I figure I know my networks well enough—after all, I installed and configured them, so if something comes up, it should be easy to figure it out and fix it, right? And most of the time I can do that, but as networks get bigger and more complex, it gets harder and harder to remember it all. Plus, it's an integral part of the service I provide for my clients to have seriously solid documentation in hand to refer to after I've left the scene and turned their network over to them.

So while I'll admit that creating documentation isn't something I get excited about, I know from experience that having it around is critical when problems come up—for myself and for my clients' technicians and administrators, who may not have been part of the installation process and simply aren't familiar with the system.

Using SNMP

Simple Network Management Protocol (SNMP) is used to gather information from and send settings to SNMP-compatible devices. SNMP gathers data by polling the devices on the network from a management station at fixed or random intervals, requiring them to disclose certain information. This is a big factor that really helps to simplify the process of gathering information about your entire internetwork.

SNMP uses UDP or TCP to transfer messages back and forth between the management system and the agents running on the managed devices. Inside the UDP packets (called *datagrams*) are commands from the management system to the agent. These commands can be used either to get information from the device about its state (SNMP GetRequest) or to make a change in the device's configuration (SetRequest). If a GetRequest command has been sent, the device will respond with an SNMP response. If there's a piece of information that's particularly interesting to an administrator about the device, the administrator can set something called a *trap* on the device.

Figure 12.4 shows how a host updated a network management station (NMS) about a problem it has.

FIGURE 12.4   SNMP NMS station receiving a trap

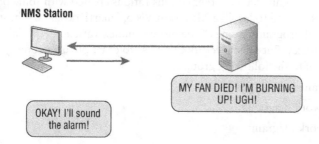

So, no whining! Like it or not, we're going to create some solid documentation. I'm guessing you really don't want to redo it, so it's a very good idea to keep it safe in at least three forms:

- An electronic copy that you can easily modify after configuration changes

- A hard copy in a binder, stored in an easily accessible location

- A copy on an external drive, to keep in a really safe place (even off-site) in case something happens to the other two or the building or part of it burns to the ground

Why the hard copy? Well, what if the computer storing the electronic copy totally crashes and burns at exactly the same time a major crisis develops? Good thing you have that paper documentation on hand for reference! Plus, sometimes you'll be troubleshooting on the run—maybe literally, as in running down the hall to the disaster's origin. Having that binder containing key configuration information on board could save you a lot of time and trouble, and it's also handy for making notes to yourself as you troubleshoot. Also, depending on the size of the intranet and the number of people staffing the IT department, it might be smart to have several hard copies. Just always make sure they're only checked out by staff who are cleared to have them, and that they're all returned to a secure location at the end of each shift. You definitely don't want that information in the wrong hands!

Now that I've hopefully convinced you that you absolutely must have tight documentation, let's take a look into the different types you need on hand.

Schematics and Diagrams

Now, reading network documentation doesn't exactly compete with racing your friends on jet skis, but it's really not that bad. It's better than eating canned spinach, and sometimes it's actually interesting to check out schematics and diagrams—especially when they describe innovative, elegant designs or when you're hunting down clues needed to solve an intricate problem with an elusive solution. I can't tell you how many times, if something isn't working between point A and point B, a solid diagram of the network that precisely describes exactly what exists between point A and point B has totally saved the day. Other times these tools come in handy is when you need to extend your network, and you want a clear picture of how the expanded version will look and work. Will the new addition cause one part of the network to become bogged down while another remains underutilized? You get the idea.

Diagrams can be simple sketches created while brainstorming or troubleshooting on the fly. They can also be highly detailed, refined illustrations created with some of the snappy software packages around today, like Microsoft Visio, SmartDraw, and a host of computer-aided design (CAD) programs. Some of the more complex varieties, especially CAD programs, are super pricey. But whichever tool you use to draw pictures about your networks, they basically fall into the following groups:

- Wiring diagrams/schematics
- Physical network diagrams
- Logical network diagrams
- Asset management
- IP address utilization
- Vendor documentation

Wiring Schematics

Wireless is definitely the wave of the future, but for now even the most extensive wireless networks have a wired backbone they rely on to connect them to the rest of humanity.

That skeleton is made up of cabled physical media like coax, fiber, and twisted-pair. Surprisingly, it is the latter—specifically, unshielded twisted-pair (UTP)—that screams to be pictured in a diagram. You'll see why in a minute.

As a quick refresher from Chapter 9 (you should already know this info), we'll start by checking out Figure 12.5, (the figure colors will not show up in the printed book, only in the e-book), which shows how UTP cables use an RJ-45 connector. (*RJ* stands for *registered jack*.)

FIGURE 12.5 An RJ-45 connector

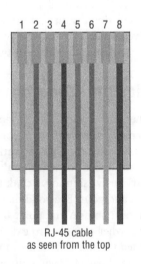
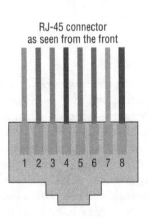

RJ-45 connector
as seen from the front

1 2 3 4 5 6 7 8

1 2 3 4 5 6 7 8

RJ-45 cable
as seen from the top

As you can see, pin 1 is on the left and pin 8 is on the right, so clearly, within your UTP cable, you need to make sure the right wires get to the right pins. No worries if you got your cables premade from the store, but making them yourself not only saves you a bunch of money but also allows you to customize cable lengths, which is really important!

Table 12.1 matches the colors for the wire associated with each pin, based on the Telecommunications Industry Alliance and Electronic Industries Association (TIA/EIA) 568B wiring standard.

TABLE 12.1   Standard TIA/EIA 568B wiring

Pin	Color
1	Orange/White
2	Orange
3	Green/White
4	Blue
5	Blue/White
6	Green
7	Brown/White
8	Brown

Standard drop cables, or *patch cables*, have the pins in the same order on both connectors. If you're connecting a computer to another computer directly, you should already know that you need a *crossover cable* that has one connector with flipped wires.

Specifically, pins 1 and 3 and pins 2 and 6 get switched to ensure that the send port from one computer's network interface card (NIC) gets attached to the receive port on the other computer's NIC. If you are using 1000BaseT4, all four pairs of wires get crossed at the opposite end, meaning pins 4 and 7 and pins 5 and 8 get crossed as well.

Figure 12.6 shows what this looks like.

Crossover cables were also used to connect older routers, switches, and hubs through their uplink ports.

This is where having a diagram is golden. Let's say you're troubleshooting a network and discover connectivity problems between two hosts. Because you've got the map, you can know the cable running between them is brand new and custom-made. At this point, you can go directly to that new cable because it's may be poorly made and therefore causing the snag.

FIGURE 12.6 Two ends of a crossover cable

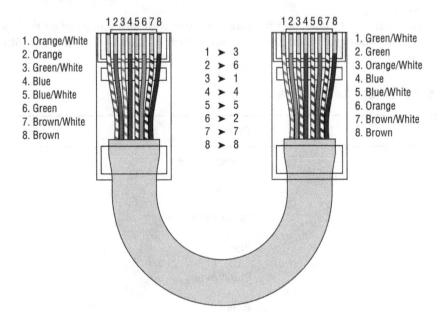

Another reason it's so important to diagram all things wiring is that all wires have to plug into something somewhere, and it's really good to know what and where that is. Whether it's into a hub, a switch, a router, a workstation, or the wall, you positively need to know the who, what, where, when, and how of the way the wiring is attached.

After adding a new cable segment on your network, you need to update the wiring schematics.

Knowing someone's or something's name is important because it helps us differentiate between people and things—especially when communicating with each other. If you want to be specific, you can't just say, "You know that router in the rack?" This is why coming up with a good naming system for all the devices living in your racks will be invaluable for ensuring that your wires don't get crossed.

Okay, I know it probably seems like we're edging over into OCD territory, but stay with me here. In addition to labeling, well, everything so far, you should actually label both ends of your cables too. If something happens (earthquake, tsunami, temper tantrum, even repairs) and more than one cable gets unplugged at the same time, it can get really messy scrambling to reconnect them from memory—fast!

Documentation and Diagrams

Ending up with a great network requires some really solid planning before you buy even one device for it. And planning includes thoroughly analyzing your design for potential flaws and optimizing configurations everywhere you can to maximize the network's future throughput and performance. If you blow it in this phase, trust me, you'll pay dearly later in bottom-line costs and countless hours consumed troubleshooting and putting out the fires of faulty design.

Start planning by creating an outline that precisely delimits all goals and business requirements for the network, and refer back to it often to ensure that you don't deliver a network that falls short of your client's present needs or fails to offer the scalability to grow with those needs. Drawing out your design and jotting down all the relevant information really helps in spotting weaknesses and faults. If you have a team, make sure everyone on it gets to examine the design and evaluate it, and keep that network plan up throughout the installation phase. Hang on to it after implementation has been completed as well because having it is like having the keys to the kingdom—it will enable you to efficiently troubleshoot any issues that could arise after everything is in place and up and running.

High-quality documentation should include a baseline for network performance because you and your client need to know what "normal" looks like in order to detect problems before they develop into disasters. Don't forget to verify that the network conforms to all internal and external regulations, and that you've developed and itemized solid management procedures and security policies for future network administrators to refer to and follow.

Physical Network Diagram

A physical network diagram contains all the physical devices and connectivity paths on your network and should accurately picture how your network physically fits together in glorious detail. Again, I know it seems like overkill, but ideally, your network diagram should list and map everything you would need to completely rebuild your network from scratch if you had to. This is actually what this type of diagram is designed for. But there's still another physical network diagram variety that includes the firmware revision on all the switches and access points in your network. Remember, besides having your physical network accurately detailed, you must also clearly understand the connections, types of hardware, and their firmware revisions. I'm going to say it again: You will be so happy you have this documentation when troubleshooting! It will prevent much suffering and enable you to fix whatever the problem is so much faster!

If you can't diagram everything, at least make sure all network devices are listed. As I said, physical network diagrams can run from simple, hand-drawn models to insanely complex monsters created by software packages like SmartDraw, OmniGraffle (my personal favorite), Visio, and AutoCAD.

Never forget to mirror any changes you make to your actual network in the network's diagram. Think of it like an updated snapshot. If you give the authorities your college buddy's baby picture after he goes missing, will that really help people recognize him? Not without the help of some high-tech, age-progression software, that's for sure—and they don't make that for networks, so it's better to just keep things up-to-date.

Logical Network Diagram

Physical diagrams depict how data physically flows from one area of your network to the next, but a logical network diagram includes things like protocols, configurations, addressing schemes, access lists, firewalls, types of applications, and so on—all things that apply logically to your network.

And just as you mirror any physical changes you make to the network (like adding devices or even just a cable) on your physical diagram, you map logical changes (like creating a new subnet, VLAN, or security zone) on your logical network diagram. It is important that you keep this oh-so-important document up-to-date.

IP Address Utilization

Documenting the current IP addressing scheme can be highly beneficial, especially when changes are required. Not only is this really helpful to new technicians, but it's very useful when identifying IP addressing issues that can lead to future problems. In many cases, IP addresses are configured over a long period of time, with no real thought or planning on the macro level.

Current and correct documentation can help administrators identify discontiguous networks (where subnets of a major network are separated by another major network), which can cause routing protocol issues. Proper IP address design can also facilitate summarization, which makes routing tables smaller, speeding the routing process. None of these wise design choices can be made without proper IP address documentation.

Vendor Documentation

Vendor agreements often have beneficial clauses that were negotiated during the purchase process. Many also contain critical details concerning SLAs and deadlines for warranties. These documents need to be organized and stored safely for future reference. Creating a spreadsheet or some other form of tracking documentation that alerts you of upcoming dates of interest can be a huge advantage!

Seven-Step Troubleshooting Process

As shown in Figure 12.7, Cisco has created a seven-step troubleshooting process for help desk technicians to have a step-by-step approach to help find and fix issues.

1. Define the problem.
2. Gather information.
3. Analyze the information.
4. Eliminate possible causes.

5. Propose a hypothesis.

6. Test the hypothesis.

7. Solve the problem and document the solution.

FIGURE 12.7   Cisco's seven-step troubleshooting process

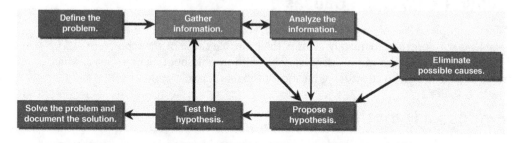

Define the Problem

As soon as a report is created, you need to identify the problem, such as the application, physical location, servers, network devices, and so on.

A symptom can be an application not responding, the network being slow, the Internet not being accessible, and so on. You can look at the SNMP NMS and Syslog console messages for information, as well as gather all the user complaints.

This is really a time for asking questions and investigating further in order to localize the problem. For example, is this a single device? A full branch office? A particular application? A subnet or VLAN?

It is likely that trouble tickets will be assigned to a network engineer. The help desk should have a type of trouble ticket software that can also track the progress of each ticket.

In addition, the software or application may have a self-service web page for customers/users to submit tickets, look up current known problems, and get the status of their tickets.

Gather Information

This is an important step in identifying servers, hosts, routers, and so forth that can be part or fully the problem. To perform this step, you must have access to the devices in question, and the information about these devices must be documented.

At this point, a technician or help desk personnel will gather and document more symptoms.

Analyze the Information

After you gather as much information as possible, you must consider and identify all possible causes of the problem.

This information needs to now be interpreted and analyzed using the documentation and network baselines created in the past, researching possible manufacturers' online documentation, conducting Internet searches, and getting advice and information from other engineers and technicians.

Eliminate Possible Causes

When multiple causes of an issue are reported, you must work hard to reduce the possible problems with urgency, to quickly identify the probable cause or the reports.

Most of the solutions can be identified only with troubleshooting experience, which is very valuable in quickly identifying the most probable cause.

Propose a Hypothesis

After you find and agree on a probable cause of the problems and report, you then must work on a solution to this problem.

At this stage, troubleshooting experience is very valuable when proposing a plan of attack.

Test the Hypothesis

In order to test your possible solutions, you need to understand the urgency of the issue and the impact your solution will have on the business.

When you implement the solution, will it cause a network outage? Does some critical infrastructure need to be rebooted, reconfigured, or shut down? Many solutions might need a change window that is implemented after hours. If this is the case, you can employ a workaround until the time window can be scheduled.

Solve the Problem

Okay, finally! You solved the problem. Woohoo! Now what? Happy hour, pizza day, and high fives all are in order, but maybe we should tell the customers too.

Inform your teammates and/or customer, as well as everyone else involved in the troubleshooting process, that they can all now breathe a collected sigh of relief because the problem has been solved.

But, wait, you're not done yet. It is important to properly document the problem's both cause and solution, as this can help other support help desk personnel and IT staff when they are trying to prevent and solve similar problems in the future.

Now, since we just talked about problems, reporting, analyzing, and solving issues, you may know that one of the tools that can help you provide solutions is a network analyzer. Let's look at the most popular network analyzer now.

Wireshark

Sometimes when you're troubleshooting an issue, it's useful to pull out a magnifying glass to see what the actual packets are doing. This is called doing a packet capture, for which you use a tool like Wireshark to see all the packets that are flowing through your computer's network connection. Once you perform a capture, the next step is to do packet analysis, which is a fancy way of saying check for any errors that could explain your issue.

This allows you to identify problems that may not be immediately obvious, such as retransmitting packets or other errors. This process is known as doing packet analysis because you're inspecting the protocols at the packet level to potentially find problems.

In order for Wireshark to be useful, you do need to have a good understanding of how the protocols you are looking at work. Fortunately, using the tool is rather easy. Simply download it from www.wireshark.org, install it on your PC or Mac, and then open it up.

Once Wireshark loads, you need to select the interface you want to do a packet capture on (see Figure 12.8). If you have multiple interfaces in your computer, you'll need to select the one that has the traffic you are interested in seeing.

FIGURE 12.8   Selecting an interface

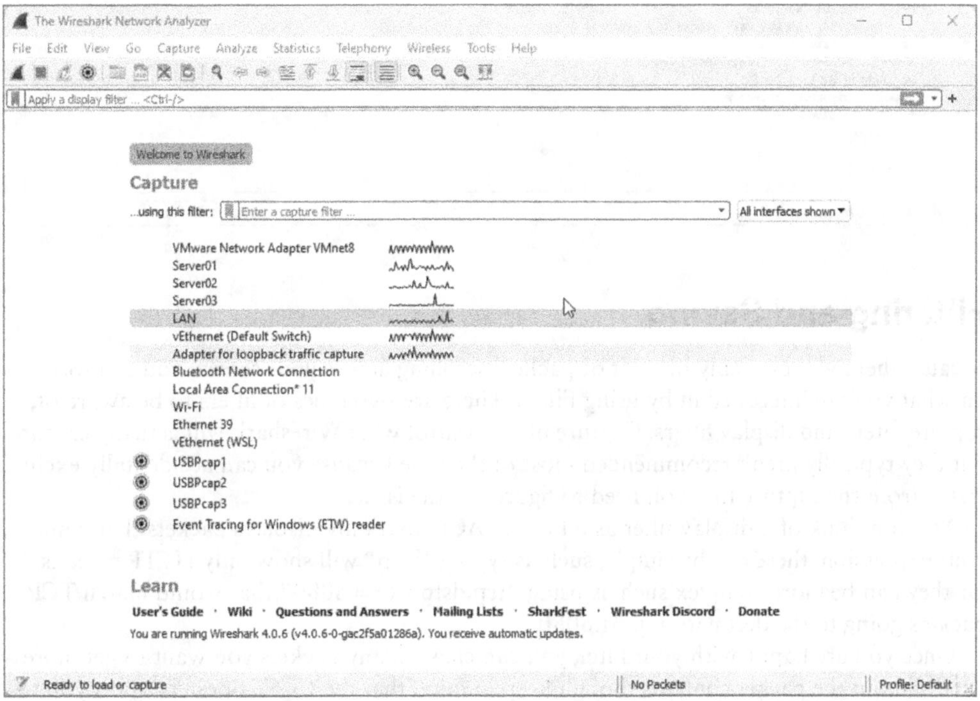

At this point, the packet capture is running, as shown in Figure 12.9. The next step is to try to replicate the issue you are trying to fix, such as navigating to a web page that isn't working or opening an application that isn't connecting to the network properly.

FIGURE 12.9   A running packet capture

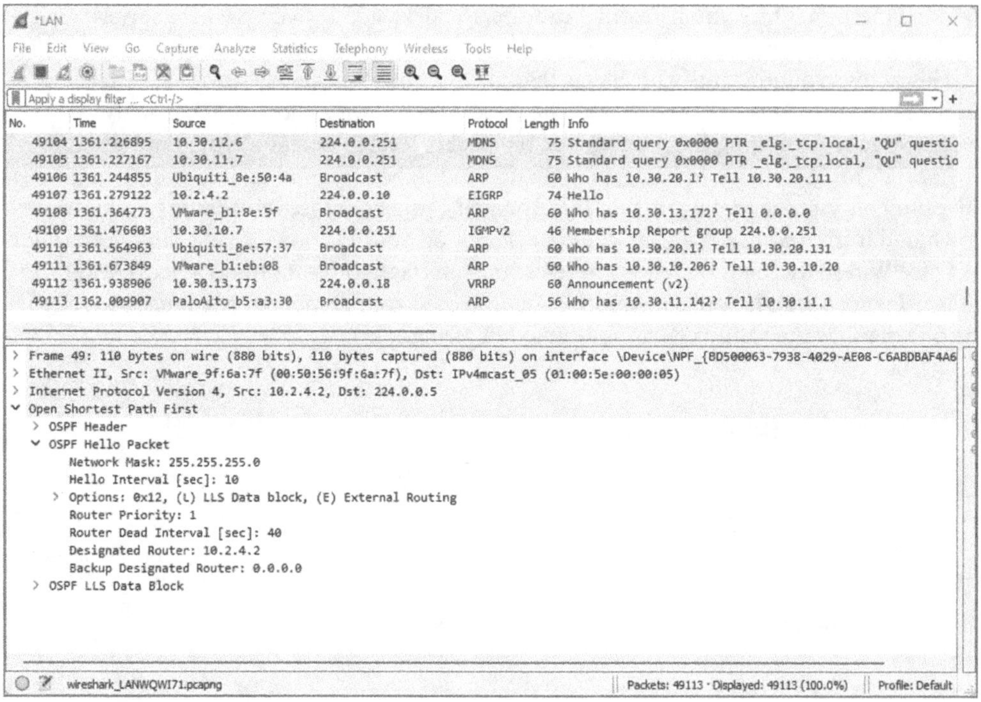

Filtering and Saving

Because there will probably be a lot of packets scrolling across your screen, you can focus on what you are interested in by using filters. There are two types of filters to be aware of, capture filters and display filters. Capture filters control what Wireshark will actually capture, but they typically aren't recommended most of the time because you can accidentally exclude traffic from the capture that you need to figure out the issue.

You can think of a display filter as a kind of ACL, that only displays packets that match your expression, these can be simple, such as typing "http" will show only HTTP packets. Or they can be more complex such as using **"tcp.dstport == 8080"** that would match TCP packets going to the destination port 8080.

Once you are happy with your filter, you can click on any packets you want to get more details about the packet contents though keep in mind that the CCST doesn't expect you to be able to packet analysis at this level. In fact, Wireshark has its own certification program that is focused on making sense of packets.

Finally, once you have the packets you want, you should save them as .pcap or .pcapng files so they can be reviewed later or shared with other people.

To save a capture, you first need to stop the capture by pressing the red square button or by selecting the Capture menu and choosing Stop. Then, select the File menu and choose Save or Save As, as shown in Figure 12.10.

FIGURE 12.10   Saving a packet capture

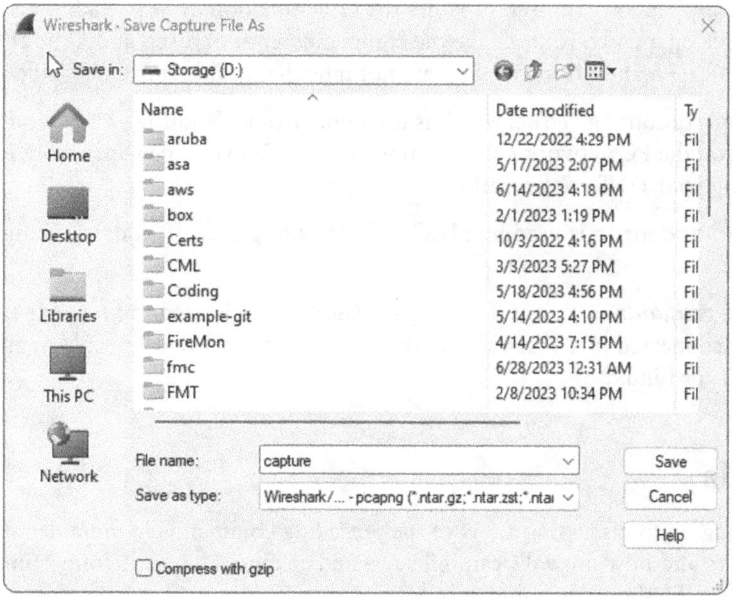

Diagnostic Commands

Chapter 9 covered a few IOS commands you can use to gather information about Cisco devices. It's important to remember those commands, so go back and review that section if necessary.

This next section will cover the basic commands that you can use to help troubleshoot your network from both a PC and an IOS device.

I'll then move on to define terms such as bandwidth, latency, delay, and throughput, and finally touch on the difference between a speed test and iPerf. Let's start by defining the basic troubleshooting commands:

ping   ping uses ICMP echo request and replies to test whether a node IP stack is initialized and alive on the network.

traceroute traceroute displays the list of routers on a path to a network destination by using TTL time-outs and ICMP error messages. Note that traceroute won't work from a command prompt.

tracert tracert serves the same function as traceroute, but it's a Microsoft Windows command and won't work on a Cisco router.

arp -a arp -a displays IP-to-MAC-address mappings on a Windows PC.

show ip arp show ip arp provides the same function as arp -a but displays the ARP table on a Cisco router. Like the commands traceroute and tracert, the commands arp -a and show ip arp are not interchangeable through Windows and Cisco.

ipconfig ipconfig /all, which is used only from a Windows command prompt, shows you the PC network configuration. The /all switch provides more information, including your DNS configuration.

ifconfig ifconfig is used by MAC and Linux to get the IP address details of the local machine.

ipconfig getifaddr en0 ipconfig getifaddr en0 is used to find your IP address if you are connected to a wireless network; use en1 if you are connected to an Ethernet for MAC or Linux.

Firewalls

Before moving on to discussing a few of the preceding commands in more detail, it is important to understand how firewalls can influence and change the results from running and performing troubleshooting commands.

Cisco has a very high-end firewall, which they purchased from SourceFire in 2014, called Cisco Secure Firewall, commonly known as Cisco Firepower. It's a great next-generation firewall (NGFW) that provides layer 7 deep packet inspection (DPI).

Many companies now provide and sell NGFWs, and they all inspect traffic up to layer 7, so this is a generic discussion on how firewalls can cause a disruption in your troubleshooting; it is not specific to Cisco devices.

The troubleshooting command ping uses ICMP echo request and echo replies to verify if a host is alive on the network—and what a great tool it is! However, it can also allow someone to not only find a host but also to create a denial-of-service attack or more, and, with an ICMP unreachable packet, draw out your network. However, with a firewall, most ICMP requests would or should be denied.

Figure 12.11 shows an alert when a firewall blocks ICMP from responding to an ICMP echo request.

FIGURE 12.11 ICMP being blocked by the Cisco NGFW

Action	Reason	Initiator IP	Initiator Country	Responder IP	Responder Country	Ingress Security Zone	Egress Security Zone	Source Port / ICMP Type	Destination Port / ICMP Code	Application Protocol	Client
Block		🖥 10.1.105.11		98.139.225.43	🇺🇸 USA	inside	outside	8 (Echo Request) / icmp	0 (No Code) / icmp	🗔 ICMP	🗔 ICMP client
Block		🖥 10.1.104.71		23.15.128.251	🇺🇸 USA	inside	outside	8 (Echo Request) / icmp	0 (No Code) / icmp	🗔 ICMP	🗔 ICMP client

The tool `traceroute` was invented in 1987 and is used with the ICMP protocol to trace or draw out a path a packet takes to a destination. It does this by using Time To Live (TTL) error responses. When a packet leaves a host when `traceroute` is implemented, the first packet TTL is set to 1. This means it goes one hop, times out, and then sends that error response back to the sending host where the error occurred. The next packet will be sent with a TTL of 2, and so on, until it reaches the destination, unless it's blocked on the way to or from.

By using `traceroute` (`tracert` with Microsoft), which uses ICMP, you can see the path, but also where the IP packet is dropped:

```
C C:\Users\Todd Lammle>tracert 172.16.20.254

Tracing route to 172.16.20.254 over a maximum of 30 hops

1     1 ms     1 ms     <1 ms   10.1.1.1
2     *        *        *       Request timed out.
3     *        *        *       Request timed
```

Since you can test a host by using more than just the ICMP protocol, you can configure a firewall to block any type of request and response that you feel is invalid or a risk to your network.

With that under our belt, let's go through the most widely used troubleshooting commands.

IP Config

It's a fact that at some point in your Cisco studies, you'll need to know how to verify and change the IP address on the operating system you're using. Doing this is really helpful for labs that use PCs for testing since you can adjust the IP to suit your lab environment.

Clearly, being good at this is vital in the real world because most servers use static IP addresses. Not every subnet will have DHCP running, and you'll probably need to troubleshoot an end user's connection from time to time.

Windows 10

On Windows operating systems, you can set the IP address from Network Connections. The easiest way to get there is to type **ncpa.cpl** in the search bar or from the Run command.

You can also get there through the Control Panel by selecting Network and Sharing Center then Change Adapter Settings. Once you're in, just right-click the network adapter you want to set the IP address of, and then click Properties, as shown in Figure 12.12.

The Properties page has a bunch of protocol-related information about the network adapter that you can adjust. For now, I'm going to choose Internet Protocol Version 4 (TCP/IP) and click Properties, as shown in Figure 12.13.

If you want to change the IPv6 address, you should go into the Version 6 properties instead.

FIGURE 12.12 The Network Connections page

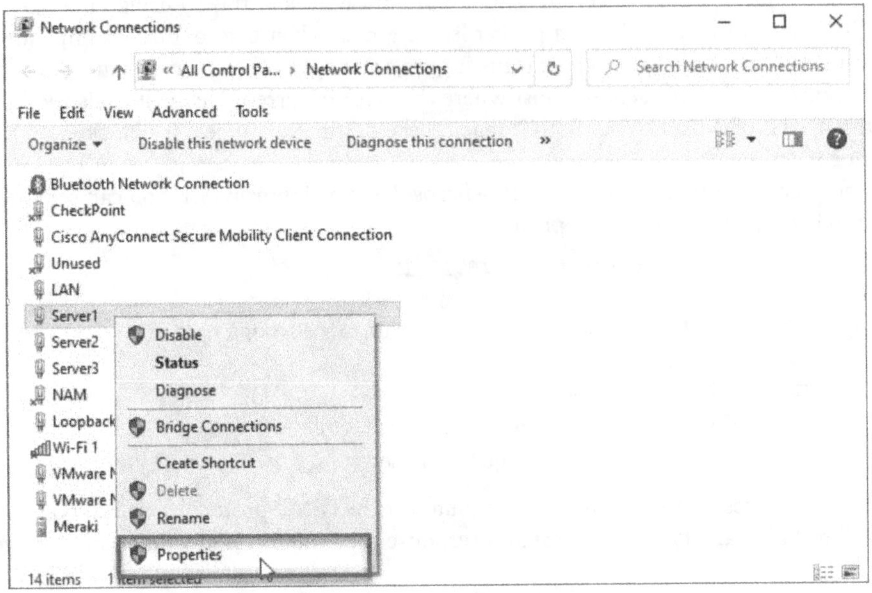

FIGURE 12.13 The IPv4 Properties page

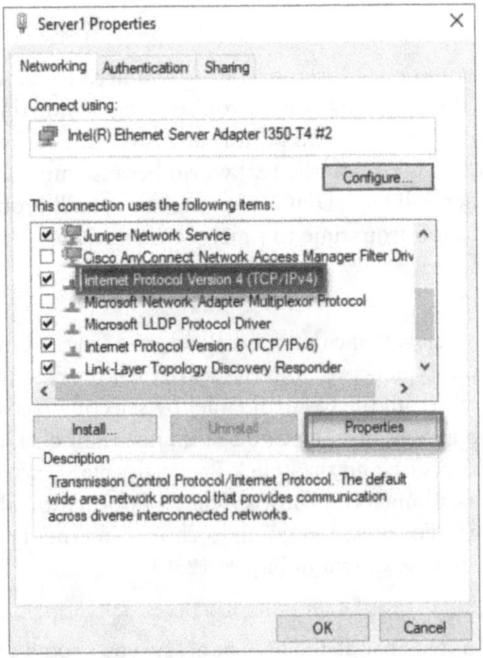

On the next page (Figure 12.14), I can finally set my IP address information, including the IP address, subnet mask, and the default gateway the network adapter will use. And because I'm statically setting an IP address, I've also got to statically set the DNS address used to resolve domain names too, as the network adapter won't be learning it via DHCP.

FIGURE 12.14   Setting the IP and DNS addresses

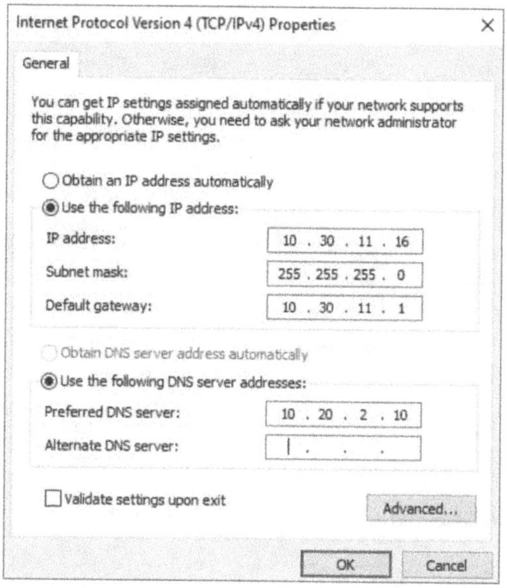

Now that the network adapter's IP and DNS are set, I could just hit OK to apply the changes. But I'm not going to do that just yet because first I want to introduce you to a couple of important items under the Advanced tab. This is where you can add additional IP addresses under the interface. This is like adding a secondary IP address on a Cisco router interface, where you can add as many additional IPs as you want. Check out Figure 12.15.

This comes in really handy for web servers, where each website may want to bind to a different IP address on the system.

Like a Cisco router, Windows also has a routing table. So, if you have multiple active interfaces on your computer, you can choose to adjust the interface metric, making it either more or less desirable when the computer needs to pick an interface to route traffic out of.

The last thing I want to point out here in the properties is the DNS tab. This is where you can choose to add more DNS servers, if you have more than two, as shown in Figure 12.16.

Oh, and I can also choose to append domain names to my DNS queries! For example, if I want to add "testlab.com," I just need to type web01 to get web01.testlab.com; the name will be appended for me. Cool!

With all that out of the way, I'll hit OK on all the dialogs until I'm back to Network Connections screen.

FIGURE 12.15 The IP Settings tab

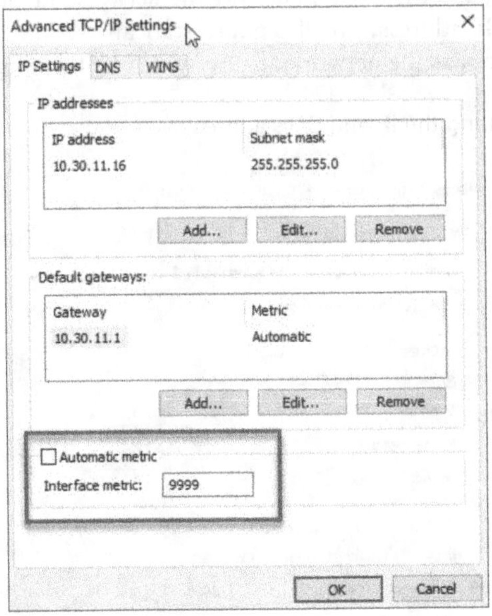

FIGURE 12.16 The DNS tab

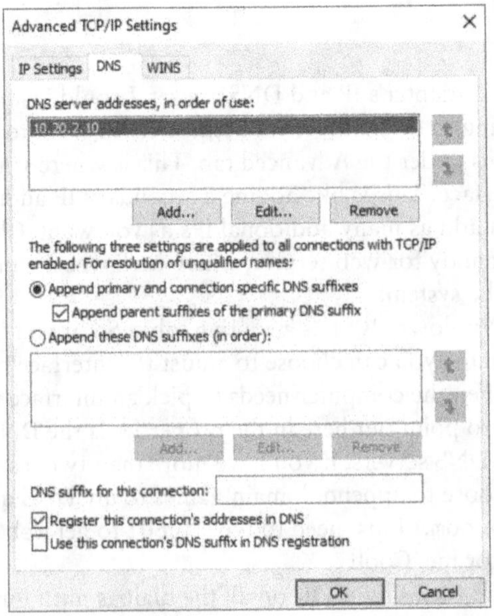

And if I want to verify the IP change from Network Connections, I'll just double-click the network adapter and then click Details. From there, I can see the IP information, as shown in Figure 12.17.

FIGURE 12.17 Verifying IP information

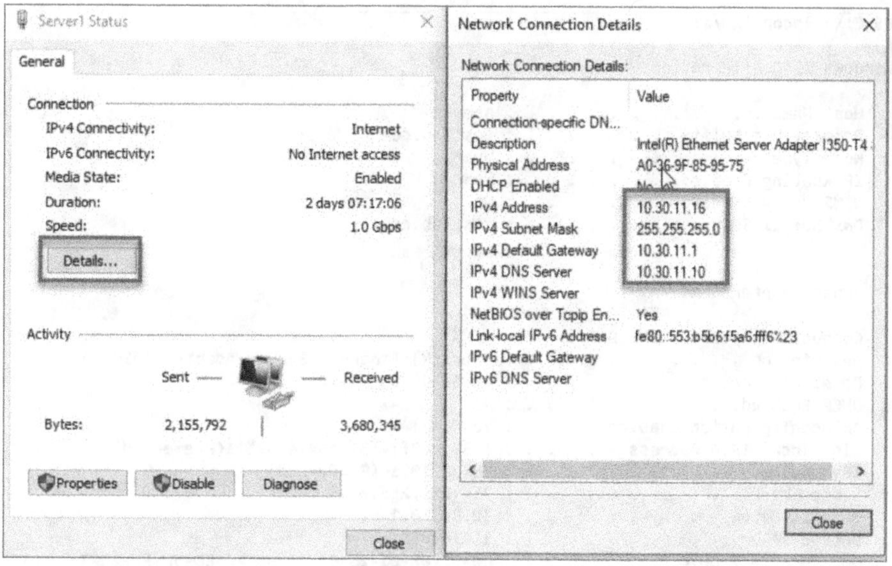

You can also use the `ipconfig` command to get the IP address information from Windows's command prompt. This will give you the IP address, subnet mask, and default gateway for each interface, as shown in Figure 12.18.

FIGURE 12.18 `ipconfig`

```
PS C:\> ipconfig

Windows IP Configuration

Ethernet adapter LAN:

   Connection-specific DNS Suffix  . :
   Link-local IPv6 Address . . . . . : fe80::c8f:7f3f:e84:4953%11
   IPv4 Address. . . . . . . . . . . : 10.30.10.16
   Subnet Mask . . . . . . . . . . . : 255.255.255.0
   Default Gateway . . . . . . . . . : 10.30.10.1

Ethernet adapter Server1:

   Connection-specific DNS Suffix  . :
   Link-local IPv6 Address . . . . . : fe80::553:b5b6:f5a6:fff6%23
   IPv4 Address. . . . . . . . . . . : 10.30.11.16
   Subnet Mask . . . . . . . . . . . : 255.255.255.0
   Default Gateway . . . . . . . . . : 10.30.11.1
```

If you want to check out information like DNS servers as well, just go with the `ipconfig/all` command to see all the information about the network adapters on the system, as shown in Figure 12.19.

FIGURE 12.19   *ipconfig /all*

```
PS C:\> ipconfig /all

Windows IP Configuration

    Host Name . . . . . . . . . . . . : home01
    Primary Dns Suffix  . . . . . . . : testlab.com
    Node Type . . . . . . . . . . . . : Hybrid
    IP Routing Enabled. . . . . . . . : No
    WINS Proxy Enabled. . . . . . . . : No
    DNS Suffix Search List. . . . . . : testlab.com

Ethernet adapter LAN:

    Connection-specific DNS Suffix  . :
    Description . . . . . . . . . . . : Intel(R) Ethernet Server Adapter I350-T4
    Physical Address. . . . . . . . . : A0-36-9F-85-95-74
    DHCP Enabled. . . . . . . . . . . : No
    Autoconfiguration Enabled . . . . : Yes
    Link-local IPv6 Address . . . . . : fe80::c8f:7f3f:e84:4953%11(Preferred)
    IPv4 Address. . . . . . . . . . . : 10.30.10.16(Preferred)
    Subnet Mask . . . . . . . . . . . : 255.255.255.0
    Default Gateway . . . . . . . . . : 10.30.10.1
    DHCPv6 IAID . . . . . . . . . . . : 111163039
    DHCPv6 Client DUID. . . . . . . . : 00-01-00-01-25-0B-09-00-40-8D-5C-FF-2C-34
    DNS Servers . . . . . . . . . . . : 10.30.11.10
                                        10.20.2.10
    NetBIOS over Tcpip. . . . . . . . : Enabled

Ethernet adapter Server1:

    Connection-specific DNS Suffix  . :
    Description . . . . . . . . . . . : Intel(R) Ethernet Server Adapter I350-T4 #2
    Physical Address. . . . . . . . . : A0-36-9F-85-95-75
    DHCP Enabled. . . . . . . . . . . : No
    Autoconfiguration Enabled . . . . : Yes
    Link-local IPv6 Address . . . . . : fe80::553:b5b6:f5a6:fff6%23(Preferred)
    IPv4 Address. . . . . . . . . . . : 10.30.11.16(Preferred)
    Subnet Mask . . . . . . . . . . . : 255.255.255.0
    Default Gateway . . . . . . . . . : 10.30.11.1
    DHCPv6 IAID . . . . . . . . . . . : 211826335
    DHCPv6 Client DUID. . . . . . . . : 00-01-00-01-25-0B-09-00-40-8D-5C-FF-2C-34
```

Okay, so you know that the `ipconfig` method works fine, but it's an older command. The new way to do things in Microsoft products is to use PowerShell instead of the CMD. The main advantage is that you can filter the output you get back, instead of getting all the network adapters every time you type `ipconfig`.

In PowerShell, you can use the `Get-NetIPAddress` cmdlet to get the IP address and netmask, and I can opt to just see my Server1 interface and only IPv4 addresses.

Note that PowerShell likes to keep its commands very focused, so it won't return any default gateway or DNS information. So, I would need to use the

`Get-DnsClientServerAddress` command to get DNS information, and `Get-NetRoute` to see routing information, as shown in Figure 12.20.

FIGURE 12.20   PowerShell

```
PS C:\> Get-NetIPAddress -InterfaceAlias Server1 -AddressFamily ipv4

IPAddress          : 10.30.11.16
InterfaceIndex     : 23
InterfaceAlias     : Server1
AddressFamily      : IPv4
Type               : Unicast
PrefixLength       : 24
PrefixOrigin       : Manual
SuffixOrigin       : Manual
AddressState       : Preferred
ValidLifetime      : Infinite ([TimeSpan]::MaxValue)
PreferredLifetime  : Infinite ([TimeSpan]::MaxValue)
SkipAsSource       : False
PolicyStore        : ActiveStore
```

MacOS

To verify IP address information on a Mac, open Network Preferences by either clicking the wireless signal on the upper right of the desktop or by opening System Preferences and selecting it from there, as shown in Figure 12.21.

FIGURE 12.21   MacOS

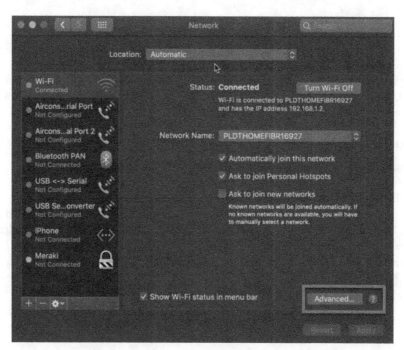

From there, you can see the IP address by choosing the network you're connected to. You won't see any other information unless you click Advanced. Once you do, you'll get the screen shown in Figure 12.22.

FIGURE 12.22   The MacOS TCP/IP tab

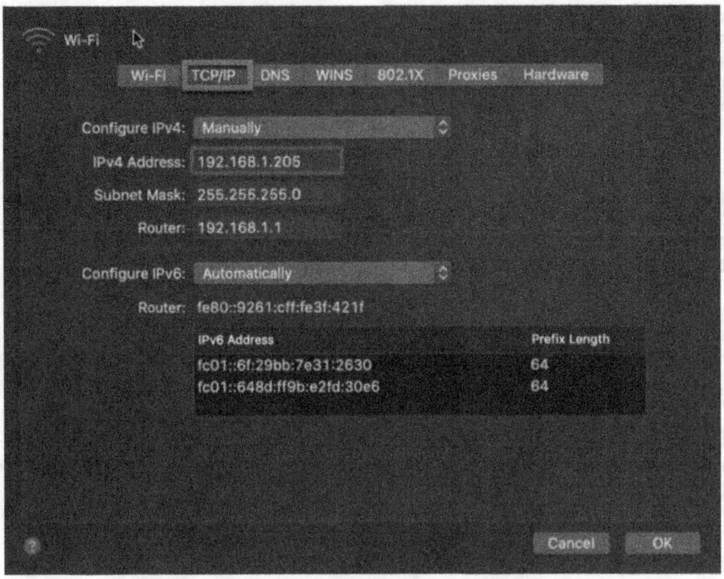

Under the TCP/IP tab, I can set the IP address, subnet mask, and gateway.

Under the DNS tab, as shown in Figure 12.23, I can add the IP addresses of DNS servers, which appends domain names to DNS queries, just like in Windows.

If I want to verify the IP information from the command line, I can use the `ifconfig` command, which can also be used to set an IP address. Just know that the static IP address won't survive a reboot. Check out Figure 12.24.

Ubuntu/Red Hat

Both Ubuntu and Red Hat-based Linux desktops actually go through the same steps to change an IP address via the GUI. They only differ in how you change the IP address in the Linux shell.

To verify or change an IP address in Ubuntu or Fedora/Centos, open Settings and then Network. You can also click the network on the top right of the screen and then select the connection's settings, as shown in Figure 12.25.

From there, click the gear icon to see the network information on the Linux box, as shown in Figure 12.26. This is where you can adjust the IP address, subnet mask, default gateway, and the DNS servers.

FIGURE 12.23 The MacOS DNS tab

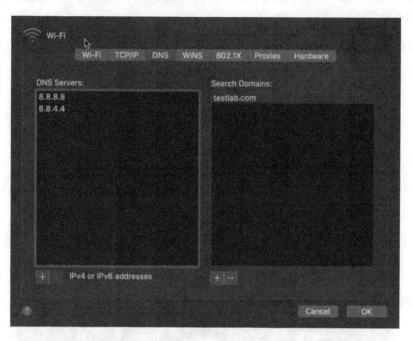

FIGURE 12.24 The MacOS *ifconfig* command

```
Donalds-MacBook-Pro:~ drobb$ ifconfig en0
en0: flags=8863<UP,BROADCAST,SMART,RUNNING,SIMPLEX,MULTICAST> mtu 1500
        options=400<CHANNEL_IO>
        ether a4:83:e7:c4:e8:b8
        inet6 fe80::b8:9238:1f3c:a398%en0 prefixlen 64 secured scopeid 0x6
        inet 10.30.10.114 netmask 0xffffff00 broadcast 10.30.10.255
        nd6 options=201<PERFORMNUD,DAD>
        media: autoselect
        status: active
Donalds-MacBook-Pro:~ drobb$ 
```

When you're done, just click the Apply button to make the changes active.

Finally, to verify the IP address, use the ifconfig command, just like we did in the MacOS example.

Using Diagnostic Commands to Solve Network Issues

A customer calls and says they cannot get to the server they use to run payroll. Obviously, this is a serious issue and needs to be fixed asap! The payroll server is on a remote network, so we need to start testing locally to see where the problem is and then get this working ASAP!

FIGURE 12.25 Ubuntu IP Settings

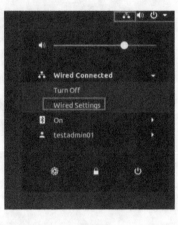

FIGURE 12.26 The Linux gear icon

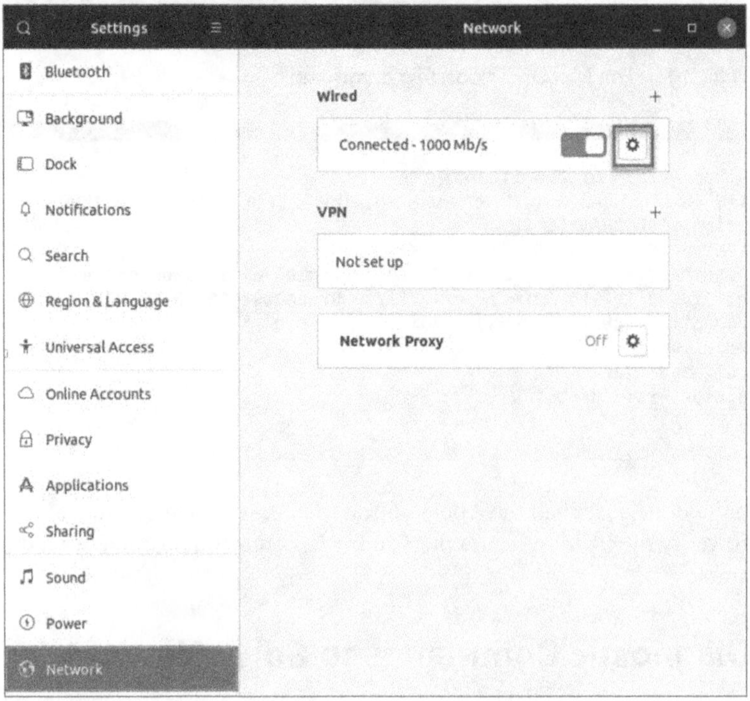

Settings	Network
Bluetooth	
Background	**Wired** +
Dock	Connected - 1000 Mb/s ⚙
Notifications	
Search	**VPN** +
Region & Language	Not set up
Universal Access	
Online Accounts	**Network Proxy** Off ⚙
Privacy	
Applications	
Sharing	
Sound	
Power	
Network	

We need to first determine if this is a local issue or a remote issue, so let's start by looking at the local PC.

We'll first check out the PC configuration by using the `ipconfig` command (or we can use an `ifconfig` on a Mac or Linux device):

```
C:\Users\Todd Lammle>ipconfig

Windows IP Configuration

Ethernet adapter Local Area Connection:

   Connection-specific DNS Suffix  . : localdomain
   Link-local IPv6 Address . . . . . : fe80::64e3:76a2:541f:ebcb%11
   IPv4 Address. . . . . . . . . . . : 10.1.1.10
   Subnet Mask . . . . . . . . . . . : 255.255.255.0
   Default Gateway . . . . . . . . . : 10.1.1.1
```

We can also check the route table on the host with the `route print` command, to see if it knows the default gateway:

```
C:\Users\Todd Lammle>route print
[output cut]
IPv4 Route Table
=======================================================================
Active Routes:
Network Destination        Netmask          Gateway       Interface  Metric
          0.0.0.0          0.0.0.0          10.1.1.10     10.1.1.1   10
[output cut]
```

Between the output of the `ipconfig` command and the `route print` command, we can rest assured that the hosts are aware of the correct default gateway.

Let's verify that the local IP stack is initialized by pinging the loopback address of the host:

```
C:\Users\Todd Lammle>ping 127.0.0.1

Pinging 127.0.0.1 with 32 bytes of data:
Reply from 127.0.0.1: bytes=32 time<1ms TTL=128
Reply from 127.0.0.1: bytes=32 time<1ms TTL=128
Reply from 127.0.0.1: bytes=32 time<1ms TTL=128
Reply from 127.0.0.1: bytes=32 time<1ms TTL=128

Ping statistics for 127.0.0.1:
    Packets: Sent = 4, Received = 4, Lost = 0 (0% loss),
Approximate round trip times in milli-seconds:
    Minimum = 0ms, Maximum = 0ms, Average = 0ms
```

This first output confirms the IP address and configured the default gateway of the host. Then I verified the fact that the local IP stack is working. Our next move is to verify that the IP stack is talking to the LAN driver, by pinging the local IP address:

```
C:\Users\Todd Lammle>ping 10.1.1.10

Pinging 10.1.1.10 with 32 bytes of data:
Reply from 10.1.1.10: bytes=32 time<1ms TTL=128
Reply from 10.1.1.10: bytes=32 time<1ms TTL=128
Reply from 10.1.1.10: bytes=32 time<1ms TTL=128
Reply from 10.1.1.10: bytes=32 time<1ms TTL=128

Ping statistics for 10.1.1.10:
    Packets: Sent = 4, Received = 4, Lost = 0 (0% loss),
Approximate round trip times in milli-seconds:
    Minimum = 0ms, Maximum = 0ms, Average = 0ms
```

And now that we know the local stack is solid and the IP stack is communicating to the LAN driver, it's time to check our local LAN connectivity by pinging the default gateway:

```
C:\Users\Todd Lammle>ping 10.1.1.1

Pinging 10.1.1.1 with 32 bytes of data:
Reply from 10.1.1.1: bytes=32 time<1ms TTL=128
Reply from 10.1.1.1: bytes=32 time<1ms TTL=128
Reply from 10.1.1.1: bytes=32 time<1ms TTL=128
Reply from 10.1.1.1: bytes=32 time<1ms TTL=128

Ping statistics for 10.1.1.1:
    Packets: Sent = 4, Received = 4, Lost = 0 (0% loss),
Approximate round trip times in milli-seconds:
    Minimum = 0ms, Maximum = 0ms, Average = 0ms
```

I'd say our host is in good shape. Let's try to ping the remote server next to see if our host is actually getting off the local LAN to communicate remotely:

```
C:\Users\Todd Lammle>ping 172.16.20.254

Pinging 172.16.20.254 with 32 bytes of data:
Request timed out.
Request timed out.
Request timed out.
Request timed out.

Ping statistics for 172.16.20.254:
    Packets: Sent = 4, Received = 0, Lost = 4 (100% loss),
```

Well, it looks like we've confirmed local connectivity but not remote connectivity, so we're going to have to dig deeper to isolate the problem. But first, and just as important, it's key to note what we can rule out at this point:

1. The PC is configured with the correct IP address, and the local IP stack is working.

2. The default gateway is configured correctly, and the PC's default gateway configuration matches the router interface IP address.

3. The local switch is working because we can ping through the switch to the router.

4. We don't have a local LAN issue, meaning our Physical and Data Link layers are good because we can ping the router. If we couldn't ping the router, we would need to verify our physical cables and interfaces.

Let's see if we can narrow the problem further using the `traceroute` (`tracert` with Microsoft as shown) command:

```
C:\Users\Todd Lammle>tracert www.google.com

Tracing route to www.google.com [142.251.33.68]
over a maximum of 30 hops

  1     1 ms     1 ms    <1 ms   10.1.1.1
  2     *        *        *       Request timed out.
  3     *        *        *       Request timed
```

We have connection to the router from the inside host but packets cannot pass through the router to a remote network, which means, of course, that we can't get a response from the remote end.

At this point, we'd want to look at the router's configuration and routing table to determine the problem of getting to the remote network. This last step is covered in my *Cisco Certified Network Associate (CCNA) Study Guide* and not something you need to know when studying for the CCST exam—but it's something to look forward to once you pass the CCST exam.

Once the routing is fixed, we can now test out the network path with the `tracert` tool from the source to the remote network:

```
C:\Users\Todd Lammle>tracert www.google.com

Tracing route to www.google.com [142.251.33.68]
over a maximum of 30 hops:

  1    <1 ms    <1 ms    <1 ms   10.1.1.1
  2     2 ms     2 ms     2 ms   50.99.126.65
  3    19 ms    20 ms    20 ms   154.11.12.217
  4    22 ms    22 ms    23 ms   74.125.50.110
  5    21 ms    20 ms    21 ms   142.251.229.135
```

```
6    18 ms    19 ms    18 ms  142.251.50.243
7    19 ms    18 ms    19 ms  sea09s28-in-f4.1e100.net [142.251.33.68]
```

Looks great!

Network Bandwidth and Throughput

To help you troubleshoot your networks, you need to understand some basic terms, including bandwidth, throughput, latency, and delay.

Bandwidth and throughput both indicate network performance, and the terms are used interchangeably, although they shouldn't really be. Here is the definition of each:

- *Bandwidth* is the total capacity of the bounded or unbounded media.

- *Throughput* is how much data can be transmitted in the media.

You can see how these terms are basically interchangeable. Remember, however, that although the terms are similar, they are not the same thing. To make things worse, latency and/or delay can be thrown in here as well because these define the speed the data can travel across the network.

- *Latency* is the round-trip time it takes for a packet to travel from its destination point back to its source point.

- *Delay* is how long the data takes to reach its destination.

You'll typically find that people use the terms *bandwidth*, *throughput*, *latency*, and even *delay* when describing network speed; however, speed is defined primarily by the amount of latency on the network.

If the latency is high for a link, this indicates a delay, which is also referred to as *lag*.

Bandwidth and latency typically don't affect one another, but you can still use the two to analyze your network performance, and you won't see, or more likely notice, much latency unless you are using a high-bandwidth link. But who doesn't these days? Since high throughput networks are so common, we typical have less or low latency, or little lag, that affects our speed.

There are an enormous number of places and ways to test the bandwidth, throughput, latency, and delay of your networks. Let's look at that in our final section of the chapter.

Speed Tests vs. iPerf

Speed tests are used constantly now, by almost everyone and at every company. Speed test websites allow you to see your download and upload speed as well as latency and delay. This is popular because you just need to use a standard host on the inside of your network to assess the Internet bandwidth and test your connections.

The clients will look for the best server based on your location and select with the one it thinks will have the lowest latency. Understand that these are public servers and get overloaded, so it's important to test multiple times, to multiple different sites.

People use speed tests because of their simplicity. You just open a browser and go. In the past, they were clunky and didn't work that well, but that was then and this is now, and now is better. Reliable and detailed, speed tests are used for good reason.

Figure 12.27 shows the details available from the site `www.fast.com`, which Netflix created for you to test your Internet connection. This is the site I like the best.

FIGURE 12.27 Fast.com

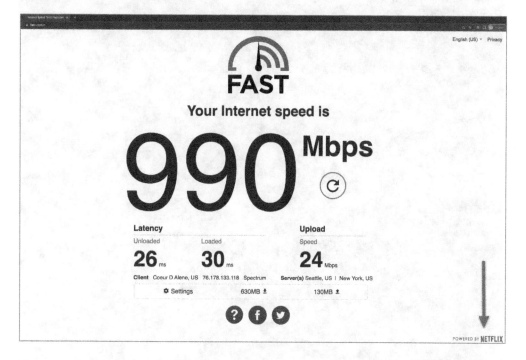

As I've mentioned, a lot of sites are available, so take your pick of what you'd like to use. Be sure to use multiple servers to get the best average result.

Another site I like is `https://speedof.me`, which has a very nice graphical interface and output, as shown in Figure 12.28.

In addition to the hundreds of speed test HTTPS sites, there are CLI version's as well. One popular version that I like can be found at `www.speedtest.net/apps/cli`. It's literally the same test but with a CLI output. It even provides an URL at the end of each test to give you a GUI result.

If you want more detail and options regarding your bandwidth and latency, iPerf is a tool that actively measures the maximum possible bandwidth in IP networks. iPerf can be found at `https://iperf.fr`.

iPerf offers different tests for different protocols (TCP/UDP/SCTP). Each test reports the bandwidth, loss, and other parameters. You can use either IPv4 or IPv6 with iPerf.

FIGURE 12.28 *Speedof.me*

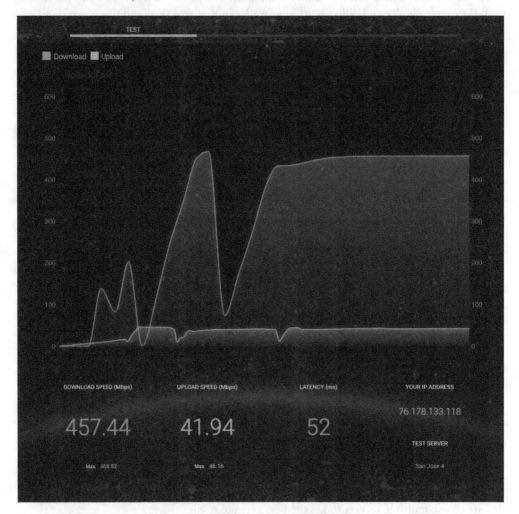

What is the difference between a speed test and iPerf? The main difference between the two programs is a speed test does not require a "speed test server" to be set up; rather, it automatically chooses a server on the Internet. iPerf, however, requires an endpoint program, which must be installed on a separate server, typically on your own network, so there is more administrative overhead to get started.

The results of iPerf bandwidth tests depend on the following three values:

- The connection speed of the client's network interface card
- The bandwidth available between the source and destination
- The connection speed of the server's network interface card

Speed test sites do not offer any configuration options, so people who need options prefer iPerf. You can choose TCP or UDP with iPerf. When using TCP, the sender generates as much data as supported by the network, and when using UDP mode, the user has to define the rate of transmission.

TCP mode returns the maximum bandwidth available between two hosts, and UDP mode returns the jitter, packet loss, and bandwidth.

TCP and SCTP measure bandwidth, report on maximum segment size (MSS)/maximum transmission unit (MTU) size and observed read sizes. With the UDP tests, the client can create streams of specified bandwidth and measure packet loss and delay jitter. UPP tests are multicast-capable.

You can download iPerf for various operating systems at `https://iperf.fr/iperf-download.php`.

All this said, there are actually a few public iPerf servers for testing at `https://iperf.fr/iperf-servers.php`.

Most people use the various GUI speed test sites because they are the easiest to run, and they are fast and efficient, and typically spot on. For more detail, you'd want to set up iPerf servers and clients.

Summary

This chapter started by discussing the help desk, including its purpose, policies and procedures, ticketing, documentation, and information gathering. I also showed you Cisco's seven-step troubleshooting process for help desk personnel to find and solve problems.

The chapter then introduced you to Wireshark and its purpose, how to use it, as well as save and open a file.

Finally, the chapter wrapped up by guiding you through some important Cisco basic IP and network troubleshooting techniques to ensure that you're well equipped with these key skills.

Exam Essentials

Remember the Cisco seven-step troubleshooting process. Cisco created the following seven-step troubleshooting process for help desk technicians to find and fix issues:

1. Define the problem.
2. Gather information.
3. Analyze the information.
4. Eliminate possible causes.
5. Propose a hypothesis.
6. Test the hypothesis.
7. Solve the problem and document the solution.

Understand the troubleshooting tools that you can use from your host and a Cisco router.   The `ping 127.0.0.1` command tests your local IP stack, and `tracert` is a Windows command to track the path a packet takes through an internetwork to a destination. Cisco routers use the command `traceroute`—or `trace` for short. Don't confuse the Windows and Cisco commands. Although they produce the same output, they don't work from the same prompts. The command `ipconfig /all` will display your PC network configuration from a DOS prompt, and `arp -a` (again from a DOS prompt) will display IP-to-MAC-address mapping on a Windows PC.

Understand the terms bandwidth, throughput, and latency.   *Bandwidth* and *throughput* both have to do with network data. Network bandwidth defines how much data can possibly travel in a network in a period of time. Network throughput refers to how much data actually transfers during a period of time. Bandwidth and throughput are also sometimes confused with latency, which is understandable because latency refers to the speed at which data travels across the network to its destination.

Know the difference between iPerf and speed tests.   The main difference between the two programs is that a speed test does not require a "speed test server" to be set up; rather, it automatically chooses a server on the Internet. iPerf, however, requires an endpoint program, which must be installed on a separate server, typically on your own network, so there is more administrative overhead to get started.

Review Questions

You can find the answers to these questions in Appendix, "Answers to Review Questions."

1. Which of the following defines the term *latency*?

    A. Network latency refers to the amount of bandwidth and delay over a period of time.

    B. Network bandwidth refers to how much data can possibly travel in a network during a period of time.

    C. Network throughput refers to how much data actually transfers during a period of time.

    D. Network latency refers to the speed at which data travels across the network to its destination.

2. Which of the following defines the term *bandwidth*?

    A. Network bandwidth refers to the amount of latency and delay over a period of time.

    B. Network bandwidth refers to how much data can possibly travel in a network during a period of time.

    C. Network throughput refers to how much data actually transfers during a period of time.

    D. Network latency refers to the speed at which data travels across the network to its destination.

3   Which of the following defines the term *throughput*?

    A. Network throughput refers to the amount of delay over a period of time.

    B. Network bandwidth refers to how much data can possibly travel in a network during a period of time.

    C. Network throughput refers to how much data actually transfers during a period of time.

    D. Network latency refers to the speed at which data travels across the network to its destination.

4. Which of the following describes a speed test in contrast to iPerf? (Choose two.)

    A. iPerf requires a speed test server to be set up.

    B. A speed test requires a speed test server to be set up.

    C. A speed test requires an endpoint program, which must be installed on a separate server.

    D. iPerf requires an endpoint program, which must be installed on a separate server.

5. Which of the following diagnostic commands provides a step-by-step output of the path a packet takes on the way to a destination?

    A. `ping`

    B. `route print`

    C. `ipconfig /path`

    D. `traceroute`

6. Which of the following diagnostic commands provides the routing table of a Windows host?

    A. `ping`

    B. `route print`

    C. `ipconfig /path`

    D. `traceroute`

7. Which of the following diagnostic commands provides output that tells you a host is up and running on the network?

    A. `ping`

    B. `route print`

    C. `ipconfig /path`

    D. `traceroute`

8. Which of the following would you perform after analyzing a problem described in a trouble ticket?

    A. Gather information.

    B. Solve the problem.

    C. Define the problem.

    D. Eliminate possible causes.

9. What is the first thing you should do after loading Wireshark on your computer?

    A. Read the first frame you just received.

    B. Choose the interface on which you want to receive the packets.

    C. Open all TCP packets, which always show the problem.

    D. Save the file.

10. Which of the following would you perform after proposing a hypothesis of the problem described in a trouble ticket?

    A. Test the hypothesis.

    B. Solve the problem.

    C. Define the problem.

    D. Eliminate possible causes.

Appendix

Answers to Review Questions

Chapter 1: Internetworking

1. B. The contents of a protocol data unit (PDU) depend on the PDU because they are created in a specific order and their contents are based on that order. A packet will contain IP addresses but not MAC addresses because MAC addresses are not present until the PDU becomes a frame.

2. C. You should select a router to connect the two groups. When computers are in different subnets, as these two groups are, you will require a device that can make decisions based on IP addresses. Routers operate at layer 3 of the Open Systems Interconnection (OSI) model and make data-forwarding decisions based on layer 3 networking information, which are IP addresses. They create routing tables that guide them in forwarding traffic out of the proper interface to the proper subnet.

3. C. Replacing the hub with a switch would reduce collisions and retransmissions, which would have the most impact on reducing congestion.

4. B. Wireless LAN controllers are used to manage anywhere from a few access points to thousands. The APs are completely managed from the controller and are considered lightweight or dumb APs, as they have no configuration on the AP itself.

5. C. Firewalls are used to connect a trusted internal network such as the demilitarized zone (DMZ), also called a screened subnet, to the untrusted outside network—typically the Internet.

6. D. The Application layer is responsible for identifying and establishing the availability of the intended communication partner and determining whether sufficient resources for the intended communication exist.

7. A, D. The Transport layer segments data into smaller pieces for transport. Each segment is assigned a sequence number so that the receiving device can reassemble the data on arrival. The Network layer (layer 3) has two key responsibilities. First, this layer controls the logical addressing of devices. Second, the Network layer determines the best path to a particular destination network and routes the data appropriately.

8. C. The IEEE Ethernet Data Link layer has two sublayers, the Media Access Control (MAC) sublayer and the Logical Link Control (LLC) sublayer.

9. C. Wireless APs are very popular today and will be going away about the same time that rock n' roll does. The idea behind these devices (which are layer 2 bridge devices) is to connect wireless products to the wired Ethernet network. The wireless AP will create a single collision domain and is typically its own dedicated broadcast domain as well.

10. A. Hubs operate on the Physical layer, as they have no intelligence, and send all traffic in all directions.

Chapter 2: Introduction to TCP/IP

1. B. Secure Shell (SSH) protocol sets up a secure session that's similar to Telnet over a standard TCP/IP connection and is employed for doing things like logging into systems, running programs on remote systems, and moving files from one system to another.

2. B. Address Resolution Protocol (ARP) is used to find the hardware address from a known IP address.

3. A, C, D. The listed answers are from the OSI model and the question asked about the TCP/ IP protocol stack (DoD model). Yes, it is normal for the objectives to have this type of question. However, let's just look for what is wrong. First, the Session layer is not in the TCP/IP model; neither are the Data Link and Physical layers. This leaves us with the Transport layer (Host-to-Host in the DoD model), Internet layer (Network layer in the OSI), and Application layer (Application/Process in the DoD). Remember, the CCENT objectives can list the layers as OSI layers or DoD layers at any time, regardless of what the question is asking.

4. C. A Class C network address has only 8 bits for defining hosts: $2^8 - 2 = 254$.

5. A, B. A client that sends out a DHCP Discover message in order to receive an IP address sends out a broadcast at both layer 2 and layer 3. The layer 2 broadcast is all Fs in hex, or FF:FF:FF:FF:FF:FF. The layer 3 broadcast is 255.255.255.255, which means any networks and all hosts. DHCP is connectionless, which means it uses User Datagram Protocol (UDP) at the Transport layer, also called the Host-to-Host layer.

6. B. Although Telnet does use TCP and IP (TCP/IP), the question specifically asks about layer 4, and IP works at layer 3. Telnet uses TCP at layer 4.

7. RFC 1918. These addresses can be used on a private network, but they're not routable through the Internet.

8. B, D, E. SMTP, FTP, and HTTP use TCP.

9. C. The range of multicast addresses starts with 224.0.0.0 and goes through 239.255.255.255.

10. A. Both FTP and Telnet use TCP at the Transport layer; however, they both are Application layer protocols, so the Application layer is the best answer for this question.

11. C. The four layers of the DoD model are Application/Process, Host-to-Host, Internet, and Network Access. The Internet layer is equivalent to the Network layer of the OSI model.

12. C, E. The Class A private address range is 10.0.0.0 through 10.255.255.255. The Class B private address range is 172.16.0.0 through 172.31.255.255, and the Class C private address range is 192.168.0.0 through 192.168.255.255.

13. B. The four layers of the TCP/IP stack (also called the DoD model) are Application/Process, Host-to-Host (also called Transport on the objectives), Internet, and Network Access/ Link. The Host-to-Host layer is equivalent to the Transport layer of the OSI model.

14. B, C. ICMP is used for diagnostics and destination unreachable messages. ICMP is encapsulated within IP datagrams, and because it is used for diagnostics, it will provide hosts with information about network problems.

15. C. The range of a Class B network address is 128–191. This makes our binary range 10*xxxxxx*.

Chapter 3: Easy Subnetting

1. D. A /27 (255.255.255.224) is 3 bits on and 5 bits off. This provides 8 subnets, each with 30 hosts. Does it matter if this mask is used with a Class A, B, or C network address? Not at all. The number of subnet bits would never change.

2. D. A 240 mask is 4 subnet bits and provides 16 subnets, each with 14 hosts. We need more subnets, so let's add subnet bits. One more subnet bit would be a 248 mask. This provides 5 subnet bits (32 subnets) with 3 host bits (6 hosts per subnet). This is the best answer.

3. C. This is a pretty simple question. A /28 is 255.255.255.240, which means that our block size is 16 in the fourth octet. 0, 16, 32, 48, 64, 80, etc. The host is in the 64 subnet.

4. C. A CIDR address of /19 is 255.255.224.0. This is a Class B address, so that is only 3 subnet bits, but it provides 13 host bits, or 8 subnets, each with 8,190 hosts.

5. B, D. The mask 255.255.254.0 (/23) used with a Class A address means that there are 15 subnet bits and 9 host bits. The block size in the third octet is 2 (256 – 254). So, this makes the subnets in the interesting octet 0, 2, 4, 6, etc., all the way to 254. The host 10.16.3.65 is in the 2.0 subnet. The next subnet is 4.0, so the broadcast address for the 2.0 subnet is 3.255. The valid host addresses are 2.1 through 3.254.

6. D. A /30, regardless of the class of address, has a 252 in the fourth octet. This means we have a block size of 4 and our subnets are 0, 4, 8, 12, 16, etc. Address 14 is obviously in the 12 subnet.

7. D. A point-to-point link uses only two hosts. A /30, or 255.255.255.252, mask provides two hosts per subnet.

8. C. A /21 is 255.255.248.0, which means we have a block size of 8 in the third octet, so we just count by 8 until we reach 66. The subnet in this question is 64.0. The next subnet is 72.0, so the broadcast address of the 64 subnet is 71.255.

9. A. A /29 (255.255.255.248), regardless of the class of address, has only 3 host bits. Six is the maximum number of hosts on this LAN, including the router interface.

10. C. A /29 is 255.255.255.248, which is a block size of 8 in the fourth octet. The subnets are 0, 8, 16, 24, 32, 40, etc. 192.168.19.24 is the 24 subnet, and since 32 is the next subnet, the broadcast address for the 24 subnet is 31. 192.168.19.26 is the only correct answer.

11. A. A /29 (255.255.255.248) has a block size of 8 in the fourth octet. This means the subnets are 0, 8, 16, 24, etc. 10 is in the 8 subnet. The next subnet is 16, so 15 is the broadcast address.

12. B. You need 5 subnets, each with at least 16 hosts. The mask 255.255.255.240 provides 16 subnets with 14 hosts—this will not work. The mask 255.255.255.224 provides 8 subnets, each with 30 hosts. This is the best answer.

13. C. You cannot answer this question if you can't subnet. The 192.168.10.62 with a mask of 255.255.255.192 is a block size of 64 in the fourth octet. The host 192.168.10.62 is in the zero subnet, and the error occurred because `ip subnet-zero` is not enabled on the router.

14. A. A /25 mask is 255.255.255.128. Used with a Class B network, the third and fourth octets are used for subnetting with a total of 9 subnet bits—8 bits in the third octet and 1 bit in the fourth octet. Since there is only 1 bit in the fourth octet, the bit is either off or on, which is a value of 0 or 128. The host in the question is in the 0 subnet, which has a broadcast address of 127, since 112.128 is the next subnet.

15. C. A /28 is a 255.255.255.240 mask. The first subnet is 16 (remember that the question stated not to use subnet zero), and the next subnet is 32, so our broadcast address is 31. This makes our host range 17–30. 30 is the last valid host.

Chapter 4: Network Address Translation (NAT) and IPv6

1. D. An IPv6 address is represented as eight groups of four hexadecimal digits, each group representing 16 bits (two octets). The groups are separated by colons (:). Option A has two double colons, option B doesn't have 8 fields, and option C has invalid hex characters.

2. A, B, C. This question is easier to answer if you just take out the wrong options. First, the loopback is only ::1, so that makes option D wrong. Link local is FE80::/10, not /8, and there are no broadcasts.

3. A, B. ICMPv6 router advertisements use type 134 and must be at least 64 bits in length.

4. B, E, F. Anycast addresses identify multiple interfaces, which is somewhat similar to multicast addresses; however, the big difference is that the anycast packet is delivered to only one address—the first one it finds defined in terms of routing distance. This address can also be called one-to-one-of-many, or one-to-nearest.

5. C. The loopback address with IPv4 is 127.0.0.1. With IPv6, that address is ::1.

6. B, C, E. An important feature of IPv6 is that it allows the plug-and-play option to the network devices by allowing them to configure themselves independently. It is possible to plug a node into an IPv6 network without requiring any human intervention. IPv6 does not implement traditional IP broadcasts.

7. A, D. The loopback address is ::1; link-local addresses start with FE80::/10; site-local addresses start with FEC0::/10; global addresses start with 200::/3; and multicast addresses start with FF00::/8.

8. C. A router solicitation is sent out using the all-routers multicast address of FF02::2. The router can send a router advertisement to all hosts using the FF02::1 multicast address.

9. A, E. IPv6 does not use broadcasts, and autoconfiguration is a feature of IPv6 that allows for hosts to automatically obtain an IPv6 address.

10. B. IPv6 anycast addresses are used for one-to-nearest communication, meaning an anycast address is used by a device to send data to one specific recipient (interface) that is the closest out of a group of recipients (interfaces).

11. B, D. To shorten the written length of an IPv6 address, successive fields of zeros may be replaced by double colons (::). In trying to shorten the address further, leading zeros may also be removed. Just as with IPv4, a single device's interface can have more than one address; with IPv6 there are more types of addresses, and the same rule applies. There can be link-local, global unicast, multicast, and anycast addresses all assigned to the same interface.

12. B. There are no broadcasts with IPv6. Unicast, multicast, anycast, global, and link-local unicast are used.

13. B, D, F. NAT is not perfect, but there are some advantages. It conserves global addresses, which allows us to add millions of hosts to the Internet without "real" IP addresses. This provides flexibility in our corporate networks. NAT can also allow you to use the same subnet more than once in the same network without overlapping networks.

14. C. Another term for Port Address Translation (PAT) is *NAT Overload*, because that is the keyword used to enable PAT.

15. A. An inside local address is considered to be the IP address of the host on the private network before translation.

16. A, C, E. You can configure NAT in three ways on a Cisco router: static, dynamic, and NAT Overload (PAT).

17. A, C, E. NAT is not perfect and can cause some issues in some networks, but most networks work just fine. NAT can cause delays and troubleshooting problems, and some applications just won't work.

Chapter 5: IP Routing

1. B. The show ip route command is used to display the routing table of a router.

2. A, B. Although option D almost seems right, it is not; the mask option is the mask used on the remote network, not the source network. Since there is no number at the end of the static route, it is using the default administrative distance of 1.

3. C, F. The switches are not used as either a default gateway or other destination. Switches have nothing to do with routing. It is very important to remember that the destination MAC address will always be the router's interface. The destination address of a frame, from HostA, will be the MAC address of the Fa0/0 interface of RouterA. The destination address of a packet will be the IP address of the network interface card (NIC) of the HTTPS server. The destination port number in the segment header will have a value of 443 (HTTPS).

4. B. Hybrid protocols use aspects of both distance vector and link state—for example, EIGRP. Be advised, however, that Cisco typically just calls EIGRP an advanced distance-vector routing protocol. Do not be misled by the way the question is worded. Yes, I know that MAC addresses are not in a packet. You must read the question carefully to understand what it is really asking.

5. A. Since the destination MAC address is different at each hop, it must keep changing. The IP address, which is used for the routing process, does not.

6. B, C. The distance-vector routing protocol sends its complete routing table out of all active interfaces at periodic time intervals. Link-state routing protocols send updates containing the state of their own links to all routers in the internetwork.

7. B. The 150 at the end changes the default administrative distance (AD) of 1 to 150.

8. B. RIP has an administrative distance (AD) of 120, whereas EIGRP has an administrative distance of 90, so the router will prefer routes with a lower AD than 90 to the same network.

9. D. Recovery from a lost route requires manual intervention by a human to replace the lost route.

10. A, B, C. The advantages are less overhead on the router and network as well as increased security.

Chapter 6: Switching

1. D. Here's a list of ways VLANs simplify network management:

- Network adds, moves, and changes are achieved with ease by just configuring a port into the appropriate VLAN.

- A group of users that need an unusually high level of security can be put into its own VLAN so that users outside of the VLAN can't communicate with them.

- As a logical grouping of users by function, VLANs can be considered independent from their physical or geographic locations.

- VLANs greatly enhance network security if implemented correctly.

- VLANs increase the number of broadcast domains while decreasing their size.

2. A. Layer 2 switches and bridges are faster than routers because they don't take up time looking at the Network Layer header information. They do make use of the Data Link layer information.

3. `show mac address-table`. This command displays the forward filter table, also called a content-addressable memory (CAM) table.

4. B. Gateway redundancy can be solved with Hot Standby Router Protocol (HSRP), which provides dynamic default gateways.

5. `ip default-gateway`. The command `ip default-gateway` provides a way for the management traffic to traverse between VLANs.

6. Spanning Tree Protocol (STP). STP is a switching loop avoidance scheme used by switches.

7. C. *Frame tagging* refers to VLAN identification; this is what switches use to keep track of all those frames as they're traversing a switch fabric. It's how switches identify which frames belong to which VLANs over trunk links.

8. C. The management IP address of the switch is called the management VLAN interface, which is a routed interface on every Cisco switch and called interface VLAN 1.

9. B. The command `show vlan` provides the VLAN port assignments.

10. A, B, D. Address learning, forward/filter decisions, and loop avoidance are the functions of a switch.

Chapter 7: Cables and Connectors

1. B, C. Plenum-rated means that the cable's coating doesn't begin burning until a much higher temperature of heat, doesn't release as many toxic fumes as PVC when it does burn, and is rated for use in air plenums that carry breathable air, usually as nonenclosed fresh-air return pathways that share space with cabling.

2. D. UTP is commonly used in twisted-pair Ethernet like 10BaseT, 100BaseTX, 1000BaseTX, and so on.

3. D. Unshielded twisted-pair has standards from Category 2 through 8 for use on Ethernet networks. There is no Category 9 defined.

4. C. UTP usually connects with RJ-45. You use a crimper to attach an RJ connector to a cable.

5. A. Single-mode fiber allows for the maximum cable run distances.

6. B. In a star topology, each workstation connects to a hub, switch, or similar central device but not to other workstations. The benefit is that when connectivity to the central device is lost, the rest of the network lives on.

7. C. Fiber-optic cable transmits digital signals using light impulses rather than electricity; therefore, it is immune to EMI and RFI.

8. B. Remember that fiber-optic cable transmits a digital signal using light impulses. Light is carried on either a glass or a plastic core.

9. B. The difference between single-mode fibers and multimode fibers is in the number of light rays (and thus the number of signals) they can carry. Generally speaking, multimode fiber is used for shorter-distance applications and single-mode fiber for longer distances.

10. C. Standards limit UTP to a mere 100 meters. Different fiber-optic types have different maximum lengths, but fiber-optic is the only cable type that can extend well beyond 100 meters.

11. B. A logical grouping of hosts is called a LAN, and you typically group them by connecting them to a hub or switch.

12. D. Routers are used to connect different networks together.

13. D. A typical WAN connects two or more remote LANs together using someone else's network (your ISP's) and a router. Your local host and router "see" these networks as remote networks and not as local networks or local resources. Routers use proprietary serial connections for WANs.

14. D. LANs generally have a geographic scope of a single building or smaller. They can range from simple (two hosts) to complex (with thousands of hosts).

Chapter 8: Wireless Technologies

1. B. WPA3 Enterprise uses GCMP-256 for encryption; WPA2 uses AES-CCMP for encryption; and WPA uses TKIP.

2. C. The IEEE 802.11b and IEEE 802.11g standards both run in the 2.4 GHz RF range.

3. D. The IEEE 802.11a standard runs in the 5 GHz RF range.

4. C. The IEEE 802.11b and IEEE 802.11g standards both run in the 2.4 GHz RF range.

5. C. The minimum parameter configured on an AP for a simple WLAN installation is the SSID, although you should set the channel and authentication method as well.

6. A. WPA3 Enterprise uses GCMP-256 for encryption; WPA2 uses AES-CCMP for encryption; and WPA uses TKIP.

7. A. The IEEE 802.11b standard provides three nonoverlapping channels.

8. C. WPA3 is resistant to offline dictionary attacks where an attacker attempts to determine a network password by trying possible passwords without further network interaction.

9. D. The IEEE 802.11a standard provides a maximum data rate of up to 54 Mbps.

10. D. The IEEE 802.11g standard provides a maximum data rate of up to 54 Mbps.

11. B. The IEEE 802.11b standard provides a maximum data rate of up to 11 Mbps.

12. C. The 802.11 "open" authentication support has been replaced with Opportunistic Wireless Encryption (OWE) enhancement, which is an enhancement, not a mandatory certified setting.

13. D. Although this question is cryptic at best, the only possible answer is option D. If the SSID is not being broadcast (which we must assume in this question), the client must be configured with the correct SSID in order to associate to the AP.

14. B, E. WPA uses Temporal Key Integrity Protocol (TKIP), which includes both broadcast key rotation (dynamic keys that change) and sequencing of frames.

15. A, D. Both WEP and TKIP (WPA) use the RC4 algorithm. It is advised to use WPA2, which uses AES encryption, or WPA3 when it is available to you.

16. C. Two wireless hosts directly connected wirelessly is no different from two hosts connecting with a crossover cable. They are both ad hoc networks, but in wireless we call this an independent basic service set (IBSS).

17. A, C. WPA, although using the same RC4 encryption that WEP uses, provides enhancements to the WEP protocol by using dynamic keys that change constantly, as well as providing a pre-shared key method of authentication.

18. B. To create an extended service set (ESS), you need to overlap the wireless BSA from each AP by at least 15 percent in order to not have a gap in coverage, so users do not lose their connection when roaming between APs.

19. A. Extended service set ID means that you have more than one access point, and they all are set to the same SSID, and all are connected together in the same VLAN or distribution system, so users can roam.

20. A, B, D. The three basic parameters to configure when setting up an access point are the SSID, the RF channel, and the authentication method.

Chapter 9: Cisco Devices

1. C. The command `show cdp neighbors detail`, which can be run on both routers and switches, displays detailed information about each device connected to the device you're running the command on, including the IP address. The command `show cdp neighbors` does not show the IP address of your neighbor devices; only `show cdp neighbors detail` provides that information.

2. B. Secure Shell (SSH) creates a secure channel between devices and provides confidentiality and integrity of the data transmission. It uses public-key cryptography to authenticate the remote computer and allow the remote computer to authenticate the user, if necessary.

3. C. The Cisco IOS command `show ip interface brief` is a very useful output that provides all of a device's interfaces, including the logical address and interface status at layers 1 and 2.

4. D. This is a very simple cable for a 10/100Mbps straight-through connection. If you want gigabit (of course you do!), you need all 8 wires connected. But since this is 1 to 1, 2 to 2, etc, this is a cable for connecting from host to switch.

5. B. This is a crossover cable. It is using all 8 pins, so it can be used for higher speeds, such as between gigabit ports. Crossover cables are used to connect like devices, such as host to host, switch to switch, etc.

6. B. This is a rolled cable and is used for a connection from a host to a console port.

7. B. The command `show mac address-table` provides the known MAC address of local hosts and which port they are connected on.

8. D. The `show cdp neighbors` command (`sh cdp nei` for short) delivers information about directly connected devices.

9. C. A VPN allows you to connect securely to a remote location and appear local to that network.

10. D. The command `show switch` on a stack of Cisco Catalyst switches shows the base MAC address, the priority to become Master, the version, and the state of the switch.

Chapter 10: Security

1. A, D. TACACS+ uses TCP, is Cisco proprietary, and offers multiprotocol support as well as separated AAA services.

2. B. Unlike TACACS+, which separates AAA services, this is not an option when configuring RADIUS.

3. B. MFA, biometrics, and certificates are all password alternatives.

4. B, D. There are quite a few denial-of-service attacks, but from the options in this question you have command-and-control (C&C), DDoS, and ping of death.

5. A, B, C, E. Unstructured, structured, external, and internal threats are the types of threats that are important to understand when trying to implement CIA.

6. A, B, D. RADIUS, TACACS+, and Kerberos are the three types of security server protocols supported by Cisco routers.

7. D. An exploit occurs when a threat agent takes advantage of a vulnerability and uses it to advance an attack.

8. B, C, D. Multifactor authentication is when two or more of the following factors are being tested:

   - Something a user knows (password)
   - Something a user is (retinas, fingerprint, facial recognition)
   - Something a user possesses (smart card)
   - Somewhere a user is (location)
   - Something a user does (behavior)

9. A. ACLs typically reside on routers to determine which packets are allowed to route through them based on the requesting device's source or destination Internet Protocol (IP) address or layer 4 ports.

10. C. A firewall protects your LAN resources from invaders who prowl the Internet for unprotected networks while simultaneously preventing all or some of your LAN's computers from accessing certain services on the Internet.

Chapter 11: Cloud & IoT

1. B. There are many different service type offerings from the cloud providers. IaaS, or infrastructure as a service, is when the cloud vendor provides the hardware platform and the company installs and manages its own operating systems.

2. C. Pretty much everything in your life would eventually be an IoT endpoint, but can you imagine an out-of-control weed trimmer? Let's hope this never happens.

3. B, C, D. The benefits of using cloud computing include more fault tolerance, constant availability, access from anywhere, and, although there will be increased performance, it's unlikely anything will be faster when moving your data off-site. Certainly, some things can be, but that's not really a guaranteed benefit as much as the three listed here.

4. B, D, E. Here are the advantages to a cloud service builder or provider:

   Cost reduction, standardization, and automation

   High utilization through virtualized, shared resources

   Easier administration

   Fall-in-place operations model

5. A, B, C. Here are the advantages to cloud users:

   On-demand, self-service resource provisioning

   Fast deployment cycles

Cost-effective

The centralized appearance of resources

Highly available, horizontally scaled application architectures

No local backups

6. A. Remote auto phones through IoT cell clouds is a useful IoT and VoIP integration.

7. A. IaaS delivers computer infrastructure—a platform virtualization environment—where the customer has the most control and management capability.

8. B. The vendor provides the hardware platform or data center and the software running on the platform, allowing customers to develop, run, and manage applications without the complexity of building and maintaining the infrastructure typically associated with developing and launching an application. An example is Windows Azure.

9. C. The vendor provides the entire solution. This includes the operating system, infrastructure software, and the application. SaaS consists of common application software such as databases, web servers, and email software that's hosted by the SaaS vendor. The customer accesses this software over the Internet. Instead of having users install software on their computers or servers, the SaaS vendor owns the software and runs it on computers in its data center. Microsoft Office 365 and many Amazon Web Services (AWS) offerings are perfect examples of SaaS.

10. C. **Private cloud:** This is a solution owned and managed by one company solely for that company's use.

Public cloud: This is a solution provided by a third party. It offloads the details to the third party but gives up some control and can introduce security issues.

Hybrid cloud: This is some combination of private and public. For example, perhaps you only use the facilities of the provider but still manage the data yourself.

Community cloud: This is a solution owned and managed by a group of organizations that create the cloud for a common purpose.

Chapter 12: Troubleshooting

1. D. Bandwidth and throughput both have to do with network data. Network bandwidth refers to how much data can possibly travel in a network during a period of time. Network throughput refers to how much data actually transfers during a period of time. Bandwidth and throughput are also sometimes confused with latency, which is understandable because latency refers to the speed at which data travels across the network to its destination.

2. B. Bandwidth and throughput both have to do with network data. Network bandwidth refers to how much data can possibly travel in a network during a period of time. Network throughput refers to how much data actually transfers during a period of time. Bandwidth and throughput are also sometimes confused with latency, which is understandable because latency refers to the speed at which data travels across the network to its destination.

3. C. Bandwidth and throughput both have to do with network data. Network bandwidth defines how much data can possibly travel in a network during a period of time. Network throughput refers to how much data actually transfers during a period of time. Bandwidth and throughput are also sometimes confused with latency, which is understandable because latency refers to the speed at which data travels across the network to its destination.

4. A, D. The main difference between the two programs is that a speed test does not require a speed test server to be set up; it automatically chooses a server on the Internet. iPerf, however, requires an endpoint program, which must be installed on a separate server, typically on your own network.

5. D. ICMP uses echo request and replies to test whether a node IP stack is initialized and running on the network. `traceroute` displays the list of routers on a path to a network destination by using TTL time-outs and ICMP error messages. Microsoft uses `tracert`.

6. B. `route print` provides the routing table of a Windows host. ICMP uses echo request and replies to test whether a node IP stack is initialized and running on the network. `traceroute` displays the list of routers on a path to a network destination by using TTL time-outs and ICMP error messages. Microsoft uses `tracert`.

7. A. ICMP uses echo requests and replies to test if a node IP stack is initialized and alive on the network. `traceroute` displays the list of routers on a path to a network destination by using TTL time-outs and ICMP error messages. Microsoft uses `tracert`.

8. D. Cisco created a seven-step troubleshooting process for help desk technicians to find and fix issues.

9. B. Once Wireshark loads, you need to select the interface you want to do a packet capture on. If your computer has multiple interfaces, you'll need to select the one with the traffic you are interested in seeing.

10. A. Cisco's seven-step troubleshooting process is as follows:
    1. Define the problem.
    2. Gather information.
    3. Analyze the information.
    4. Eliminate possible causes.
    5. Propose a hypothesis.
    6. Test the hypothesis.
    7. Solve the problem.

Index

1000 router with 6G, 274
1000Base-T wiring, 283
2G, 230
3G, 230
4G, 230

A

AAA (authentication, authorization, accounting), 325
   RADIUS (Remote Authentication Dial-In User Service), 326
   TACACS+ (Terminal Access Controller Access-Control System Plus), 326
AAA (authentication, authorization, and accounting), 320
access links, 175
ACI (Application Centric Infrastructure), 320
ACK (acknowledge), 17
acknowledgments, positive with retransmission, 20–21
ACLs (access control lists), 322–323
   NGFWs (next generation firewalls), 323
   port filtering, 323
AD (Active Directory)
   DC (domain controllers), 330
   groups, new users, 331
   new users, 331
AD (administrative distance), 154–155, 157
advanced distance vector routing protocols, 156
Android, networking and, 260–264

answers to review questions
   cables, 402–403
   Cisco devices, 404–405
   cloud computing, 406–407
   connectors, 402–403
   internetworking, 396
   IoT (Internet of Things), 406–407
   IP routing, 400–401
   IPv6, 399–400
   NAT (Network Address Translation), 399–400
   security, 405–406
   subnetting, 398–399
   switching, 401–402
   TCP/IP, 397–398
   troubleshooting, 407–408
   wireless technologies, 403–404
antennas
   directional, 220
   omnidirectional, 220
AP (access point), 9
APIPA (Automatic Private IP Addressing), 46
Apple, networking and, 256–260
Application layer (layer 7), OSI, 12, 13, 14
arp -a command, 374
ARP (Address Resolution Protocol), 62–64
   ND (Neighbor Discovery), 129–130
AS (autonomous system), 154
ASA (Adaptive Security Appliance), 10, 332
ASIC (application-specific integrated circuit), 25
authentication, 232–233
   AAA (authentication, authorization, accounting), 325

X–Y–Z

Online Test Bank

To help you study for your CCST Cisco Certified Support Technician Networking certification exam, register to gain one year of FREE access after activation to the online interactive test bank-included with your purchase of this book! All of the chapter review questions and the practice tests in this book are included in the online test bank so you can practice in a timed and graded setting.

Register and Access the Online Test Bank

To register your book and get access to the online test bank, follow these steps:

1. Go to www.wiley.com/go/sybextestprep. You'll see the **"How to Register Your Book for Online Access"** instructions.
2. Click "here to register" and then select your book from the list.
3. Complete the required registration information, including answering the security verification to prove book ownership. You will be emailed a pin code.
4. Follow the directions in the email or go to www.wiley.com/go/sybextestprep.
5. Find your book on that page and click the "Register or Login" link with it. Then enter the pin code you received and click the "Activate PIN" button.
6. On the Create an Account or Login page, enter your username and password, and click Login or, if you don't have an account already, create a new account.
7. At this point, you should be in the test bank site with your new test bank listed at the top of the page. If you do not see it there, please refresh the page or log out and log back in.